The United States Army in China, 1900–1938

ALSO BY ALFRED EMILE CORNEBISE
AND FROM MCFARLAND

The Shanghai Stars and Stripes: *Witness to the Transition to Peace, 1945–1946* (2010)

The United States 15th Infantry Regiment in China, 1912–1938 (2004)

The CCC Chronicles: Camp Newspapers of the Civilian Conservation Corps, 1933–1942 (2004)

The United States Army in China, 1900–1938

A History of the 9th, 14th, 15th and 31st Regiments in the East

ALFRED EMILE CORNEBISE

McFarland & Company, Inc., Publishers
Jefferson, North Carolina

LIBRARY OF CONGRESS CATALOGUING-IN-PUBLICATION DATA

Cornebise, Alfred E.
 The United States Army in China, 1900–1938 : a history of the 9th, 14th, 15th and 31st Regiments in the East / Alfred Emile Cornebise.
 p. cm.
 Includes bibliographical references and index.

 ISBN 978-0-7864-9770-6 (softcover : acid free paper) ∞
 ISBN 978-1-4766-1905-7 (ebook)

 1. United States. Army—Foreign service—China—History—20th century. 2. United States—Military relations—China. 3. China—Military relations—United States. 4. United States. Army. Infantry Regiment, 15th—History—20th century. I. Title.

 UA26.C58C67 2015
 356'.1130973—dc23   2015018328

BRITISH LIBRARY CATALOGUING DATA ARE AVAILABLE

© 2015 Alfred Emile Cornebise. All rights reserved

No part of this book may be reproduced or transmitted in any form or by any means, electronic or mechanical, including photocopying or recording, or by any information storage and retrieval system, without permission in writing from the publisher.

Printed in the United States of America

McFarland & Company, Inc., Publishers
 Box 611, Jefferson, North Carolina 28640
 www.mcfarlandpub.com

For Jan Miller Cornebise,
fellow writer and constant companion

Acknowledgments

I would like to acknowledge the support of Bonnie S. Henning and Paul C. Jensen at the Institute of Heraldry, along with other agencies, for their assistance in getting copies and information regarding the coats of arms of the 9th, 14th, 15th and 31st Infantry regiments. Also thanks to the staff at the China Marine organization for permission to use a photograph of the 15th Infantry. Jody Gripp, at the Tacoma Public Library, provided valuable information and illustrations regarding the return of the 15th Infantry to Fort Lewis, Washington, from China in March 1938. Jamie Carstairs at the University of Bristol, in the UK, gave me permission to use a photograph from their Historical Photographs of China collection. Colonel Tim R. Stoy, a veteran of the 15th Infantry Regiment and the historian and president of the 15th Infantry Regiment Association, provided me with much information about service in the regiment. He also discussed details of the lives of certain soldiers thereof, especially during the 1930s. I would like to thank Grant Woods for his map of Shanghai as of 1932. Hearty thanks to my wife, Jan Miller Cornebise, for her patient, careful editing of the manuscript, and for creating an illustration for the study.

Lynn Smith and other staffers at the Hoover Presidential Library, West Branch, Iowa, have been of considerable assistance in finding materials concerned with the U.S. involvement in the Boxer Uprising.

Ann Squier and Joyce Ehlert at the General Forrest Harding Memorial Museum in Franklin, Ohio, provided me with much information on the general. Joanne D. Hartog, the director of the George C. Marshall Foundation's library in Lexington, Virginia, extended much help to me. At Archives II in College Park, Maryland, Mitchell Yockelson and Timothy Nenninger ably assisted me in locating numerous relevant materials, as did Trevor Plante at Archives I in Washington.

Table of Contents

Acknowledgments vi
Preface 1

Part I: The Era of the Boxer Uprising

1. Introduction 10
2. The Boxer Uprising 29
3. Aftermath 38
4. Assessment, Consequences and Conclusions 48

Part II: The 15th U.S. Infantry Regiment's Service in China, 1900–1938

5. The 15th Infantry Regiment in the Boxer Uprising 60
6. The 15th Returns to China, 1912–1938 67
7. Life in the 15th Infantry Regiment in China 80
8. Going Home and the Regiment's Legacy 100

Part III: Notable Alumni of the 15th Infantry's Service in China

9. A Gallery of Generals 116

Part IV: The U.S. Army and the First "Shanghai Incident": With the 31st Infantry Regiment in China, January–June 1932

10. Introduction — 182
11. The 31st United States Infantry Regiment in China — 194
12. Dénouement — 217

Conclusion — 229
Chapter Notes — 249
Bibliography — 273
Index — 283

Preface

The scenario of East versus West is a long-standing one in the history of humankind.

Early manifestations included the Greeks versus the Trojans, where the truism, regarding the Trojan horse, "beware the Greeks bearing gifts" might also plausibly be stated as "beware the gifts bearing Greeks." Later struggles included the Greeks versus the Persians, the Romans versus the Jews, and the Crusades pitting Western Christians against the Muslim world. The confrontations between the Asians and Europeans, eventually involving the United States and Japan, came along later, being especially important as the 19th century evolved. By this time, especially after Marco Polo, a "yen" for the world of "yin and yang" was noteworthy. Also, Western imperialism and colonialism had intruded upon the huge landmass of Asia, which counted its span in the framework of 5,000 years. As for the United States, with its 200-year history as a nation, this time frame required some getting used to. When the Americans arrived in Asia, "Manifest Destiny" was in full flower: the United States not only included the land arching from "sea to shining sea" on its own continent, but extended into Asia as well.

In any event, the West was driven by an intense desire for trade, and Christianity strongly longed to take on the "Great Gawd Budd" and Confucius. Rudyard Kipling's pen has delineated what was at stake. Much of this was portrayed in such poems as "The Ballad of East and West," though its famous "Oh, East is East, and West is West, and never the twain shall meet" became outdated. "Never the twain shall part" was more accurate. Kipling was also prophetic in his poem "The Naulahka," noting that it was not good for the Christian's health, "to hustle the Aryan [Asian] brown," because while the "Christian riles" the Aryan "simply smiles" and "weareth the Christian down." The end of the strife was well known, being "a tombstone white with the name of the late deceased," and "the epitaph drear: 'A Fool lies here who tried to hustle the East.'" When Kipling wrote, however, the East was being "rustled" as well as "hustled," and it would be over a century before the East would cease being subjected to those excesses. Kipling also foretold events in his poem "Recessional," wherein he predicted that the "tumult and shouting" would cease, and the "captains and Kings" would depart, at least from China and India. Before then, though, there would be much "tumult" indeed.

Beyond these considerations, China had—and has—a strong appeal in various ways. One suggested answer as to why the Occident was in the Orient was set forth by a Western commentator who noted, "He must be dead to all noble thoughts who can tread the venerable continent of Asia without profound emotion"—certainly about the Chinese portion of that continent, as its size rarely failed to impress. It is, after all, one-third larger than Europe, and if the United States and Alaska were laid upon China, there would be room left for several British Isles. Regarding such matters, Marco Polo (1254-1324) once stated that, as to China, "he did not write half of what he saw; he knew that he would not be believed," which is as true today as then.[1] In addition, regarding Marco Polo, it should be noted that in his *Travels* he presented China (Cathay) as the epitome of wealth and power, and claimed that there was certainly "no court as splendid, no realm as vast, no economy as large, and no cities as grand in fourteenth-century Europe." Accordingly, a dream—perhaps better styled as a desperate desire, propelled by an immense thrust—of getting to China was ignited, and emerged as "the imaginative thread that runs through the history of early-modern Europe's struggle to escape from its isolation and enter the wider world."[2]

One member of the United States 15th Infantry Regiment, in China from 1912 to 1938, Captain David D. Barrett, an instructor in the Chinese language all officers of the regiment were required to study, clearly loved the Chinese language, especially the pure crystalline structure of the Pekinese form. But he loved more than the language. He admired the Chinese people and loved contact with them, "in the way that so many Western travelers, missionaries, merchants and scholars have enjoyed it through the ages ... because of the pervasive charm and excitement of Chinese life on the personal plane." Pearl S. Buck agreed, writing, "It is true that we have always liked the Chinese people ... since it is impossible not to like them when one understands them. They are almost universally liked and likable."[3] Other observers have noted something of a haunting sense of timelessness that they experienced there, adding to China's appeal. One Englishman who grew up in Tientsin reported that once, when observing a procession, what he had just watched seemed to "have been taking place many hundreds of years before. Time had disappeared in the swirling wind, and past, present and future were one. More than once during my boyhood in China, I was to know this sensation of timelessness."[4]

The American writer Nora Waln was another who was similarly impressed. She wrote that "time in China has no immediacy as in America. Here I find the swift passage of our few earthly years accepted as naturally as the fall of flower and leaf. This philosophical acceptance of the individual life as just a part of the life of the race, which goes on as the life of the tree goes on, makes time limitless. A century past or a century in the future is not considered far off." She observed that even the grammar of Chinese language has no tense: "Both scholars and illiterates, in ordinary daily speech, tell an event of centuries ago as casually as an incident of the hour." As a rickshaw driver explained to her on the way to market one day, "Events that happen are not put away in books. That would not be fair. Only a few folk have leisure to read, and history belongs to everyone. It flows in every mother's milk and is digested by every babe. Thus it becomes a part of everyone's experience to use when needed. That which happens is not past. It is all a part of our now." As Waln further explained, "Hours, days, weeks, and months glided smoothly by in the cycle of seasons, from which serenity we were occasionally summoned by the special festivals."[5]

The former American secretary of state Henry Kissinger observed that "a special feature of Chinese civilization is that it seems to have no beginning. It appears in history less as a conventional nation-state than a permanent natural phenomenon." Those who act in China appear to be "reestablishing, not creating, an empire." Kissinger quotes the Abbé Régis-Evariste Huc, a 19th century traveler and missionary, who wrote, "Chinese civilization originates in an antiquity so remote that we vainly endeavor to discover its commencement. There are no traces of the state of infancy among this people." Kissinger concluded that "the Chinese never generated a myth of cosmic creation. Their universe was created by the Chinese themselves, whose values, even when declared of universal applicability, were conceived of as Chinese in origin."[6]

Though many foreigners beheld the Chinese through "jaundiced eyes," some Westerners possessed the acumen and insight to see much substance and depth in the Orient and its people. One of these was Martha J. Opie, who, in a poem, simply entitled "China," captured something of the multifarious sides of China, further delineating its lure:

> Dear old China quaint, fantastic,
>   Like a bit of Dresden rare;
> Art and nature strangely blending
>   In your dark dust-laden air,
> And your brilliant bursts of sunshine,

> Sunny skies of azure blue
> Fretful, smiling, gay, beguiling,
> Winsome, wayward, false and true.

Opie wanted to know just where its "charm is hidden." Was it perhaps in the "coolie throng?/With their rickshas gaily gliding/And their pigtails dangling long?" It might, perhaps, have been in their "shrines and temples," with their "glittering tinted tiles," or maybe it was simply personified by "the curious curio dealer/Answering to the name of 'Smiles.'" It surely would also include the Great Wall that rises as the "Ancient mark of kingly power/And upon your brick and mortar/We would place our choicest flower," and other achievements, which, nonetheless, are "Doomed to crumble and decay-/While the glory of the heaven/ Smiles into a perfect day."[7] Finally, China boasted a high culture that had persisted for thousands of years. Furthermore, it was accustomed to a central fact: "The strength of her superior civilization until now [the later 19th century] had conquered every invader." Certainly, its literary and artistic heritage was most impressive, which appealed to many, and its language enjoyed a longevity denied most of the world's other tongues.[8]

In any event, in the period from 1839, with the coming of the First Opium War and extending to 1949, with the triumph of Mao's communism, China existed in what they commonly regarded as its "Century of Shame." This present study is concerned specifically with the years 1900 to 1938, during that "Century," when the United States military forces, with a special consideration of the U.S. Army, were involved from the time of the Boxer Uprising to March of 1938, when the 15th Infantry Regiment was withdrawn from China. The focus will be on the 9th and 14th Infantry Regiments involved in the Boxer Uprising, as was the 15th, which then departed for a short time only to return in 1912, remaining for 26 years. The study will then discuss the 15th from 1900 to 1938. This will be followed by details of the 31st Infantry Regiment's involvement in Shanghai in 1932, during the first Japanese-Chinese conflict, a prelude to the coming of World War II in Asia in 1937.

It is intended to consider the roles, actions, and consequences of the presence of the U.S. Army in China for the period noted. Throughout, the focus will be on what life was like for those who were "soldiering in the Orient." For example, a firsthand account by an officer of the 9th Regiment describing what occupation duty was like in Peking (Beijing) in 1900 is included. Regarding the 15th Infantry Regiment, a short story has surfaced that illuminates experiences and attitudes concerning the Chinese population in Tientsin in the 1920s. Several letters and memoirs relating to the 15th's service in the 1920s and 1930s, both from the viewpoint of family members and the soldiers themselves, also add dimension to what service in China denoted. The occasion of the 15th's return to Fort Lewis in March of 1938 has been described closely detailing that event.

When the book *The United States Fifteenth Infantry Regiment in China, 1912–1938* was published in 2004, several readers and reviewers responded to statements therein that numerous officers who had served in the 15th later attained general officer rank, often proceeding to illustrious careers. The

Left: Coat of Arms of the 9th Infantry Regiment, courtesy of U.S. Army Institute of Heraldry. *Right:* Coat of Arms of the 14th Infantry Regiment, courtesy of U.S. Army Institute of Heraldry.

Left: Coat of Arms of the 15th Infantry Regiment, courtesy of U.S. Army Institute of Heraldry. *Right*: Coat of Arms of the 31st Infantry Regiment, courtesy of U.S. Army Institute of Heraldry.

author was queried as to their names. Some are well known, such as Generals George Marshall and Joseph Stilwell, but there were many more who were lesser known. Charles G. Finney, who served in the 15th as an enlisted man in the late 1920s, in his book, *The Old China Hands*, has written that the numbers involved were quite "impressive" and that clearly the "old China days were … formative in their careers." He wondered "what other regiment of those days can boast of such an alumni list?" Perhaps somewhere in the job description of the 15th Regiment might be the notation that it served as a "nursery of generals." Part Three of this study was created in part to answer such queries. These legacies add dimension regarding what the U.S. Army's service in China involved.

Other legacies of the U.S. Army's China experience will be delineated. These were of two sorts. In the first place was the negative impact of the West upon China; the U.S. Army was a part of that. On the positive side, the involvement of U.S. military forces in China contributed to those forces' esprit de corps and traditions, enhancing their sense and understanding of the parameters of duty, especially in foreign climes. In this respect, the focus is on the influence of China on Americans, and Americans on the Chinese, being, in turn, a significant part of Chinese history. But the thrust of Asian service was perhaps greater in American history, as the men involved were subsumed by Chinese atmospherics and conditions and turned their experiences to useful ends during the years to come, especially in World War II. The army's service there also accelerated its significant reforms in the 1930s, particularly those ascribed to Generals Marshall and Stilwell and others. This had bearing on developments at the schools at Fort Benning and the army's service schools at every level. All of this enhanced the formation of the "New Army" as distinct from the force that emerged from World War I, which in turn, fought World War II. Conditions in China beyond that time, however, require continual, ongoing reevaluations. Some aspects of these matters are discussed in the concluding chapter.

Part I: The Era of the Boxer Uprising

"somewheres east of Suez"
—Rudyard Kipling

Hinc illae lachrymae ("Hence these tears").
—Terence, *Andria*

1
Introduction

The involvement of the U.S. in China in particular and Asia in general, as in the Philippines, for example, is quite complex, if lacking the more profound dimensions of, say, the British in the Orient. Here it is necessary to attempt to make the "inscrutable scrutable." As to the West versus the East, it has been observed that the English, who in the time of what became known in China as its "Century of Shame"—which lasted from 1839, with the coming of the First Opium War, to 1949, with Mao's triumph—were global adventurers, "half-pirate, half-pastor," and dominated Asia "on an awesome scale."[1] Whether as proconsuls, neocolonialists, adventurers, or missionaries, they possessed interesting connections and characteristics, often with significant consequences that persist to this day. This study focuses on the United States and China from the perspective of the United States Army units that served there from 1900 to 1938 as illustrative of the larger issues of East and West contacts and conflicts in a more general sense, some forecasting future developments.

Contacts between China, i.e., the "East," and the Europeans and Americans, the "West," began essentially with the arrival of the Portuguese in about 1516. Then came the Spanish to the Philippines in 1563, where they also encountered Chinese in large numbers. The Dutch followed shortly thereafter, in 1598. In the ensuing struggles among these people, the Portuguese were driven to seek a place for themselves in far southern China at Macao, arriving there in 1662, where they would remain.

The conflicts with the Chinese therefore pitted the late arrivals—the West—against the Han Chinese, who boasted a high culture that had persisted for thousands of years. A watchword recently current in China was "5,000," denoting the length of the existence of China's "civilization" enumerated in years. During this time it was also accustomed to a central fact: "The strength of her superior civilization [until the mid–19th century] had conquered every invader." Therefore, from the vantage point of the "Middle Kingdom," ruling under the auspices of the "Mandate of Heaven," China was central to the whole of earthly creation. Certainly, its literary and artistic heritage was most impressive, and its language has enjoyed a longevity denied most of the world's other tongues.

Marco Polo (1254–1324), in his *Travels*, presented China (Cathay) as the epitome of wealth and power, stating that there was certainly "no court as splendid, no realm as vast, no economy as large, and no cities as grand in fourteenth-century Europe." Accordingly, a dream developed in Europe—perhaps better regarded as a desperate desire propelled by an immense thrust—of getting to China and emerged as "the imaginative thread that runs through the history of early-modern Europe's struggle to escape from its isolation and enter the wider world."[2]

The West was also driven by a collective ego, arrogance and sense of power generated after the Renaissance and the Enlightenment, coupled with the rise of science and technology and the industrial revolution, especially by the 19th century. Then, too, there was the compelling Western preoccupation with Christian missionary zeal, ever looking for new fields "white unto harvest." They never seemed whiter than in Asia, though Africa would run a close second. The Chinese, however, resisted this force as it did all the others.[3]

In fact, the Chinese essentially saw all foreigners as *fan qui*, or "foreign devils," with various results. In the main, however, as the Englishman Sir Robert Hart—the inspector general of the Chinese Imperial Customs and Posts, who subsequently headed the establishment, making it a major force in China until his resignation in 1907—once wrote that it was little wonder that the Chinese detested "foreign devils." "'We did not invite you foreigners here,' they say; 'you crossed the seas of your own accord and more or less forced yourselves on us.'" Furthermore, "Chinese were accustomed to considering theirs the chief of kingdoms and all others tributaries," and they expected from all who approached them "an acknowledgment of superiority and a submissive tone and attitude." When, on the contrary, "men of the West ... laugh at their pretensions, question their superiority, refuse them obedience, and make them accept dictation," the Chinese are profoundly shocked; they hardly saw themselves as a benighted people. This attitude was reinforced by their "innate pride—pride of race, pride of intellect, pride of civilization, [and] pride of supremacy," which had been so hurt "by the manner of foreign impact that the other good points of Chinese character have, as it were, been stunned and cannot respond." Therefore, the Chinese, "an intelligent, cultivated race, sober, industrious, and on its own lines civilized, homogeneous in language, thought, and feeling ... after thousands of years of haughty seclusion and exclusiveness," had been pushed "by the force of circumstances and by the superior strength of assailants into treaty relations with the rest of the world." While some Western wise men might be tolerated, none were loved, and the Chinese were determined to end the foreign presence, "their minds full of the memories of the good old times when for thousands of years China had lived her own life and been untroubled by the intrusion and restless competition of aliens and barbarians." As Hart concluded, "Just as one can paralyse the body or corrupt the soul of a human being, so too it is possible to outrage the spirit and antagonise the nature of a people."[4] Accordingly, as the Westerners—and later the Japanese—became more pervasive, the Chinese were determined to limit their influence, and, while tolerating some trade arrangements, initially confined them to Shameen Island near Canton.

Far more significant were Chinese contacts with the English, the French and the United States, especially in the 19th and 20th centuries. The first involved the English in 1635, when four ships of the English East India Company sailed into Canton. They demanded trading rights and sought to negotiate them, but they soon had recourse to fire and sword. Accordingly, as early as 1684, they established themselves in Canton, where they enjoyed limited rights.

Much later, in June 1834, a British commission headed by Lord Napier arrived in Canton intent upon negotiating far-reaching formal trade agreements with the Chinese. The haughty Chinese, however, refused to accept the delegation.

Events in these years, among other things revolved around the poppy plant, the source of opium. Small quantities of opium had been used medicinally in China since ancient times, but the first large quantities were brought to China by Portuguese sailors at the beginning of the eighteenth century. In later years, opium poppies were grown in India, where, under careful and efficient British management, large quantities of the drug were harvested and shipped under the protection of the British navy to seaports in Southern China. Thus ensued "one of the cruelest chapters in China's degradation at the hands of the West," the Opium Wars.[5]

Beginning in 1838, events which led to the so-called First Opium, or Anglo-Chinese, War of 1839–42, were set in train. Alarmed by the enormously damaging effects of opium on the minds and bodies of his subjects, in 1838 the Manchu emperor Tao Kuang attempted to break the "British Connection." He ordered one of his officials, Lin Tse-hsu, to end the import of the drug. Arriving in Canton (Guangzhou), Lin confiscated all the opium in the possession of foreign traders and had it publicly burned.

Having done this, he was unable to extract a pledge that no future shipments would be made. Angered by the traders' arrogant refusal, Lin threatened to ban all foreign commercial traffic. Britain, who had long planned a war against China so as to gain more trade concessions, used Lin's actions as a pretext "to fire the first shot." The Chinese were no match for the military and naval might of the British challengers and during the conflict, Canton, Nanking, and several coastal ports were captured. Consequently, the Chinese, on August 29, 1842, signed the humiliating Treaty of Nanking, the first of the so-called unequal treaties China was forced to conclude with western powers in the years to come.

One of the document's stipulations was that China formally agreed to open five ports to British trade and the right of British citizens to reside therein. These were Canton, Amoy, Foochow, Ningpo and Shanghai. The Chinese also ceded Hong Kong, which the British had occupied in January 1841. In addition, China was to limit the tariff it could impose on imported goods and pay an indemnity of twenty-one million pounds for the opium Lin had confiscated. The opium trade was also resumed, bringing with it the destruction of human life on a huge scale. This treaty was supplemented by the Treaty of Bogue signed on October 3, 1843. It included the major concession of extending extraterritorial privileges to British subjects whereby they would be tried only in their own courts rather than those of China. The treaty also granted Britain most-favored-nation status thereby granting that country any privileges granted to other powers.

The continuing unrest led to a series of episodes and confrontations known as the Second Opium War (1856–60), during which Anglo-French forces seized Canton and forced China to sign the Treaties of Tientsin on June 26–29, 1858, with Great Britain, France, the United States and Russia. China opened eleven additional ports and permitted legations at Peking. The treaties also established a maritime customs service headed by a foreign inspector-general and legalized the importation of opium. Foreigners could also travel into the Chinese interior, though only missionaries could live there. Foreign ships were allowed to sail up the Yangtze River. The Chinese, however, initially refused to ratify the treaty that led to the second phase of the war. When the Chinese refused to allow foreign diplomats to enter Peking as provided for by the treaties, French and British troops occupied the city and burned the sumptuous Summer Palace in 1860, a crime which still rankles in the hearts of the Chinese. The second phase resulted in the Peking Conventions of October 24 and 25, 1860, with Britain and France, which provided for increased indemnities. In addition, the French secured the right for Catholic missions to own land. On November 14, the Russians obtained the cession of China's Maritime Province, upon which Vladivostok was founded shortly thereafter.

The Chefoo Convention of 1876, forced by Britain following the murder of an interpreter, opened ten additional ports and improved the status of foreigners in China. In the years 1881 to 1885, France made many gains in Indochina. By the terms of a second Treaty of Tientsin on June 9, 1885, China acceded a protectorate to the French in Annam in return for a reciprocal promise to respect China's southern frontier. On July 24, 1886, the British protectorate in Burma was recognized in return for the continuance of a decennial tribute. On December 1, 1887, Portugal secured cession of Macao on its promise not to alienate it.

Clearly, all the gains that were further wrung from the Chinese were the results of military force or the threat of it. This involved a growing number of Western nations, including France, Germany, Russia, Japan, Italy and even Belgium and Austria-Hungary. Within the treaty ports that were opened, certain areas called concessions were reserved for the use of the foreign residents, though foreigners were also allowed to reside among the Chinese beyond the ports. Within the concessions, the foreigners carried on business and trade, were governed entirely by themselves, were not subject to Chinese law, and were judged by their own courts, all while being protected by their own military and naval detachments. Thus, key among these was the principle that underlay every treaty and ran through every treaty stipulation—and which, as the Chinese saw it, was "unhappily ... at the bottom of all the mischief"—i.e., extraterritoriality, called "extrality" for short. This recognized the right of foreigners to live under their own laws rather than those of the host country. This still deeply rankles the Chinese psyche, even in the 21st century.

One British writer with considerable knowledge of China, Simon Winchester, has noted, regarding the concept, that it was "something the sheer strangeness of which should not be forgotten." He argued that "by today's standards it was a bizarre arrangement—as outlandish and unimaginable as, say, letting Japanese warships patrol today's Mississippi to protect a Honda plant in Hannibal, or allowing Chinese gunboats to sidle among the punts on the Isis to look out for the interests of Beijing students." But, of course, at the time, "the Chinese were too debilitated and powerless to prevent such high-handedness."[6] Robert Hart, for another, identified it as a "special affront" that was especially detested. It far outweighed even the aggressive, sharp commercial practices and Christianity. It was, in fact, the imperium in imperio that simply had far too much of that which "humiliates and disintegrates." Hart counseled "could we but give up this ... relations would at once right themselves, rancour disappear, and friendliness rule instead."[7]

The undoubted consequences of these foreign depredations and actions were foreseen by Wen Hsiang, the Chinese Prime Minister in the early 1860s. He observed that "You [the West] are all too anxious to awake us and start us on a new road, and you will do it; but you will all regret it, for, once awaking and started, we shall go fast and far—farther than you think—much farther than you want!" The same minister further observed, during negotiations with the West in 1868, that the West should "take away your opium and your missionaries, and you will be welcome!" He further concluded: "Do away with your Extra-territoriality clause, and merchant and missionary may settle anywhere and everywhere; but retain it, and we must do our best to confine you and our trouble to the treaty ports!" Indeed, as one often heard in China, "Really, you [Westerners] are too short-sighted, and you are forcing us to arm in self-defense, and giving us grudges to pay off instead of benefits to requite."[8]

The Americans willy-nilly also became involved in China in these decades, though there was a lull during the American Civil War. By the latter part of the 19th century, America had arrived as a world power. Beginning with the purchase of Alaska from the Russians on March 30, 1867, the tiny islands of Midway in the Pacific were the next to be added to America's growing overseas acquisitions, on August 28 of the same year.

Throughout America's involvement in China, trade was in the forefront of America's concerns, but the activities of missionaries were never far behind. Though arriving later than most other Westerners, Americans were not exempt from Chinese hostility. Having no formal concessions in China, America demanded certain rights that had been obtained by other nations by treaty. The first American agreement with China, the Treaty of Wanghsia of July 3, 1844, was modeled on the Treaty of Nanking.

Later, when the Spanish became increasingly oppressive in their relations with Cuba, after much turmoil, on April 18, 1898, the U.S. Congress passed a joint resolution that amounted to a declaration of war against Spain. This declared Cuba to be free, demanded the withdrawal of Spain, and directed President William McKinley to use armed force to achieve these goals. Reluctantly, McKinley consented, and the Spanish-American War began. This resulted in the prompt defeat of Spain. The Treaty of Paris, signed on December 10, 1898, stipulated that Cuba was to be free and Spain also ceded the Philippines, Puerto Rico and Guam to America. Meanwhile, on July 7, 1898, the U.S. Congress passed a joint resolution annexing the Hawaiian Islands. The division of the Pacific island of Samoa between Germany and the United States was agreed to in 1899. These developments led to the rise of American imperialism, generally known as Manifest Destiny, an aggressive view that brought America front and center into Asia and China.

Many accounts glorifying Manifest Destiny appeared, including the popular history, *The Story of the Philippines: The Eldorado of the Orient*, penned by Murat Halstead. This American historian was duly accredited by President William McKinley to the War Department, under the Secretary of War, Russell A. Alger, to accompany Major General Wesley Merritt, commander of the Military Expedition to the Philippines on that venture. Merritt was later the Governor-General of the Philippines. America's involvement in the East was considerably enhanced by the Spanish-American War in 1898, Halstead explained, and her victories there seemed to be a result of a natural progression. As to the Philippines, one had to consider that the U.S. possessed a front on the Pacific Ocean consisting of the Western states of Washington, Oregon and California. From this vantage point, conquest of the Philippines could not be said to "be out of the scope of reasonable American expansion and is in the right line of enlarging the area of enlightenment and stimulating the progress of civilization." In any event, the victory of the U.S. Navy there under Commodore George Dewey had salutary results: "The unexpected has happened, but it is not illogical. It must have been written long ago on the scroll of the boundless blue and the stars." Accordingly, America now held "the golden key of a splendid archipelago of a thousand beautiful and richly endowed islands." Waxing poetic, Halstead declared that "the Philippines are southwest from our western front doors. They have been the islands of our sunsets in the winter. Now they look to us for the rosy dawn out of which will come the clear brightness of the white light of mornings and the fullness of the ripening noons, all the year around."

Other results seemed even more dramatic to Halstead. He asserted that America was now destined to be truly an Asian power, with its influence extending well beyond the Philippines. If Americans were comparative strangers in the East in 1898, Halstead declared, "we shall not be [for] long." American power now resided in Asia as well as back toward Europe. Indeed, he said, "Our Course of Empire is both east and west." This was easily explained: "With our bulk of the North American Continent bulging into both the great oceans it was foreordained since the beginning when God created the earth, that we, the possessors of this imperial American zone, should be a great Asiatic Power." The result would be that America henceforth could sit at the head of the table "when the empires of the earth consult themselves as to the courses of empire." Indeed, it was claimed that all of this had been forecast by the American drive to the Pacific, following a natural progression of western expansion from colonial times, such as the course laid out by President Jefferson with the launching of the Lewis and Clark expedition to Pacific shores. In the crossing of that ocean it was "but the logic of going beyond the great western rivers, prairies and mountains [earlier]." In short, "we walk in the ways of the fathers when we go conquering ... along the Eastward shores of Asia."[9]

Meanwhile, friction between China and Japan over Korea led to the Sino-Japanese War, 1894–1895. Korea had been a tributary of the Manchus since 1637. The Japanese easily won both naval and military victories, which resulted in the Treaty of Shimonoseki, April 17, 1895. According to this, China recognized the independence of Korea and ceded to Japan the island of Formosa, the Pescadores Islands, and the Liaotung Peninsula, paid a large indemnity and opened four more ports to foreign commerce. Russia, Germany and France intervened, however, and obliged Japan to return the Liaotung Peninsula to China in exchange for further indemnities. Then France, Germany, Russia and Britain made loans to China, and by the Russian-Chinese Treaty of June 3, 1896, Russia obtained the right to build and operate the Chinese Eastern Railway across northern Manchuria as a link to the Russian Trans-Siberian Railway to Vladivostok. A commercial treaty with Japan on July 21, 1896, gave Japan most-favored-nation status and granted all the treaty powers the right to operate industrial enterprises in the treaty ports. On November 14, 1897, the Germans occupied Kiaochow Bay, including Tsingtao, a result of the murder of two missionaries in Shantung.

All of these developments precipitated a general Western "scramble for concessions" by 1898, at which time the British secured agreements, in February, to open inland waters to foreign steamers and stipulated that China was not to alienate any part of the Yangtze River Valley to any other power, and it was to employ a British inspector-general of customs. On March 6, Germany extracted a 99-year lease of Kiaochow Bay; on March 7 and May 7, Russia extorted a 25-year lease on the southern part of the Liaotung Peninsula, including Darien and Port Arthur. Fearing that this endangered its own position, on June 6, 1898, Britain obtained a 99-year lease to Kowloon, opposite Hong Kong, and on July 1 added a lease of Wei-hai-wei, which was to continue in force as long as the Russians maintained their occupation of Port Arthur.

The American response to this state of affairs, which seemed to portend the carving up of China into separate spheres of influence, was the "Open Door Note" of September 6, 1899. In this missive, the American secretary of state John Hay proposed to Great Britain, France, Russia, Germany and Japan that there be a free, open market and equal trading opportunities for merchants of all nationalities operating in China. This was to be based in part on the most-favored-nation clauses already in place in several treaties formerly signed. The document's most important stipulation stated that within its sphere of interest or leasehold in China no power would interfere with any treaty port or vested interests therein. The intention was also to respect China's administrative and territorial integrity. Though most of the nations agreed in principle, no formal treaty was signed. Hay, however, acted as though they existed, and his initiatives, while establishing a basis for subsequent U.S.-China relations, remained, to a degree, in the realm of an idea. The Open Door therefore only amounted to an affirmation of the pious hopes of the United States that these principles would be in force in China.

The articulation of the Open Door policy did represent the growing American interest and involvement in East Asia by the turn of the century. It also contributed to the notion of a Sino-American "special relationship" that, somewhat at least, distanced the U.S. from other foreign powers and their attempts to further penetrate China, though this was true only to a degree.

By the end of the 19th century, pressures within China approached a boiling point and led to an inevitable eruption. This was known, inaccurately, as the Boxer Rebellion. "Rebellion" is clearly the wrong word; the Chinese were not in "rebellion" against Westerners because, at least technically, they did not rule them, though, of course, they were greatly influenced both negatively and positively by them in many ways. The correct term is "uprising," because they did, in fact, rise up against the hated, heavy-handed, "foreign devils." The uprising extended from 1899 to the conclusion of the Boxer Protocol of September 7, 1901, which terminated the matter, though not the matter's consequences. The main belligerents were the forces of the anti-foreign faction of the Qing, or Manchu, Dynasty, focusing on the Empress Dowager Tz'u His—also called Cixi—and the Boxers, and to a greater or lesser extent, the foreign Eight-Nation Alliance consisting of Japan, Russia, the United Kingdom, France, the United States, Germany, Austria-Hungary, and Italy.

Earlier events and circumstances had cast their long shadows. As Sir Robert Hart observed, "On the Chinese side there is pride, innate pride—pride of race, pride of intellect, pride of civilization, pride of supremacy; and this inherited pride, in its massive and magnificent setting of blissful ignorance, has been so hurt by the manner of foreign impact that the other good points of Chinese character have, as it were, been stunned and cannot respond." The Occident's blandishments sounded to Chinese ears something like this: "You are pagans, but we are Christians—your laws are not our laws—your judges are corrupt—injustice prevails—torture is practised—punishments are barbarous—jails are hells—and we therefore withdraw our people from your jurisdiction, and send missionaries to make you think as we do: but there is money to be made in your trade, and therefore you must share that trade with us, even though it be along your coasts and on your inland waters, and you must accord us—for are we not strangers and guests?—the commercial privileges which go hand in hand with the principle on which we have made treaties, and you had better not violate these treaties, or you'll have to pay for it!" Thus, "China, the proudest of the proud, is wounded to the core."[10]

Another factor that contributed to the disturbances in China at this time was the presence of numerous secret societies that existed for different purposes and causes in every province, though this in itself did not necessarily mean revolt or disturbances. Nonetheless, even the existence of such as the relatively benign and widespread Elder Brethren Association—the *Ko-lao-hui*—or the more famous *San-ho Hui*, or Triad Society, were their members to become aroused, could cause serious trouble.[11]

More important regarding the events of 1900 were the "Boxers." Members of this society were sometimes aided, abetted and supported by the Qing dynasty, under the control of the Empress Dowager Cixi, though there was no consistency in this policy. The "Boxers," i.e., the *I Ho Tuan*, the "Righteous Fists of Harmony Society," was a violent quasi athletic and patriotic organization dedicated to expelling all foreigners from China and rooting out all foreign influences and installations, such as, in particular, the railways and telegraph systems. It was also closely focused on the so-called Western spheres of influence present in many Chinese cities, principally the ports, and shared the hatred of the "unequal treaties." The ire of its members extended to Chinese Christians and all Chinese who had been associated with foreigners and their life and ways. Equally hated were the extensive rights accorded missionaries, who could live in their own enclaves even deep in the interior of the country and conduct aggressive proselyting as well as establish schools and other institutions. In addition, they usurped various rights and privileges offensive to the Chinese public. The Boxers were especially concerned with the Christian converts being assisted in court cases. Sometimes even criminals, appealing to the rather naive missionaries, found legal covering for their illegal operations.

Though it had been founded earlier, the Boxer movement began to emerge as a significant force in northwest Shantung during 1898. Among the average Chinese there were mixed responses to them, some seeing them as a danger but others hailing them as patriots. Though the Boxers were without leaders in the usual sense of the word, in the face of foreign encroachment in China and the drought that plagued the Shantung Peninsula in the years 1898 and 1899 they spread rapidly, recruiting farmers and the urban poor of many professions. Even young women formed their own organizations to support their men, one being the "Red Lanterns Shining."

It was the supernatural element of the Boxer claims, however, which gave them their powerful hold on the popular imagination and faith. They worshipped gods of a heterogeneous sort, many of the gods being deified heroes of extant dynasties whose spirits were thought to animate the believers to such an extent that they could do the very deeds which had been wrought ages ago. These characters were well known throughout China, their existence having being popularized and disseminated by pervasive theatrical performances and universal storytellers, which were of considerable importance in Chinese culture. They were presented by traveling players, normally men who played women's parts, which, as one observer noted, was done so skillfully that they appeared to be women. The plays were performed on stage with no scenery, as in Shakespeare's time, "but so vivid was the acting that it created the impression of background."[12]

Much of the worship was carried out in temples or in the presence of images of the deities. In the course of the worship, devotees were seized by spasms similar to catalepsy or epilepsy before passing into a trance. Having emerged from this, and protected by a myriad array of spiritual defenders, worshippers professed to be able to resist blows of swords, bullets, or even cannonballs, all of which could be swept aside by a wave of the hand. The Boxers also believed, as did so many Chinese, in the secret forces, the spirits, both good and evil that prevailed throughout the land.[13]

The Boxers adopted informal uniforms that usually featured red, black or yellow turbans and red leggings. In these guises, and for these reasons, they rapidly grew in numbers to tens of thousands and were a force to be reckoned with by the Qing Dynasty and foreigners alike. The antiforeign actions were attributed not only to the secret societies, but also to tracts. One of these was by Ma Kien Chang, the manager of the China Merchant's Company from 1884 to 1891. Entitled *Pi-hsieh shih-lu*, this tract was a shortened version of a Chinese anti–Christian document that first appeared in 1861. It was repeatedly reissued and widely distributed in a variety of forms.[14]

There was another concern that was manifested among the many superstitious Chinese. This was that the year 1900 had an intercalary *eighth* moon, and wise men thought that this meant inevitable trouble. The Chinese mind not only expected it, but was also inclined "to help along untoward occurrences." Various dates were suggested when significant events might occur, such as June 1, June 9, and September 8. Of these, June 1 fell on the *Wu-yueh-chieh*, i.e., the "5th month festival," the spring event when graves of ancestors were swept and offerings made to them. Another day of note was June 9, the God of War's birthday, called by the Chinese *Kwan-Lao-yeh mo tao*, i.e., "the God of War whets his sword!" Others favored the *Pa-yueh-chieh* falling on

September 8, the "8th month festival," i.e., the harvest festival. These beliefs reveal the importance of astrology in China.[15]

Meanwhile, internal conditions in China precluded much improvement. During the year past, there had been insufficient rain. The concern with the drought led to the appearance of diatribes featuring catchy jingles in doggerel verse, one of which went "No rain comes from Heaven/The earth is parched and dry/And all because the [Christian] churches/Have bottled up the sky."[16] Furthermore, the railways and telegraphs, and other hated inventions of foreigners began to be targeted, their existence described by Boxer propagandists as further causes of the long-continuing drought, especially in Chihli in the Peking area. It was explained that the ponderous locomotives and the rumbling trains pressed heavily on the head of the dragon who ruled the skies, disturbing the feng shui of the area and consequently, no clouds could form in the heavens. Beyond this, the manifestations of Western technology such as steamships and railroads produced massive unemployment, putting Chinese river barges and their crews out of work. The railroads did the same for those engaged in land transportation. These unemployed became ideal candidates for Boxer recruitment. In addition, the foreign passengers on the trains were regarded as invaders. These unbidden guests roamed at will over the country. They also passed their summers in delightful places among the hills, and in the process they trampled unsparingly upon Chinese prejudices and norms of conduct. For example, they showed small respect for the sacred precincts of Peking and "peered curiously into all its nooks and corners." Beyond this, they even obtained admission to the Imperial Palace and held audiences there with the Son of Heaven himself.[17]

Among the first victims of the Boxer Uprising were missionaries, and especially initially, Chinese converts, the latter being called "secondary devils." Cordially hated, many were massacred early in 1899, though there were numerous encounters on many occasions before this. Some Westerners opined that the missionaries had only themselves to blame because "it is no business of theirs to go to foreign countries to worry the natives."[18]

Indeed, the matter of the missionaries is a complex one. It can plausibly be argued that missionaries were not only a major bone of contention for the Chinese generally, but they were also a significant cause of the Boxer Uprising. As one commentator with wide experience in China has indicated, missionaries generally regarded themselves as members of "a righteous and consecrated crusade that strove with love to win China to Christ." The results, however, "did much to shatter a civilization that had endured for millennia."[19]

During this time, a well-known slogan among Christians was that the goal was to "win the world for Christ in our time." As to the nature of the

Protestant incursion, at least, one scholar has observed, "Finally, Protestant nineteenth-century America, that strange mixture of philanthropy and intolerance, was ready to resume the missionary tasks which seventeenth-century Catholic Portugal had been forced to relinquish." This was, however, a formidable challenge, because the Chinese "had proved remarkably resistant—almost impermeable—to religious conversion."[20]

More to the point, the attitudes of some missionaries were quite harsh, one observer reporting that he had heard one declare "that Christianity should be spread through China at the point of the sword." Another distinguished missionary insisted "that every Chinaman should be seized, and should have the choice given him of becoming a Christian or having his head cut off."[21] The American writer Admiral Kemp Tolley had some acute observations on Western missionaries, noting that they were in competition with each other, as in sort of a game, and were "attempting to reform and 'civilize' a people who were highly civilized a thousand years before the nations they represented knew the meaning of the word, when they were, in fact, roaming wild in the woods."[22]

The missionary ventures also reflected America's developing Manifest Destiny ideals. This was clearly annunciated in an oration by a young U.S. senator from Indiana, Albert Jeremiah Beveridge, entitled "The March of the Flag," which he gave in numerous public appearances and also on the floor of the Senate. He asserted that "the Philippines are ours forever," and just beyond was China. "We will not retreat from either.... We will not abandon one opportunity in the Orient. We will not renounce our part of the mission of our race, trustee under God, of the civilization of the world."[23]

Americans, then, were swept into "the mid-current of enthusiasm in a great world crusade of that day." Yet, they did not go, one argued, "with a will to destroy, but to fulfill, and sought to include each value from the past in the new order. Just as East and West had inevitably come together in the economic conditions of trade, we wished to share also the deepest values of our civilization."[24]

To be sure, some missionaries went to great lengths to better understand the Chinese and dug deep into their life, history, and customs. One of these was James Legge, of the London Missionary Society and one of the most knowledgeable of Western missionaries. He translated many of the great Chinese classics, so important for centuries in selecting—by rigid exams—the intellectuals of China.[25]

Another prominent missionary, Arthur Henderson Smith, who, in addition to his Christian work, undertook serious studies of China and its culture and civilization and published several acclaimed books. In 1872, Smith, a

Congregationalist minister, was sent to China with his wife, Emma Jane Dickenson, by the American Board of the Commissioners for Foreign Missions. In China, he and his wife lived for several decades in the north China village of Penjiazhuang, where they aspired to "fit in as 'natives.'" Indeed, they succeeded in getting into the Chinese world to the fullest extent possible for a Westerner at that time.

Smith's most widely read book, *Chinese Characteristics*, grew out of articles that were first published in the *North China Daily News* in Shanghai in 1889. The initial book edition appeared in Shanghai in 1890, followed by revised editions in 1892 and 1894. It was widely acknowledged, both in China and the West, that this book "was the most widely read American book on China at the turn of the twentieth century." It remained so until the publication of Pearl Buck's *The Good Earth* (1931).[26]

Nonetheless, despite his often profound observations, Smith, true to the usual missionary stance, expressed views both salutary and noxious, concluding in *Chinese Characteristics* that "the face of every Western land is towards the dawning morning of the future, while the face of China is always and everywhere towards the darkness of the remote past." This was a "most pregnant fact," he continued, and "one which we beg the reader to ponder well." Yet, he further observed that reform in China was both necessary and possible. The solution? "What China needs is righteousness, and in order to attain it, it is absolutely necessary that she have a knowledge of God and a new conception of man, as well as of the relation of man to God. She needs a new life in every individual soul, in the family, and in society. The manifold needs of China we find, then, to be a single imperative need. It will be met permanently, completely, only by Christian civilization." Indubitably, despite his long experience with China and the truthful, factual accounts that he wrote, his works nonetheless bear the considerable baggage of familiar Western biases.[27]

Accordingly, hand in hand with the development of the foreign concessions in the treaty ports, Christianity emerged and eventually flourished, but there was always dissent. To be sure, the devotion, zeal and good works of the missionaries were widely recognized, and they had "everywhere been teaching good lessons, and benevolently opening hospitals and dispensing medicine for the relief of the sick and afflicted, but wherever they go trouble goes with them, and instead of the welcome their good intentions merit, localities and officials turn against them."[28]

The reasons were many. Most important was that their presence was considered a standing insult, "for does it not tell the Chinese their conduct is bad and requires change, their cult inadequate and wants addition, their gods despicable and to be cast into the gutter, their forefathers lost and themselves only to be saved by accepting the missionary's teaching?" It was horrifying to the Chinese that Confucianism would be called into question. The Chinese never forgot that Confucius was born about 2,400 years ago, centuries before Christ. Also, his teachings were, as the Chinese argued, essentially a way of life. The whole of Chinese society rested upon them and emphasized ancestor worship that stressed humanity and supported the unity of the family and the state. The need for all to labor, especially to nurture the land, was central to its beliefs and practices as well. These notions featured the worship of Mother Earth as the source of all, and Heaven as the giver of light and rain. The result was a practical, coherent scheme designed to undergird and enhance life in the temporal world.

Christian critics argued, though, that Confucianism was essentially only a moral code and not a true theology with a hope of eternal life, which further failed to take into account the definitive Holy Word of God and its manifold, profound message which only Christians understood and affirmed. Confucianism was also severely limited in that it led to such conservative views that "whatever is, is right," and that "custom" was sacred. This was especially onerous to women, who were accorded few rights. All Chinese must focus their thought and action on the family, especially the parents, which often led to excessive spending on their behalf, as on elaborate funerals, which often chained the poor to their poverty. This also led to selfishness and provincialism, a narrow sphere that did not accord well with concepts of a modern state. By the nineteenth century the nation-state was central to Western life and the mighty engine of its lesser god, progress. As one Christian concluded, "Confucianism therefore is China's weakness as well as [its] strength, the foe of all progress, the stagnation of all life."[29]

The missionaries' presumptions and their assumed right to remain and work and their actions and stances were understandably disturbing to the Chinese. This can perhaps be better understood by a consideration of the manner in which Arthur Judson Brown, an American missionary, once observed that "no self-respecting nation can [impede] its citizens who go abroad to do good."[30]

The official policy of the United States was made clear by the action of the U.S. Secretary of State in the early 1870s, J.C.B. Davis, in a note sent to the United States Minister at Peking on October 19, 1871: "The rights of citizens of the United States in China are well defined by treaty. So long as they attend peaceably to their affairs they are to be placed on common footing of amity and good-will with subjects of China, and are to receive and enjoy for themselves, and everything appertaining to them, protection and defense for all insults and injuries." Furthermore, he went on, "They have the right to reside at any of the ports open to foreign commerce, to rent houses and places of business, or to build such upon sites which they have the right to hire. They have secured to them the right to build churches and cemeteries, and they may teach or worship in those churches without being harassed, persecuted, interfered with, or molested. These are some of the rights which are expressly and in terms granted to the United States, for their citizens, by the Treaty of 1858."

But the treaties referred to were exacted from China by force and the Chinese were not the only critics of the missionaries. For various reasons, adverse judgments of them by other Westerners were commonplace, someone even referring to them as "the Left Hand of God." An American on the staff of the Chinese Maritime Customs Service who spent many decades in China was perhaps typical. The missionary system, he asserted, "should be expunged from China, and it should never have been referred to among treaty rights and obligations." More harshly, he noted that, while there were laudable missionaries, "those who do the damage are ... so often of the half-baked variety, of little education...." Furthermore, they were "often sickly sentimental, [and] infected with the *bacillus furiosus sinensis* so badly as to be unable to mind their own business."[31]

An American businessman working for the Texaco Company in China entertained similar—if more benign—notions, observing that in Szechuan, for example, "most of the missionaries, with the exception of doctors, are away for the worst months of the heat and misery in their cool bungalows in the mountains. I would certainly raise the salaries of the medical missionaries and the teachers who teach hygiene; the others I would send back home."[32] An anonymous American soldier, who in the mid-1920s served in the U.S. Army in China as part of the 15th United States Infantry Regiment, which was stationed there from 1912 to 1938, likewise manifested an uncharitable view of western missionaries in a poem he published in the regiment's troop newspaper, *Sentinel*. His stanzas remind one of Kipling's "Recessional," and "White Man's Burden":

The Missionary Speaks

"Brothers are we," the Preachers say
From their pulpits 'neath the Cross,
"Your skin is naught to the One above,
To Him all flesh is dross.
And when on the final day you come
To His throne for your just deserts,
He'll reck no more of your yellow skins

Than he does of the White Man's shirts.
But think you must as the White Men think
And bow to the White Man's rule,
For the only God is a White Man's God
And He hateth the face of a Fool."[33]

Especially noxious to the Chinese was the failure of missionaries to live among the natives, the missionaries often opting to reside in private compounds. The missionaries were well aware, however, that it would do little good to live in such poor straits; their own health and that of their families would be endangered by living among the Chinese.[34] To be sure, the missionaries' steady endurance in the face of great suffering, deprivations, dangers, and loss of lives, especially of their children, should be noted.[35]

Another irksome matter involved the missionaries' propensity to ride in green sedan chairs, which had a special signification, being normally reserved for the Chinese elites such as governors and viceroys. This was regarded as a usurpation and bespoke missionary aspirations to be equal to anyone in the land even at the highest levels. The missionaries argued that they needed to elevate themselves so as better to influence the Chinese middle and upper classes, and this they could not do without assuming the trappings of an upper-class life for themselves.[36] Neither did Chinese Christian converts win the esteem or goodwill of their fellows. In the first place, they offended public feeling by deserting Chinese for what were regarded as foreign cults. Many Christian converts withdrew from the local community and therefore did not take up their social and cultural responsibilities, refusing, as Christians, to take part in or share the expenses of village festivals. In addition, Chinese Christians regarded themselves as exempt from local laws and they shocked the official mind and popular opinion by getting their religious teachers to interfere on their behalf in litigation, for example.

Many Westerners have read Pearl S. Buck's *The Good Earth* (1931), but few have read her, in many ways, more important work, an autobiography published as *My Several Worlds*.[37] Herein, she presents cogent analyses of much of significance about the Chinese scene, including provocative commentaries on what the West had done to China, its assaults on Chinese civilization, culture and life in general, with special notice to Western missionaries and the impact they had, for both good and evil. She was the daughter of Presbyterian missionary parents, Absalom and Caroline Sydnestricker, and spent her first years in China, though she was born in West Virginia on June 26, 1892. She would live forty years in China, principally in Chinkiang (Zhenjiang), a small city at the junction of the Yangtze River and the Grand Canal. From childhood, Pearl spoke both English and

Chinese and was taught by her mother and a Chinese tutor, Mr. Kung. Her autobiography, therefore, contains much firsthand information and personal knowledge of the Chinese scene.

She was fortunate, she stated, in that she did not encounter racism exhibited by her missionary parents. They were the only missionaries that she remembered who welcomed Chinese guests to spend the night in their home and eat at the table with them. To be sure, these were usually Chinese of a rather lofty social and educational station, but they were careful to draw no distinctions between Westerners and Chinese. Her parents did not, however, live totally among them. The reason given by her mother was that—while it was desirable that there be even closer contacts and perhaps "we white people ought never to have built a separate place for ourselves"—but they wanted to "so that we could keep our children." As it was, Pearl noted, her mother and father buried four children in China, all lost to disease. Three were buried in Shanghai and one in Chinkiang.[38] Though Pearl Buck grew up in China and held the Chinese in great esteem, she had no desire to follow in her parents' footsteps. Calling the missionary venture "that dangerous business," she simply could not "proclaim my religion superior to all others," nor could she "preach or persuade people to change their religion."[39]

As to Chinese attitudes toward missionaries, Buck explained "it did not occur to the Chinese, actually, that missionaries were in China for any purpose except their own, and being an incomparably tolerant people, accustomed to individualism, they interfered only when the missionary was personally objectionable." Also, while Americans took no part in the wars so oppressive to the Chinese, when any other country, usually Britain, forced a new treaty upon China, the Americans demanded that "its benefits be extended also to us. The famous Open Door Policy of the United States was useful to China but certainly it was as useful also to us." The United States could claim only self-interest regarding China, "enlightened though it might be," and the Chinese, "who are accustomed to all sorts of self-interest and hypocrisy, even in the subtlest forms, are not and never have been deceived about anybody, including the Americans." "We have therefore," she concluded, "no honest claim to gratitude from them."[40]

In the end, Buck was profoundly disturbed by "the whole disgraceful story of the Western Powers and how they were still robbing the great peaceful countries of Asia, which on principle had never developed the use of gunpowder and modern weapons." There was in particular, "the arrogance of the white man in Asia, unmatched ... since the days of the cruel Roman empire," she concluded.[41]

In the upshot, the Chinese found much to abhor regarding Western involvement in China, including missionary ventures, and in the end would not willingly assent to it. They would ever deplore the fact that the "Red Hairs," or "Ocean People," had established effective control over much of China's territory, governmental functions and affairs in all areas of life. With a nod to Kipling, it was the East that was being "hustled," until the Chinese themselves at length possessed both the will and the means to alter the situation. And it was not the Chinese who trampled the Christian message underfoot; it was the Westerners. It was the Christian nations that taught that it was by fire and the sword that "Right" in this world was powerless unless it was supported by armed "Might." The Chinese therefore noted the lesson and would learn it well. It would then be woe for Europe when the lesson had been fully digested. The Chinese nation of 400,000,000 would then be armed, a nation that, until the West came, "had no better wish than to live at peace with themselves and all the world." Certainly, therefore, the Chinese could be forgiven if they saw missionaries as a horde of locusts about which the Bible had something to say, an invasion of that insect being recognized as one of the gravest calamities to befall any nation. As one observer concluded, "In the name of Christ you have sounded the call to arms! In the name of Confucius, we respond!"[42]

2
THE BOXER UPRISING

Over the years, riots and disturbances became commonplace. For instance, in September 1883, houses of foreigners on Shameen Island near Canton were attacked. Other riots occurred along the Yangtze Valley in 1890. At Chungking, and later at Wuhu in May 1891, the culprits were identified as members of a secret society, the *Ko-lao-hui* (Society of Brothers and Elders), known to be strongly anti-dynastic as well as antiforeigner. It was apparently aiming its blows at the Chinese monarchy as well as at foreigners.[1]

The Western powers often brought strong pressure to bear on the Chinese government to act but its response was sporadic, although on occasion arrests were belatedly made and some guilty parties were beheaded. Also, the French and British received some financial compensation.[2] The results of these riots were a determination by the foreign legations in Peking that the Chinese government "must be taught by hook or by crook that intercourse means more than toleration—it means adequate recognition and full protection." When further disturbances occurred in September of 1891, the Chinese government was advised that Western gunboats would shell Wu Chang if necessary to cover the retreat of missionaries and the landing party sent for their rescue if this occurred, though this apparently did not come to pass.[3]

Later, in May 1895, at Chengtu, Szechwan, rampaging Chinese destroyed the French mission there, although their anger was also directed at British and American Christian establishments. More seriously, on August 1, 1895, at Ku-t'ien in the hills of Fukien, a rising against British and American missionaries occurred aimed at those who had gone there for the summer. Five English missionary girls, four other adults and two children were killed.[4]

But then things changed decidedly for the worst. Hart noted that the decisive phase of the Boxer movement dated from the appointment of Yu-hsien as governor of Shantung, in March 1899, where the Boxers were especially active and to whom he was sympathetic. Tension increased as a consequence, and the alarmed and persecuted Christian converts appealed to their white friends and teachers, who in turn presented these matters to the Ministers of their respective countries, pointing out the growing dangers and violations of treaty rights.

The foreign envoys demanded that the Chinese government suppress such lawless organizations and noted that China had signed solemn treaties guaranteeing the protection of both missionaries and their Chinese converts. In reply, the Tskungli Yamen—the Chinese foreign office—belittled the Boxer movement; the Boxers, they averred, were simply robbers and were mainly "only boys practicing gymnastics."

Soon, in May, August, and October 1899, attacks on London Missionary Society outposts occurred. By early October, foreign newspapers began to report these events and identified the Boxers as the perpetrators. On December 31, 1899, the Rev. Sidney M. Brooks, a missionary of the Society for the Propagation of the Gospel in Foreign Parts, traveling between stations in a lonely part of Shantung, was set upon by Boxers and beheaded. He was the first foreign victim of Boxer vengeance.[5]

Consequently, on January 27, 1900, Britain, the United States, France, Germany and Italy sent notes to the Zongli Yamen—China's foreign office—requesting suppression of the Boxers. Almost immediately rumors spread that members of the Big Knives and Boxers (*I Ho Ch'uan*, "Righteous Harmony Fists") were on their way to Peking and many feared the future.[6]

Events accelerated, and by mid April of 1900, warships from European countries began arriving in Chinese waters near the Taku forts southeast of Tientsin, at the mouth of the Hai Ho River. These ships guarded the ports there that served Peking. By May, Boxer upheavals had spread beyond Shantung, though the Boxers initially directed their violence mainly against native Christians. The Boxers' fury also led to attacks on railway and telegraph installations. On May 28, they destroyed the Fengtai station on the Peking-Tientsin railway only ten miles from Peking. This caused the foreign envoys in Peking to request a special legation guard, drawn from the ships at Taku. This unit pulled into the Peking railroad station on May 31, 1900, and was a major turning point in the struggle. These troops were to be the backbone of the forces subsequently defending the legations. They numbered about 350 in all, including some 56 U.S. Marines from the U.S. ships *Newark* and *Oregon*, about three officers and 76 men of the British Marine Light Infantry, three Royal Navy ratings, and other men from Russia, France, Italy and Japan.

The news of this foreign intervention precipitated the first attacks on foreigners since the death of the British missionary Sidney Brooks. By June,

2. The Boxer Uprising

Boxers from the countryside were streaming by the thousands into both Peking and Tientsin. These developments caused Empress Cixi to reassess the official stance against the Boxers with much vacillating as she veered from a position of opposing them to sanctioning official support and cooperation with them. In early June, the policy seemed to be to suppress them, and clashes occurred between the Boxers and military units of the Qing army at the command of several Qing Viceroys.

At the same time, the foreigners increased their fleet at Taku to about 24 vessels, which steadily mounted in numbers. Also, on June 10, the British minister in Peking, MacDonald, asked the British navy and certain allied forces congregating in Tientsin for a relief mission to protect the legations. He, however, did not ask the Chinese court's permission, leading to great alarm there. This effort, soon underway, was headed by Vice Admiral Sir Edward Seymour of the British navy, and consisted of 916 British soldiers and seamen, as well as 540 Germans, 312 Russians, 158 Frenchmen, 112 Americans, 54 Japanese, 40 Italians and 25 Austrians. He hoped to reach Peking by nightfall but soon found that the railroad was destroyed along the way. After several sharp, armed encounters, Seymour began a retreat to Tientsin on June 18, having had a harrowing experience and a narrow escape. He had sustained the loss of 62 killed and 228 wounded. On June 22, the ill-fated expedition came upon the Hsiku Arsenal, just to the northwest of Tientsin, and by the next day had captured it and its welcomed supplies of water, food, ammunition and arms. The admiral wisely decided to hole up there until they could be rescued by the allied forces being assembled in Tientsin.

Meanwhile, in a situation of mounting tension in Tientsin, on June 13, the Boxers attacked an important Tientsin railway station, which was saved by Russian troops. On June 15, the Boxers attacked the Chinese City portion of Tientsin, and on the following day, they moved against the foreign concessions. The serious situation in Tientsin alerted the commanders of the foreign naval squadrons anchored off Taku that stern measures must be taken. One June 16, the foreign powers issued an ultimatum to the Chinese government to surrender the Taku forts by 2:00 a.m. on June 17 or face a general assault. The Chinese responded by shelling allied ships, resulting in a spirited general attack against the Chinese. By 8:00 a.m. on the morning of June 17, the forts fell to the allies.

At the same time, on June 16 and 17 the Chinese court once more debated what its stance should be toward the Boxers: accommodation or annihilation. The former was chosen because the Boxers by then had much popular support and the court feared a rebellion if the Boxers were destroyed. Then, when on June 19 news of the Taku ultimatum reached the court, it issued its own ultimatum on June 21, declaring war on the allies and demanding that the foreign envoys vacate the capital within 24 hours. On the following day, the German envoy, Baron Clemens von Ketteler, on his way to an appointment with the Zongli Yamen, was shot dead by a Chinese soldier. This convinced the other envoys to stay put in their legations in Peking.

By this time, on June 20, the siege of the legations in Peking, which would last for 55 days, had begun. Soon scenes of arson and slaughter became commonplace and as one observer has noted, such could occur "in no city of a million without stirring the populace to frenzy." Chaos reigned. All law, restraint and social order disappeared. Thus, "what Paris was under the Terror, that was Peking in the mad throes of the Boxer revolt." In those days, there was ceaseless and frantic turmoil, and the nights were periods "of clamor and alarms." While the Chinese were naturally peaceful and apathetic, under the stress of passion they were noisy, riotous and cruel. This was easily explained: "All the fury of fifty years of enforced association with the hated foreigner seemed concentrated in one continuous howl of rage which broke over the wall with such fearful distinctness that men grew grave, the faces of women blanched with fear and little children stopped their play in very awe. The cry was 'Sha, sha yang kuei-tze' kill, kill the foreign devils."[7] Another of their chants went like this:

> Never mind soya for our noodles,
> We're going to smash the Legation Quarter.
> We're going to smash the British Embassy.
> Never mind vinegar for our noodles,
> We're going to smash the West Arsenal.[8]

Meanwhile, on June 16, approximately 25,000 Boxers had surrounded Tientsin and began burning houses between the Concession and the city. The siege that then began lasted for 29 days, until July 14. The Boxers were countered by allied forces, initially principally British and Russian, though it also included U.S. Marines. These actions also involved the rescue of the Seymour Expedition holed up in the Hsiku Arsenal, which was accomplished on June 25.[9]

By this time, troops began to pour into the Tientsin area from the ships in increasing numbers. The Americans had only belatedly considered sending troops to China, but on June 18, in Washington, Adjutant General Henry C. Corbin ordered General Arthur MacArthur, the commander of the U.S. forces in the Philippines and the military governor-general of the Philippines, to dispatch American troops to Taku. The regiment sent in was the 9th, under the command of Colonel Emerson H. Liscum. Unfortunately, a typhoon delayed the regiment's departure for China from the Philippines until June 27.

2. The Boxer Uprising

The regiment arrived at the port near Taku on the transport *Logan* on July 6. Liscum indicated that their orders were from the State Department and that they were to proceed to Tientsin, then march on to Peking to protect the U.S. Minister and other Americans. They were to participate with seven other foreign military contingents.[10]

While conducting operations at Tientsin, concern for the residents of the foreign legations in Peking rose, while those in Peking did not know of the failure of the Seymour Expedition, and, though they became aware of the capture of the Taku forts, had no knowledge as to how or when they might be rescued.

As the battle in Tientsin continued, in view of the grave dangers there, many Westerners were evacuated from the city. One was Mrs. Anna Drew, wife of Edward Bangs Drew, an American commissioner for the Imperial Chinese Customs Service in Tientsin, i.e., one of Sir Robert Hart's men. Mrs. Drew and others left Tientsin by launch on July 4, 1900, together with many wounded American army officers, bound for Taku, Tientsin's port. There, on July 7, Mrs. Drew and several other evacuees were soon on board the U.S. Army transport *Logan*, which had just arrived the night before from Manila with men of the U.S. Army's 9th Infantry Regiment.

During this hectic time, Mrs. Drew kept a detailed account, with much interesting information concerning events in Tientsin, at the port of Taku, and on the U.S. Army transport USS *Logan*.[11] The 9th had been in Cuba during the Spanish-American war and had then spent a year in the Philippines. Mrs. Drew noted that many of the officers were "very young and boyish, and full of life and fun. When I went down to lunch in my large dining saloon, and saw them all come trooping in laughing and joking, I felt as if they were a lot of college boys." Many of these men were married and had left their wives at home or in Manila, though a few of the wives had come up to Nagasaki "to be as near as possible to their husbands."

Before debarking, however, the men on the *Logan* enjoyed a night of festive celebration, at which they sang songs by soldier-composers in their ranks, attesting to their verve and high morale as they proceeded into action. Only a few days hence, many of them, including their commanding officer, Colonel Liscum, were dead or wounded, casualties of the rapidly developing struggle. These pieces of music were copied down by Mrs. Drew, a member of the "appreciative audience." One was a reminder of where they had just sailed from, a Kiplingesque piece entitled, "On the Road to San Roque":

> By the good fort San Filipe, looking westward to the sea
> Lives a little Philippino, and I know she thinks of me
> For the bugle is sounding and I hear her sweetly say

> Come you back you Yankee soldier
> Come you back to San Roque.
>
> [Chorus] On the Road to San Roque where old Dewey's squadron lay
> You can hear the bells a chiming far across Cavite Bay
> On the Road to San Roque where the [little niños] play
> And the dawn comes up like thunder
> From Manila cross the Bay.

True to the spirit of Kipling's poem "Mandalay," in the song "Mandalay," the girl alluded to, Esmeralda, when he first saw her was "smoking at a whacking big cheroot/And wasting precious kisses on a blooming second Lieut." The poet naturally wanted to be "somewhere west of 'Frisco, where the best is like the worst/Where there are no ten Commandments and man can raise a thirst." No doubt with an eye to the immediate future, when he expected to be in combat, he simply wanted to be:

> On the road to Americee, far across the deep blue sea
> Is the land of peace and plenty
> Where my sweetheart waits for me
> On the Road to Americee
> Yes, gladly I would be
> A traveling due eastward to a country of the Free.

Subsequently, on July 10, the 9th debarked with its 1st and 2nd battalions, reaching Tientsin on July 11. Anna Drew watched some of the soldiers leave, but confessed to being "inexpressibly sad," as she understood the danger they were headed for. She also recorded that some of the troops "gave a very terrible sort of war whoop which the few invalided men left on board ... responded to." She described it as "an awful sounding yell—which I am told they give sometimes when they are going into battle."

Immediately following, the men of the 9th participated in the last phase of the furiously fought Battle of Tientsin. While other Americans, principally Marines, had been steadily involved previously, the 9th was fully committed on July 13 and 14. Though the latter period of the Battle of Tientsin was to be the Americans' first major engagement in China at this time and was to result in a victory, it was disastrous for the 9th Regiment. On the 13th, Colonel Emerson H. Liscum was killed, and his command reverted to Lieutenant Colonel Charles A. Coolidge. By the end of the day, in addition to its commanding officer, the 9th had lost 22 other officers and men killed, and three officers and 70 men wounded. On the following day, July 14, the siege of Tientsin was lifted and the battle ended. In the struggle, three of the 9th's soldiers performed feats winning them the Medal of Honor. Subsequently, Liscum's dying words, "Keep up the fire, men," became the regiment's motto. Their China exploits also produced the regiment's nickname: "Manchus." They would go on to play a major role in the relief of the legations at Peking.[12]

By the time that Tientsin had been secured, the U.S. War Department had decided that even more troops must be dispatched to China. Many in the allied forces estimated that perhaps as many as 80,000 troops would be required to relieve the foreign legations—if these were still in existence. Intelligence was so limited that the fate of the people there was often in doubt. The army had further determined that a general officer should be appointed to command the U.S. Army's forces in China. They selected a Major General of Volunteers, 58-year-old Adna Romanza Chaffee, a veteran of the Civil War, the Indian Wars and the Spanish-American War.[13]

Chaffee arrived in Nagasaki on July 24, and made his way to Taku, arriving on July 29. He took command of the U.S. forces there, which included the 14th Infantry Regiment, Colonel Aaron Simon Daggett commanding, the 14th having arrived with him. Following conferences of the allies, it was calculated that about 20,000 troops would proceed to Peking, and though the Chinese Imperial troops and their Boxer militias outnumbered them by far, "the foreigners were confident that their superior weapons and training would prevail. There was also the growing belief that if they did not march soon, there might be nothing left to rescue."[14]

In due course, an international force, the China Relief Expedition for the rescue of the legations in Peking was organized. It was commanded by British Lieutenant-General Alfred Gaselee. How many troops were engaged is not clear, though the number approximated 19,000 to 20,000 men and apparently included 8,000 Japanese, 4,800 Russian, 3,000 British, 2,100 American, and 500 French troops. The Italians later fielded a small force, and the Austrians and Germans also arrived later with additional troops. Reinforcements continued to appear at the advancing front and eventually about 2,500 Americans, commanded by Chaffee, reached Peking. His force consisted of 2nd and 3rd battalions of the 14th Regiment; the 9th U.S. Infantry Regiment, despite its being severely mauled at Tientsin; Captain Henry J. Reilly's Light Battery F of the 5th Artillery; Batteries A, D, I, and O of the 3rd Artillery; Headquarters and 1st and 3rd Squadrons, 6th Cavalry (though no horses had yet arrived and the remainder of the cavalry regiment remained in Tientsin); and a composite battalion of the 1st Marine Regiment.[15]

The overall commander of the China Relief Expedition was Field Marshal Alfred von Waldersee of Germany but he did not arrive in China until after the relief of the legations. In the interim, the British general Sir Alfred Gaselee was in charge. The expedition departed Tientsin on the afternoon of

August 4, stopping first at the Hsiku Arsenal, which had earlier been captured by Admiral Seymour's column.

In the ensuing days before the relief of the legations, which came in mid–August, the U.S. Army acquitted itself well, while suffering its share of casualties. One of the main foes was the persistent scorching heat, leading to several deaths from heat exhaustion. During the first of the action, on August 5, the Americans were mainly engaged in maneuvering with other allied forces, arriving at the village of Tao-Wa-She, near the town of Yangtsun. The major engagement of the expedition's march to Peking was the Battle of Yangtsun, in which both the 9th and 14th were closely engaged. This ended on August 7, when the Chinese retreated.[16]

On August 7, the allied commanders convened a war council at Yangtsun. There the German, Italian, Austrian and French contingents decided to turn back for Tientsin; their numbers were few and the loss of combat power was negligible. The British, Japanese, Americans and Russians elected to proceed toward Peking. Meeting only scattered enemy opposition, it remained for the expedition to cope with the temperatures, which exceeded 100 degrees. They would proceed by marching up along the Pei Ho River to Tungchow, just east of Peking. There they would plan the final assault on the city.

Tungchow was first reached by the Japanese forces on the morning of August 12, and another council of war ensued. There the Russians decided that they needed a full day's rest before continuing. They were overruled, however, and it was determined to spend August 13 making a reconnaissance of the situation. In the final plan, several gates into the Tartar City and the Chinese City were assigned to each of the armed units: the Russians were to assail the Tungchihmen Gate at the northeast corner of the Tartar City, where the besieged legations were located. The Japanese were assigned the Chihuamen Gate, also entering into the Tartar City. The British were to push into the Shawomen Gate in the Chinese City, but with the possibility of moving into the legations from there. The Americans, aided by the French, were to proceed to the Tungpienmen Gate, where the Tartar City and the Chinese City joined.

In the event, however, the attack did not go as planned. The failures were mainly the result of an ever-present factor: national rivalry. The Russians discovered that the defenses around the Tungpienmen Gate, which the Americans were scheduled to assault, were light. Accordingly, the Russian commander, General Lineivitch, decided to steal a march on his allies early in the morning of August 14. Only discovering the Russian actions hours later, the remainder of the allied forces rushed into action. Unfortunately for the Russians, they were promptly pinned down for some hours and the other allied forces proceeded to move against their assigned gates. The British soldiers, by way of the Shawomen Gate, were soon inside the Chinese City. About 3:00 p.m. they thereupon arrived at the besieged legations, being the first to be greeted by the greatly relieved residents.

The Americans appeared at their assigned gate only to be confronted with the Russian encroachment. A famous event then transpired. Colonel Aaron Simon Daggett, in command of the 14th Regiment, asked for a volunteer to attempt to scale the wall to the right of the shattered gate. Corporal Calvin P. Titus, bugler of E Company, declared, "I'll try, sir!" Unarmed, he made his way up, and found that the enemy had fled. He then assisted other troops to mount the wall, and soon raised the Stars and Stripes.[17]

Subsequently, the 14th Regiment ground its way forward, followed and supported by the 9th. They were surprised and chagrined when they entered the legation area at about 4:30, to learn that the British had arrived over an hour earlier. The Russians belatedly came into the legation area about 5:50. The Japanese had a harder time than the others and made it into the legation quarter only late in the evening. The French arrived on the following morning, the 15th.

Most of the allied commanders resolved to celebrate their success, but General Chaffee opted to begin immediate operations against the Imperial City on the morning of August 15. Though the Americans persisted in their attempts to move into the Imperial City, the other allied commanders held another war council and persuaded Chaffee to withdraw from the city gates where they had been actively engaged. It was agreed that the Imperial City was not to be entered until the following day, August 16. One painful loss of the day was that of Captain Reilly of the Light Battery of the Fifth Artillery. He was felled by a bullet about 9:00 a.m. during the attacks on the gates.[18] By this time, with the relief of the legations, the primary mission of the China Relief Expedition was concluded.

3

AFTERMATH

After the end of the siege, Peking was placed under martial law, but many excesses then ensued. With the mission accomplished, international rivalries, personal greed, and lax leadership resulted in widespread murder, rape, and theft over the next months. It became commonplace to ascribe degrees of guilt. None was declared innocent and the German contingent, having arrived late, became the most notorious, followed closely by the Russians and the French. Civilian ministers frequently amassed large fortunes derived from stolen property. These considerations led one student of the Boxer Uprising to conclude "of all the actors in this story, the Boxers, despite their violence, were perhaps the least sinning."[1]

Following the capture of Peking on August 14, the Empress Dowager and her court, conceding defeat, fled to Sian (now Xi'an).[2] Subsequently, Peking, Tientsin and other cities in northern China were occupied for more than a year by the international expeditionary force under the command of a German, General Alfred Graf von Waldersee. This phase was ended by the signing of the Boxer Protocol of September 7, 1901. Negotiated by the ambassadors from nine European powers, the United States, and Japan, and two Chinese representatives, it was signed at the Spanish Legation in Peking on September 7, 1901. Officially it was known as the "Austria-Hungary, Belgium, France, Germany, Great Britain, Italy, Japan, Netherlands, Russia, Spain, United States and China—Final Protocol for the Settlement of the Disturbances of 1900," though it was usually referred to simply as the "Boxer Protocol." This stipulated that the Chinese would pay an indemnity of 450 million taels (about 335 million in U.S. gold dollars, at the 1900 rate of exchange, or about $4,355,000,000 at current rates), to be paid over thirty-nine years. The final figure was arrived at by determining that each of China's estimated 450 million people would theoretically be accountable for one tael. Russia received the far largest portion: 28 percent. Germany was to get 20 percent; France, 16 percent; Great Britain, 11 percent; Japan 8 percent; the United States and Italy 7 percent each; remaining portions going to Belgium, Austria-Hungary, The Netherlands, Spain, Portugal, Sweden and Norway. The Americans eventually used their proceeds to fund the education of foreign—mainly Chinese—students in the United States.

Other stipulations included a two-year ban on weapons imports, and all anti-foreign societies were declared illegal. The Taku forts were to be destroyed, and the allies were permitted to station permanent garrisons in Peking and Tientsin and other points between Peking and the coast. No Chinese troops were to be stationed anywhere near Tientsin. Shortly thereafter, the nations involved decided that to implement the Protocol; an international force consisting of American, British, French, German, Russian and Japanese troops would be permanently stationed in China to guard their vital lifeline, the Peking-Mukden Railway, which ran to the sea, and to protect the lives and commercial enterprises of foreigners.[3]

There was also to be recognition by the Chinese government that the Legation Quarter would be reserved for the use of foreign governments and placed under their exclusive control, with the right of each Power to maintain a permanent guard in that quarter for its defense. No Chinese were permitted to reside there. The Chinese were to apologize for the murders of Baron von Ketteler and the Japanese Chancellor of their Legation during the siege, Minister Sugiyama, and make honorable reparation for their deaths. In fact, von Ketteler's killer had previously been found, arrested and decapitated on the spot of his murder. The Chinese were also to erect a commemorative monument on the site of his assassination. There would be punishment of designated Chinese officials guilty of war crimes against foreign governments and their nationals. In the event, some 100 executions of minor officials occurred, but no major leaders were executed.

In effect, however, despite the severe demands of the Protocol, the Qing Dynasty scored some triumphs: they remained in power, though the Empress Dowager was forced to step down and be permanently banned from office.[4] And China lost no territory. Nonetheless, political power began to be more fully exercised by the provincial governors. Various reforms were instituted, such as the former reliance on the Confucian examination system, which was replaced by a Western educational system. The Qing's loss of power was to result, in 1912, in a revolution, at which time China declared itself a republic.[5]

There were other legacies for the Chinese of the Boxer era. The Boxers naturally took on other aspects. While they were viewed as "the enemy" by the Western powers and Japan, in China they were regarded negatively, mainly because they brought the wrath of the West down upon China, but especially because they failed in their efforts. In the days of Mao's China, they were considered heroes because they had forthrightly challenged the "foreign devils." It is no accident that after 1949, all things foreign were expelled from China. At long last, the Boxers, and so many of China's other anti-foreign elements, were vindicated. Subsequently, with peace restored, many of the Allied forces were withdrawn. Meanwhile, Russian troops and legation left Peking, and between September 4 and October 10, 1900, Russia seized control of southern Manchuria. The Russian minister returned to Peking only in October 1900.

Meanwhile, numerous expedients were undertaken to create law and order and to begin the process of reestablishing contact with the Chinese. To these ends, Peking was divided into districts, each administered and policed by military forces of one of the allied powers. In Peking and its environs, as had been true earlier in Tientsin, chaos and looting were rampant. Certainly, looting was a usual occurrence in such conditions and was not unknown in China throughout its history. Nonetheless, at this time, much was made of it and various measures were taken to eliminate it, or at least to curtail or control it. As for the Americans, one observer, the British explorer, writer, painter and anthropologist Arnold Henry Savage Landor, who was in Tientsin before joining the march to Peking, stated that American newspaper accounts reporting that the American soldiers did no looting were absolutely false. Still, he went on, "the American soldier was no worse, indeed, but decidedly no better, than any other soldier present." Landor noted that the average American soldier "possibly ... lacked some of the feeling and artistic taste to be found in some of the other nationalities...." The American soldier exhibited little interest in "artistic embroideries, nor for rare bronzes and china ware, nor can he understand why anybody else does." An American would, he went on, "pick up a costly vase which has been preserved for centuries in the house of a high official, and to save himself the trouble of putting it gently down in the place from which it came will drop it on the floor. Its companion piece at the other end of the sideboard meets a similar fate, the noise of smashing crockery giving more wild delight to his unmusical ears than the beautiful design, the patient work of years, on the vase, before it was broken, gave pleasure to his artistically untrained eye." The visit of American soldiers to one rich Chinaman's house produced the same results as if the house had experienced "a severe shock of earthquake."[6]

Even more onerous to the Chinese was that between the autumn of 1900 and spring of 1901, the practice was established by the Allies of sending out what were called "punitive expeditions" into the countryside. These operations were justified on the ground that barbarous or semi-barbarous people could be taught only by example. They had murdered the citizens of the nations represented, hence their blood must be shed. Certainly, many hundreds of innocent Chinamen were killed as a consequence. Many of these expeditions, however, were simply excuses to extend the range of looting, though ostensibly they were to pursue elusive Boxer bands.

These operations were also undertaken while the troops awaited the arrival of the commander of the international relief expedition, Field Marshall Alfred von Waldersee of Germany. He became closely associated with these ventures and often pressed them beyond what most of the other allies were doing. This was no doubt because he was determined to justify his belated presence and his not having participated in the relief of the legations. It was not until mounting outcries in the international press that focused on these nefarious activities began to have effect that Waldersee was persuaded to curtail them. Nonetheless, the Americans generally curtailed their activities in the punitive measures, though they did participate in a few, and on occasion killed Chinese.[7]

Considerable insight into the activities, attitudes and roles of the U.S. Army in China in 1900 and 1901, and what they experienced on occupation duty in China, can be obtained by perusing an account by one member of the 9th Regiment during those months. He was First Lieutenant William I. Naylor, who commanded that unit's F Company. As a colonel, he returned to China in 1924 as the commander of the U.S. 15th Infantry Regiment, based at Tientsin. They had arrived there in 1912, when the Chinese Manchu Ming Dynasty was toppled, causing unrest. This led various foreign nations to send in troops to maintain their concessions, i.e., territory at certain cities and ports in China since the middle of the 19th century. While in China in 1925, Naylor was approached by a reporter on the staff of the 15th's troop newspaper, the *Sentinel*, with a request that he write an article describing his experiences and adventures as part of the 9th Regiment in Peking and he complied. It should be noted that the 15th Regiment had also, for a brief time, been present in China in 1900 and 1901, though Naylor had no contact with it at that time. His story follows as it appeared in the *Sentinel*:

"Christmas in China During the Boxer Rebellion, 1900"

Personally, there are many things about China that I don't like and there are other things that I do. In fairness, we must admit that this statement can be applied to most any place, for one has yet to find an earthly heaven and even the exact site of the Garden of Eden is in doubt. With the approach of the holidays, with Christmas and New Year's festivities before us, my mind turns back to another Christmas and the Holidays spent in a different environment.

After the capture of the Forbidden City [at Peking] in August of 1900, my company joined the others of the regiment in guarding sacred gates, caring for the needy and shoveling up refuse and filth principally the latter. We cleaned up so much and so often that the Chinese boys used to yell "sowza" at us and duck out of sight. I don't know what the epithet meant, but it was not intended to be complimentary.

A short time after the fall of the city, most of us were moved to a new camping ground in a large walled enclosure nearly a half-mile square in which were located the buildings and "compounds" of the Temple of Agriculture. This enclosure was situated in the southern part of the Chinese City of Peking across the way from the Temple of Heaven. The buildings were large and stately and were places to which the emperor went either to pray for a good harvest, or to return thanks for one already had or do something bizarre in connection with agriculture. In the surrounding grounds were large cedar trees and long grass here and there. The paucity of buildings and the desire for fresh air *for others* on the part of our high command decided them to rule that we should hibernate for the coming winter under canvas. The higher-ranking officers, with true Spartan spirit of self-denial, arranged to have some of the buildings renovated and fixed up as their winter habitats. Of course, all the company officers and the "bucks" appreciated this demonstration of affection towards them. That winter's experience has so prejudiced me against tents that I feel a subconscious desire to run away and hide when anyone suggests a camping party....

We had a good spirit in the old outfit and always made the most of what we couldn't prevent, so after laying out our camp, we set about fixing up. In those days we possessed the old army spirit of doing for ourselves, and the company had two mottoes, the first, "God helps those who help themselves," and the second, "God help anyone caught helping himself around here," meaning to another fellow's stuff. These mottoes were most appropriate for my company, Company "F," which was endearingly known in the regiment as the "40 Thieves." I don't know who was Ali Baba nor why a company made up almost entirely of Irishmen should be thus branded, for the palms of our hands never itched any more than those of anyone else. There is one thing that I am here to swear to, and that is, there never was a squarer bunch of "Micks" that lined up back of a 125-lb. lieutenant than old "Battery 'F,'" of the 9th Infantry. They would get drunk and they would raise h—, but whenever there was anything doing, the 40 Thieves were always "Johnnie on the Spot."

I recall one afternoon, shortly after we arrived in the Temple of Agriculture, a hurry order came for a battalion to march out of the West Gate of the Chinese City to repel 5,000 Boxers who were supposed to be, but actually weren't, just outside of the gate. This was a chance for adventure so the 40 Thieves turned out in force. We arrived at the Gate a little before dark and, after placing guards, went into bivouac. That wasn't so bad as the night was warm and we could get into houses out of the dew; fleas were thick but

3. Aftermath

didn't annoy us as we were used to them and anyway the fleas were taking as many chances as we were.

Shortly after "chow" next morning, an order was received by the major to leave the company having the most men out on the wall for a week, and of course the 40 Thieves had to have the most men, so there we stuck while our pals marched back. "All's well that ends well" as we were to find out later. Being philosophers, we decided to make the most of it and try to be comfortable. We had hardly disposed of the question when a man came to me with some large grapes and a hat full of peaches. He said, "Ain't so bad, Lieutenant. All the truck farmers pass through this gate each morning with vegetables and fruit for market, so we get first crack at it." Of course, we paid for what we took. Ahem. At all events the bunch lived on the fat of the land and with the little "hootch" we could pick up here and there, we eked out a fairly good existence.

But let me get back to our camp. We decided to fix [it] up. In the first place, our tents were of the round Sibley type so we had difficulty in fitting the Helen Gould (Gold Medal) cots we had for sleeping purposes. Seven privates and a corporal, in other words a squad, were assigned each tent. We paved all the floors with [a]dobe bricks and built up a sort of brick oven about three feet square and two feet high in the middle of the tent. On top of this oven, we placed our Sibley stoves, making a grate out of round iron for the bottom on which to build a fire and which would prevent the coals from dropping through. The iron tripod that holds the center pole was scrapped for the time being, the end of the pole being set in mortar on top of the oven. The pole was covered with tin or zinc to prevent its being burnt and, with the stovepipe attached, it was run through the canvas top flap which the Sibley tent of those days had. To prevent this flap from being burned, a tin, circular, funnel-shaped fender was run around both pole and pipe flush with the sloping peak of [the] tent. The ubiquitous Standard Oil 5-gallon can was called into service and was converted into a hot water boiler built around the stovepipe in such a manner as not to interfere with the pole. Packing boxes were utilized to make storm doors to protect the entrances to the tents and small holes were cut at one or two places in the sloping sides into which window glass was fitted and fastened into place with battens.

The officers' quarters were the large hospital tents reinforced by framework, and lined with felt, or heavy paper. The Sibley stoves were fixed up similar to those of the men. Taken by and large, we were all pretty comfortable except during a dust storm, when so far as I know no one is comfortable anywhere in China.

We "rigged-up" mess shacks out of [a]dobe brick similar in design to the houses in the average Chinese farmer village. The only source of supply for vegetables and poultry was the outlying districts beyond the Wall and each day a company chosen by roster would go out all day to rustle. We always tried to pay for what we took, that is if we could find the lawful owner, for we found that it paid in the long run. Aside from the fact that looting is bad for discipline, the practice has a tendency to scare off the people so that after one such trip the natives will make off with their "stuff" and strip the country. If you are determined to loot, get it all on the first trip for there will be nothing to be found on subsequent trips.

"F" Company's turn for foraging finally came around, so bright and early on the designated day, off we went, everybody present and everybody happy. Just what will happen when one starts out with a bunch of Murphys, Conroys, Caseys, half a dozen Sullivans, unassorted Kennedys, Flynns, Regans, etc., no one can foretell. To express it classically "the day bid fair to be portentous."

We marched out by the main thoroughfare leading to the West Gate, sending patrols on the side streets and alleys, for sniping had not entirely died down. Scarcely a living being other than a dog, was to be seen. Just where the tens of thousands of Chinese inhabitants of the Chinese City were hiding out I don't know, but they had almost completely vanished. Now and then, a squad would root out a poor old man or woman or a beggar. The soldiers would drop into the various stores or shops to look around, now and then finding the cringing owner who "kowtowed" and hit his head on the ground and swore, on all the books of Buddha and Confucius, that he loved the foreign devil as himself. Many of them had already been to the Provost Marshal for help and had been given a "Safe Guard" for the protection of their property. Violation of a Safe Guard among civilized people is punishable with death. The Chinese who had received these Safe Guards, "pieces of paper" as the Chinks called them, were unmolested. Consequently, Safe Guards were in great demand. Most of the Chinese, not knowing that the Provost Marshal was the one to whom to apply, would hold up the first American soldier they would encounter and ask him for the "piece of paper" that would prevent all intrusion. With genuine Yankee ingenuity, the soldiers hit on this scheme. They would accompany the poor guileless Celestial to his abode or place of business, give a sort of "show down" inspection or—once over—making mental notes of its contents, which might be anything from watches down to liquor, and then would write out or print on a card something like this: "Come in boys, this fellow has a fine line of tobacco," or whiskey, or cakes or whatever it might be. The poor Chink, not being able to read, would supinely paste this above his door, thus branding it, and wonder why the boys still insisted on coming in. The practice was not condoned by us and was prevented and seriously punished when malefactors were discovered. In an atmosphere where property rights are so little respected as in a punitive expedition such as the relief of Peking unquestionably was, it is small wonder that private property rights were violated, and while not wishing to excuse any of our weaknesses unwarrantedly, and while not claiming virtues for a soldier, particularly an American, which he does not possess, it was my observation that a lawful owner went unmolested by an American when his identity was unquestioned. I do not recall a case of an American soldier unlawfully taking advantage of anyone who was helpless or came to him for protection.

Well, we continued on and arrived at the site of our old friend the West Gate. Passing through, we soon found ourselves out in an open farm coun-

3. Aftermath

try where vegetables and fruit of all kinds were in abundance. It wasn't long before we had gathered together a supply of potatoes, pumpkins, green corn, eggplant, turnips, radishes, [and assorted] fruit for the regiment, and were ready to start back. It took some time to herd together transportation but we were finally successful, so with a caravan of Peking carts, rickshas, horse and mule pack animals, we got underway.

After passing inside the wall, we fell out in the field near the West Gate to rest and for chow. Shortly after arrival, one of the men, who had been scouting around on his own hook, came up to me and said, "Lieutenant there is a big 'Kamal' over yonder," pointing. I went with him to a few houses on an eminence and looked in the direction he pointed and there was a double-humped camel wandering about in the fields with no apparent owner. I told the soldier to go get him, and while he was gone, I started "buscaring" around on my own hook. I hadn't gone far when I heard the worst cackling of chickens, gobbling of turkeys, quacking of ducks and hissing of geese imaginable. I investigated the noises and finally landed in a large walled yard where there were more fowl than I had ever seen or heard about before. No owner was about, and from the racket it was apparent that feeding time had been passed by several times. I sent the man with me back to bring up the company, for it would have been a pity to have left the dear fowl go unattended [any] longer. The company came on the run, one dragging along the "Kamal." If you have never tried it, try to lead a camel faster than he wants to go and see how far you get. He takes his own gait and that's all there is to it.

With our minds set on Thanksgiving and Christmas, we decided to lay in a supply of poultry. We gathered in a few more donkeys and ponies—there were many in the open gardens along the inside of the wall where they had wandered for food when their owners had fled—and, harnessing them to the carts that we found close at hand, we began to load on our bag. There were plenty of wicker baskets about and when the supply was exhausted, we tied the fowls' legs together in bunches. The camel came in handy as transportation—all we had to do was to tie ducks or geese together by the legs leaving enough slack cord between and then throw one bunch over the camel's back leaving the other bunch hanging down on the near side. Thus festooned, they rode quite well. I didn't count all the fowl assorted that we had any further than the geese, of which number we had six hundred.

The afternoon was wearing away so we had to start back. Organizing the party so that it would make sure progress, we started out. We hadn't been going long when we came to a public watering trough so the tenderhearted "nut" with the camel decided to give him a drink. I never before fully realized the significance of the saying—"A camel can go eight days without a drink." If the quantity of water drunk and time spent has anything to do with it, that camel got enough water to last him for the rest of his life. He drank for a flat half hour before he even paused for breath. Take my advice and never stop to water a camel. If you must work on the water squad of a circus, pick out the elephant—it is easier.

We finally succeeded in prying our camel loose and got started again.

Along our line of march no one was taken unawares, for the racket made by our captives could be heard for blocks. As we neared the sally port of the Temple of Agriculture, everyone turned out to welcome us, not quite so much because of brotherly love but in order to get a fowl of some kind. Of course, we had to send the Department Headquarters a few to keep them from coming over and taking more. Next morning we erected a big poultry yard and turned our bunch loose. By the time Christmas came around, they were all fat and plump, and we roasted enough so that each man had a two- to three-pound chicken all to himself while roast goose and duck [were] served as an entree. There was nothing remarkable about our dinner unless it was the beer and punch that was served right along with the food. That was during the days before the "Big Drought" when it was considered no crime to drink beer and stronger stuff if one wanted it.

If you look at your own kitchens here in the Compound with their cooking ranges and other fairly modern equipment, just imagine trying to cook a good Christmas dinner in a Buzzacott oven. A Buzzacott is just a modification of a Dutch oven, yet our cooks, for this dinner, baked cocoanut and chocolate cakes, made pumpkin and other kinds of pies, and in fact cooked about everything and in a most delectable manner.

That night, we had a show in the mess shack, putting on a bunch of Chinese jugglers and tumblers. After the jugglers had finished, we put on a prizefight, and believe me, an Irish Company can put on a good one. We "rung down the curtain" with a fight between two of our coolies, one introduced as "Ah Hell" and the other as "Hung Loo." These two hopefuls had never learned that their hands could be used for anything other than food passers or their fingers for other purposes than scratching "cooties." When turned loose in the ring, stripped to the waist, they functioned more like Dutch windmills than anything else and a spectator in a ringside seat was really in as much danger of their flying fists as they were. The fight wound up with Ah Hell getting a grip on Hung Loo's pigtail, right next to his skull, with one gloved hand while with the other he literally knocked h— out of him. By this time, everybody was hilarious or asleep, so we all knocked off and went to sleep in our own bunks.

I soldiered with that bunch of Micks for some time thereafter, and when I finally left them, it was with many regrets. Even now, 25 years afterwards, I hear from some of them now and then.

When passing through 'Frisco about a year ago, who should be down at the pier but ex–Musician Jimmie McFadden of old "Battery 'F,'" with his wife and two of the cutest-looking little Irish kids you ever saw. He said he wanted his children to meet the Colonel, for we both had started soldiering together. McFadden now owns a very nice little shoe store in 'Frisco. I never pass through 'Frisco that there isn't someone of the old bunch down to see me. The time before last, it was Sergt. Oscar Winters, over 80 years old, who commenced his service in the Civil War. Oscar has crossed the Great Divide, as have many of the others, but I am willing to bet that few went the southern or hotter route. With all their faults, they were a bunch of as square shooters as anyone will meet in many a day.[8]

3. Aftermath

Subsequently, on April 28 and May 1, 1901, orders from General Chaffee's headquarters officially ended the American involvement in the China Relief Expedition. There were further instructions for the 9th Regiment. General Orders No. 15, Headquarters, China Relief Expedition, directed that its Company B be increased to 150 men under the command of Major Edgar B. Robertson. They were to remain in Peking as the American legation guard. Later, on August 18, 1905, the detachment was relieved from this duty and returned to the United States, replaced by a U.S. Marine unit.[9]

4
Assessment, Consequences and Conclusions

An assessment of some of the consequences of the Boxer Uprising is in order. William E. Bainbridge, the Second Secretary of the American legation in Peking, and the personal secretary of the U.S. Minister to China during the siege, Edwin Hurd Conger, and who, together with his wife, endured the events of that time, observed a touching scene following the relief of the legations when the usually forbidden foreigners entered the Forbidden City on August 28. He explained that he saw "an able and progressive [Chinese] man," who "stood with averted face beside one of the splendid pillars and wept." Had he dared to speak, Bainbridge asserted, he might have said, "Many years ago you Westerners came to us humbly petitioning the right to trade. The profits of our trade helped to make you rich and powerful and then, grown bolder, you forced us at the cannon's mouth, to sign the treaties which you now call sacred. When China lay prostrate before the rising power of Japan, you came with mailed fist threatening her territory, desecrating her temples, reviling her gods. If we have sinned, will the God you worship and call 'the Just' hold you guiltless?" Bainbridge recognized that the man "would have spoken the truth. The Boxer movement was the spontaneous outburst of an injured people's wrath. If it teaches anything it is that among nations as with individuals the way of Peace is the way of Righteousness and that no international comity can long endure whose roots grasp not the eternal principles of Justice."[1]

The discussions of the Boxers by Sir Robert Hart were important in such considerations. The Boxer uprising had untoward effects for him. During the siege of the Western legations his fine home was destroyed together with many invaluable—even priceless—records. Despite the severe stress that he, and all others involved, were under, Hart's composure and ability to analyze

4. Assessment, Consequences and Conclusions

The 15th Infantry on parade in the American Compound (*Mei-Kuo Ying-P'an*), Tientsin, China, 1927. National Archives, Washington, D.C. (111-SC-106241).

events in a penetrating and dispassionate manner were remarkable. He wrote and published six articles in the journals *Fortnightly Review* and *North American Review* concerned with the events of the summer and autumn of 1900 and their implications.²

A major theme that Hart projected was that common sense must prevail. He further hoped that recent events might contribute to better feelings and relations between China and non–China. He also surmised that the Boxer Uprising would lead China to be a different China than before and "that foreign invasion will be met in another way next time." He felt that his articles were of a certain value because "the writer has eaten, digested, and assimilated Chinese thought and feeling on the questions treated of."³

Hart explained that he did not plan "to excuse the Chinese but to simply explain how intercourse has affected the Chinese mind and led to what exists." Though he did not wish to be a prophet, nonetheless he concluded that as a consequence of the Boxer Uprising, "China will go on along a new road to gather strength and that foreign invasion will be met in another way next time." While the Boxers were discredited, in the future "the arming of the people, of a people in fact, will be taken in hand more seriously and the future will have a different China to deal with." In the short term, he hoped that the Chinese might undertake serious reform, "but these people are very wise in their own conceit and they often take the bit in their mouth and have their own way. It is all very interesting, but very tragic—and yet it is comical to see how these Pigmies [Westerners] think to bind Gulliver!"[4]

In all of the backing and filling, Hart never lost his farsighted views of the Chinese. He was often weary of the Chinese tendencies to do nothing about reforms, or to proceed very slowly, and these conditions were "like trying to make a fishing-line out of jadestone!" Yet, China would eventually "arrive!" He held these views, he asserted, because "I never lose heart." He noted, with a reference to Tennyson, that his "faith is large in Time, and that which shapes it to some perfect end" would prevail. He was confident that circumstances "will force this [Chinese] Govt. to take action in various directions and in the end all will come right, but I am sure of one thing: China will grow strong and then international relations will be of another kind." Hart went on to state that the Boxer Uprising therefore was "not meaningless," but rather it was "the prelude to a century of change and the keynote of the future history of the Far East: the China of the year 2000 will be very different from the China of 1900!"

By now, he went on, Chinese national sentiment was a constant factor that must be recognized and taken into account: "The one feeling that is universal in China is pride in Chinese institutions and contempt for foreign: treaty intercourse has not altered this—if anything, it has deepened it, and the future will not be uninfluenced by it." Indeed, China "had slept long, as we count sleep, but it is awake at last, and its every member is tingling with Chinese feeling—'China for the Chinese and out with the foreigners!'" Many of these developments were destined to lie well beyond his own era but his faith was eventually justified.[5]

The American admiral Kemp Tolley similarly remarked upon the rise of the awesome Chinese crowds that had come into their own during the uprising. Indeed, since 1900, the Imperial Court no longer effectively represented any section of the Chinese population. Accordingly, "the common people were for the first time in history actively displaying in strikes and boycotts, mass reaction to both Imperial do-nothingness and foreign influence." This created conditions for the collapse of the Qing empire in 1911, by which time China was overripe for a major change.[6]

Yet, if the Chinese were changing as a consequence of the Boxer era's

4. Assessment, Consequences and Conclusions

events, many Westerners remained unaltered. The well-known missionary Arthur Henderson Smith, who had been present in Peking during the siege and who knew the Chinese better than most Westerners, stubbornly clung to the stodgy, staid position earlier embraced by many Western missionaries. His account of the Boxer Uprising, *China in a Convulsion*, reveals little tendency to change earlier positions, and he concluded that it was important "to recognize the indisputable and vital fact that China is in need of a new moral life" that only Christianity could provide.[7]

Pearl S. Buck—herself a missionary kid, or "mishkid"—also cogently discussed the failures of the West in the Boxer era in her often neglected or ignored memoirs, *My Several Worlds*, written shortly after the Communist takeover of China. Therein, we read that "the Chinese are a proud and envious people, as a nation and as individuals, and they do not love their superiors and never did, and the truth is they have never believed that their superiors could exist." This was one of the explanations of anti–Americanism, she wrote, coupled with the attitudes of white missionaries and traders and diplomats who considered themselves, whether consciously or unconsciously, superior to the Chinese. This smoldering fury, which white men could not or would not recognize, had lived on in Chinese hearts for more than a century. It was later the chief reason why Chiang Kai-shek lost his country and the Communists won it. In fact, if he had been wise, he would have boldly expressed his own anti–Western feelings and thereby retained his leadership. He thought, however, that he could win by American power and this his people could not forgive him. Accordingly, Mao Tse-tung seized the opportunity Chiang threw away, and the power of history in Asia therefore turned against the West.

To reverse matters, Pearl Buck suggested, Americans in particular must prove to the Asians that they were not totally involved in suppressing the Chinese. They were therefore relatively innocent of much of the past. They were not to be confused with the British, who once ruled India and in China won the Three Opium Wars and heavily taxed the people. Nor were they like those officials in England who allowed Japan to remain in Manchuria, thereby establishing the basis for the Japanese imperial war. Americans should prove to Asia that they had not been as other white men had been. Nevertheless, this posed many difficulties, because Americans were "only relatively innocent." Americans, for instance, in 1900 participated in suppressing the Boxer Rebellion, which was not a rebellion but rather a revolt against the white man. During this venture, Americans played a part in the destruction of palaces and the looting of incalculable quantities of the nation's treasure in Peking, Tientsin and elsewhere. Buck indicated that Americans did not heed or understand—and did not yet understand—what the results of these actions would be, for Americans were numbered among the white race.

Consequently, Buck continued, after the storm and the defeat of the Chinese, the West went back again to China without a lesson learned, and in fact, persisted as before. They returned to complacency, thinking that they had taught the Chinese a lesson by force and that the Chinese would never again rebel against the white man's rule. Westerners were allowed to come and go as they pleased in China, and their merchant ships and naval vessels could sail Chinese waters and dock at any port, unhindered by rules and restrictions. Missionaries were given the freedom to live where they wished and to open schools teaching subjects foreign to the Chinese, though the schools were a boon as well. They could establish hospitals that practiced foreign medicine and surgery. Medical aid, like education, was one of the positive sides of Western missionary intervention. Perhaps most devastating of all, missionaries were free to preach a religion entirely alien to the Chinese, insisting that their religion was the only true one and declaring that those who refused to believe were condemned to hell. Buck, having grown up in China, and therefore possessing a firsthand knowledge of these matters, concluded that "the affrontery [sic] of all this still makes my soul shrink." Buck's tutor—a Mr. Kung—further warned her that there would surely be a reckoning "until justice is done," though he said it "gravely and with infinite pity."[8] It is interesting to reflect that in 21st century China, there are still remembrances of the invasion of Chinese territory by the Eight-Nation Alliance in 1900, a major event that set a benchmark for outrages the Chinese suffered at the hands of the West.[9]

In Kipling's terms, trying to "hustle [and rustle] the East" has had a mixed legacy, resulting in more error and failure than success, as is perhaps understandable when the scale and complexity of China and its history, culture and traditional attitudes are considered. Nonetheless, driven by desires to tap China's apparently limitless markets, an often chimerical lure, and by religious missionary zeal, the Occident was determined to venture into China. In so doing, as one scholar has observed, "early travellers arriving from West, amongst a people utterly alien to themselves in almost every detail—language, dress, habits, modes of thought, ethical ideals and general view of life—would have done well to walk very warily and, in the Confucian phrase, 'to reserve their judgment on what they saw and heard around them.'"[10] But this they failed to do, and they became altogether imperialistic in attitude and conduct. Accordingly, Chinese contacts with the West were largely negative.

In the more extreme cases, cruelty, rapaciousness, arrogance and debauchery of Western traders and men of commerce became a byword in

4. Assessment, Consequences and Conclusions 53

China, as did the conduct of foreign soldiery. One observer has noted, regarding the latter, "Army life is not a school of virtue anywhere, particularly in Asia where a comparatively defenseless people open wide opportunities for evil practices and where Asiatic methods of opposition infuriate men. In almost every place where the soldiers of Europe landed, they pillaged and burned and raped and slaughtered like incarnate fiends."[11] A Chinese proverb underscores these characteristics, observing that "nails are not made from good iron; honest citizens never become soldiers," or as Kipling has stated it in his poem "Tommy," soldiers "don't grow into plaster saints." Finally, the failure of the West to learn from the Boxer Uprising contributed to the West's prevailing general shortsightedness and inabilities to understand Asia and China, their history, and their 5,000-year-old culture and civilization, which prevails, in varying degrees, to this day.

As to the U.S. Army, it might be asked, what ends did they serve in China? To some extent, the U.S. presence contributed to the negative aspects of the Century of Shame and the great impact this had on the Chinese. For instance, some U.S. troops were undoubtedly engaged in looting during the Boxer era, though apparently they were not as involved as were other Westerners. Pearl Buck so asserted, but noted that the American involvement as compared to others was a matter of degree. The same was true of the punitive expeditions launched after the legations were rescued, though Americans were less involved than other forces. The Chinese, though, often drew no such distinctions and considered all Westerners as drawn from the same mold. American "boots on the ground" have not always been a good thing and should only be employed with caution.[12]

One explanation of the Western attitudes that Buck describes can be seen in General Daggett's book on the Boxer Uprising, in which he observed that during that time, "everyone felt that he was engaged in a righteous cause, and was stimulated to energetic exertion thereby." This was coupled with a sense of the heroic, among the American forces, at least, which reflected the temper of the times. This attitude also emphasized that the flag was being honored, "as it always has been where American soldiers have borne it." These considerations of "my country right or wrong" loomed much larger than even the dangers encountered and the losses sustained by the combatants. Indeed, in the Boxer Uprising days, reflecting U.S. views of Manifest Destiny, many Americans felt that they were serving the international good, and according to the lights of those times, showing the flag and protecting American interests, notably those of the business and missionary communities, were all regarded as worthy aims. To be sure, insofar as the American Relief Expedition's actions were in keeping with the time-honored and generally accepted practices of support of diplomatic personnel on foreign soil, they were performed in an acceptable manner. To the extent, however, that they contributed to the suppression and exploitation of the Chinese nation and people, they were reprehensible and in support of a perfidious cause.[13]

In any case, while there, American service personnel abroad enlarged their views and knowledge of China and Asia, which in many instances would have significance in later years. The military units involved in the Boxer Uprising also enhanced their honors, their sense of worth and prestige, and an exaltation of glory, adding illustrious chapters to their histories. In any event, American soldiers and their various organizations recognized and lauded their own bravery and sacrifices, their own "band of brothers" relationships, and participation in those occurrences, which in their time were considered earth-shaking, desirable, and sought-after ventures.

The 9th Regiment emerged with the sobriquet "Manchus," and the 14th was known ever afterward as the "Golden Dragons." The 15th obtained its own motto, "Can Do," as a consequence of its quarter-century stint in China. Its coat of arms retains to this day the image of a dragon. Not to be overlooked are memorabilia such as silver bowls and accouterments, including the 9th Regiment's "Liscum Bowl," the 31st's "Shanghai Bowl," and the 15th's similar silver dishes, all attesting to the regiments' significant involvement in Asia. Also concerning the 9th, a monument, paid for by officers of the regiment, was erected in Tientsin, in 1903, in memory of Colonel Liscum in the Japanese Concession, where he fell.[14] These considerations would also include records of major decorations, especially the Medal of Honor, which was founded in 1861 when it was authorized for the U.S. Navy and extended to the U.S. Army the following year. There were special medals, much rarer in those days, struck by both the army and navy—the latter being awarded to the Marines as well—for those who participated in the Boxer Uprising. Lest one underestimate the utility of such decorations or accouterments and

Ninth Infantry Punch Bowl. There were similar bowls for the 31st and the 15th Infantry Regiments,. All of them were in recognition of the service of the regiments in China (original photograph courtesy of New York Public Library).

the remembrances they evoke, it might be well to recall that Napoleon Bonaparte, who understood something about military leadership, reinstituted military decorations that had been abolished during the revolution, especially the *Légion d'Honneur*. He admonished scoffers, asserting, "You call these baubles. Well, it is with baubles that men are led.... Do you think that you would be able to make men fight by reasoning? Never. That is good only for the scholar in his study. The soldier needs glory, distinctions, and rewards."[15]

Something of the later history of U.S. Army units earlier engaged in China will put this service in perspective, with the recognition that their future accomplishments were at least partially influenced and enhanced by their previous engagements there. Regarding service in the Boxer era, there was the 14th Regiment. This unit, unlike many major American infantry regiments, did not take part in combat in World War I. Neither was it engaged during World War II until the spring of 1945, when it participated in the final battles in Germany. It was more fully involved in the Korean War, fighting in such storied places as the "Punchbowl" and "Porkchop Hill." It was also employed in a major way as part of the U.S. Army's 3rd Brigade from 1966 to the early 1970s in Vietnam. Later ventures included Somalia in 1993, Bosnia in 1997, and Iraq in 2003–2005.

The 9th Regiment, after the Boxer Uprising, returned to the Philippines in 1901 and 1902, though a detachment remained in Peking until 1905 as the legation guard until relieved by U.S. Marines. In 1902, the bulk of the 9th deployed once more to the United States, not departing again until World War I, when, as part of the famed "Indianhead" 2nd Division, it was in France, fighting at Chateau-Thierry, in the Meuse-Argonne, the Aisne-Marne, and elsewhere. After the armistice, it was part of the U.S. Army of Occupation in Germany, 1918–1919. Following that it returned to the United States.

It was engaged during World War II, arriving at Omaha Beach on 7 June, and fought on the Brittany Peninsula and later at the Battle of the Bulge and crossed the Siegfried Line into Germany and Czechoslovakia. It returned home in July of 1945. In the Korean War, from July 31, 1950, it was again part of the Indianhead Division. It participated in the breakout of the Pusan perimeter and proceeded almost to the Yalu, when the Chinese attacked on November 25, 1950, driving the American forces far to the south again. The 9th was savaged and later withdrew to Seoul to regroup. It then fought along the 38th Parallel, participating in the struggle at "Heartbreak Ridge," among other encounters.

At the end of the Korean War, the regiment was ordered to Alaska, then again into Germany from 1963 to 1966, and from there to Hawaii. In December 1967, it was in Vietnam, there to stay for four-and-one-half years. After Nam, it was used in various trouble spots—Panama from 1989 to 1990, Cuba in 1995, and Iraq in 2004, 2007 and 2009.

The 6th Cavalry Regiment, after its involvement in the Boxer Uprising, saw little action until World War II when it landed at Utah Beach in July 1944. It then became part of Patton's Third Army, seeing action in the Ardennes and at the Battle of the Bulge, assisted in the breaching of the Siegfried Line and the crossing of the Rhine and participated in the drive into Germany.

Following World War II, on December 20, 1948, the 6th was reorganized as the 6th Armored Cavalry and numerous reorganizations followed. Eventually, in the summer of 1974, it was once more transformed in a major way, becoming part of an air cavalry combat brigade. In 1990, units were involved in Iraq in "Operation Desert Shield" and "Desert Storm." Numerous deactivations and reactivations followed, until in February 2003, when units of the organization were deployed to Kuwait preparing for the 2003 invasion of Iraq, and it became part of "Operation Iraqi Freedom." By the year 2007, aviation squadrons of the old 6th Cavalry Regiment were known as Air Cavalry Reconnaissance Squadrons.

Many of the personnel who served in China in these outfits, then or later, attained the rank of general with its concomitant major responsibilities, some of which reflected the effects of their Asian service. Among those who had experience in China was Lieutenant General Adna Romanza Chaffee, Sr. He had served in the 6th United States Cavalry during the Civil War. He later fought with distinction in numerous battles against the Indians in the Southwest. During the Spanish-American War, as a major general of U.S. Volunteers, he became chief of staff to the governor-general of Cuba. There he also commanded the troops that participated in the last military operations prior to the ending of the struggle. Following that war, he was discharged from the Volunteers and was reappointed brigadier general, U.S. Army, on April 13, 1899. On July 19, 1900, he was made a major general of Volunteers once again and ordered to command U.S. troops with the Allied armies in China discussed elsewhere in this study.

On the reorganization of the Regular Army in 1901, he became a major general and commander of the Military District of the Philippines and on January 8, 1904, he was promoted to lieutenant general. From August 19, 1904, to January 14, 1906, he was the army's chief of staff. He then retired, having spent forty-five years in the U.S. Army. He died in 1914 and is buried at Arlington National Cemetery.

Another example of how important the China deployment could be was

4. Assessment, Consequences and Conclusions 57

the case of General Charles Pelot Sommerall. He, after the demise of Captain Reilly, commander of Battery F (usually referred to as the "Reilly Battery") of the 5th U.S. Field Artillery Regiment before the gates leading to the Imperial City on August 15, 1900, took over the battery. He then proceeded to forge a significant military career in the years following. Sommerall himself recognized the importance of his being placed in charge of Battery F. He stated that it was in the Philippines, and especially in China, where he served with that battery, that "I got my head out of the crowd. From then on, I had an individual reputation and standing in the army."[16]

He was then on duty in the American West and at Camp Skagway and Fort Seward in Alaska. He was then senior instructor of artillery tactics at West Point from 1905 to 1911. From 1912, he commanded summer camps for the Army and National Guard artillery, was assistant chief of the Militia Bureau, a member of the Boards of Ordnance and Fortifications, and was in charge of National Guard artillery from 1915 to 1917. In 1917, he was attached to a U.S. military mission to British and French armies. He became a brigadier general in the National Army in August 1917 and was soon promoted to major general. He, then in succession, commanded the 1st Division and V Corps during the Cantigny, Soissons, St. Mihiel and Meuse-Argonne operations in 1918. For a time, he later commanded IX and IV Corps, and after the armistice served on the American Peace Commission at the Peace Conference in 1919.

Demoted following the conflict, as were many officers, he commanded the 1st Division in 1919 and 1920, receiving promotion to brigadier general once more in February 1919, and to major general in 1920. He then commanded the Hawaiian Department from 1921 to 1924. After commanding the 8th and 2nd corps areas from 1924 to 1926, he was appointed army chief of staff on November 21, 1926, completing his term on November 20, 1930, after obtaining his four stars as general in February 1929. He retired from the army in 1931 and became president of the Citadel in Charleston, South Carolina, from 1931 to 1953. He died in Washington, D.C., on May 14, 1955, and is buried at Arlington National Cemetery.

Another officer of note who participated in the Boxer Uprising was Joseph Theodore Dickman. He became Chaffee's chief of staff in Peking, though not until immediately after the siege of the legations had been lifted. He did participate in the punitive Battle of Pa-ta-Chao on September 26, 1900. His earlier military experience included Indian wars in the 1880s and the Spanish-American War, where he participated in the battle of San Juan Hill and El Caney, at Santiago, Cuba. During the Philippine-American War from 1899 to 1902, he served on the staff of General Joseph Wheeler.

From 1902 to 1905, Dickman was on the Army General Staff, and, in

1905, graduated from the Army War College, remaining from 1905 to 1912 as an instructor. He was the U.S. Army Inspector General from 1912 to 1915, then served as commander of the 2nd U.S. Cavalry in 1915, and the 85th Infantry Division in 1917. In November 1917, he assumed command of the 3rd Infantry Division, taking it to France. He led the division into combat at Chateau-Thierry in May 1918, where it earned its nickname, "Rock of the Marne." He then commanded the IV Corps during the Saint-Mihiel Offensive in August 1918. In October, as commander of I Corps, he led his men into battle during the Meuse-Argonne offensive.

Following the armistice, General Pershing created the U.S. Third Army, designated the Army of Occupation of Germany, with headquarters at Coblenz, making Dickman its commanding general.[17] Subsequently, back in the U.S., Dickman, among other things, served as commanding general of VIII Corps, 1919–21. Retiring from the army on October 6, 1921, he was recalled for a time to preside over the army's downsizing board in 1922. Again retiring, he died in Washington, D.C., on October 23, 1927, and is buried at Arlington National Cemetery.[18]

Undoubtedly, during the Boxer Uprising members of the United States military forces acquitted themselves well. Nonetheless, it was the larger issues of why any of the Westerners—and Japanese—were there at all. The Chinese saw things much differently, recognizing that they still lacked much regarding being in charge of their own affairs. There would then ensue further years of protracted suffering and hardship before the foreigners would be expelled. China's own revolution in 1911 and 1912, failed to establish that country on solid ground. As to the U.S. Army, these events would bring another infantry regiment once more to China's shores: the 15th U.S. Infantry, which had also been engaged in the Boxer Uprising. It would then return to the United States, with some service in the Philippines during the following decade until 1912, and would subsequently remain in China from that year to 1938. It is to these developments that this narrative now turns.

Part II: The 15th U.S. Infantry Regiment's Service in China, 1900–1938

"Can Do" is a true expression,
Of the spirit that lies within,
The heart of we "doughboy" soldiers,
Here in this far away city, Tientsin.
—Pvt. John B. Houchin,
"Ode to Our Motto Heaven-sent,"
Sentinel, April 25, 1931

5

THE 15TH INFANTRY REGIMENT IN THE BOXER UPRISING

In addition to the 9th and 14th Regiments, and the other units involved in the Boxer Uprising, the U.S. Army's 15th Infantry Regiment, under the command of Colonel Edward Moale, also participated, though it arrived only after the relief of the besieged legations.[1] It was on July 7, 1900, that the 15th received orders from the War Department to prepare for service in China to participate in the relief of the foreign legations in Peking. The 1st Battalion, the Regimental Band, and the Regimental Headquarters were equipped for the field, with some additions from the 2nd and 3rd Battalions. The regiment embarked at San Francisco on the U.S. Army transport *Sumner* on July 17, 1900. Sailing across the North Pacific, the ship first landed at the Japanese port of Kobe and then crossed the Inland Sea to Nagasaki, arriving on August 10. There the *Sumner* was ordered to Manila, and the regiment was transferred to another ship, the *Indiana*. On this they made their way to the Taku Bar, the port area of Tientsin, China, at the mouth of the Hai Ho River on August 16, two days after the siege had been lifted in Peking. At the time, its strength was 22 officers and 1,058 men. From Taku, the regiment proceeded to Tientsin via the railroad, arriving there on August 19. There, a few days later, the regiment camped in tents on the west bank of the Hai Ho River just south of the European quarter of Tientsin, establishing quarters in the American Methodist Mission. The Americans then joined troops of many nationalities in various encampments. Because the siege in Peking had been relieved by then, the 15th was mainly employed from September to November in guarding fleets of junks transporting supplies to the American forces in Peking under the command of General Adna Romanza Chaffee. The railroad had been destroyed by the Boxers and thus it was necessary to utilize water transportation. The route was from Tientsin to T'ung Hsien, the head of navigation about fifteen miles southeast of Peking. Fleets numbering from ten to about twenty junks were established.

Before these events, however, General Arthur Dorward, commander of the British troops in Tientsin and the provisional governor of the Tientsin Military District, received word that Boxers were assembled at the walled town of Tiu-liu, about thirty miles up the Grand Canal. He decided to send a joint expedition, consisting of American, British, Japanese, Russian and Italian units, to the threatened town to capture or destroy the hostile detachment, and then burn the town, in order to prevent its use as a hostile base on the flank of the Allies' line of communications. About 3,600 men were ordered to this duty. On the morning of September 9, this force, in three columns, set out. First Lieutenant John M. Palmer commanded the two companies of the 15th assigned to the mission. To Palmer, "the march in such a column was a marvelous experience for the American doughboy of that day. His younger brothers of this generation who have served in every part of the globe can have no conception of the dreamlike quality of that experience. After generations of isolation, the doors of the wide world had at last begun to open. It then seemed unbelievable to boys bred in Illinois and Kansas and New Hampshire that they were carrying the American flag along the Grand Canal of China with Sikhs from India marching ahead of them and Italians with rooster feathers in their hats behind them."[2] Unfortunately, for the Chinese it would be another experience altogether.

As has been previously noted, one of the perennial aspects of the Boxer venture from the Allied forces' point of view was that of looting. Palmer noted something of this when he asserted that the troops began to harvest melons, fruit and all manner of vegetables. The medical officer of the detachment, however, noted that fresh foodstuffs were contaminated by their soil, which was permeated by human and animal waste and therefore unsafe to eat without much processing. Only the fruits from trees obtained his sanction.[3]

Arriving at Tiu-liu, the force halted and prepared for the anticipated struggle. It was discovered, however, that the Boxers were not present and Palmer doubted that they had been there in the first place. In his view, Tiu-liu was "simply a Chinese trading town whose peaceful inhabitants were frightened almost to death by a savage horde of foreign devils, which included Company D, 15th U.S. Infantry, commanded by First Lieutenant John McA. Palmer."

Palmer expressed fears that as soon as the Japanese and Russian contingents entered the town, "there would be the usual orgy of loot and destruction. So I reminded the men that they were American citizens, as well as soldiers, and that it was against our principles as well as our Army Regulations for any officer or man in the American uniform to appropriate any private property to his own use. We were authorized to take what was strictly needed for military purposes, but that whatever we took, we took for the military service of the United States and not for ourselves."

Outrages were soon underway, and the unit's medical personnel did what they could to mend numerous broken bones and the many bayonet wounds the Chinese suffered at the hands of members of the Allied contingent. As the day progressed, buildings were destroyed and their contents confiscated or trampled in the mud, while the Chinese citizens, burdened with heavy bundles of household goods on their back, fled to the countryside. In one instance, Palmer heard "ear-piercing shrieks from two coolies" who were being dragged along by their queues. He was informed that the victims were about to be executed as Boxer spies. But Palmer discovered that they were "our private servants," and they were rescued only with great difficulty. He surmised, "No doubt many of the alleged Boxers who were executed in North China were as innocent as these poor devils." All-in-all, Palmer concluded, "Here were all the evils of an international military force with no effective international command to control it."

But if it could not be controlled, then perhaps it might be profitably managed, at least as far as the looting went. General Dorward appointed a board to divide up the loot that began to appear, especially that found in pawnshops, which in China often served as banks. When apprised of the fact that he was to serve on the board as an American representative, Palmer protested that American orders were in place forbidding looting. His British counterpart then stated that he would take into account this "technical defect in your Army Regulations," and that he would see that the Americans got their share when they returned to Tientsin. Palmer was astonished that this procedure was followed, and concluded that "when we got back to Tientsin each American officer [there was no mention of enlisted men] who took part in the Tiu-liu campaign received a bundle from [the board]." He himself admitted that this was the only loot that he acquired in the Boxer campaign, mainly retaining only a bolt of fine Chinese silk with the imperial seal woven into the cloth, which his wife later used to cover several of the family's chairs.

British looting was no doubt accompanied on occasion by the perpetrators reciting from Kipling's famous enthusiastic poem, "Loot," in his "Barrack-Room Ballads." Palmer had written in his memoirs that on one evening, while the 15th Regiment was sailing to China, a company member was strumming his mandolin as an accompaniment to Kipling's songs. His rendering of "On the Road to Mandalay" just as the sun was going down "like thunder" into the Yellow Sea was greatly appreciated by the listeners. The musician then "gave us Kipling's 'Loot, Loot, Loot,' which led to a discussion of the song's subject." Thereupon, one of the senior officers scolded the men for the discussion, reminding them of the current Army Regulations on the subject. Yet, undoubtedly, all foreign troops were engaged in looting to a greater or lesser extent. Lieutenant Charles Pelot Sommerall, attached to Captain Henry J. Reilly's battery in Peking, has noted that "although Captain Reilly sternly forbade the taking of anything [Chinese], a certain amount of looting became accepted, and our men and officers had a small share. Some officers even accumulated rich stores of treasure."[4]

On September 11, the Allied contingent began the march back to Tientsin, with one British detachment left behind to complete the burning of the town. This example of Allied punitive activity was the basis of one of the *Letters from John Chinaman*, in Dickinson, wherein it was observed that regarding cruelties inflicted on the Chinese by the troops of the Christian nations, one must "ask the once fertile land from Peking to the coast; ask the corpses of murdered men and outraged women and children; ask the innocent mingled indiscriminately with the guilty; ask the Christ, the lover of men, whom you profess to serve, to judge between us who rose in mad despair to save our country and you who, avenging crime with crime, did not pause to reflect that the crime you avenged was the fruit of your own iniquity," and it was this that had caused the Boxer Uprising in the first place.[5]

Following the return to Tientsin, Palmer was put in charge of one of the junk fleets that carried supplies from warehouses in Tientsin to Peking for the American forces still on duty there. On September 27, his little fleet was underway. He had 12 junks under his command, each about 30 to 40 feet long. A hold amidships was used to stow the freight. He established his headquarters in a shelter tent, also amidships, on the deck of the leading junk. Two of his soldiers occupied a single shelter tent ahead of the mast near the bow. The detachment cook and his coolie kitchen staff and two soldiers were assigned to the second junk. Each of the other junks carried two soldiers as guards. An American flag flew from each junk's mast. This was necessary to prevent those from other Allied forces, such as the Russians, Germans, or Japanese, from attempting to requisition the junks, which were in rather short supply and needed greatly. Two tugboats pulled the junks past the walled city and then dropped them off and proceeded upriver. Along much of the route, six coolies towed each junk with a tow rope attached to the top of the mast, while the pilot manned the rudder and kept the bow of his vessel off the shore. Where the river widened, and if a favorable breeze blew up, each junk hoisted its big square sail and the coolies came aboard from the towpath. Thus the flotilla proceeded up the Pei Ho. The junks tied up each night and

Junks on the Pei Ho River bound for Peking during the Boxer Rebellion sailed by men of the 15th Infantry Regiment (Library of Congress).

5. The 15th Infantry Regiment in the Boxer Uprising   65

The 15th Infantry's regimental band on parade in the American Compound, 1927 (National Archives, Washington, D.C. 111-SC-106231).

the cook built his fire on the shore and prepared the meals. The usual army fare of bacon, beans and coffee was served, while the coolies ate the rice that had simmered throughout the day on a little charcoal burner near the junks' sterns.

After almost a week of sailing, the junks arrived on October 2 at T'ung-Hsien at the U.S. Army supply base a few miles from Peking. Palmer had wanted to visit Peking, but General Chaffee, in need of all the supplies he could get, sent him back downstream almost immediately the same afternoon. Following his return to Tientsin, Palmer was notified of his six-year-old son's death, so he did not return upriver. At length, Palmer was ordered to Fort Porter in New York, and he sailed from China on November 27, eventually arriving at San Francisco on January 1, 1901. While at Fort Porter in New York, in the summer of 1901, Palmer was ordered to West Point as instructor in the Department of Chemistry.

Other companies of the 15th were stationed at Tientsin Arsenal on

Officers and men of the 15th Infantry Regiment. Note the sharp uniforms for which the regiment was noted (courtesy of chinamarine.org).

September 6, and others were at the port at Tongku from September 22. Until the latter part of November, men of the 15th participated in expeditions against small bands of Boxers in nearby villages, as Palmer recounted of one such venture.

On November 25, 1900, the 15th was ordered aboard the transport *Rosecrans*, which sailed first to Nagasaki and then proceeded to the Philippines, arriving there on December 13. The regiment's 2nd and 3rd battalions soon joined the 1st there from the United States. It remained on duty in the Philippines engaged in the arduous and dangerous tasks of "pacifying" the Filipinos until July 1902, when it returned to the United States and took up garrison duties at Monterey, California, in September and built the Presidio. Three years later, on December 3, 1905, the 15th was again in the Philippines, remaining until late in 1907. Returning to the United States, the 15th proceeded to Fort Douglas, Utah, where it was engaged in garrison duty. There it remained until 1912, when duty called it to serve in China once more.

6

THE 15TH RETURNS TO CHINA, 1912–1938

As for American involvement in China in the early years of the 20th century, while trade and missionary work was in the forefront, American armed forces were also involved. Earlier, the navy had been the first in the field. As far back as 1831, when Levi Woodbury became secretary of the navy, it was clear that American vessels trading in Asia were not being protected from pirates and other depredations. Accordingly, American ships were dispatched by President Andrew Jackson to seek treaties with such locales as Cochin-China, Siam and Muscat to secure safety for American shipping. Some treaties were successfully negotiated, and in 1935, Commodore Edmund P. Kennedy established the first significant permanent U.S. Navy presence in Asia, the East India Squadron.[1]

This squadron was subsequently engaged in significant ways during the First and Second Opium wars (1839–1842 and 1856–1860) as well as in the opening of Japan to U.S. trade during the 1850s. In 1868, the East India Squadron was disbanded and merged with the new U.S. Asiatic Squadron. This unit participated principally in protecting commerce with China and Japan, though it was also engaged in Korean operations, as in 1871. Its most important involvement was in the Spanish-American War of 1898, being heavily engaged against Spanish forces in the Philippines and in the capture of Guam from Spain. From 1899 to 1902, the Asiatic Squadron participated in the Philippine-American War.

The Asiatic Squadron was superseded by the creation of the United States Asiatic Fleet in 1902. Its principal occupation from that time until 1942 was the protection of the Philippine Islands and Guam, and upholding the "Open Door Policy" in China. For a brief period, from 1907 to 1910, the fleet was downgraded, becoming known as the First Squadron of the United States

Pacific Fleet. On January 28, 1910, however, it was reorganized as the Asiatic Fleet.

Another important body of water, the Yangtze River, from 1854 to 1941 was patrolled by vessels, principally gunboats, of the U.S. Navy's East India and Asiatic Squadrons. In 1922, the Yangtze Patrol was more formally established as a component of the Asiatic Fleet. Indeed, from 1854 to the end of its life in 1941, the Yangtze Squadron—The "YangPat"—was one of the most important in the United States Navy in China. According to the "unequal treaties," and the doctrine of extraterritoriality, various nations had several "treaty ports" open to them for extensive commercial operations. The Yangtze River, the longest in China, was central to much of this activity. It was navigable as far inland as Chungking, 1,300 miles from sea at Shanghai, and even beyond. Accordingly, its patrol was an important assignment for the United States Navy.

Another branch of the United States armed forces, the U.S. Marine Corps, was also heavily involved in China. Though the event was of no permanent significance, the U.S. Marines landed in Shanghai in 1854, again in Shanghai and Hong Kong in 1855, Canton in 1856, Shanghai once more in 1859, and New Chwang, Tung Chow Foo and Shanghai in 1866, to protect American diplomatic personnel. It was not until December 1894 that the Marines went ashore for an appreciable time. This came about during the Sino-Japanese War of 1894. As Japanese forces advanced, antiforeign riots broke out, and the American minister in Peking, Colonel Charles Denby, requested that the Marines send in a guard detachment. The Marines duly landed and proceeded to Tientsin. Because the emperor would not permit them into Peking, however, they languished in Tientsin until 1895, when, after six months in China, they were withdrawn.[2]

Once more, in 1898, there was civil unrest in China that convinced American and other foreign nations to request that guards be sent to Peking. This time, in November, eighteen United States Marines and one officer duly arrived. They remained until March 1899.[3] The Marines were closely involved in the Boxer Uprising in 1900, as has already been noted. Also in mid–August, additional Marines had entered China but did not participate in relieving Peking. In early September, many of the Marines had returned to the ships from whence they came, and by the end of the month, most of those remaining in China were ordered back to the Philippines.

The Marines had acquitted themselves well during this time and 33 Medals of Honor were conferred on them. In addition, many other decorations and much official recognition came their way, and eventually three officers who served in the Boxer Uprising later became commandants of the Marine Corps.[4]

6. The 15th Returns to China, 1912–1938

The exit of most of the Marines by September 1900 did not mark their final departure from China. In 1900, a company-size detachment from the 9th U.S. Infantry Regiment, by then having been withdrawn to the Philippines, was maintained as the American legation guard at Peking. On September 12, 1905, the U.S. minister to China, W.W. Rockhill, requested that a marine detachment be returned to Peking as the permanent guard, a request that was granted. Included among those then in Peking was a band and a thirty-man mounted detachment, referred to rather jocularly by some as the "Horse Marines." Subsequently, from that time until Pearl Harbor, the Marines remained on duty in the Chinese capital, until they were forced to surrender to Japanese forces on December 8, 1941.[5]

On several occasions after 1900, U.S. Marines intervened in China, for example to reinforce the legation guards in 1911 and 1912. Also, in the 1920s, as civil wars swept over China, the legation guards were reinforced, as in 1922, and again in 1925. With the International Settlement in Shanghai, Marines reinforced that area as well, though they were withdrawn the following year. In 1926, another Marine unit intervened at Chinwangtao, on China's northeast coast, "to protect American interests" there. Much more significant were the Marines' presence in Shanghai when a provisional battalion landed there on February 8.

In the following year, 1927, intensification of civil unrest led to the 4th Marine Regiment's being summoned from San Diego; the 4th arrived in Shanghai on February 14. They were to be a familiar, colorful presence there until 1941. These Marines were sometimes referred to as the "Old China Hands." Soon, however, their numbers seemed insufficient. Accordingly, the Marine commandant, Major General John A. Lejeune, decided that they should be brought up to brigade strength. This consisted of the 6th Marine Regiment, reinforced by the 10th Marine Artillery Regiment, and the brigade armed with artillery, tanks and an aviation force. The brigade, designated the 3rd Marine Brigade, was commanded by Brigadier General Smedley D. Butler, a controversial figure of note, mainly because of his leftist political views. This force, consisting of 238 officers, 18 warrant officers and 4,170 enlisted men, arrived in Shanghai on May 2, 1927. It was decided in early June that the 3rd Brigade, less the 4th Marine Regiment, which remained in Shanghai, should proceed to Tientsin, there to join the U.S. 15th Infantry Regiment, which had been in that city since 1912.[6]

In January 1929, after Chiang Kai-shek had, to a degree, established control over a united China, the 3rd Brigade returned to the United States, though the 4th Regiment remained in Shanghai. At this time, the U.S. military presence, not including the U.S. Navy, consisted of the 15th Infantry in Tientsin, the legation guard in Peking, and the 4th Regiment in Shanghai, subsequently often referred to as the "China Marines."

The 15th's first ventures in China occurred during the Boxer Uprising as recounted above. Subsequently, from 1912 to 1938, the regiment was a familiar fixture on the landscape of Tientsin, China. Accordingly, a brief history of the 15th Regiment from its inception to the time of its arrival in China in 1912 is justified.[7]

The first 15th Infantry unit was organized on July 16, 1798, for the "Quasi-War" with France. It saw no service in this venture and was deactivated in 1800. Its second manifestation came on the occasion of the War of 1812 when an act of Congress, approved by President James Madison on January 11, 1812, created the Fifteenth Infantry. It consisted of ten companies and was first commanded by Colonel Zebulon Montgomery Pike of New Jersey. It participated in the capture of Toronto [York] and Fort George in April and May of 1813, subsequently fought in the Champlain Valley campaign in 1814, and participated in the October offensive in Ontario and other minor activities late in the war. It was again deactivated in May 1815.[8]

It was not until February 11, 1847, that the 15th reemerged as an organized unit in the U.S. Army for service in the war with Mexico. Arriving at Vera Cruz, the 15th moved inland to join General Winfield Scott's army in its advance to Mexico City. It participated in the battles of Contreras and Churubusco, among others, and was finally engaged in the storming of the walls of Chapultepec. Following the war, the 15th was involved in occupation duties in Mexico City and Cuernavaca before returning to the United States, where it was once more deactivated in August of 1848.

The official records of the 15th Infantry date only to General Order No. 33 of May 3, 1861, in the Civil War. The earlier incarnations are not recognized. During the Civil War, the 15th was headquartered at Wheeling, West Virginia; Cleveland, Ohio; Newport Barracks, Kentucky; and Fort Adams, Rhode Island. During the war, it fought in 22 major engagements, including Chattanooga, Chickamauga, Murfreesboro, and Atlanta, as part of General William Tecumseh Sherman's armies.

After the Civil War, the 15th was engaged in occupation duty in Alabama until 1869. Subsequently, it was deployed in the West, first in New Mexico and Arizona for twelve years. It was then in Colorado, involved in operations against the Apaches in both Colorado and New Mexico. In the autumn of 1882, it was transferred to the Department of Dakota and served there for eight years.

In 1890, some of the 15th's units remained in Dakota Territory and headquartered at Fort Sheridan in Illinois. Other units, meanwhile, were stationed

6. The 15th Returns to China, 1912–1938

in Alabama, Florida, and Louisiana. In the following year, 1891, the 15th was reunited in Illinois. It then became part of the Department of Missouri until October 5, 1896, then served in the Department of Colorado from October 19, 1896, to October of 1898.

With the outbreak of the Spanish-American War, in October of 1898, various units of the regiment converged on Camp Force, near Huntsville, Alabama, for training. Though the fighting had ceased by this time, it departed from Savannah, Georgia, on November 27 bound for Nuevitas, Cuba, for occupation duty. There it remained until January 5, 1900, at which time it sailed home, taking up posts in Vermont and New York.

The coming of the Boxer Uprising intruded upon the peace of the world and the 15th was to be engaged, though it was hardly the first in the field, as has been recorded above. Following its actions at that time, on November 25, the regiment was relieved from duty with the China Relief Expedition, and set sail for Manila, where warring factions of Filipinos were engaged in action against American occupying forces. There, for some months, units were variously engaged in action. By February of 1902, men of the Second and Third battalions had joined the First in action in the Philippines, though the entire regiment sailed for the United States in September 1902, taking up its post at Monterey, where it undertook much of that base's Presidio construction from 1902 to 1905. Some insight into the attitudes of the average infantryman during these years can be gleaned from a study by Victor Vogel. He noted that, "for the most part, the regular army enlisted man of pre–World War II days was reliable, cheerful, willing, respectful, physically tough, proud of his outfit, and above all, patriotic. If there were horseplay and mischief at times, it was because he was young and led an active life. He considered his profession an honorable one and service to his country serious business."[9]

This interlude was broken once more by a return to the Philippines in November of 1905, the 15th taking up station in Mindanao, where it remained until 1907, when it returned to the United States, being assigned to Fort Douglas, Utah. There then ensued a four-year stretch extending to late in 1911, when elements of the outfit began to move to Asia in November of that year.

The 15th's return to China in 1912, after a decade's absence, stemmed from the deterioration of China's condition and stability associated with massive changes occurring there. The defeat of the Chinese by the Western powers in 1900 and the signing of the protocol of September 1901, eventually led to a series of internal crises beginning on October 10, 1911, and culminating in the unseating of the Chinese boy emperor P'u-i. This paved the way for the proclamation of the Chinese Republic by Dr. Sun Yat-sen in January of 1912, thereby ending the Manchu Dynasty, which had reigned in China since 1644.

Sun Yat-sen, however, proved unable to rule and he resigned in favor of Yuan Shih-ka'i, a warlord who was elected provisional president of the Chinese Republic on February 12. Fearing a recurrence of the events of 1900, the international community began to increase its armed contingents beyond those that had been stationed there since the Boxer Uprising and provided for in the protocol of 1901, raising their numbers to over 10,000 troops. The first precaution taken by the U.S. War Department in Washington was to order the 15th Infantry Regiment, then at Fort Douglas, Utah, to the Philippines, where it arrived on December 3, 1911. There it equipped and brought its First Battalion to war strength, obtaining reinforcements principally from the 7th, 12th, 13th and 20th infantry regiments then in the Philippines.[10] When, on January 5, 1912, the U.S. State Department requested advice from the American minister in Peking, W.J. Calhoun, that official urged a speedy dispatch of additional forces, although he thought that a regiment would suffice. On January 9, the State Department accepted his recommendations but noted that only 500 troops would be sent initially. Accordingly, on the same day, the War Department ordered the commander of the Philippines Division, Major General James Franklin Bell, immediately to dispatch troops to China. In response, on January 10, he ordered the 15th's First Battalion and its Machine Gun Platoon, under the command of Major James M. Arrasmith, the First Battalion's commanding officer, forthwith to board the waiting U.S. Army transport *Logan* and proceed to China, reporting to Calhoun upon his arrival. Sailing on January 12, the battalion, by then designated the American China Expedition, reached the port city of Chinwangtao on January 18. In keeping with the intent of the Boxer protocol of September 7, 1901, which permitted the international powers to maintain forces in China, the expedition's aims were the protection of American citizens, business interests and missionaries, and, more specifically, "to keep open railway communication between Peking and the sea." There was also the political consideration of maintaining American prestige and upholding "the commitment of the United States government to share with other powers the burden of stabilizing China."[11]

In Chinwangtao, the American China Expedition received more specific instructions from Calhoun. He informed the troops that they were under his orders—that is, under the control of the State Department—though they remained operationally under the War Department and the Philippines Division—later called the Philippine Department.[12]

A few days later, at 7:30 a.m. on January 22, the China Expedition departed the port by rail and made its way inland, dropping off detachments to guard the railway along the way at Leichuang, Tangshan, Kuyeh, Wali, Linsi and Kaiping. The main body arrived in Tientsin at 5:30 p.m. on the

6. The 15th Returns to China, 1912–1938

same day. They were met by troops and the band of the Royal Tunskilling Fusiliers, British soldiers then stationed at Tientsin.[13]

Soon, some of the American troops saw limited action. Following instructions from Calhoun, in Peking, who feared a developing situation reminiscent of the Boxer Uprising days, a detachment of six officers and 221 enlisted men left Tientsin on March 3, 1912, to reinforce the Legation Guard. But the Chinese government soon had the situation in hand, and the 15th's detachment, relieved by U.S Marines from Taku, and from the USS *Abarenda* then on the coast, returned to Tientsin on March 11. Simultaneously, the fury of the Chinese Revolution engulfed Tientsin, and the entire native Chinese city was burned and looted by revolutionaries, though the foreign Concessions were spared, no doubt because of the presence of foreign troops.[14]

Meanwhile, Calhoun thought the situation dictated that additional troops be brought into China. On March 4, General Bell issued General Orders No. 20 providing for the dispatch of the 15th's Third Battalion, and for the headquarters staff and band to depart on the USAT *Warren* on March 9. Under the command of Lieutenant Colonel Edwin A. Root, the regiment's executive officer, the troops arrived off Taku Bar on March 15 and were in Tientsin two days later. Meanwhile, in Manila, the regiment was raised to its statutory strength when the Second Battalion was fully armed and equipped for action. Its numbers were appreciably increased by an influx of troops mainly from the 19th Infantry Regiment then in the Philippines. The 15th Regiment's commanding officer, Colonel Frank B. Jones, who had been ill for some time at the Army and Navy Hospital in Hot Springs, Arkansas, arrived in China in late April, and on the 25th, he took command of his regiment and the China Expedition.[15]

When the 15th first arrived in Tientsin on January 22, 1912, its men were escorted to a barracks on Rue Dillon in the city's French Concession because America had no Concessions in China. Thus began, as one writer has noted, "a five-year attempt to resolve the problem of the billeting of the entire regiment," which often had to make do with godowns (warehouses) and similar buildings, such as former wool and cotton mills scattered in various parts of Tientsin, usually in the French and British Concessions. They were finally better established in barracks at the corner between Dagu Road and Yantai Street near the Hai Ho River.[16]

Some troops continued to be stationed at various sites along the railroad and at Leichuang, in particular—where for some years the regiment maintained its firing range—and the industrial and coal city of Tongshan, which also housed extensive railroad shops. Finally, in 1917 the 15th was able to occupy the American Compound and "spent the next twenty years expanding, trying to build 'a little bit of America' in the heart of China." The new compound, called in Chinese *Mei-Kuo Ying-P'an*, occupied about a city block in the former German Concession, which, after the Germans departed in World War I, was taken over by the Chinese and designated the First Special Area. The Chinese leased parts of the area to the U.S. Army and in 1917 constructed three parallel lines of buildings running east and west forming three courtyards, the largest being 260 feet by 90 feet, the area in which regimental ceremonies were subsequently usually held.

Designed by a lieutenant of engineers of the U.S. Army, the buildings were constructed by the Oriental Real Estate Company under the supervision of German architects. Not knowing precisely when or if the Americans might depart, the Chinese hedged their bets by building the structures for easy conversion to apartment houses. The new structures were three stories high and were in a combination American/Dutch/German style. The buildings were rather poorly constructed and it was difficult to keep them in good repair, but they provided a fairly satisfactory barracks, especially after several renovations were undertaken. Two companies were housed in each barracks building, except for Headquarters Company, which occupied a double barracks building. Kitchens and mess rooms were in the basements. The hospital was constructed specifically for that purpose, as was a large building, known as the recreation hall, that had a stage and was utilized for indoor athletics, theatricals and the cinema. The guardhouse was located in the basement of the hall, as were the shower baths. The post exchange occupied part of a barracks building, though it was later moved.[17]

Other buildings on the north side of the Compound dated to the period when the Germans occupied the area.[18] These included the Headquarters Building, the Service Club with a restaurant, the Quartermaster Department with its storage facilities and motor vehicle garages, and quarters occupied by the Bureau of the First Special Area and the Oriental Real Estate Company, which was responsible for the compound's maintenance, heat, water and electricity. In the same locale were also coal storage bins, the magazine, carpentry and paint shops, a small radio station and a medical laboratory and morgue.

Located across Shansi Road to the west of the compound were the wagon park, the stables, the corral, forage and coal storage facilities, wagon and harness sheds, the veterinary hospital, an ice plant—which also provided distilled water—a bakery, and later, the post exchange.

There were persisting limitations on the use of these buildings as barracks. They lacked sufficient storage space and, more inconvenient, there were inadequate bathing facilities, which, being initially located in the Recreation Hall, made treks in all weather conditions a constant nuisance. The hall, which had been built specifically for recreation, was regarded as simply a large, unsightly barn, generally ill appointed and inefficiently arranged. It soon deteriorated and in early 1921, the roof was declared unsafe and the hall was closed. It was not until July of 1922 that contracts were signed with the Oriental Engineering and Construction Company to completely tear down and rebuild the hall, a task that was completed by year's end. In addition, at the same time, the barracks were renovated and repainted.[19]

Annual reports of the commanding general of the United States Army Forces in China routinely noted that renovations of the quarters were ongoing, one stating that by the mid-1920s, showers were finally installed in all barracks. These reports generally stated, as a matter of course, that the buildings were "poorly constructed" and left much to be desired. Nonetheless, the constant repairs, including those to the stables and other outlying structures, kept conditions fairly tolerable.[20]

Another change in the compound came in 1925 when an energetic, competent chaplain, Luther D. Miller, recruited sufficient volunteer help and official sanction to move the chapel from the inadequate Recreation Hall into a spare room in the General Headquarters Building, greatly facilitating religious services. Somewhat later, a more visible change came to the compound when, in June of 1928, a large flagpole was raised in front of the headquarters building. The flag was then removed from the top of the water tower, a prominent structure, where it had long waved.[21]

In the early 1920s a development of note occurred that subsequently had some impact on the regiment's life and morale. This was the devising of the regiment's coat of arms. This consisted of fields of blue and white, the colors of the infantry; four red acorns, which stand for the four major battles of the Civil War; a stone mountain commemorating the Battle of Chickamauga, where the unit fought so valiantly in that struggle; and a five-toed Chinese imperial dragon in recognition of service in China. The "Can Do" motto of the regiment of "Old China Hands," was, in laconic "pidgin English," that of an "honest Chinaman," which also referred to the unit's quarter of a century in China.[22]

A much more significant transformation came to the compound on April 1, 1923, when a new command, designated the American Forces in China (AFC), was created. It consisted of all troops and agencies of the U.S. Army then serving in China—principally the 15th Regiment—and it reported directly to the War Department instead of the Philippine Division (later the Philippine Department). Accordingly, a general officer was designated to head the new entity, the first being Brigadier General (later Major General) William Durward Connor. This organization generally functioned as a corps

Top: One of the five remaining buildings of the former American Compound, Tientsin, China, 2011. It is now part of a medical school campus. *Bottom:* Another of the remaining buildings of the former American Compound, Tientsin, China, 2011 (both photographs by the author).

6. The 15th Returns to China, 1912–1938

area headquarters in the United States, though with much fewer personnel. Further changes came on June 23, 1924, when the War Department labeled these troops as the United States Army Forces in China [USAFC]. While the 15th was the major part of this force, its commanding officer still had considerable control over his regiment.

Connor arrived at his post on April 12, 1923. He was born on February 22, 1874, in Beloit, Wisconsin. Graduating from the United States Military Academy on June 11, 1897, he was assigned to the Corps of Engineers and served in it until he was promoted to brigadier general on June 26, 1918. He served in the Philippines during the Spanish-American War, where he participated in the capture of Manila and later engaged in the campaigns against the Philippine insurrectionists. Subsequently, he attended the U.S. Army War College, graduating in 1909. In the years 1912–1916, he was a General Staff officer at the War Department. During the Great War, he was successively the assistant chief of staff, G-4, GHQ, AEF; chief of staff of the 32nd Division; commander of the 63rd Brigade; commanding general of Base Section, No. 2, AEF; and chief of staff of the SOS (Services of Supply). Finally, on September 1, 1919, Connor assumed command of American Forces in France, the liquidating agency for the AEF, withdrawing from France on September 1, 1919. Later, Connor was commandant of the U.S. Army Engineer School, director of the Inland and Coastwise Waterways Service, and then deputy chief of staff, G-4, at the War Department. Ordered to China, he served there from 1923 to 1925, and when he was promoted to major general on September 1, 1925, he withdrew from China, taking command of the Second Division at Fort Sam Houston in Texas. From 1927 to 1932, Connor was commandant of the U.S. Army War College and from 1932 to 1938, he commanded West Point. While at the War College, Connor initiated major revisions in the curriculum and launched a general reform of its activities.[23]

Of the two generals who commanded the USAFC, Connor was well liked by his men, as well as by the Chinese, and he left behind an impressive legacy of goodwill. The second and last general to command the USAFC in China, Joseph C. Castner, was much more controversial. In the first instance, he placed, in the minds of many, far too much emphasis on physical preparedness, often ordering elaborate marches for extended distances well beyond the usual. He was once ordered to cease and desist by a visiting representative of the inspector general in Washington. He also was often unfavorably compared with the much more popular—and cerebral—Connor. Nonetheless, he was well qualified for command in many respects and had a long, and even illustrious, record. He was born in New Brunswick, New Jersey, November 18, 1869. He graduated from Rutgers College with a degree in civil engineering in 1891.

On August 1, 1891, he was commissioned a second lieutenant in the United States Army and assigned to the Fourth Infantry. In 1895, he attended the U.S. Infantry and Cavalry School and was promoted to first lieutenant in the Fourth Infantry in 1898. For a time, while a lieutenant, Castner served in Alaska, gaining the reputation as an indefatigable hiker and explorer. Sailing to the Philippines during the Spanish-American War, he first became a captain in the Philippine Squadron of Cavalry, then rejoined the Regular Army as a captain in the Fourth Infantry on February 2, 1901. He subsequently took command of the Second Battalion, Fourteenth Infantry. On December 4, 1908, Castner arrived on Oahu, Hawaii, as construction quartermaster and began the construction of the Waianae-Uka military reservation on the Leilehua Plain, later known as Schofield Barracks. He later served as construction quartermaster at Yellowstone National Park. On August 27, 1913, Castner was promoted to major in the Twenty-first Infantry and was later adjutant general of the District of Columbia National Guard. In 1915, he attended the War College.

With the coming of the Great War, he was first promoted lieutenant colonel of the Sixth Infantry on May 13, 1917, followed a few months later by promotion to colonel of the Thirty-eighth Infantry, on August 5 of the same year, instilling in it the "fighting spirit which won for that regiment its fame as the 'Rock of the Marne.'" When American forces sailed for Europe, Castner was promoted to brigadier general on April 12, 1918, and took command of the Ninth Brigade of the Fifth Division. Castner took his brigade into action in the St. Mihiel Offensive and then in the Meuse-Argonne Offensive, seeing much combat and enjoying considerable success, Castner being awarded the Distinguished Service Medal for his services. He remained with the Fifth Division in the Grand Duchy of Luxembourg as an occupation force until its return home in July of 1919. In 1920, Castner graduated from the General Staff School at Leavenworth and a second time from the War College in 1921. The same year, he was appointed a brigadier general in the Regular Army and assigned to command a brigade in the First Cavalry Division. For a time, he commanded the division itself. Headquartered at Fort Bliss, Texas, the First Cavalry was the largest mounted organization then in the U.S. Army.[24]

Shortly after Connor's departure and the arrival of Castner, changes in the command structure were made. Effective December 10, 1926, both the headquarters of the USAFC and the 15th—and the American Barracks—were consolidated. For a time, known as Headquarters, U.S. Army Forces in China and American Barracks, it was brought under the orders of the commanding general. The colonel commanding the 15th accordingly found his position and powers reduced. He was then essentially the administrative head of his organization, though he still had to provide the necessary guard for the post and be responsible for the policing of the grounds occupied by the command and for the interior of all buildings occupied by the 15th Infantry.

Attached to the centralized command were its own Finance, Quartermaster, Ordnance and Signal detachments. The Medical Detachment was assigned to the Station Hospital and administered by the senior medical officer on duty there. The commanding general also emerged with an enhanced staff, bringing in several personal appointees, some of whom were from the 15th, as well as an enlarged personnel contingent.[25]

The USAFC continued as an entity until midnight, March 16/17, 1929, when Washington decided, following Chiang Kai-shek's establishing, at least nominally, a unified Chinese nation, that the operational control of the USAFC should once more pass from the War Department to the commanding general, the Philippine Department. The General Headquarters and some of its offices, such as that of the chief of staff and the adjutant general, were eliminated, and superfluous personnel, both officers and enlisted men, were transferred to the 15th Regiment, sent to Manila or put on a homeward-bound ship.[26] Castner then sailed for home on March 16,1929, taking command of the 3rd Infantry Division at Ft. Lewis, Washington. (Some of the other departing officers included Colonel Joseph Warren Stilwell, who had been chief of staff, USAFC; Major Henry B. Lewis, the adjutant general of the USAFC; Major Harry A. Auer, who headed the organization's Judge Advocate General's Office; and Captain Louis H. Price, the finance officer. Castner's aide in China, Lieutenant Otto L. McDaniel, of the Field Artillery, rejoined Castner at Ft. Lewis. There was only one other Field Artillery officer at Tientsin at that time: Captain Woodrow W. Woodbridge, a Chinese linguist, who served as "dean" of the 15th's Chinese language college).[27]

On April 15, 1929, a new commander of the 15th Regiment, Colonel James D. Taylor, arrived in China and was concurrently named the commanding officer of U.S. Army Forces in China and the 15th Regiment, but the designation USAFC was soon altered to United States Army Troops in China [USATC].

7

LIFE IN THE 15TH INFANTRY REGIMENT IN CHINA

The military aspects of the American experience in the 15th Regiment in China have been discussed at length in the study by this author in a work published as *The United States 15th Infantry Regiment in China, 1912–1938*.[1] Memoirs and letters help round out the picture of life in the 15th Infantry with which this narrative is principally concerned. Two letters containing much information about service in the 15th are by Private William R. Steele, a rifleman in the regiment from 1936 to 1938, after which he returned to the United States with the unit. He arrived in Tientsin, China, in February of 1936. Prior to this time, he had served in the U.S. Army Field Artillery. After his discharge, he reenlisted for the 15th in Tientsin in August 1935. Upon his arrival in China, he was assigned to Company I. He—and other new arrivals—were restricted to the compound until they had completed their eight weeks of basic infantry training. In addition, they were required to attend Chinese language school for three months "to teach us enough Chinese to ask our way when our restriction was lifted and we went to town." They were ordered, for health reasons, to drink no water when they did get into town. When the men went on pass, they were issued a box of condoms. Then, if they "had intercourse, we were to use a condom then go to the nearest medical station and take a prophylactic." If they failed to follow these instructions and contracted VD, they were court-martialed. The minimum sentence was six months in the guardhouse and loss of two-thirds of their pay. In addition, this was classed as "bad time," and the miscreant would have to make it up prior to the end of his enlistment. These drastic measures were attempts to keep the 15th's notoriously high VD rate in check.

In other routine matters, it was customary for uniforms to be tailor-made. They were inspected by company commanders for proper fits. In addi-

7. Life in the 15th Regiment in China

tion, there were no KP duties, nor were the men required to clean their own barracks. These tasks were performed by Chinese laborers, and each man of the regiment had four dollars deducted from his pay, the base of which for a private was $18.75 monthly, paid in American dollars, to obtain these services.

One of the distinctions of the 15th Infantry, often commented on and strongly stressed by the regiment's high command, was the Chinese Language School. By the mid–1930s, enlisted men were required to study Chinese for three months. They were taught in classrooms with about twelve students under the charge of an instructor. Enlisted men could volunteer for the advanced course. Private Steele did so, graduating after many months. He then appeared before a three-man board made up of officers who had passed the advanced course for testing, one of which, in Steele's case, was Lt. Joe Stilwell, Jr. Having passed his exam, Steele was awarded a certificate, signed by the regimental commander—at this time, Colonel George A. Lynch. In addition, he could then wear a sleeve patch on his uniform, the "Chung." This prized cloth ornament was in red against a green background and was the character for "Chung Kuo," meaning the "Middle Kingdom," i.e., China, which, incidentally, mystified the Chinese. Officers were required to take the entire course and graduate. They were instructed on a one-on-one basis.

By the late 1930s, the entire regiment participated in a yearly weeklong hike and maneuvers while engaging in a tactical problem with an assigned objective. They were to march fully equipped. The "enemy" was the regiment's own Headquarters Company, who were mounted on Mongolian ponies and able to gallop from position to position, making their capture difficult, if not impossible. Traditionally, the men were welcomed back to the compound after maneuvers by the regimental band's rendition of the "Beer Barrel Polka," the unit's "official" song. The yearly firing for qualification of various weapons was conducted at "Camp Burrowes," near Chinwangtao. Often, after firing, the men could visit the Great Wall of China, where it meets the sea near Shankaikwan.

Private Steele was once granted a temporary assignment (TDY) to Peking. Being accommodated in the Marine barracks, where he observed the drilling of the famous "Horse Marines," he took in the usual sights, including the Forbidden City.

In Tientsin, Steele noted that one of the highlights of the regiment's daily round was a close watch by all personnel on the guard mounts to see who was picked as the "Commander's Orderly." A prestigious, highly competitive selection, the successful candidate was chosen by the officer of the day. He was regarded as the best-dressed and best-informed soldier of the guard on that occasion. His reward was a 24-hour pass, a free movie ticket, and a free quart of beer! Such recognition might have helped reconcile the men to the fact that it was most difficult to obtain promotions to private first class or corporal. Accordingly, privates were in the vast majority, one consequence of the army's pinched financial condition in depression era America.²

The officers and men of the 15th were often unclear about their exact status as members of the American armed forces in China in the 1920s and 1930s. They were not alone; there is evidence that certain members of the U.S. Marines had similar thoughts. Colonel James C. Breckinridge, who commanded the U.S. Marine Legation Guard in Peiping from 1930 to 1932, once wrote "A Military Soliloquy" in which he probed some aspects of the very existence of military power that applied more cogently to service abroad. All military men, he began were "trained in the science of destruction," which was their raison d'être. But they were not self-created, nor were they "the instigators of our being, our actions, or of philosophy." They were "but the instruments of another's will. We do not decide if, when, and whom, we are to destroy." Military men were "the effect and not the cause of the decisions of others. We are the last word of the politician, and the ultimate argument of the statesman." They were also "the great reflection on what is called civilization," but they were also "the weakest link in the chain of human ethics" because they were "the stultification of logic, the cessation of reason, and the terminus of sense." That being the case, military personnel should not be held accountable if things did not work out when force was employed. Rather, those who were really responsible were to blame, in the last analysis, even for the "causes which bring us into being" (and without those causes "we would cease to exist"). Even when force was evoked, this was an admission of their own failures, "and we are the deadly weapon with which they clinch their final efforts." In the act of proceeding, "our responsive obedience reflects the ascendency of brutality, and the climax of futility." Those, then, who are truly responsible should "devote themselves to the eradication of those causes that maintain us as a menace to each other, and denial of human progress."³

One indication of how diverse the rank and file of the 15th was at any given time is the presence of a Papago Indian from Arizona with the Anglicized name of James McCarthy. He had begun his military service in the U.S. National Guard in April of 1917 along the Mexican border. He then participated in subduing striking miners, the "Wobblies," in the Bisbee, Arizona, area. Shipped to Camp Kearney near San Diego, California, for training, McCarthy was soon on his way to Camp Dix for shipment overseas. Proceeding from Liverpool, McCarthy and the other men were shipped out of Dover bound for France. Taken by train to Chateau-Thierry, McCarthy was

7. Life in the 15th Regiment in China   83

assigned to Company D, 109th Infantry Regiment, of the 28th Infantry Division and participated in the Meuse-Argonne operation, where he was gassed and later on, after being struck by grenade shrapnel, was captured and held as a prisoner of war for the last few weeks of the conflict. McCarthy rejoined the 109th in time to leave with it from Le Mans and sailed from Saint-Nazaire in April 1919. Landing at Philadelphia, he was demobilized at Camp Dix on May 8 and promptly joined the Regular Army, choosing China and the 15th Infantry for his first tour of duty.[4]

After delays and sometime in 1919, McCarthy boarded the USS *John A. Logan* in San Francisco bound for China. The usual route was followed, first to Honolulu, where the men were given passes to see something of the sights, then Guam, and on to Manila, where the men were sent to Fort McKinley for a short stay. The next stop was Nagasaki, Japan, where the ship took on coal, which was loaded by a chain of Japanese women who carried big baskets of coal on their heads and dumped the coal into the ship's bunkers. Sailing from Japan, the ship made its way to Vladivostok, Siberia, where the 31st Infantry Regiment was stationed. The final stop was Chinwangtao, China, where the men bound for the 15th boarded a train for the journey to Tientsin.

Typical rickshaw boys at ease in Tientsin. This form of transportation was ubiquitous and the rickshaw boys were examples of close U.S. troop contact with the Chinese (courtesy of Historical Photographs of China, http://visualisingchina.net/).

The countryside en route reminded the Arizona Indian of the deserts of his home state. Arriving in Tientsin, McCarthy was assigned to Company D, of the First Battalion, a machine-gun outfit. The new trooper easily fell into the regiment's routine, greatly appreciating the "easy living for us Americans." Each soldier had Chinese boys to do their cleaning, shine their shoes, fix their beds, and clean their clothes, all for about one American dollar per month. McCarthy, obviously a thrifty person, received thirty dollars per month, which was paid in gold. He drew a ten-dollar and a twenty-dollar gold coin, but accepted only five dollars per month, turning the remainder back to the paymaster for safekeeping.

Coveted "Chung" given to officers and men who completed the prescribed course in the Chinese language in the 15th Infantry Regiment (illustration by Jan Miller Cornebise).

McCarthy was engaged in athletics, especially baseball and basketball, at which he was skilled, having played on numerous teams in various Indian schools he had attended, such at the Santa Fe Indian School. Like almost everyone else, he used the rickshaws for sightseeing around and about Tientsin, noting that one could go almost anywhere for a dime. One of his friends once persuaded him to witness executions, which were a common event in the China of the day. McCarthy described the scene, at a site about twelve miles north of Tientsin, as follows: "The killings were done in a big graveyard about a mile long and half a mile wide. I was surprised to find that there were many American soldiers there to watch." Preceding the prisoners, a parade of men carried signs indicating that these prisoners had been condemned to death and would be executed. "That day," McCarthy, went on, China "killed forty-five men. They brought them forward one at a time and a policeman shot them in the head with a pistol. There was a trench about forty or fifty feet long and six feet deep. Every time one was shot, men would throw his body in the pit. They let us get close to the shooting. I had a little camera with me and I still have some pictures of the shootings." He soon grew sickened by the experience and departed, never to return, though, he ruefully admitted, "some of the soldiers would watch every time there were executions."

McCarthy was a machine gunner. The guns were mounted on a little cart pulled by a mule. His job was to train and manage the mule, which he was able to do because he had worked with mules at the Santa Fe Indian School and "knew how to treat them." This was no doubt the reason that he and his mule, and other members of the company, were selected to take part in a contest held in the Philippines in the summer of 1920. There, at Fort McKinley, the team was in competition with several others, the object being to unlimber and fire the gun in a prescribed fashion in the shortest time from various locations, in one instance after having scaled a ten-foot wall while carrying the gun. McCarthy's squad won handily and returned to Tientsin in triumph. After his return, he sometimes worked in the bakery and often served as an MP. He did sports, baseball and basketball on company teams. There was baseball and basketball but no football team. Instead, the men played pushball. The ball was about eight feet high and teams tried to outpush one another. He also did some boxing.

McCarthy noted that the winters were very cold in Tientsin and the troops had to wear their big, long overcoats and heavy caps with earflaps. He also stated that many of the boys did not want to go to the Philippines when the First Battalion was transferred there. Some had been in China for a long time, and some had families. One of his friends was married to a pretty Japanese woman and had four daughters. Others had married Chinese or Korean girls—or simply lived with them.[5]

One feature of Company D was that it had a mascot, a seven-year-old Chinese boy who had been abandoned and left to die when he was very small. Naming him "Spud," some of the soldiers took charge of him and made him their mascot. He always wore the miniature army uniform the soldiers made for him and, speaking good English, he was often used as an interpreter by the company. McCarthy on one occasion used his language skills when he visited Peking, the Great Wall, the Forbidden City, and other sites commonly visited by men of the regiment.

Subsequently, in September of 1921, Major Noble J. Wiley, the commander of the regiment's First Battalion, which was then with the regiment in Tientsin, was ordered to move his outfit to Camp Eldridge, at Los Baños, on Laguna de Bay in the Philippines, about fifty miles east of Manila. Late in 1923, the battalion moved to Fort William McKinley, at Rizal, about nine miles from Manila. There, it was garrisoned with troops of the 57th and 45th Infantry regiments, both Philippine Scout units, and brigaded with the 31st Infantry Regiment as part of the 24th Infantry Brigade of the Philippines Division. Calling themselves the "Lost Battalion," condemned to "eating our bread among strangers," the men nonetheless found service at McKinley to be "most pleasant," as one soldier admitted. Here, the First served the parent

15th in useful ways, one being that men assigned to China often passed through its ranks for initial training and classification. Recently arrived officers and men were placed on probation for three months. Those failing to measure up to desired standards were not sent on to Tientsin.[6]

Meanwhile, after a year or so in the Philippines, McCarthy's enlistment ended, and he returned to the Presidio, at San Francisco. There he received his discharge on July 22, 1922, his army career over.

Further, as to life in the 15th, the yearly firing on the range at various camps, such as Nan Ta Ssu and later at Camp Burrowes, both located near the port city of Chinwangtao, was a pleasant break and a relief from the day-to-day routine at the American compound, not to mention the torrid summers in Tientsin. All who were there, officers and men alike, not to mention their families, were invigorated by the experience. Not surprisingly, numerous poems appeared in the regiment's troop publication, *Sentinel*, on the subject. One anonymous soldier-poet fondly remembered what it was like to be at Nan Ta Ssu in the mid–1920s:

> Sand.
> A torquoise [sic] bay murmuring.
> Forests of jade-green locust trees.
> The shrill whir of locust wings,
> "Glory," ever new, floating over all.
> Vistas of distant village roofs,
> Like a gray sea, petrified.

He was touched by the many sights and sounds there: soldiers, beggars, an American lady "like a rose-tinted porcelain cup, filled with amber wine." There were Sikh fortune-tellers, and coolie fishermen, "naked, chanting, straining at their nets," that produced "heaps of gleaming, silvered fish." There were straw-mat huts, donkeys, and "the plaintive note of a Chinese flute, sounding through the trees, interrupted by "the staccato bark of rifles, and the put-put of machine guns." These also masked the "soft pit-pat of slippered feet, treading over the singing sands," and "the far-off clang of bronze gongs." Finally, at day's end, came night, "a velvet canopy, diamond-spangled, flung o'er the earth," and then "silence and sleep, and the mystery caravan of fragrant dreams."[7]

Many of the enlisted men of the 15th Regiment did not have opportunities to bring their families to China, a privilege limited to top-ranking NCOs. The female relationships among the rank and file accordingly were along the usual avenues of prostitutes and other "camp followers," some of whom were more or less abetted or tolerated by the regiment's high command. There are a few accounts of various "houses" in which the women were closely monitored weekly by the post's medics, who normally used any expedient they could to keep the regiment's venereal rate down. One "Old China Hand," Howard W. Palm, who served in the regiment in the late 1930s, recalled that one such establishment was located "across from our bowling center a few blocks from our compound." In these conditions, "[the] girls weren't prostitutes," he insisted, though how he arrived at that conclusion is not clear. As he described the establishment, it was similar to USO operations in the United States, and "the girls were all young and actually wholesome looking. If you wanted to select one of the girls you paid the Chinese madam the equivalent of around 30 cents for a visit." He was unsure as to "how this was kept from the poor mothers in the U.S," but he justified the practice. "Though it may seem crude," he explained, "society has been trying to keep the oldest profession in the world checked but still has not succeeded," nor, he might have added, kept soldiers and women separated. Palm had been in the U.S. cavalry earlier and noted that "when we used to take our weekly or sometimes two weeks hikes ... the girls followed us and set up camp each night a little distance away from our bivouac. The poor chaplains, how they must have suffered," he concluded. There are no indications that the 15th Regiment followed this practice.[8]

Other 15th soldiers were fascinated by the tradition of having concubines in China. Accordingly, many soldiers availed themselves of arrangements of their own involving their common-law wives, or "shack squaws," as they were called, or "sleeping phrase books," and gave them credit for helping them learn the Chinese language. At least, this served as a convenient excuse for their actions. These were often Chinese women recruited from the ranks of the many White Russian damsels in China in those years after the Bolshevik Revolution in Russia. This upheaval had led to a mass exodus from Russia of White Russians and others who had emerged on the losing side in what was now the USSR under Bolshevik rule. Many of them had made their way to China, and major cities such as Shanghai and Tientsin received a great influx of Russian refugees. Men of the 15th were often attracted to these willing consorts who had arrived unexpectedly—and were most welcomed—in their midst. A soldier of the 15th returning to the compound after firing on the range—then known as Camp Burrowes—had some "poetic" words to address to his Russian girl back in Tientsin to the tune of "For Seven Long Years I Courted Nancy":

> It's seven long weeks since I saw Russky!
> Hai Ho, the rollin' river.
> It's seven long weeks since I saw Russky!
> I'm comin' home on the Tientsin special.

> She'd better have some supper waitin'!
> Hai Ho the rollin' river.
> She'd better have some supper waitin'!
> I'm bound for home on the Tient-tsin special.

He hoped that she would greet him at the station and they would soon be home to their evening meal, with its inevitable "quart of beejoe on the table!"[9]

The preoccupation of the men of the 15th with les femmes often revealed antifeminist attitudes common in the era of the 1920s and 1930s generally and sometimes similarly prevalent racial biases vis-à-vis the Chinese. Both of these prejudices were manifested in a short story written by a certain Private Haydock, a member of the Regiment's Company K in 1920. Entitled "His Belle of the Orient," it is a jarring, rather explicit piece of fiction revealing attitudes—and perhaps adventures and experiences—of at least certain soldiers of the 15th in those days. It was published in the *Sentinel* in that year, and reprinted in the paper's October 7, 1927, issue.[10]

The story is filled with a measure of excitement as a newly arrived American soldier sought to come to grips with another culture, at once foreign, appealing, and even exotic. It also reveals the stain of racism common to many foreigners in China. Americans were hardly exempt from such sentiments. No doubt autobiographical in its essentials—or an account of someone whom Haydock knew—the story suggests something about how first impressions are often changed, sometimes in dramatic ways and with unexpected consequences, and concludes with an evocative pathos and sense of disillusionment, not only with a certain Chinese girl and her family, but also with the incident that no doubt resulted in a substantial reassessment by the soldier of China in particular and Asia in general. The story follows as it appeared in the *Sentinel*:

"His Belle of the Orient"

> She was a Chinese girl body and soul: just an ordinary yellow-faced, slant-eyed Chink girl who wore "pants" as most Chinese girls do. But being a Chink girl mattered nothing to her, and she did not know that she wanted to be anything else, even if she could. Her entire world lay within the big city of Tientsin, in which she first saw the light of day, and out of which she had never been.
>
> One day she was riding in a ricksha through a narrow street of the city [when] a "rookie" saw her, and for an instant their eyes met in passing. What a beautiful Chink girl! said the rookie to himself, as the vision of her large oval face loomed up before him and seemed to haunt him. Till then he had always regretted coming to China, and swore if ever he should meet the smooth-tongued recruiting officer who had induced him to quit follow-

7. Life in the 15th Regiment in China

ing his father's plow, to take a trip to the land of the slant eyes, one or the other must die.

Of a sudden, China had become a place on the map to him, the face of the beautiful girl had smitten him, and he muttered to himself "I owe the recruiting officer an apology." I know it is wrong to notice boys, soliloquized the Chink girl, "but it was an accident and at any rate I can't help it," [and] she gave herself up to the picturing [of] the pleasing face of the rookie in her mind. That night as the rookie lay asleep, he dreamed of seeing the beautiful girl in the ricksha once again, and as he lay dreaming, the girl of his dream also lay dreaming and it was of drinking tea beneath a willow tree with him.

They were destined to meet again, and both thought it queer. It was in a tea house, into which the rookie had ventured out of curiosity. Upon his entering, the beautiful girl, [who] was seated in one of the theatre-like boxes that ran along each building, immediately espied him and simultaneously the rookie, as if attracted by her presence, recognized her. Although their faces betrayed no signs of recognition, their eyes seemed to say to each other "How do you do," and both their hearts beat the faster for it. The rookie seating himself just near enough to her [so] that he might observe and admire her, was understood by the girl, and she turned her face full upon him as much as to say—"Help yourself; you're welcome to observe me as much as you please," and the rookie did. As he looked upon her big, flat, oval face, it enchanted him. He noted the big dreamy eyes that slanted: the soft, velvety, flawless yellow skin: the lips that pouted sweetly and parted just enough to exhibit a mouthful of beautiful pearly teeth: the small baby-like nose: the smallness of the ears from which dangled large pink ear drops, and the abundant head of hair, black and glossy as the raven's coat dressed tastefully, and descending upon her low, broad forehead like the wings of a bird. All these things so pleasing the rookie noted, nor did he fail to notice the slender and graceful form that a tight-fitting costume of black satin set off so admirably.

Upon the stage, four sing-song girls endeavored with their songs and musical stringed instruments to entertain the audience. Their efforts were successful, for the audience, most of whom were indulging in sipping scalding tea out of bowls, seemed affected by the music, and looked so calm and serenely happy as if they had not a care in the world. The shrill screaming voices of the entertainers, the rasping tone of their stringed fiddles, accompanied by the loud clang of cymbals, [and] the beating of the tom-tom and Xylophone, formed a medley of sound that would have at any other time sounded harsh to the rookie, [but] now inspired him with awe. The weird and the lovely Oriental Belle entranced him. A mist seemed to rise before his eyes and dim them, and out of the dimness arose the sweet face of the girl who had captivated him. The face at first indiscernible to him, gradually came nearer and nearer and finally stood about a foot away from him. No face was ever so beautiful he thought, nor had ever an artist painted one so rare. He drank in its beauty, and the soft, gentle breeze that fanned him through an open window, he mistook for the warm breath upon his cheek.

Suddenly this delightful illusion was interrupted by one of the waiters who wished to serve him with tea and immediately the lovely face disappeared from before him and he realized that he had been in a trance.

The rookie did not want any tea and was about to tell the waiter so, when suddenly it flashed into his mind that the bowls of his Oriental beauty and her elderly companion, who he presumed rightly to be her mother, might need replenishing, and directed the waiter to offer to fill them. Intently he watched the face of the lovely girl as the waiter made known to her and her mother his kind attention. He saw the girl look askance at her mother about the propriety of accepting it, and after a brief deliberation between them, accepted.

For the first time, the girl favored him with a smile, and being in earshot of him, startled him pleasantly by saying in a rich musical voice—"Thank you very much." So overjoyed was the rookie that he could scarcely [restrain] himself from joining her company but when he remembered that she might consider it improper of him, he reluctantly refrained, and acknowledged her thanks by saying politely—"You are very welcome." The ice was broken between them, and the rookie knew all that was needed, was for the girl to leave the tea-house, and he would follow and join her company. He had not long to wait, for soon after, the beautiful girl and her mother arose to leave, and on passing his seat, the girl smiled and said to him—"I'm going now," and the rookie answered, "I am too."

Outside the theatre with the permission of the mother, whose dignity kept her aloof, the rookie was invited by the girl to accompany her home, and he gladly consented, [and] all three got into rickshas. With many twistings and turnings through the streets both broad and narrow, the rookie lost track of his whereabouts, but finally when they stopped, he recognized the broad, flowing Pei-tao-ho River. The girl conducted him into a house of the Chinese type that was her home and entered through a large doorway that opened into a courtyard that was protected by the popular Chinese devil screen, which, if failing to turn the devil, is at least fairly serviceable as a means of screening the courtyard from prying eyes. As the rookie entered the home, a dog snapped viciously at him, and it was not until the girl, its mistress, procured a switch that it cowered at [the] sight of it. But it was too late, the beautiful mistress seized the fierce brute by its collar, and forced it to lay down and whipped it unmercifully. Finishing her cruel task, she laughingly turned to the rookie and remarked—"What a happy world it would be, if we were all whipped there and then, each time we committed a fault." That such a beautiful girl could be so cruel, fairly made the rookie gasp with astonishment, and the girl, noticing it, regretted her display of cruelty before him. Without waiting for him to speak, she begged him to be seated and opening wide the rear doorway of the courtyard, revealed the Pei-tai-ho sweeping by.

Left to themselves, they chatted on different topics and were very happy in each others company. The time to depart came all too soon, and the girl proposed that they should take a boat ride which she explained would take him as far upon his way to the Compound as the Russian Park. This proposal, of course, delighted the rookie and he promptly agreed to it, and soon, at the girl's command, a craft manned by two oarsmen made its appearance. The boat was small and of the fishing type with a cabin, and its little deck was spotlessly clean and shipshape. Seating themselves on grass mats upon the deck, the boat pulled off. Down the stream the boat gently glided, the dying sun in its last moments, casting a soft, yellow hue over the earth, turned everything to gold. The rookie felt happy; happier than he had ever been. The soft splashing of the oars, as they were dipped into the water, was sweet music to him. Beside him was the most charming girl in all the world, and it seemed to him, that it was almost too much like a beautiful fairy story from the Arabian Night's, to be true. The face of his lovely, smiling companion turned toward his own causing him to pour forth his great love for her. He praised her great beauty to her, and called her his "Oriental Belle," and the girl chuckled with delight at the many compliments that greeted her ears. When the boat pulled up at the landing place on the opposite shore from the Russian Park, the two lovers had pledged to meet the following evening, and ere they parted the girl, heedless of the presence of the boatmen, permitted her lover to embrace her, and turned up her face to his and submitted her lips to be saluted with the joy of her lover's first kiss.

Next day to the rookie's great sorrow, he found himself on guard, and try as he did to get excused from it, he could not. It was a bitter twenty-four hours he spent on guard, imagining that his girl would think him faithless, but it was some consolation to him that he could see her the following evening and explain. But when the following evening did come it was to find him ill in the hospital, and truly his cup of sorrow was running over.

A whole month went by in which he was confined to the hospital, and he could find no means to acquaint the girl he loved [as to] why he was absent, which fairly distracted him. Many great changes [had] taken place in a month of time, and even Rome was destroyed in a day. During the month the rookie was in the hospital, the family of his beautiful belle had fallen upon hard times. The family was reduced to almost poverty, and almost all that was left to them was the home, and even it was in grave danger of being lost to them.

The luxuries of the home were dispensed with, and the servants discharged, and the rookie's beautiful belle was compelled to weave cloth and do other things in the home to help to keep the wolf from the door. As the days went by, and her soldier lover did not put in his appearance, she concluded that he was faithless, just as he feared and decided that he was lost to her. Her mother being sore pressed to save the home, decided that her only course was to sell her beautiful daughter, and to this course the daughter felt herself compelled to agree.

One afternoon while she was seated in the courtyard of the home with her married sister and her two babies, indulging in a feast of locust, the rookie unexpectedly made his appearance. The sight of his Oriental belle seated eating locust in company with her slovenly-appearing sister and her two babies at her naked breast was not very pleasing to him, but just the same, he was glad to greet his beautiful belle again. She gave a cry of joy as she caught sight of him, and led him in to the reception room of the home but before entering, he had time enough to detect the skin of an animal hanging up, and he recognized it at once to be the skin of the dog that he had seen chastised. "Poor old thing," said the girl to him, as she saw him observing it. "It will never bite at you more," and laughed heartily as she said it, and ere the shocked rookie could reply, he was ushered into the hall. Of the misfortune that had overtaken her family the girl quickly informed him, and that to save even the home itself, she was to be sold. The rookie was overcome with the sad intelligence, and felt that his beautiful girl was lost to him, for the cost of her was entirely out of his reach. "Say that you will buy me," was the girl's plaintive plea, and the rookie, not knowing how it would be possible for him to do so, answered "Yes." Just as a ray of sunshine breaks forth in the heavens to light up the earth with its brilliance upon a gloomy day, the rookie saw the girl's gloomy countenance light up with joy, and the next moment she was frantically hugging and kissing him.

After her frantic joy had somewhat subsided, she left him to return again in a jiffy with a pot of tea and a dish of locust, which he declined, and thinking in her kindness that [he] disliked locust, she fetched him a bowl of meat. To accommodate her, the rookie found himself obliged to partake of something, but when he saw the meat his mind instantly reverted to the skin of the dog, and to ease his mind of the ugly thought he had, he inquired what kind of meat it was. The girl, who was busily engaged in chewing a piece of it, [paused] long enough to answer him, "Dog," and went on chewing. The poor rookie was dumbfounded. In an instant, his belle of the Orient's loveliness had faded from before his eyes, and instead, he saw a common Chink girl unconcernedly eating dog. His head seemed to swim, and in his mind a mental picture of his being married to her arose. He imagined he could see her as untidy and heedless of her appearance as her sister and surrounded by squealing children and performing her particular ablution in the same filthy bowl as she prepared his food, and so much was he engrossed in his mental picture, that he failed to notice the girl observing him. To arouse him, she selected a choice piece of meat out of the bowl and approaching him, held it up before him, expecting him to snap at it as she would have done, had she been so tempted. Awakened by this act that made her forever a repulsive and detestable creature to him, he sprang to his feet and sent her sprawling upon her back and fled the house, never more to return.

Often when the wind blows round his quarters at night, his thoughts turn to the Chinese girl: just the ordinary, slant-eyed, yellow-faced Chink girl, whose entire world lays all within the city of Tientsin and who had been his Belle of the Orient.

So ends "His Belle of the Orient."

Further insights into the American experience in Tientsin can be obtained by an examination of how the civilian contingent of the regiment viewed their lives in China. Among the most useful of these are accounts of some of the soldiers' dependents who accompanied them to Asia. One of the more interesting memoirs is that of John W. Leonard, Jr., the son of then Major John W. Leonard, who came out to the 15th Regiment in 1933 as a commander of the regiment's 2nd Battalion. John Jr. entitled his unpublished work "A Lucky Life."[11] The major's family included his wife, née Eileen O'Brien, two daughters, Eileen and Natalie, in their early teens, and his son, John Jr., about ten years of age. John Jr. began with a narrative of the voyage out, which included his father, mother, two sisters and himself. They spent some time en route in the Panama Canal Zone, with his father visiting colleagues in army cantonments there. The venture there was concluded by a trip across the isthmus by rail. Other stops along the way to China included Hawaii, Guam and the Philippines. In Manila, visits were made to Corregidor and another fortified island nearby which resembled a battleship and hence was called the SS *Drum*, where the Coast Artillery troops were decked out in sailors' caps. A pleasant stay was arranged at the so-called American capital at Bagio in the hills where servicemen and their families took refuge in the summer from the stifling climate of Manila.

From the Philippines, the army transport proceeded to Chinwangtao, arriving there on July 6, 1933. From there they took the train to Tientsin, where the U.S. Army compound was located. As Major Leonard observed, "China is a big gravy train!" It certainly was for the officers and their families. Six servants were present in their home, with the boss, named Shao, being "Number One Boy." He answered the door and served drinks and dinner. A coolie cleaned the house; two cooks, one for the family, the other for the crew who lived in the basement, managed the meals. Two female servants, called amahs, washed and sewed. The total monthly salary for all six was twenty-six dollars plus room and board. In addition, Leonard remembered, "we left the sugar [sitting] out" because the Chinese exhibited a sweet tooth, which needed to be assuaged. "Number One Boy" also obtained a routine "squeeze"— a commission, or "kickback"—from the garbage man, all food suppliers and other shopkeepers and merchants with whom the family did business. Some of the households maintained their own rickshaw, complete with a rickshaw boy.

The Leonard family lived at 294F Race Course Road in the British Concession. It was one of about six houses in a row fronting Taylor Field, an athletic field. Other officers' families lived in the neighborhood and therefore there were plenty of playmates with whom to play soccer or baseball. They sometimes played with Chinese or British children, though John Jr.'s mother did not want them playing with the Chinese kids, as "she was sure we would get lice from them, as we both headed the ball." It was the British kids, who for some reason John called "Salvation Army kids," sons of British military personnel who were interesting but prone to stone-throwing fights—while attacking or defending a garage, perhaps—and bleeding cuts were regarded as badges of honor. These worthies therefore soon proved "too tough," and the Americans ceased playing with them. John wondered what happened to them and hoped that "the Brits got them out before 1941."

As to schooling, there were three choices: a French convent school, which John's sisters attended, a British school, and the Tientsin American school, in which John was enrolled. It was several miles from home and the students were transported every day in a World War I ambulance pulled by two mules. A U.S. Army MP was in charge. He also transported the students home for lunch each day. There were two classes to a room and while one class was engaged in activities the other did homework, so there was less homework to do at home. At home, John and his sisters did few chores. Everything was done by the Chinese. For instance, a coolie handed John his books and Number One Boy handed him his jacket as John went out the door. The coolie had, in the meantime, rushed to the ambulance to help him in.

Taylor Field was the site of many of the 15th's parades as well as athletic events, including baseball, basketball, and sometimes football matches, especially between the 15th and the U.S. Marines, usually from the Legation Guard in Peiping. There were also Olympic-style track meets, which usually included tug-of-war contests, especially among the Americans, British and French. Various bands performed on the field as well, always well received by large crowds, soldiers and civilians alike.

Major Leonard routinely took 24-mile horseback rides with his daughters, but John was not yet sufficiently skilled to join them, though he later learned to ride. Initially, he instead took trips into the countryside on his own, some of several days' duration.

Major Leonard also, as was usual with both officers and men of the 15th, took lengthy trips, sometimes hunting expeditions, hiking or traveling by boats, on mule or horseback or in Peking carts that were usually drawn by oxen. Leonard also visited with missionaries at their far-flung posts. The Catholic major took scotch, pipe tobacco and radio tubes as gifts to the padres. John Jr. once accompanied his father to visit a group of German Fathers located at Yu Ping Fu, where, in addition to their clerical duties, they found time to manage their own brewery.

Opposite: **Colonel David D. Barrett was active in the life of the 15th Infantry, notably as a language instructor, and in China as a military attaché, and other duties, on into the years of World War II and afterward (U.S. Army Signal Corps photograph).**

7. Life in the 15th Regiment in China

Men and families of U.S. military personnel took other trips, the traditional destination being Peiping, where the usual sites were visited: the Great Wall, the Forbidden City, the Temple of Heaven, the Summer Palace, and the Ming tombs. Some ventured to the summer resort frequented by Westerners from Peiping and Tientsin, Pei To Ho, south of the port of Chinwangtao on the Gulf of Chihli.

But the venture that was most frequently anticipated and long talked about was the one to the firing range, then called Camp Burrowes, which the troops proceeded to every summer. Each battalion spent six weeks there, though the families could spend the entire summer. It was located just southwest of the port city of Chinwangtao, where the U.S. Army transports normally docked. The city was a major naval port of call and coaling station maintained by the British-owned Kailan Mining Administration. John observed how the coal was loaded onboard the ships: the coal trains pulled down to the dock on the long pier, which could accommodate about six ships at a time. Planks were placed from the coal cars to the ships' holds and "an endless conveyor line" of coolies, with bags on their shoulders, manually carried the coal from railcar to ship, a typical use of China's massive reservoir of manpower. Among the British ships present were some destined for notable action in World War II such as the carrier HMS *Hermes* and the cruiser HMS *Exeter*. John, who faithfully recorded their names, admitted, however, that a favorite of his and his friends was the much smaller gunboat, the *Flamouth*, which John and his pals were invited to board. There they were subjected to a curious trick played on them by British seamen: A bowl with money in it was offered to them to pick from. But to do so, they had to stand on a mat wired to an electrical outlet, and accordingly the boys were shocked. "Eventually," John confessed, "after much torture," and no doubt many laughs for the crewmen, "they would either move us off the mat or throw the switch. We still enjoyed it." He could only conclude, "Kids are strange." Although he did not mention it, so apparently were certain British seamen!

At Camp Burrowes, John and his buddies lived a veritable Huck Finn and Tom Sawyer existence—a "Lucky Life" indeed. In addition to their observing and boarding the ships, there were also the trains that brought the coal to the ships for them to investigate. The trains had guards on them to protect against stealing. Often, as the trains slowed to enter a town, Chinese children would jump aboard and throw off coal lumps for retrieving later. Occasionally shots were fired in their general direction and naturally this appealed to John and his companions. As he admitted, they occasionally stole some coal "but were disappointed at the lack of shooting."

Inland of Camp Burrowes were large sand dunes that the boys were not allowed to visit, presumably because of threats posed by Chinese bandits said to be lurking in the area. This made the dunes all the more appealing and boys naturally ventured there; but when found out, as John once admitted, "I was put to bed without dinner, complete with a good lickin.'" On other occasions, when he was learning to ride horseback he was allowed to enter the dunes but only with several soldiers along as escort.

Fishing was also pursued, but rather violently, by use of pistols and sometimes grenades, though these pursuits were no doubt conducted by soldiers rather than the lads. The boys were allowed to visit the firing ranges in search of ejected cartridges, but as John ruefully noted, "between the penny-pinching Army and the Chinese, it was slim pickings."

The setting at Camp Burrowes, especially from the point of view of officers and their dependents, especially the latter, was almost idyllic. To be sure, all personnel were housed in tents but those of the dependents and officers boasted substantial flooring, some even having carpets placed over bricks, as well as other amenities. Most families were accompanied by some of their Tientsin servants, who helped in serving their meals and in other ways. For instance, on hot days coolies pulled ropes attached to hanging fans suspended from the roof battens of various buildings, such as the mess hall, which helped to circulate the air. As John also remembered, the food was good and "ice cream was plentiful."

They could also enjoy a nice beach only a short distance from the camp on the Gulf of Chili. In addition, the seaside was the scene of much fishing activity by Chinese fishermen who provided interesting viewing entertainment. There, the fishermen hauled their nets out in two boats about half-a-mile apart, proceeding out for a considerable distance. They then slowly and laboriously pulled both ends into shore, chanting as they worked, much to the fascination of the onlookers. They subsequently poured out their haul on the sands and a fast and furious buying and selling spree ensued until every scrap of their yield was claimed.

There was a complete athletic program maintained for the camp; tennis and other sports, swimming programs, riding ventures, and especially organized sports for the kids, including boxing instruction supervised by a "rah, rah" army officer who took it all quite seriously. When John tired of these activities, he adjourned to the post exchange, where he played games or "budded up with the soldiers." There John and his friends learned to play checkers, blackjack "and other valuable things," though, at least officially, root beer and sarsaparilla "were the drinks of choice."

Adults, in addition to the rounds of entertaining that accompanied military camp life, could go into Chingwangtao, where the British had established their "typical colonial ... setup," including a country club with a nine hole golf course," which was "sporty, complete with burial mounds," those ever-present, numerous specters which dotted the Chinese landscape in that area. Indeed, John judged the Camp Burrowes establishment to be altogether "pukka."

John had fond memories of the Chinese, "a friendly cheerful people, overly kind to kids" but "mean as hell to animals. Dogs got a kick; donkeys were beaten unmercifully." The answer seemed to him to be that "everyone needs to feel better than somebody." He also noted that the 15th's officers could speak Chinese and were required to learn the language, "at penalty of a portion of their pay." Not so the British, however. Their attitude was: "Let the blighters speak English—English spoken loud enough and slow enough is plain enough for any blighter to understand!" As for the Japanese, they were clearly "unlovely" and could "clearly mistreat people." Regarding the Koreans, John noted that "both Chinese and Japs looked way down on [them]. Being kids, we went along with it."[12]

As to other officers that were associated with the 15th, John Jr. had met Colonel Joseph Stilwell. He had heard that the Stilwells were regarded by other Americans as "funny" because when they were in Peiping they lived in the Chinese section of the city and wore Chinese clothing while at home. It was also known that Stilwell found the architecture of the American Compound "disgusting," and he himself had come to "love the clean and simple lines of ... Chinese homes."[13] Admittedly, however, John Jr. noted, "even in the 1920s and 1930s, Stilwell was recognized as the Army's expert on China," and may simply have desired to live and think like a Chinese so as better to learn as much about them as he could.[14]

One example of how the 15th Infantry affected the U.S. Army's history did not occur in China but at Fort Benning, where men who were alumni of the 15th, especially in the 1930s, "were thick on the ground." After Marshall departed Tientsin, he made his way to Fort Benning. He was not to be the only member of the 15th to gravitate there in the late 1920s and early 1930s. Among other "Old China Hands" to arrive was Major Edwin Forrest Harding, who had commanded the 15th's 2nd Battalion from October 30, 1923, to July 26, 1924, He then commanded the regiment from July 26, 1924, to September 9, 1924, when he again resumed command of the 2nd to his departure date from China, May 1, 1927.

Indeed, members of "that Damned China Crowd (the DCC)" might be more important than has been imagined. Others present at the same time in the late 1920s and early 1930s included Harding, who was an instructor at the Infantry School at Benning from September 7, 1929, to June 25, 1933. There

7. Life in the 15th Regiment in China 99

he joined Marshall, the assistant commandant under the commandant, General Campbell King, who had commanded the 15th regiment in the early 1920s and arrived at Benning in 1932. Others included William B. Tuttle, who was the provost marshal, Dennis McCunniff, and Charles L. Bolte. This group was sometimes singled out for criticism, their presence being regarded either as "rueful or gleeful." Whether snide or admiring, some observers complained about the "chop suey at the Officers Club [on] Thursday nights" as well as Marshall's insistence on much horseback riding. Certainly, there were impromptu reunions of the Old China Hands with abundant merriment, singing, recitations of Harding's poetry, circa China in the 1920s, and prominent nose thumbing at "Volsteadism."[15]

Much more important were the developments of U.S. Army doctrine and innovations calculated to move the army beyond the lessons learned in the Great War, and what might be expected in any war to come. There was inculcated at Benning at this time a "new tone," which sought to rub out the "old military scholasticism" heretofore prevalent. This had been characterized by "overindulgence in 'lessons learned' between July and November of 1918," which was regarded as "hazardous for an army that needed to be thinking about the 'first six months of the next war.'" Marshall, the kingpin of much of this development, insisted that battle problems had given the students too much structure, leaving far too little time for them to exercise their imagination and initiative. As he expressed it, "The main problem 'next time,' would not lie with *what* decisions to make but rather with *when* to make them." "Pernicious in the extreme," he went on, was Benning's fascination with "prolix order-writing." Simplicity was to be the new order of emphasis, because in any new conflict the army would have to employ a great number of "partially trained officers and men."[16] In this way, "That Damned China Crowd"—drawing in part from their involvement with the army in China, particularly while members of the 15th Infantry—contributed to the development of America's "new army," which was to fight World War II.[17]

8

Going Home and the Regiment's Legacy

As the 1930s unfolded, the regiment rocked along in its well-worn paths, but as the international situation deteriorated, when the Japanese conquered Manchuria in 1932 and began the systematic conquest of Chinese territory, its position became increasingly precarious. Colonel James D. Taylor, who commanded from 1929 to 1932, was succeeded by Colonel Reynolds J. Burt, from 1932 to 1935. He was followed by Colonel George Arthur Lynch, who came aboard in May 1935. Lynch departed early, after two years in command, having been made chief of infantry by President Franklin D. Roosevelt, and proceeded to Washington. He was replaced by Colonel Joseph A. McAndrew, who assumed command on May 14, 1937, and was in charge when the 15th was withdrawn from China.

Meanwhile, tensions were steadily increasing by the mid–1930s. Private Tom Mason, performing duties as driver for the 15th's commanding officer, noted that on one occasion in the spring of 1935, he and the C-in-C, Colonel George A. Lynch, were at the pedestrian overlook of Tientsin's East Station when they observed a Japanese troop train loaded with Japanese troops and artillery pieces. He remarked to Mason that " if you are writing to the folks at home you may tell them that you have just seen the start of WW II."[1]

Tense incidents in the previous weeks and months had been almost routine as 1937 unfolded, some of which could have erupted in exchanges of fire between Japanese and American troops. As the Japanese began military operations against Tientsin, even men in the 15th came under fire. One incident developed when, in conjunction with the movement of the 3rd Battalion of the 15th Infantry, from Camp Burrowes, a freight car carrying machine guns, ammunition and other valuable government property had arrived at that site when the Chinese and Japanese were engaged in a battle for its possession, which, unfortunately, ended with the Japanese capture of Tientsin. A guard of enlisted men who had been posted in the freight car became isolated and cut off from all outside communication. The unit's commanding officer, First Lieutenant Joseph W. Stilwell, Jr., set out to obtain trucks in order to remove the guard and the property. During this operation, he and members of the guard and the truck drivers were "subjected to sporadic rifle, machine-gun, and infantry mortar fire and were exposed to bombs from airplanes engaged in the bombing of nearby buildings," though there is no evidence that the Americans were specifically singled out in the general action. The lieutenant and his men, by their "heroic conduct in face of danger ... aided materially in preventing the possible loss of human life and the destruction of Government property." This event resulted in the awarding of medals—a rare occurrence in the U.S. Armed Forces between the world wars. The words of the citation delineated events of the action: "the President of the United States of America [then FDR] ... [takes] pleasure in presenting the Soldier's Medal "to First Lieutenant Joseph W. Stilwell, Jr. ... for heroism at the risk of life not involving conflict with an armed enemy at East Station, Tientsin, China, 29 July 1937." Others decorated for this incident—also with the Soldier's Medal—included Privates Armand A. Roy, Kenneth C. Platt, Glenn D. Cohee, and Merle J. Pyle.[2]

Another incident threatening American troops occurred when Japanese troops began maneuvering in a menacing fashion near the borders of the encampment at the Camp Burrowes firing range at Chinwangtao, made all the more ominous because women and children were present. Also at Chinwangtao, on August 20, 1937, when American troops on their train at the rifle range allegedly photographed a nearby Japanese troop train, an armed clash was narrowly averted. The Japanese threatened that if further incidents occurred, the U.S. would not be permitted to use the railway at all. In response, the regiment's command ordered all of its troops to avoid anything that might be provocative.[3]

Inherently more dangerous to American armed forces in China in those weeks was the *Panay* incident of December 12, 1937, when Japanese warplanes sank a U.S. Navy Yangtze patrol boat near Nanking with loss of life. Because of the *Panay* incident, and much else, isolationist America, with the War Department in the van, and even finally, the State Department, decided that the 15th Infantry had long outlived its usefulness. Indeed, it simply was in an ever-more-dangerous situation. Because the *Panay* incident led only to apologies and an indemnity from Japan, Tom Mason, an Old China Hand, was of the opinion that the incident was "more or less swept under rug." This was true, he went on, because "apparently international affairs in Europe rated a higher priority than an obsolete gunboat and a handful of white hats stationed halfway around the world and away from the hallowed Halls of Congress."[4]

There seems little doubt that the *Panay* affair was one of the most important of the many events and pressures that then prevailed. Plainly, America was determined to keep out of war, and accordingly "discreetly backed out of Nippon's swashbuckling way," as one account described it.[5] The 15th's withdrawal—and the earlier *Panay* affair—naturally did not come without official explanation. One instance was a long rambling, obfuscated address delivered by the American secretary of state, Cordell Hull, in Washington on March 17, shortly before the 15th's arrival in Tacoma. In it, he reiterated America's salient position: that the "maintenance of peace should be constantly advocated and practiced," and further stated that "the primary objectives of our foreign policy are the maintenance of the peace of our country and the promotion of the economic, the social, and the moral welfare of our people." He admitted, however, "unfortunately, the means of attaining these objectives involve today so many factors of great complexity that their real significance is frequently misunderstood and misinterpreted. Nonetheless, he urged upon all nations the need "through voluntary self-restraint, [to] abstain from use of force in pursuit of policy and from interference in the internal affairs of other nations." These powers should, he went on, "seek to adjust problems arising in their international relations by processes of peaceful negotiation and agreement." Finally, they "should uphold the principle of the sanctity of treaties and of faithful observance of international agreements." As to China, he asserted that "from time immemorial" it had been the practice of civilized nations to afford protection "by appropriate means and under the rule of reason, to their nationals and their rights and interests abroad."[6]

This policy had always been pursued by the United States, though the methods and means of affording protection abroad varied according to time, place and circumstance. Secretary Hull noted that the case of China, where "unusual local conditions were such that the protection afforded by local authorities did not suffice to give security against excited and lawless elements, there have occasionally been sent—not by this country alone but by a number of countries—armed forces, to contribute to the affording of such protection as is due under the rules of international law and the provisions of treaties." American forces thus sent to China had never had any mission of aggression, and, indeed, "it has been the practice of the American Government to withdraw such forces whenever and as soon as the local situation so develops as to warrant the view that their withdrawal can be effected without detriment to American interests and obligations in general." Surely, the conditions then existing in China hardly fit this pattern, nonetheless, given the drastic conditions then existing in eastern China, one could say that it would be folly for the 15th Infantry Regiment to remain in beleaguered Tientsin.[7]

This speech by Hull was a further manifestation of the passive, hunkered-down American stance of several years' standing, especially prominent in the 1930s, reflecting Washington's preoccupation with the depression and much else, including the strong isolationism then rampant in the U.S. The historian Akira Iriye has correctly observed, "Numerous official memoranda written at this time [by various American officials] on the East Asian question were rationalizations for the basic lack of policy and of interest in East Asia. Moral globalism and political parochialism could only be reconciled by tortured argument, and the officials were engaged in countless experiments in such argument after 1933." Debates were involved as to what America's interests in Asia truly were. Were they fundamentally economic? Should missionaries be strongly supported? What of the growing stridency of Japan? Should not America avoid provoking the Japanese empire? There was the role of the Chinese Communist Party to consider. Was its example a threat to depression-plagued America? Should not China solve its own problems without American intervention? Isolationism and pacifism also became stronger on the American domestic scene as the 1930s unfolded, with increasing public demands that American forces in Asia be completely withdrawn.[8]

While America always hoped to act in accordance with the principles enumerated by Hull, his remarks certainly could not have influenced the Japanese, who would hardly have perceived any menace therein sufficient to pay any heed. It is worth noting that as to America's being, or remaining, in China, early in World War II, the American ambassador to France, William C. Bullitt, reminded FDR that "we have large emotional interests in China, small economic interests, and no vital interests."[9] This passage speaks volumes about what was at stake in China as viewed from Washington and explains much about America's sporadic policies there in the early decades of the 20th century.

Undoubtedly, during those hectic last weeks of the 15th's being in Tientsin, the American compound became a virtual prison as the Japanese consolidated their hold over the city and its surrounding area. Furthermore, the Japanese often verbally taunted the American troops, hoping to create incidents that might lead to hostilities.[10] Indeed, as early as 1935, growing tensions produced numerous conflicts and altercations between U.S. and Japanese civilians and troops. The intensity of the darkening picture dictated that the timetable for the 15th's withdrawal be moved up from May 25, as originally set, to March 2.[11]

By now, plainly the 15th had outlived any possibility of usefulness to their nation's imprecise, insipid Asian policy. But if there had been mixed feelings among U.S. officialdom as to its necessity, the atmosphere when they departed Tientsin, and following their arrival in Tacoma (home of Fort Lewis), revealed no serious compunctions among the soldiers about their going home. Their departure was characterized by various farewell ceremonies and other developments in the few days preceding it. The 15th was replaced by a 200-man U.S. Marine detachment from the U.S. Legation Guard in Peiping, who took over the American Compound on March 1, 1938. Commanded by Lieutenant Colonel William C. James, the ranks included the unit's mascot, "Sergeant Trooper," a bulldog decked out in appropriate uniform. The formal transfer of command occurred with the changing of the guard at the compound early on March 2, 1938.[12]

As to the 15th's departure, one British lad, Desmond Power, who had grown up in the British Concession, recounted the details in his memoirs. To him, "that was the hardest part to take—the departure of fine fellows, the severance of warm ties. We taught them cricket ... they taught us American baseball. We went to their homes at Thanksgiving and Halloween ... and there was that incredible celebration at Can Do Field on the Fourth of July." The British children were invited to participate—especially in eating ice cream. "Hey kid, over here!," a soldier would call out, and "he'd plop three scoops: pink—white—brown into a gigantic cone. Heaven! Sheer heaven!" Accordingly, he concluded, "March 2, 1938, must surely be counted as one of Tientsin's most heart-stirring days."

By mid-morning, British policemen, firemen, Boy Scouts—including Desmond—and soldiers of the Lancashire Fusiliers were in position along Victoria Street in the British Concession to honor the passing parade. Troops of the British Volunteer Defense Corps and soldiers of the French 16th Colonial Infantry Regiment were also lined up as the Americans proceeded along their concession on the Rue de France. French policemen and firemen were also present, as were a troop of French Boy Scouts and an Italian band. The Yanks, appearing from the American compound on their way to Tientsin's East Train Station, marched to their band's "crashing out *Stars and Stripes Forever*." The men were "grinning sheepishly at the ovation," which was deafening, what with the "shouting, cheering, hand clapping and the fire-crackers." Many women broke through the ranks and flung themselves on their departing sweethearts. Then it was suddenly over, and Desmond confessed "a strange feeling of emptiness fill[ed] the air." "Tientsin would never be the same," he declared. There would be "no more Friday Night Fights. No more baseball at Can Do Field. No more hockey at Can Do Rink," and, he ruefully concluded, "no more ice cream on the Fourth of July." But a Chinese youth, one of Desmond's friends, named Jefferson Wu, when Desmond noted that it was "pretty sad for all of us" retorted that it was "not so. It's a happy day, happy for China, happy for America." His statement was borne out by the many firecrackers. "It's a tradition with us. It's our way of celebrating a joyous event. And they'll be celebrating in America too. Bet you anything you like most people over there believe strongly that it was wrong for their soldiers to be used as an occupation army. And as for that other army of occupation, the British, there's going to be an even happier, noisier celebration when they leave." When Desmond protested that these Western forces were protecting them, Wu responded, "we don't need their protection, never did."[13]

An American Army officer, Frank Dorn—later a brigadier general—also witnessed the regiment's exodus, and wryly observed—on the whole, accurately—that the 15th Infantry, "having long enjoyed the good life at Tientsin, was ordered to depart its cushy post for reassignment in the United States." After its 26 years of service in China, he wrote, "the tasks of packing up and of breaking off relations with their Chinese and White Russian women were enormous; but eventually the sad-eyed men of the regiment marched through the streets of the city, flags flying and bands playing, and boarded the trains that would take them to Chinwangtao and a transport [the U.S. Army transport (USAT) *U.S. Grant*] waiting to return them to the rigors of a discipline and training they had not known for years."[14]

As for those women left behind, Desmond observed at least one "tragic scene": "A great big hippopotamus of a woman lies collapsed on a bench, her mountains of flesh shuddering as she chokes out her heart-breaking lament." His unsympathetic friends simply dismissed it, one noting that it was "only Russian playacting, Russian emotion." "She'll be okay in no time," he declared.[15]

The regiment was underway by train by mid-morning of March 2 and by evening had set sail from Chinwangtao for Hawaii and Tacoma, arriving at the latter on March 24. The numbers involved about 716 officers and men of the 15th, together with several other military personnel attached for transportation to the United States, for a total of 808 officers and men. In addition, families consisting of 417 wives and children, including eleven Russian spouses, of the men were aboard, though some thirty-five Chinese wives, forbidden by U.S. law to be admitted to the country even if married to U.S. military personnel, were left behind in China. Numerous "shack squaws," as concubines were called, were similarly abandoned.[16]

The voyage was not smooth. There had been some storms in the China

The USAT *U.S. Grant*, the army transport bringing men of the 15th Infantry Regiment hoe from China, docked in Tacoma, Washington, on March 24, 1938. Aircraft from the 91st Observation Squadron, based at Fort Lewis, flew over in their Douglas O-46 aircraft in a welcome salute (courtesy the Tacoma Public Library, D7143-2B).

8. Going Home and the Regiment's Legacy

Seas, resulting in the inevitable seasick soldiers. Storms of another sort occurred in Hawaii when one group from the regiment "had mistaken a Portuguese apartment for a cathouse." The results were "black eyes, broken noses, cuts and bruises galore." In any event, the time of departure from Honolulu for Tacoma was a stirring one. "The band was on deck and playing Hawaiian music," one soldier, Howard W. Palm recalled, and he opined "there's something thrilling about going back as a unit."[17]

The men's arrival at the Tacoma docks on March 24, 1938, triggered joyous celebrations resembling those for World War I's returning veterans. As the *Grant* pulled up to the dock, ships in the harbor, train locomotives, and factories blew their whistles. Overhead, planes of the 91st Observation Squadron flew in formation and a dirigible also flew over, while the Fort Lewis's 10th Field Artillery band played. A huge crowd jammed the Tacoma docks along Commencement Bay to welcome them home, it being perceived that they had made fortunate "escapes," having " fled" China, being "whisked away" as Japanese bombing in the Tientsin area had intensified. Indeed, the official explanation given for the regiment's return was "because of the escalating hostilities between [China] and Japan."[18]

The welcome home was orchestrated by a reception committee that included Tacoma's "Daffodil Queen" and hosts of people bearing large bouquets of daffodils. The governor of Washington, Clarence D. Martin, Tacoma's mayor, George Smitley, and Major General Thomas Merrill, the Fort Lewis commander, headed the dignitaries' delegation of numerous state and local officials and numerous reporters and photographers. The "Can Doers" were therefore joyously received with applause and acclamation all around after 26 years in China, during which time it was declared they had helped the Chinese "fight flood and famine," among other salutary deeds.

These festivities were soon forgotten, however, and the men found themselves at nearby Fort Lewis in dispiriting circumstances. One trooper, Howard W. Palm, complained that their new surroundings were "quite depressing" after their much better accommodations in the American Compound in Tientsin, and he asserted that they had gone from "riches to rags." They were initially housed in temporary squad tents, which, while waterproof, "were still mighty cold." In any case, the regiment was eventually better cared for and was soon poised to take its place in the emerging "new" U.S. Army that was to fight World War II.[19]

By this time, some of the men may have remembered with a bit of nostalgia a poem published in the *Sentinel* in 1932 by Joan Power. Entitled "Homeward Bound," in part it went like this:

> The long trick's over; we are bound for home.
> China astern. Seen thus, it looks its best!
> The day long waited for at last has come.
> And now we are free from bondage, free to rest!

Nevertheless, her poem concluded that the men had learned a truth that "we jeered at till today," that "China is home to the old China hand."[20]

As to its China legacy, the 15th Regiment prided itself on its motto, "Can Do." It is easily imagined that some soldier might express something about it poetically, as did Pvt. John B. Houchin, of Company E in his ode to "our motto Heaven-sent," which was published in the *Sentinel* on April 25, 1931:

> "Can Do" is a true expression,
> Of the spirit that lies within,
> The heart of we [sic] "doughboy" soldiers,
> Here in this far away city, Tientsin.
> Our comrades that [sic] have gone on before us,
> Have set "Can Do" standards high,
> And *we* must carry and strengthen them,
> For the comrades we have bidden goodbye.

They were also prone to keep in mind the term and concept of their being Old China Hands. One writer has noted that the term implied contact between Chinese and non–Chinese cultures. These were especially prominent in the 1920s and 1930s, but in recent years, there is now a generation of "New Old China Hands." But between the world wars, an Old China Hand "might have been an employee of the government of China, a business person, a missionary, in maritime or military service, a refugee from Nazi Germany or Communist Russia, a civil administrator, a journalist, an adventurer or drifter, a person benign or wicked." One striking aspect of the hands was "that they were almost universally keenly aware of their heritage and take pride in having participated in this distinct and turbulent phase of China's history." Finally, when these disparate persons took up residence in China they understood was that "they changed China for good or ill, and China unmistakably changed them."[21]

Some of the Old China Hands were numbered among those "who had missed too many boats." Pearl Buck was acquainted with some of them and discussed two kinds that she was familiar with: "I used to see exiles in my Chinese world often enough but they were the white men who could never go home. Sometimes it was their fault. They had married Chinese women, or had children by them, and the little creatures they had made, inadvertently perhaps, had laid such hold upon them that they stayed until it was too late to leave them." Others "were exiles merely because they could not enjoy living in the small American towns and on the farms where they had been born. The magic of Asia had caught them, the inexplicable richness of ancient life, the ease and freedom of belonging nowhere, and they could not return to the tight circle of family and friends who could never understand the magic."[22]

In a more concrete way, among the things that the men of the 15th were proud of was a stone gateway of Chinese marble that was destined in the course of time to be sited on the grounds of Fort Benning, Georgia, near the officers' club. Erected in its Georgia setting in March of 1938, it had originally stood in the American Compound in Tientsin. It had been "respectfully presented with pleasure" in April of 1925 to the American Forces in China, which consisted mainly of the 15th Infantry Regiment, by citizens of some thirty Chinese villages in the vicinity of the American Compound. The Americans were recognized for maintaining law and order in Tientsin and the surrounding countryside when the tides of Chinese civil war surged across the area in 1924. The commander of the American Forces in China, Brigadier General Durward Connor, accepted the memorial in an address in Chinese, which he spoke rather well, "which was understood and deeply appreciated by all. It was perhaps the first time that an American Army Officer ever addressed a representation of Chinese people at a military function in their own language, and from the deep interest which was manifested, it is quite evident to those present that the few remarks made by General Connor will go far in maintaining the friendly and cordial relations which exist between China and America." Connor stated the following:

> We are gathered here today in order to perform a very pleasant task. During the war that recently destroyed the peace of this part of China, we Americans were able to do a service to certain citizens of this great country by protecting them, while at the same time performing the duties which our country has arranged with China that we shall do within her territory.

He went on to say "that Marble is a very enduring stone but I hope that long after this stone has decayed the friendship between our two countries may exist, and that as long as this stone endures it will be a memento to all the world of the friendship that grew up between us during the troubled days when China was awakening."

A poem etched in both English and Chinese on the gate stated: "A remembrance of the Golden Deeds done by Officers and men of the United States Army Forces in China during the Civil Strife, 1924," and concluded: "The sons of Uncle Sam so gallant in their deed/Day and night so strict defense took greatest heed/and through their strenuous effort and suffering/Peace among us all was kept and maintained." The villagers wished to accord "honor to those to whom honor is due."

Men of the 15th Regiment tote their duffle bags as they disembark from the *U.S. Grant* and leave for Fort Lewis, near Tacoma, Washington (courtesy Tacoma Public Library, D7143-20).

Fifteen individual local dignitaries signed the gate, as did officials of the Yu Yuan Cotton Mills and the Pei Yang First Commercial Cotton Mill, their signatures being etched in the marble. The memorial was erected near regimental headquarters in the compound where it remained as the center of regimental activities until the 15th departed China in March 1938. The gate was then disassembled and shipped to Fort Benning, where it still stands.[23]

Among the legacies of the 15th were the large number of important generals who came out of its "nursery," such as Marshall, Stilwell, and Wedemeyer,

Opposite, top: A close-up of a happy group of 15th Infantry soldiers returning to the United States. *Bottom:* The returning 15th Infantry was greeted by numerous officials. Here, the Washington governor Clarence Martin, right, shakes hands with army colonel Joseph A. McAndrew, commander of the "Can Do" regiment (both photographs courtesy Tacoma Public Library, D7143-11 and D7143-16).

among many others, sometimes referred to a bit derisively as "that damned China Crowd." Many of those generals will be discussed further in part three.

As things transpired, after the dockside celebrations the 15th moved into pyramidal tents while awaiting the construction of more permanent quarters, which were available by the end of 1938. Almost immediately, the 15th underwent intensive training, so as "to maintain its reputation as one of the best regiments in the military." During the remainder of 1938 and through 1939, the regiment was engaged in extensive field maneuvers. On January 12, 1940, it was attached to the 3rd Infantry Division, which included the famed 7th Infantry Regiment, the so-called "Cottonbalers," who had derived their name from their exploits against the British in the Battle of New Orleans under Andrew Jackson in the War of 1812. On May 15, 1940, a National Guard regiment, the 30th, rounded out the 3rd's main infantry force. The unit was called the "Rock of the Marne" Division, gaining this name during World War I.

The 3rd Division, early in 1940, participated in major maneuvers at Fort Ord, California, that included amphibious landings. It returned to Fort Lewis in May and continued its participation in amphibious operations for the remainder of 1940. It established an amphibious training camp near Olympia, having received instruction from the Amphibious Corps Pacific Fleet by navy and Marine Corps personnel from San Diego. The facility was used by all units of the 3rd Division. The regiment also established a ski patrol in the winter of 1940–1941, which conducted winter and mountain operations on Mount Rainier and tested equipment later used by the troops of the U.S. Army's 10th Mountain Division. It was during this time that Lieutenant Colonel Dwight David Eisenhower served in the 15th. Arriving in February 1940, he remained until November of that year, serving as commander of the 1st Battalion and as regimental executive officer.[24]

On May 24, 1941, the 15th departed Fort Lewis once more for large-scale maneuvers in California that included additional amphibious operations. On February 15, 1942, it was assigned the duty of defending the Washington coastline from Seattle to Canada. In May 1942, orders were received for the regiment to move to Fort Ord, California, the men receiving additional advanced combat infantry training. In September, the 15th was sent to Camp Pickett, Virginia, to await shipment overseas. This came on October 24, 1942, when the troops departed from Norfolk, Virginia, as part of the 3rd Infantry Division bound for French Morocco and "Operation Torch" in North Africa. The assault began on November 8, the 15th being engaged at Fedala.

Later operations of the 15th during World War II included the invasion of Sicily on July 10, 1943; Salerno, Italy, on September 18, 1943; and Anzio,

Italy, on January 22, 1943. Next, they were engaged in "Operation Dragoon" in southern France, beginning on August 15, 1944. The regiment entered Germany on March 13, 1945, and Austria on May 5, 1945. In all, it was in combat for 31 months during World War II. In the course of its operations, it earned 16 Medals of Honor, "more than most divisions," one of which was awarded to Audie Murphy, one of the regiment's most celebrated soldiers.[25]

Following World War II, on December 1, 1948, the 15th was transferred from occupation duty in Germany to Fort Benning, Georgia. Following the outbreak of the Korean War, on August 31, 1950, as part of the 3rd U.S. Infantry Division, it fought during the withdrawal of American forces from the Chosin Reservoir in 1950, then proceeded north to the 38th parallel in 1951, and in the Kumsong sector until the cease fire was signed on July 27, 1953. It was awarded three Medals of Honor for its actions.

The regiment returned to Fort Benning on December 3, 1954. Then, following the army's reorganization of its combat forces, the 15th maintained a presence, but under several designations. From 1957 to 1996, it was on occupation duty in West Germany. Some deactivations and reactivations then ensued. From August 20, 1990, to March 22, 1991, the regiment's 3rd Battalion participated in Operation Desert Shield and Operation Desert Storm, freeing Kuwait from Iraqi oppression. In 1993, units of the 15th were in Somalia, and in 1994 other units were in Macedonia. Further changes in organization then occurred, and units were deployed to Iraq in 2003, 2005–06, 2007, and finally in 2009. The year 2013 found the regiment engaged in Afghanistan. Battalions of the regiment still remain with headquarters at Fort Stewart, Georgia, and Fort Benning, Georgia.

Part III: Notable Alumni of the 15th Infantry's Service in China

Ah, but a man's reach should exceed his grasp, Or what's a heaven for?
—Robert Browning

9

A Gallery of Generals

This narrative will present accounts of numerous high-ranking U.S. Army officers, all of whom became generals, all of whom had served in China in the 15th U.S. Infantry Regiment sometime between 1912 and 1938. They collectively constitute one component of the regiment's Chinese legacy. A gallery of these generals, often referred to as the Old China Hands, or "That Damned China Crowd," will be considered because their tours in China were especially noteworthy. This was true, in part, because the 15th's years of service in China were more numerous than those of other U.S. Army outfits engaged there.

The historian Benjamin R. Beede, in his book *The Small Wars of the United States, 1899–2009* identified other factors, observing that the 15th Regiment's "story is less well known than the adventures of the marines in China during approximately the same period, but the stationing was a major commitment of the United States to having a voice in the Far East. A number of officers who became generals later helped lead the regiment at various times, making the story of this service all the more important."[1] In the event, the question has been asked regarding who some of these men were. Some of them were well known in this regard, such as Generals George Marshall and Joseph Stilwell, but there were many more. The following presentation is in part created to identify and discuss some of them.

A key common attribute of these officers, then, was that they had served in China, which created a common bond. This often served as a springboard for their future careers, sometimes manifested when their paths crossed in the future on some occasions, their serving once again in China or Asia. Examples included Stilwell, Stilwell's son, General Joseph Warren Stilwell, Jr., General Harold LaMaire Boatner, General Robert Battey McClure, and others who were in China or Burma with Joseph Warren Stilwell, Sr., or with General Albert Coady Wedemeyer.

9. A Gallery of Generals

To be sure, much more than their service in China accounted for their rise in rank until they crossed that magic dividing line and attained their first star as a brigadier general. Their personal drives and keen ambitions must head the list of factors leading to success, often reflecting the presence of the intense competition involved. Many were unusually talented or possessed sharp intellects. Not to be overlooked was the discipline and patience exhibited by perhaps all of those hanging on for promotions during years when there were few. Many sought to serve at favorable duty stations at home and abroad, which for some included China. Quests for honors and decorations often played some part. Also, famously, General Marshall, when he was chief of the Army General Staff during World War II, frequently had a hand in identifying and promoting many officers with whom he had served or whom he had observed, having deemed them good candidates for positions of power and responsibility. He had, in fact, first encountered several of them while in China.

There were yet other guiding stars besides being in China that made for the success of most of these generals. For some, there was service in the Philippines, though this should be deplored in many respects. Then there was involvement in World War I, with many examples of exemplary action. The army's extensive school system, including the Infantry School at Fort Benning, the Command and Staff College, and the War College, among others, played significant roles.

Soldiering at the general officer level in the U.S. Army was often a veritable family business. Many of the soldiers were born into military families, and on occasion, brothers of the same family were involved, as in attending West Point. Sons also often followed, keeping traditions alive. Sometimes they married into other military families, and on occasion, fathers-in-law contributed to the success of sons-in-law.

The role of West Point and its mystique as part of that "band of brothers" and that "long, gray line," with its emphasis on duty, honor, and country, as its motto affirms, was often important. This was well illustrated by Douglas MacArthur's farewell address to the cadets after his being recalled from Korea. In his remarks, he noted that his thoughts at the very last would be only of "the Corps, the Corps, and the Corps."[2]

As to West Point, mention might also be made of the Class of 1915, the one identified as the "class the stars fell on." This is a reference to the fact that out of a class of 164 cadets, some 59 attained the rank of general: 24 brigadiers, 24 major generals, seven lieutenant generals, two four-star generals, and two elevated to five-star rank, becoming generals of the army. One of those, Lieutenant General John W. Leonard, was also an alumnus of the 15th in China.[3]

118   Part III: Notable Alumni of the 15th Infantry's Service in China

To be sure, there were some generals who had served in the 15th who were not at West Point, including, among others, Lieutenant General Richard Kerens Sutherland, who attended Yale, Major General Joseph C. Castner, who was at Rutgers, General George C. Marshall, VMI, and General Campbell King, Harvard. These exceptions depended upon factors other than a West Point education to help them along their paths to fame and glory.

The following is hardly a complete list of general officers who had earlier served in the 15th, though it well represents those who were in China at some time in their military careers. Among those to be considered were two generals who commanded the United States Army Forces in China (USAFC) in the 1920s. Though these men have been briefly discussed above, it seems appropriate to consider them further herein. The USAFC was an organization larger than the 15th Regiment, though that unit was essentially the only force involved. This would bring more prestige for the United States, with a brigadier general in China outranking the colonel who usually commanded a regiment, thereby giving the U.S. more status.

Accordingly, on November 22, 1922, Brigadier General William Durward Connor was ordered to Tientsin. He arrived to take up his duties on April 12, 1923. Born in Wisconsin on February 22, 1874, he was appointed to West Point from Iowa, where his family had relocated. He graduated first in his class in 1897, and, as was often the case with the higher-ranking cadets, he was commissioned in the engineers. During the Spanish-American War, he served in the Philippines. From there, for a time, he was instructor in engineering at West Point. In 1907, he became the army's district engineer in Memphis, Tennessee. From Memphis, he was ordered to the Army War College as a student, following which he had a tour of duty in command of the Engineer Battalion and Engineer School, returning once more to the War College as the assistant commandant. From 1909 to 1916, he was on the Army General Staff in Washington. In 1917, promoted to colonel, he was made the deputy chief staff of the American Expeditionary Forces in France. In July 1918, he became chief of staff of the 32nd Division and, promoted to brigadier general soon thereafter, he became commander of the 63rd Infantry Brigade and fought with it in the Battle of Château-Thierry.

Following the end of hostilities, Connor was made deputy chief of staff of the Services of Supply in France and after Pershing's return to the United States, in 1919, Connor became the commanding general of U.S. Forces remaining in France. In this capacity, he was in charge of dismantling the American forces there and disposing of the vast quantities of supplies that had been accumulated.

Returning to the United States, for a time he commanded the Engineer

School. From there, he was summoned to China and remained from 1923 to 1926. Promoted to major general in 1926, he commanded the 2nd Infantry Division in the U.S. From 1927 to 1932, he was the commandant of the Army War College. He followed this by being made superintendent at West Point and served from 1932 to 1938. Retiring in 1938, he was recalled to service during World War II, and from 1941 to 1942, served as chairman of the War Department's Construction Advisory Committee. He died on June 16, 1960, at age 86 and is buried at the West Point cemetery.

Connor was highly regarded by the U.S. Amy's top brass, notably for his services in France with the AEF's Service of Supply, where he straightened out many of the difficulties with its organization and operations and for his liquidation efforts in bringing the AEF's existence to an end. But some noted that he was not only brilliant but also "imperious," and not everyone he met warmed up to him. Yet, in China he endeared himself to the Chinese, one way being to order all officers to study Chinese, which developed as a major program, enlisted men also being urged to participate. He also was keenly interested in maintaining good relations with the Chinese as well as intelligently assessing U.S.-Chinese relations and what the role of the United States should be in Asia.[4]

The man who replaced Connor was of a far different mettle. He was Brigadier General Joseph Compton Castner, who arrived in China in May 1926. Born in New Brunswick, New Jersey, on November 18, 1869, he entered the army as a second lieutenant following his 1891 Rutgers University graduation with a degree in civil engineering.[5] Castner then participated in the U.S. Army's Glenn Expedition, from June 29 to October 23, 1898, which, under the command of Captain Edwin F. Glenn, explored Prince Edward Sound, the Cook Inlet, and the Tanana River areas in Alaska. Later in 1898, as a first lieutenant, Castner served in the Santiago Campaign in Cuba in the Spanish-American War. Then came arduous service in the Philippines, at which time he, though an infantry officer, commanded the Philippine Scouts, a cavalry outfit.

Later, in 1909, as a captain, Castner was ordered to Oahu, Hawaii, where, as constructing quartermaster, he planned and built temporary military quarters, later called Schofield Barracks but initially known as "Castner Village."

Just prior to World War I, Castner graduated from the Army War College. When the United States entered World War I, Castner, first as a colonel, commanded the 38th Infantry Regiment, and then, promoted to brigadier general, from May 10, 1918, he led the 9th Infantry Brigade of the U.S. 5th Army, seeing action in the St. Mihiel and Meuse-Argonne operations. He remained with the 5th in Luxembourg, in the U.S. Army of Occupation, until its return to the United States in 1919. While there, Castner took a course at the army Center of Artillery Studies at Trier.

In 1920, Castner graduated from the General Staff School at Leavenworth and in 1921 from the War College for a second time in. Also in 1921, he was appointed a brigadier general and assigned to command a brigade in the 1st Cavalry Division, based at Fort Bliss, Texas, and for a time, commanded the division. In 1925 and 1926, he was stationed at Fort Hood, Texas.

From there, in May 1926, Castner arrived in Tientsin as General Connor's replacement. One account notes that he was "a bluff, no nonsense, hard-driving infantryman, temporarily—for four years—turned cavalryman, 'of that irritating breed of military men who pride themselves on being simple, rough, and blunt soldiers.'" Accordingly, he immediately made a distinct impression on the 15th. Finney, in his book *The Old China Hands*, described him as "an enormous man, big of bone and big of belly. He looked like a fat but very muscular giant." He was also sloppily dressed, often appearing in "an un-pressed O.D. shirt, khaki breeches faded almost white, spiral puttees, and enlisted men's shoes." Finney went on to say "it was only by the silver stars on his shirt collar that one could tell he was a general." He was also a stickler for physical fitness, a proclivity that boded ill for his tenure in Tientsin. He especially favored a great deal of physical activity, in keeping with his views that "the way to turn out a well-disciplined, rugged command was by hard drill and long hikes, the latter led by himself at a pace that forced the men at the end of the column to run most of the time." The result of all this was that for some time during his tenure he endured a running feud with many of the 15th's officers who attempted to obtain his removal on the grounds "of mental incompetence."[6]

The upshot of this came on November 12, 1928, when Castner planned a 100-mile march over a three-day period. The men made the first 30 miles as ordered, but they were too exhausted to continue. They were rescued by a visiting army inspector general, Colonel Louis I. Schaick, who had just arrived from the Philippines and had witnessed the event. Though outranked by Castner, Van Schaick was armed with the authority of the Inspector General's Office in Washington, and he threatened to cable his headquarters regarding these proceedings. Castner gave way, but not without much grumbling.

Subsequently, the army reexamined the matter of extended marches and issued orders to that effect. As Finney noted, henceforth, the most challenging march for the 15th consisted of an annual five-mile combined hike and run to test their athletic and soldierly prowess. Finney, among many others, was often mystified as to the origins of Castner's interest in extreme hiking and vigor and recorded a rumor that he had earlier in his career hiked from Alaska to Seattle, conceivably "the only white man ever to have done so." Indeed, earlier Castner was described in the 5th Division's official history, which recorded its actions in France, as "a man's man, a soldier and a leader. In mental and physical alertness, in devotion to duty, in zeal and energy, he is an example, alike to men and officers." It is not for nothing that he was known as "Roaring Joe."[7]

Certainly, the men of the 15th must have read with great interest in their troop newspaper, the *Sentinel*, that the post of brigadier general in China was to be abolished, leaving the 15th Regiment as the sole U.S. Amy force there. Castner received orders on March 10, 1929, sending him to Fort Lewis in Washington. He would have no replacement.

At Fort Lewis, Castner became the commanding officer of the 3rd Infantry ("The Rock of the Marne") Division. He retired from the Army on November 30, 1933, as a major general. He died on July 7, 1946, and is buried at the San Francisco National Cemetery. (His son, who would be with the 15th for a brief time, having to depart early because of an illness, had an interesting military career of his own but not as a general.)

Undoubtedly, one of the most important of the 15th's alumni group was Lieutenant Colonel George Catlett Marshall, the regiment's executive officer from September 8, 1924, to May 1927. He arrived when the regiment was between commanding colonels and promptly took charge. As it happened, this was a time of crisis that he handled well, following the orders of Brigadier General William Durward Connor, who was commanding the rather larger entity—of which the 15th was the major part—the United States Army Forces in China, which had been created in 1923. When the regiment's new commanding officer, Colonel William K. Naylor, arrived, Marshall was relieved of his duties on November 23, 1924, and reverted to the role of the regiment's executive officer. A year later, on December 23, 1925, with the dismissal of Naylor for alleged dereliction of duty, Marshall again took charge of the regiment, once more in a time of tension during which he again acquitted himself well. He continued to command the regiment until March 6, 1926, when Colonel Isaac Newell assumed command. Marshall then served once again as the regiment's executive officer until his departure for the United States in May 1927.[8]

George Catlett Marshall was born on December 31, 1880, in Uniontown, Pennsylvania. He entered Virginia Military Institute in 1897, and, though deficient in academics, distinguished himself as a cadet with an emphasis on leadership skills. Indeed, he had, with gusto, imbibed the soldierly virtues manifested at VMI. He graduated in 1901, having been first captain, the highest-ranking cadet at the school. He received a diploma in civil engineering. With no army commission, he took extensive exams and, passing these, was commissioned a second lieutenant in the infantry, on February 2, 1902, though he had hoped for a slot in the artillery. He married Lily Coles at this time, on February 11.

He was ordered to the Philippines with the 30th Infantry Regiment, from May 1902 to November 1903, and experienced rather arduous service on occupation duty. Returning to the United States, from December 1903 to August 1906, he was stationed at Fort Reno in Oklahoma, engaged in an extensive mapping expedition in Southwest Texas.

From August 1906 to June 1910, he was enrolled in the School of the Line at Fort Leavenworth, Kansas, first in the basic course, and the following year, 1908, in the advanced course. Also, in March of 1907, he was promoted to first lieutenant. From 1908 to 1910, he remained as an instructor. Having overcome his academic deficiencies, he emerged as an inspired teacher. It has been noted that Marshall was indeed one of the U.S. Army's great teachers of this era.

In June of 1911, he became inspector-instructor of the Massachusetts Volunteer Militia, remaining in that capacity until September of 1912. From September 1912 to June 1913, he served with the 4th U.S. Infantry Regiment in Texas and Minnesota.

Nineteen thirteen found him once more in the Philippines as aide-de-camp to Major General Hunter Liggett, then head of the Philippine Department. While there, Marshall was engaged in putting several thousand troops in maneuvers and exercises and demonstrated a high level of planning and problem-solving that well equipped him for his later service as a staff officer. He departed the Philippines in May 1916, becoming in July aide-de-camp to Major General J. Franklin Bell in San Francisco and Governors Island, New York, remaining until July 1917. Meanwhile, in October of 1916, he was promoted to captain.

In World War I, Marshall went to France in 1917 with units of the 1st Division. As assistant chief of staff, he helped plan the First U.S. Army's operations. Following June 13, 1918, he was at Pershing's headquarters, and in August, he was with the 1st Army, where he continued the plans for attack in the St. Mihiel salient and the Meuse-Argonne offensive. Here, he devised and executed the rapid shift of 220,000 soldiers from St. Mihiel, replacing them with 500,000 fresh troops who expeditiously, despite many problems with muddy, narrow roads—and even those few in number—and a shortage of transportation, proceeded to the Argonne, all in two weeks time, having moved at night and in secret. His successes at this time won him extensive praise at the higher levels of the army, marking him out as a superior staff officer and planner. This was not, in his view, however, in his best interest because he desperately wanted to command troops in the fields, the main pathway to promotion. Typically, in the "Old Army," staff officers and those assigned as military attachés and language students, for instance, were not usually considered for promotions as rapidly as were the line officers in command of troops. This continued to disturb Marshall's peace of mind until later in his career. It was certainly the case in the final weeks of World War I, when his great success as a staff officer dictated that he should remain in planning, which he did as assistant chief of staff for the U.S. First Army, remaining until November 19, 1918.

After the armistice, from November 20, 1918, to January 15, 1919, Marshall was chief of staff of the 8th Corps. In May of 1919, he became senior aide to General John J. Pershing. In this capacity, he accompanied Pershing to several European capitals for victory celebrations at the highest levels, during which he met kings, queens, presidents and masses of citizens in England, France, Italy and elsewhere. Marshall remained as Pershing's aide following the general's promotion, in 1921, to U.S. Army chief of staff, remaining in his service until June 1924, when Marshall and his wife departed for the 15th Infantry in Tientsin.

Following his three years of service there, Marshall was an instructor at the U.S. Army War College in Washington, D.C., where his wife died on September 15, 1927. Marshall then sought to leave Washington, and in November 1927 he took up his new duties as assistant commandant and chief of instruction of the army's Infantry School in Fort Benning, Georgia. There, from 1927 to 1932, he accomplished a revolution in army instruction that had far-reaching results, propelling the army to make major strides in educational reform even at other army schools. He also was able to renew acquaintances of many with whom he had served in China, there then being many Old China Hands at Benning. Furthermore, he was able to observe and influence many rising officers who would emerge as the major commanders of the U.S. Army in World War II. Marshall was, in fact, noted for his ability to choose capable commanders from the officers he had closely observed, especially at the various schools, as well as in China. Also, on October 15, 1930, during his service at Fort Benning, Marshall married a former actress and recent widow, Katherine Tupper Brown.[9]

From Fort Benning, Marshall became commander of Fort Screven, Georgia, and then was commander of Fort Moultrie, South Carolina. In 1932 and

1933, Marshall helped build and develop camps for the Civilian Conservation Corps, one of Franklin Roosevelt's creations to which Marshall fully subscribed. Marshall set up 19 camps in the South and supervised an additional 35 in the Pacific Northwest. From October 1933 to October 1936, Marshall was senior instructor with the Illinois National Guard. Here he further developed his teaching skills. Regarding these, Marshall once indicated that he had been disappointed in the quality of his education at VMI. He charged that it was too-much wedded to learning by rote memorization. This shortcoming proved to be a goad to Marshall, who, in the future, in his self-education and in his developments as a teacher in the Army, resolved to do better. As one writer put it, "Marshall spent a good part of his career as a teacher in the Army, where he had a notable, indeed historic, impact, for hundreds of the men he taught became high-ranking combat commanders in the Second World War."[10]

Obtaining his first star as a brigadier general in October of 1936, from October of that year to June of 1938 he was at the Vancouver Barracks in the State of Washington as commander of the 5th Brigade of the 3rd Division.

In July 1938, Marshall was ordered to Washington as assistant chief of staff of the War Plans Division at the War Department. Shortly thereafter, in October, he became the army deputy chief of staff, remaining until June of 1939. In the spring, FDR nominated him to succeed General Malin Craig as the U.S. Army chief of staff. Marshall was then acting chief of staff for two months from July 1, 1939, and on September 1, 1939, ironically on the first day of the outbreak of World War II in Europe when Hitler invaded Poland, Marshall became the U.S. Army's chief of staff, trading his one star as a brigadier general for the four of a full general. He was to hold the post for six years, until November 1945.

Marshall was confronted with countless responsibilities as the war loomed. He would eventually increase the army—which then included the Army Air Corps—from 200,000 men to about 8.5 million, a continuous major effort. He also attended all of the great conferences of the war, from Argentia in Newfoundland in the late summer of 1941, before Pearl Harbor, to Potsdam in Germany in the summer of 1945. He was a strong protagonist for the Europe First strategy and emphasized, and fought for the cross-channel invasion of Europe as the key strategy to be implemented. He himself strongly desired to command the Allied forces engaged there, but FDR, asserting, "I feel now that I will not be able to sleep at night with you out of the country," opted for Eisenhower. Britain's prime minister, Winston Churchill, was undoubtedly correct in calling Marshall the "true organizer of victory." Marshall also became one of the few U.S. generals to hold the rank of general of the army. This came on December 17, 1944, Congress having created the five-star rank on December 8. This was done to bring America's top military and naval officers on par with the British field marshals with whom they had to deal.[11]

Only one week following Marshall's retirement as the army chief of staff on November 20, 1945, just as he was poised to take a lengthy, well-earned vacation, President Truman asked him to undertake a mission to China as "Special Representative of the President" with the personal rank of ambassador. There, the Chinese Communists under Chairman Mao and the Nationalist forces under Chiang Kai-shek were engaged in a bitter civil war. Marshall was to attempt to bring the warring forces together. (The difficulties that he encountered may have enabled him better to understand something about Stilwell's embattled time there during World War II.) He departed the U.S. in December of 1946 but could not obtain any agreement. Remaining in China until January 8, 1947, he returned home empty-handed. In the meantime, in late 1946, he had accepted the appointment by President Truman of U.S. secretary of state, assuming those duties on January 8, 1947, when he was unanimously confirmed by the U.S. Senate. He was sworn in as secretary of state on January 21, 1947.[12]

One of the major issues then confronting the world was how to effect recovery in Europe. In a commencement address at Harvard University on June 5, 1947, Marshall introduced the basis of the European Recovery Act. He had earlier conferred with Stalin on how Europe might be resurrected, but Stalin demurred. Marshall decided that the West must act unilaterally. The result was the Marshall Plan, with its far-reaching provisions that had positive results almost from its inception. The plan officially ended on December 31, 1951, and was widely regarded as one of the most successful foreign policy initiatives in U.S. history. In addition, Marshall was one of those responsible for the establishment of NATO in 1949, which created a balance of power between the West and the Soviet Bloc, lasting until late in the 20th century when the Soviet Union collapsed. Beyond these endeavors, Marshall sought to develop greater cooperation between Latin America and the United States. By this time, in 1949, Marshall began to experience ill health and resigned as Secretary of State early in that year.[13]

Once again, however, with the coming of the Korean War on June 24, 1950, Marshall became the U.S. secretary of defense, in September, overseeing the formation of an internal force under the United Nations that eventually turned back the North Korean invasion of South Korea. He served in that office a year, retiring in September of 1951. Subsequently, in December of 1953, Marshall received the Nobel Peace Prize in Oslo, Norway, the only soldier ever to receive it. He was cited for advancing the well-being of all nations, and not only that of his own country.[14]

Undoubtedly, Marshall was one the most respected soldiers in the nation's history. When departing his office, the secretary of war, Henry L. Stimson, remarked to him, "I have seen a great many soldiers in my lifetime and you, Sir, are the finest soldier I have ever known." Churchill also noted that, while it "has not fallen to your lot to command the great armies," Marshall had in fact created, organized and inspired them. Churchill went on to say that "under your guiding hand the mighty and valiant formations which have swept across France and Germany were brought into being and perfected in an amazingly short space of time. Not only were the fighting troops and their complicated ancillaries created but, to an extent that seems almost incredible to me, the supply of commanders capable of manoeuvring the vast organisms of modern armies and groups of armies and of moving these with unsurpassed celerity" were also found when needed. He credited Marshall with developing the major strategies employed and saw him as the mainspring of "that marvelous organization, the Allied combined Chiefs of Staff," whose work had been superlative. Eisenhower weighed in with further praise, noting that Marshall had an "unparalleled place in the respect and affections of all military and political leaders with whom I have been associated, as well as with the mass of American fighting men." He concluded that "our Army and people have never been so deeply indebted to any other soldier."[15] After one of the most illustrious military careers in the nation's history, Marshall died in Washington, D.C., on October 16, 1959, and is buried at Arlington National Cemetery.

Another of the 15th's Old China Hands to attain high levels of leadership, especially regarding China, was General Joseph Warren Stilwell. Perhaps more than for any other officer who had served in Tientsin, service with the 15th most greatly influenced him in his subsequent career, much of it involving China.

Stilwell was born on March 19, 1883, in Palatka, Florida, an eighth-generation descendant of an English colonist. Though it had been planned for him to enter Yale, Stilwell's hijinks as a high schooler convinced his father that he needed discipline. Pulling political strings reaching to the office of President William McKinley, the elder Stilwell sent his son to West Point. Entering in July of 1900, Stilwell excelled in foreign languages, especially French, and sports, and was credited with introducing basketball there. He also performed well in cross-country running, rowing and football. Throughout his life, he maintained sound physical fitness, which enabled him to serve with troops in the field under arduous conditions. He obtained his commission as second lieutenant on June 15, 1904.

He then sailed for the Philippines in October 1904 for his first assignment with the 12th Infantry Regiment in Company D of the 1st Battalion. They were engaged in arduous service on Samar Island against Philippine rebels. In February 1906, Stilwell was detailed to West Point as an instructor in the Department of Modern Languages. For three years, he taught English, Spanish and French. In the following year, he switched to history and also taught tactics. In addition, he coached basketball, baseball and track and was assistant football coach. He also obtained leaves for three summers, 1907–1909, to improve his Spanish skills. He travelled first to Guatemala, during which he made a topographical survey of the country. In the following summers he was in Mexico and then Central America. During this time, he met Winifred A. Smith. They were married in October 1910. Though he requested additional summer excursions, he was required to rejoin his original regiment, the 12th. Accordingly, he and his wife set sail in January 1911, for the Philippines. This time he was posted at Fort William McKinley near Manila. In September, with three months' leave accumulated, he decided to visit Japan. He and his wife sailed on September 14, 1911, landing at Nagasaki, and toured the Inland Sea, including Hiroshima. His wife then left for the U.S. to await the birth of their first child. Stilwell continued to China for his first look. He arrived in the midst of the Chinese revolution of 1911–1912, and obtained his first significant lessons regarding the Chinese. He was to spend 17 days in China, visiting Shanghai, Hong Kong, and Canton, and journeying by riverboat on the West River to Wuchow. He returned to Manila on December 9, 1911.

Stilwell returned from the Philippines with his regiment in January 1912, being stationed at the Presidio in Monterey, California. His first son, Joe Junior, was born in March of that year in Syracuse, New York. (Joe Jr. is also an alumnus of the 15th, and he is the subject of another study below.)

In August of 1913, Stilwell returned to West Point as instructor in the Department of English and History. In the following summer, he was assigned to Madrid for further language study. He went back to the Academy in the fall, and in the summer of 1916 he was an instructor at the new school at Plattsburg, New York, for training officers for the newly expanded army provided for by the Army Act, passed in April 1916, which authorized a doubling of the army to 288,000 officers and men.

Following America's declaration of war against Germany on April 6, 1917, in the summer Stilwell was ordered to duty as brigade adjutant to the 80th Division at Camp Lee in Virginia and arrived there on August 25. In

December 1917, he received orders to report to General Pershing in France for intelligence duty as a staff officer. It seems that his knowledge of French was badly needed. He was assigned as chief intelligence officer for the IV Corps and was engaged in preparing for the American offensive at St. Mihiel, as was George Marshall, though in another unit. For several weeks at this time, Stilwell was in close contact with many French outfits while he gained intelligence for use by American planners. The American conquest of the St. Mihiel salient was followed by further decisive action in the Meuse-Argonne. Following the armistice, the IV Corps was slated for occupation duty in Germany with the U.S. 3rd Army under General Henry Tureman Allen, with its headquarters at Cochem on the Mosel. From Germany, Stilwell returned to the U.S. in July of 1919.

Only ten days following his return to America Stilwell's career took a decisive turn involving China, with which he henceforth would be engaged for much of the remainder of his military service. On August 6, 1919, he was appointed the first language officer of the U.S. Army for China. He had initially sought to study Japanese but the slots for that program were filled. Stilwell and his wife promptly left for California, where he spent the first year of his appointment studying Chinese at the University of California at Berkeley. Subsequently, on August 5, 1920, the Stilwells set sail bound for Peking, China.

Though he diligently studied the language, Stilwell, ever restless, took advantage of his opportunity to travel and work extensively in China. In the first instance, the International Famine Relief Committee asked to borrow Stilwell to serve as chief engineer for the building of a road in Shansi and Shensi provinces in north China to help bring relief to many suffering from the severe drought of 1920. This he did, from April to July 1921, and he, despite numerous difficulties, partially succeeded in accomplishing the task. Unrest in China, however, the result of activities of competing warlords, forced abandonment of the project before it was completed. Nonetheless, Stilwell, in his own words, "had functioned with Chinese under Chinese conditions," a valuable experience which subsequently helped him in numerous ways.

In addition to this work, Stilwell travelled extensively. He once more visited Japan and Japanese-controlled Korea. In April 1923, he spent a month touring three provinces on the south bank of the Yangtze in China: Kiangsi and Hunan inland, and Chekiang on the east coast. Later in June, he spent time in Outer Mongolia. Then his four-year assignment as a language student was over and on July 9, 1923, he and his family returned to the United States.

Stilwell was once more in school at the advanced infantry course at Fort Benning, Georgia. Completing this in 1924, he remained for another year as executive officer of the school under its commandant, Major General Briant

9. A Gallery of Generals

Wells. He then attended the Command and General Staff School at Fort Leavenworth from 1925 to 1926. The chance to return to China then presented itself when Stilwell was given the opportunity to serve with the 15th Infantry in Tientsin. He and his family sailed for China on August 20, 1926, his wife writing that "we all felt that we were going home." Stilwell, as a major, assumed command of the 15th's 2nd battalion. For eight months during his service in China, Stilwell was in Tientsin with Lieutenant Colonel George Marshall. At this time, the two men developed a mutual respect for each other that would have much impact on Stilwell's later career.

This was a crucial time in China's history. It marked the rise of Chiang Kai-shek and his attempt to unify China under his control. In July of 1925, Chiang's Kuomintang proclaimed itself the Nationalist government of China and began the march to the north toward Peking. As for the 15th, in 1924 General Connor, commander of the United States Army Forces in China, instituted the compulsory teaching of Chinese to all officers, though it was voluntary for enlisted men. Lieutenant Thomas S. Timberman, who will be considered below, was delegated the teaching duties. Stilwell was closely involved in this teaching program as well.

The mid–1920s was also a time of stress for the 15th. On several occasions, Stilwell, because of his facility with the language, was sent on intelligence gathering forays, one of which brought him and his sole Chinese companion into dangerous straits, in July of 1926.[16]

In January 1928, at the request of General Castner, Stilwell was shifted from troop duty to acting chief of staff to General Castner, the commanding general of the United States Army Forces in China. He was promoted to lieutenant colonel in May of that year. Meanwhile, on July 3, 1928, Chiang's troops officially took over Peking (subsequently called Peiping), bringing much of China under Chiang's control, though he would never establish a totally functioning nation. There were too many independent centers of power held by rival warlords, and there was also the growing communist movement that would be the focus of much of Chiang's concerns for years to come.

In July of 1929, Stilwell and his family returned to the United States. Colonel Marshall, by then assistant commandant and chief of instruction at the U.S. Army Infantry School at Fort Benning and fervently engaged in the revolutionizing of instruction there, desired to bring Stilwell onto the staff as head of the tactical section of the school. After he had been there for a year, Marshall declared him to be "a genius for instruction," also judging him to be "far sighted," "highly intelligent," and a "[true] leader." Marshall wrote that he was "qualified for any command in peace or war," a view from which he would never thereafter depart.[17]

General Joseph W. Stilwell surveys the situation on the Burma front, 1944. Stilwell was one of the most famous of the 15th Infantry's alumni (U.S. Army Signal Corps).

9. A Gallery of Generals

After Benning, from 1933 to 1935, Stilwell was assigned to San Diego to train the Organized Reserves of the IX Corps Area. Promoted to full colonel, he returned to Peiping on July 7, 1935, as the military attaché. His stay in this capacity was in two phases. The first was from 1935 to 1937, and the second ran from July 7, 1937, to December 7, 1941, when the Japanese began World War II in Asia by the onset of the Sino-Japanese War. To assist him in intelligence gathering, Stilwell organized a network that included five Chinese language officers, one being Captain Frank "Pinky" Dorn, who was to serve him later as aide. He also enlisted his son, Joe Jr., who had followed his father to the 15th Infantry Regiment in Tientsin. Stilwell had to follow the Chinese government when it was forced to leave its capital at Nanking up the Yangtze River to Hankow (Wuhan). From there, eight months later, the government proceeded to Chungking, where it would remain until 1945, the end of the war. Finally, on May 1, 1939, Stilwell left China with his family bound for the United States. In the years in China, he experienced many events and met major personalities who would have a profound effect on his later service in China.

Back in America, Stilwell's future was being decided in Washington. One of Marshall's first actions as chief of staff was to promote him to the rank of brigadier general, a fact that Stilwell learned on August 3 while on the ship bringing him and his family home. From that time, the remaining years of Stilwell's career would often be influenced by Marshall's decisions and actions.

Stilwell's first years after his return found him involved in the U.S. Army's expansion and training programs in anticipation of its involvement in the burgeoning war in Europe. In September, he was assigned to command the 3rd Brigade of the 2nd Infantry Division, headquartered at Fort Sam Houston in Texas. He chose as his chief aide Captain Frank Dorn, who had been with him in China. Dorn, who had graduated from West Point in 1923, was an intellectual, author, artist, and gourmet who wrote renowned cookbooks. In addition, he was a cartographer, being known, among other things, for having prepared a colorful, detailed map of the city of Peiping that continued in publication even after the Communists came to power in 1949.

Much of the activity in the U.S. Army during this time was planning for and mounting major maneuvers such as those carried out in Louisiana in May of 1940. Here Stilwell acquitted himself well, resulting in his being named the commander of the 7th U.S. Infantry Division stationed at Monterey, California, on July 1, 1940, and his promotion to major general a few weeks later, in September. He had been a brigadier general for only a year.

In the summer of 1941, the army staged further substantial maneuvers with a focus on California. Here, as previously, Stilwell's 7th Division acquitted itself favorably, and his reward was to assume command of the U.S. Army's III Corps. In August, he pitted his corps against the IX Corps at Fort Lewis, in Washington, an activity observed by Marshall and the secretary of war, Henry L. Stimson.

After Pearl Harbor, the U.S. was in a quandary as to how best to proceed. It was decided that Europe would have priority regarding major planning and preparation and Asia, despite the rapid advances that the Japanese were making in China and elsewhere in the western Pacific, was to be considered secondarily. Initially, Stilwell was considered to help plan and then command the Allied invasion of North Africa. That, however, was shelved until late in 1942. In the meantime, it was decided that China should be kept in the war, though on a secondary level. While Stilwell hoped for further employment in the European Theater, President Roosevelt and General Marshall tapped him for service in the difficult China area, to which Stilwell reluctantly agreed, averring, "I'll go where I'm sent." This decision was to cast the die for almost the entire remainder of his career.

Becoming a lieutenant general, Stilwell was designated the commanding general of U.S. Army forces in the China-Burma-India Theater, supervisor of U.S. Lend-Lease to China, and chief of staff to Generalissimo Chiang Kai-Shek. One of his functions was to maintain the Burma Road and command the Chinese forces that might be assigned to him. He would also have a hand in "Hump" operations and the activities of other routes, to keep China supplied and engaged in the war effort in Asia.

Stilwell was confronted with numerous built-in limitations to his ability to accomplish as much as he would have desired. One of his antagonists was General Claire Chennault, who, with the American Volunteer Group—the AVG—had experienced some success in dealing with Japanese air arms. Chennault enjoyed the favor of Chiang Kai-shek and his wife, Madame Chiang. Chennault, however, held to the preposterous notion that with only 105 modern fighter aircraft, supported by 30 medium and 12 heavy bombers, he could defeat Japan from the air. In the event, it would require many aircraft carriers and fleets of B-29s engaged for months and years, not to mention those involved in numerous, costly land operations, before Japan was defeated. Plainly, Chennault had little understanding of the scope of the Asian scene, while Stilwell revealed some shortsighted views regarding the use of air power.

In addition, Stilwell was confronted with Chiang's determination to use huge quantities of Lend-Lease aid from the United States, which he would only on occasion turn over to be used in land operations in Burma and China. He mainly used this equipment to bolster his best divisions to be hoarded and held so as to confront his domestic enemies, principally the Communists. As he pointedly remarked on one occasion, "The Japanese are a disease of the skin, but the Communists are a disease of the heart."

Chiang was encouraged by Roosevelt, who desired that China emerge as one of the "Big Four" of the Allied nations, together with the U.S., the British, and the Russians. In addition, Chiang was thoroughly wedded to ancient Chinese views regarding military strategy dating back to Sun Tzu's treatise, *The Art of War*, which dates to the 6th century BCE. It emphasized the employment of defense in depth, taking into account China's vast territorial expanse that could be used to exchange space for time. According to this, theoretically Japan could never subdue China. With every Japanese advance, its forces incurred ever-longer supply lines with exposed flanks. This was in direct contrast to Western views, especially those held by key American officers, who, steeped in knowledge of battles from the Napoleonic era and those of the American Civil War, emphasized massive frontal attacks, as practiced by Generals Grant and Sherman, among others. These views were assiduously taught at the Command and Staff School, the War College, and other U.S. Army educational establishments. The mutual frustrations that thus occurred between Chiang and Stilwell can be readily understood.

Beyond this, there were strong views held by the British, who, with Britain's being assailed in Europe, could only regard the China-Burma-India (CBI) Theater as a secondary front and accordingly only with great reluctance participated in operations in China or Burma. Beyond this, the British hoped to emerge from World War II with its old empire still intact, and the employment of native troops, whether Burmese or Indian, posed additional problems for them. Still, the Allied South East Asia Command, which consisted mainly of Burma and India, was led by the British admiral Lord Louis Mountbatten. Clearly, Stilwell had his hands full trying to get forces in sufficient strength engaged to defeat the Japanese.

In fact, Stilwell arrived just in time to experience the collapse of the Allied defense of Burma, which involved some American, but mainly British, Indian and Chinese troops. Trapped there himself with his staff, he personally led some 117 men and women out of Burma into Assam, India, on foot, without the loss of a single person. Thousands of others also made their way out at this time using various routes.[18]

Following his arrival at the Imperial Hotel in Delhi, India, Stilwell spoke to newsmen at a press conference, explaining matters in response to press hype that had referred to the "voluntary withdrawal," and the "glorious retreat." "In the first place," he strongly insisted, "no military commander in history ever made a *voluntary* withdrawal. And there's no such thing as a *glorious* retreat.... I claim we got a hell of a licking. We got run out of Burma, and it's humiliating as hell. I think we ought to find out what caused it, go back, and retake Burma."[19] Much of Stilwell's subsequent endeavors were dedicated to these ends.

The failure in Burma led to the blockade of China from the south. This made it necessary to mount the aerial supply line known as the "Hump." Also, plans seemed necessary that would lead to the reconquest of Burma, a goal often opposed by both the British, who did not desire it as a primary focus, and the Chinese, because Chiang did not see this as a major requirement. Stilwell understood that what China needed was to attack the problem of the Chinese army, which was not efficient, and that Chiang did not possess the necessary spirit of offensive operations, as noted above. He was content to follow another ancient dictum: Let barbarians fight barbarians and let China be on the sidelines observing. Thus, America was taking on Japan and the Japanese were resisting, a classic formula from China's point of view. Stilwell did get Chiang's reluctant permission to train Chinese in India to the projected level of thirty divisions and to equip them with American equipment.

While Stilwell also desired to obtain American divisions, China was not regarded as a primary theater in Washington either. Stilwell would never obtain significant numbers of American troops in China, though Chennault's 14th Air Force was useful and later the 10th Air Force would be formed. Even here, the forces deployed were never vast. The 14th Air Force was activated within the U.S. Army (it had been serving under Chinese control) on March 11, 1943, with Chennault being made a major general.

Nonetheless, with Chiang's reluctant assent, Stilwell began the training of Chinese troops at Ramgarh in India, 200 miles west of Calcutta, using American military personnel as instructors and advisers. The Chinese soldiers also needed medical assistance, as many of the trainees were in dire straits suffering from many tropical diseases and malnutrition was widespread throughout the Chinese army as well. Eventually, over the next two years, Stilwell would see some 53,000 Chinese troops trained and equipped in India. Brigadier General Boatner, also a veteran of the 15th, served at Ramgarh.[20]

For many months, in the summer and autumn of 1943, numerous plans and changes of plans ensued as to China's role in World War II. This culminated in the Cairo-Yalta conferences, with Stalin, FDR and Churchill meeting for major decisions. Chiang was also at Cairo, though not at Yalta. There had been a foreign ministers meeting in Moscow in October 1943, at which time China was recognized as one of the Big Four nations. Nonetheless, because Roosevelt had obtained Stalin's support for the cross-channel invasion of

9. A Gallery of Generals

Europe and the mounting of an invasion of southern France shortly thereafter, Roosevelt was inclined to downplay the role of China in planning further operations against Japan. Stilwell was authorized, however, to seek to return to Burma. To these ends, he was appointed deputy supreme allied commander under Vice Admiral Lord Louis Mountbatten. With the promise of some Chinese assistance in late 1943, Stilwell arrived at the Burmese front on December 20, 1943, assuming command of the Northern Combat Area Command (NCAC), an Allied force that had been established to reenter Burma. He was to be engaged in Burma for the next seven months, until July 1944. He now had at his disposal substantial Chinese forces from the Ramgarh program and one small American detachment, the 5307th Composite (Provisional) Regiment, called the "Merrill Marauders"—codenamed Galahad—commanded by Brigadier General Frank Merrill. The British, having fears of Japanese designs on India, were now at last committed to operations in Burma and moved from Imphal in India, employing six divisions, five Indian and one from West Africa.

Much bitter fighting ensued, which led to the Marauders being decimated under harsh conditions, suffering from scrub typhus and other tropical diseases, without relief or adequate support. In any event, after a seventy-eight-day siege, the major northwest Burmese city of Myitkyina fell on August 3, 1944. It should be noted that only a week after its fall, the Marauder force, down to only 130 effective troops out of the original 2,997, was disbanded. Stilwell's seeming harsh treatment of these men resulted in an army inspector general's investigation and U.S. congressional committee hearings, though Stilwell was not subjected to any disciplinary action. It was recorded that the season's monsoon was the wettest in many years, compounding all military operations, such as airdrops, upon which so many depended for supplies.

Despite the difficulties, the reconquest of northwest Burma made possible the building of a new road into China, the Ledo Road, later named the Stilwell Road, and a pipeline to Kunming, China, for the supplying of fuel oil and gasoline. In addition, the "Hump" could now be flown more easily, aircraft then being able to fly over much lower mountains and in better weather conditions.

Then, having been recalled from Burma in July 1944, after the fall of Myitkyina, Stilwell was engaged once more in China. Subsequently, the Allies, now mainly consisting of the British forces commanded by Field Marshall William Slim (The 1st Viscount Slim), regarded as perhaps Britain's greatest World War II general, continued the invasion of Burma. Slim's forces recaptured Mandalay in March 1945 and liberated Rangoon in May, effectively ending Japanese control of the region.

Meanwhile, while Stilwell was in Burma, the Japanese mounted major offensive operations in southeast China. Among their main goals were the airbases that Chennault's 14th Air Force was using. Here, they enjoyed considerable success. The deteriorating situation in China led to Stilwell's reappearance there, where much activity and planning ensued as to what role China was to play as the war intensified there. One option that was undertaken was to seek to contact the growing Communist forces to assist in resisting the Japanese. Chiang would have none of it, and an impasse ensued. Stilwell, having been promoted to full general on August 7, 1944, was slated to take charge of all Chinese forces, which Chiang also strongly opposed. By this time, with much vacillation in Washington, at length it was decided to recall Stilwell and replace him with Lieutenant General Albert Coady Wedemeyer—another alumnus of the 15th—who was much more acceptable to Chiang. This was done on October 19, 1944. At the same time, the CBI was broken up, with a separate China Theater being created and India and Burma continuing as their own theater.

Upon his return to the U.S., Stilwell was first placed in charge of training for the U.S. Amy's ground forces headquartered in Washington, with the promise of something more substantial if it opened up. In May 1945, Stilwell was on an inspection tour to MacArthur's area, including Okinawa, where the 10th Army was located. It was commanded by General Simon Bolivar. Just as Stilwell was departing for the United States, word was received that Bolivar had been killed by enemy artillery fire. Accordingly, on June 23, Stilwell assumed command of the 10th Army. With the surrender of the Japanese on August 14, shortly thereafter the 10th Army was broken apart. Stilwell returned to the United States on October 18, 1945, being temporarily assigned as president of the War Equipment Board. In January 1946, he was given command of the 6th Army, in charge of the Western Defense Command, headquartered in San Francisco, though he kept his connection with the Weapons Board. In this capacity, he observed two atomic bomb tests on Bikini in the Marshall Islands in July 1946.

A few weeks later, on October 3, Stilwell, having developed physical problems, was admitted to the Letterman General Hospital at the Presidio in San Francisco for surgery. The doctors found that he had stomach cancer that had spread to his liver. He died in his sleep on October 12, 1946. He was cremated and his ashes spread in the Pacific Ocean. In addition, a cenotaph was placed at the West Point Cemetery. Ironically, General Joseph Warren Stilwell, Jr., died in an aircraft crash in the Pacific while flying from California to Hawaii, and his remains are also at rest in that ocean.

Regarding the difficulties faced by Stilwell in China, he himself summarized his efforts and failures. He noted that his major job was "to change the fundamentally defensive attitude of the Chinese to an offensive attitude. They were fixed and set by long years of custom—Chiang K'ai-shek had made the defense his policy in the present war. He was going to trade 'space for time,' a very catchy way of saying he would never attack." Stilwell thought that this predilection for the defensive was based on the long succession of Chinese failures to cope with modern methods of waging war and advanced weapons. They also felt that the Japanese were superior in all aspects of waging modern war and the Chinese accordingly had no confidence in themselves. This Stilwell was able to help them develop with his training programs in India. Nonetheless, there was also the consideration that the Chinese were Taoists at heart, and this taught nonresistance. Thus, the Chinese commander hesitated to challenge fate. In addition, scapegoats were always sought for any failures, and the wise commander refused to run any unnecessary risks difficult to assess in any military venture. Finally, a Chinese command was the property of the commanding general. He normally received the payments for his troops and if he could shortchange the men by not paying them at all or not properly supplying them even with basic sustenance and by turning in inflated figures for those enrolled, then he profited. This factor also operated in that, if the commanding general lost men in action, his payments for his troops were correspondingly reduced.

Stilwell was also well aware of China's contemporary conditions. He once wrote that Chiang Kai-shek's China—especially his government—was in reality "a gang of thugs with the one idea of perpetuating themselves and their machine. Money, influence, and position the only considerations of the leaders. Intrigue, double-crossing lying reports. Hands out for anything they can get; their only idea to let someone else do the fighting; false propaganda on their 'heroic struggle'; indifference of 'leaders' to their men. Cowardice rampant, squeeze paramount, smuggling above duty, colossal ignorance and stupidity of staff, total inability to control factions and cliques, continued oppression of masses." The only factor that saved them, he went on, "is the dumb compliance of the *lao pai hsing* [the common people].... And we are maneuvered into the position of having to support this rotten regime and glorify its figurehead, the all-wise great patriot and soldier—Peanut."[21] His difficulties did not go unnoticed, however. Marshall on several occasions acknowledged that he had given Stilwell one of the most difficult assignments of any theater commander.

Another illustrious member of "That Damned China Crowd," was General Matthew Bunker Ridgway.[22] He had a rather slow start in his military career. Commissioned a second lieutenant in the army from West Point in 1917, he was not assigned to combat during World War I. Instead, he remained at the academy as an instructor in Spanish. From 1924 to 1925, he attended the Infantry School at Fort Benning. Then he was given command of Headquarters Company in the 15th Infantry Regiment in Tientsin, though he remained only from July 1925 to May 1926. He was then posted to Nicaragua in 1927. In 1930, he became an advisor to the governor-general of the Philippines and in 1935 was a student at the Command and General Staff School at Fort Leavenworth, Kansas, and in 1937 was at the Army War College. In the late 1930s, he served on the staffs of VI Corps, the 2nd and 4th U.S. armies. With the coming of World War II in Europe, General Marshall, as one of his first appointments, assigned Ridgway to the War Plans Division, where he served until January 1942, when he was promoted to brigadier general. Only a few months later, in August of 1942, Ridgway was promoted to major general and given command of the 82nd Airborne Division. His task was to convert an entire infantry division to airborne status requiring extensive effort and planning. Ridgway then helped plan the airborne part of the invasion of Sicily in July 1943 and commanded the 82nd in combat there. In 1944, Ridgway was involved in planning the D-Day airborne operations and jumped with his troops and commanded the 82nd during the first weeks of the fighting in Northern France.

In September 1944, Ridgway assumed the command of the XVIII Airborne Corps that participated in the ill-fated Operation Market Garden. From March 1945, the corps participated in further operations against the Germans, including the horrific Battle of the Bulge, and then proceeded with his men into Germany, where he was wounded on March 24, 1945.

For a time following the defeat of Germany, Ridgway was a commander at Luzon before heading U.S. Forces in the Mediterranean Theater, as deputy supreme Allied commander. Shortly thereafter, from 1946 to 1948, he was the U.S. Army representative on the military staff committee of the United Nations. In 1948, he was chief of the Caribbean Command, and in 1949 he was ordered to Washington as deputy chief of staff under the army chief of staff, General J. Lawton Collins.

In 1950, most important for Ridgway, following the death in a jeep accident of Lieutenant General Walton Walker—another alumnus of the 15th Infantry—he took over the 8th U.S. Army in Korea during the Korean War. He assumed command of the 8th at a crucial time in its career, in retreat from its advance far into North Korea under severe hammering from the invading Chinese forces. Under Ridgway's command, the Chinese offensive was brought to a halt and the Americans, in a counter offensive, stabilized the front near the 38th parallel. When General Douglas MacArthur was relieved of command in Korea by President Harry Truman in April 1951, Ridgway, promoted to full general, assumed control of Japan as military governor and command of the United Nations forces in Korea. General Omar Bradley asserted that his work in turning the tide of the Korean War was "the greatest feat of personal leadership in the history of the Army."[23] Ridgway also oversaw the restoration of Japan's independence and sovereignty on April 28, 1952. Though his roles in Korea and Japan remain the hallmark of his career, there was still much to come. In May 1952, Ridgway became the supreme Allied commander in Europe [SACEUR] in NATO. Though sometimes controversial, being regarded in Europe as perhaps too pro–American, he did help develop NATO as a major force in the world.

On August 15, 1953, Ridgway replaced General J. Lawton Collins as U.S. Army chief of staff, serving until June 29, 1955. Following an active retirement life, Ridgway died at age 98 on July 26, 1993, in Pennsylvania. He is buried at Arlington National Cemetery.

Another general of note among the alumni of the 15th Infantry was Lieutenant General Walton Harris Walker. If not as well known as some, he nevertheless has been called "the forgotten hero—the man who Saved Korea." As to his education, he spent a year at the Virginia Military Institute in preparation for study at West Point. There was little doubt that he always wanted to be an army officer. At the age of eight he had visited West Point with his parents, predicting that he would one day graduate from there and then go on to be a general. These aspirations were both realized.

Walker entered the academy in 1908 and graduated in 1912. While there, he picked up his first nickname, "Johnny Walker," after a popular whiskey brand. He would later acquire another: "Bulldog" Walker. Small of stature, if a bit heavy-set, he was unable to participate in sports at the varsity level. Riding, hunting, shooting and fencing remained his favorite activities and he was an excellent shot. Ranking 73rd in a class of 93, neither was he a brilliant student, and he had disciplinary problems as well. Nonetheless, in keeping with his basic philosophy that class standings did not forecast one's military future, he was destined for a solid career.

His first assignment was with the 19th Infantry at Fort Sheridan, Illinois. He went from there, in 1914, to Vera Cruz, Mexico, with a U.S. force under General Frederick Funston, sent there to quell Mexican forces. This involved the occupation of Vera Cruz, which grew out of an incident involving the U.S. Navy that occurred in Tampico on April 9, 1914. There, several sailors were arrested. U.S. President Woodrow Wilson demanded an apology. When the Mexican president, Victoriano Huerta, refused, Wilson sent a fleet and soldiers and Marines to the Gulf of Mexico, on April 21, 1914. Further, when reports indicated that arms were being dispatched from Germany, Wilson ordered the seizure of Vera Cruz. The U.S. Marines of the force were soon engaged in action and both leaders of an ongoing Mexican Revolution, Huerta and his rival Venustiano Carranza, condemned the U.S. action, but the Americans kept their hold on the port until November 14, 1914, when the U.S. forces withdrew. During this time, Walker was involved in patrols along the U.S.-Mexican border, and Carranza soon defeated Huerta ending the Mexican Revolution.

This did not, however, end the tensions between the U.S. and Mexico. In 1916, the Mexican bandito Pancho Villa attacked Columbus, New Mexico, killing numerous American citizens. General John J. "Blackjack" Pershing mounted a punitive expeditionary force to hunt down Villa. Walker was involved, as were George S. Patton, Jr., and Dwight D. Eisenhower. This struggle, which began for America on March 14, 1916, would continue until February 7, 1917, when Pershing ceased operations. It was called the Pancho Villa, or Mexican, Expedition, a venture which initially involved about 4,800 American troops.[24]

From 1916, following his action with Pershing, Walker organized such units as the 2nd Battalion of the 57th Infantry and the 13th Machine Gun Battalion, which he accompanied to France in 1917, commanding it from June 7, 1918. This outfit participated in the battle of St. Mihiel and the Meuse-Argonne offensive and other operations.

In early 1919, Walker served for a time in the U.S. Army of Occupation in Germany. Back in the United States in July 1919, he became an instructor at the Infantry School at Fort Benning, Georgia. Following a time when he was in the Artillery School at Fort Sill, Oklahoma, Walker returned to Fort Benning as chief of the Machine Gun and Infantry Weapons Section of the Infantry School. He then attended the advanced course at the same school.

After serving at Camp Devens in Massachusetts for a few months in 1923, he was assigned to West Point as tactical officer. Following this, in 1925, he was again in school, attending the Command and General Staff School at Fort Leavenworth, Kansas. Afterwards, he was the infantry representative of the staff and faculty of the Coast Artillery School at Fort Monroe, Virginia, a posting that continued to 1930.

In October of 1930, as a major, Walker became commander of the 2nd Battalion of the 15th Infantry Regiment in Tientsin, China. He was to remain until 1933, having acquitted himself well in that capacity. He subsequently indicated that his Chinese duty was "one of the best and happiest times in his life." He was well aware that what he learned in China was of immense help to him when he later became the commanding general of the U.S. Eighth Army in Korea.[25]

Following his duty in China, Walker was, after fifteen years, promoted from major to lieutenant colonel. He then attended the Army War College. After that he was executive officer of the 5th Infantry Brigade at Vancouver Barracks, Washington, the commander of which was Brigadier General George Catlett Marshall. The two became rather close friends. Undoubtedly, this friendship contributed to his assignment to the War Plans Division of the War Department General Staff. In April 1940, he was promoted to colonel and took control of the 36th Infantry Regiment at Camp Polk, Louisiana. In 1941, Walker became a brigadier general and was given command of the 3rd Armored Brigade. Promoted once more within a few months, Major General Walker, in 1942, assumed command of the 3rd Armored Division.

Meanwhile, General George Patton, charged with preparations for the invasion of North Africa, sought to establish a Desert Training Center for armored troops. Choosing major portions of the Mojave Desert, the rugged, desolate, blistering-hot conditions of which were selected to make training perhaps harder than even combat would be. When Patton's original forces were sent to Africa, in late 1942, Walker assumed command of the IV Armored Corps as well as the Desert Training Center. Walker commanded there until March 29,1943, when he was sent with his IV Corps to Fort Campbell, Kentucky. Temporarily detached as IV Corps commander, he was ordered to visit the North African Theater of operations as an observer. Returning to his command in October of 1943, which soon changed its designation to XX Corps, he took it to England, arriving on February 18, 1944, there undergoing further training and preparing for D-Day.

Soon afterwards, because the commander of XIX Corps was ill, Walker took it into action on D-Day for the first several weeks. Returning to his own command, XX Corps landed on Utah Beach on July 23,1944. It was subsequently engaged in the eastward action of the Americans across northern France, especially those in Patton's 3rd Army, which Walker's XX Corps was part of, crossing the Seine and proceeding to the Meuse River, crossing at Verdun, and soon capturing Metz. When the Germans launched the Ardennes offensive, the XX Corps remained on the defensive, and when the Battle of the Bulge was over, it resumed its march into Germany. Trier was their first conquest, followed by Kassel and the prison camps at Buchenwald and Ohrdruf. He then turned his force east and south and moved into Austria, where the end of the war, on May 8, 1945, found him in Linz. By now a lieutenant general, Walker had also picked up his second nickname, "Bulldog," apparently bestowed on him by Patton, who regarded him as one of his best commanders.

Following World War II, Walker returned home to command the Eighth Service Command in Dallas, Texas, transferring on May of 1946 to the Sixth Service Command in Chicago. This unit reactivated the 5th Army, which Walker subsequently commanded from June 1946 to September 1948. During this time, Walker's son, Sam Sims Walker, graduated from the U.S. Military Academy. He would eventually rise to the rank of four-star general, retiring in 1984.

Also in 1948, Walker became the commanding general of the U.S. 8th Army, which occupied Japan, a fateful posting for him. When the North Koreans invaded South Korea in June of 1950, the 8th was ordered to attempt to force the invaders back across the 38th parallel. These offensive actions were defeated, the 8th was forced to retreat, and only with difficulty was it able to set up the Pusan Perimeter on the southeast side of the Korean peninsula, nearly being evicted from Korea altogether. The American and South Korean forces, finally being sufficiently reinforced, were able to begin offensive operations, coupled with General MacArthur's Inchon landing in September of 1950. Walker's 8th Army quickly moved up the peninsula, together with men of MacArthur's × Corps, commanded by Major General Edward M. Almond, consisting of the 1st Marine Division and two army divisions, and South Korean troops.

The war seemed won, and American forces neared the Yalu River, North Korea's border with China. At this juncture, the Chinese intervened and the resulting headlong retreat of the 8th Army and × Corps found the Americans and the Republic of Korea's soldiers, between October and December of 1950, back below the 38th parallel. On December 23, 1950, Walker was killed when his command jeep collided with a truck north of Seoul. Walker was subsequently buried at Arlington National Cemetery, his illustrious military career completed. He was posthumously promoted to general in January of 1951. Ironically, General Patton, Walker's mentor, commander and friend, had died in Germany, also on December 23, in 1945, following a similar traffic accident some days before. In any event, Walker, despite the numerous setbacks in the Korean conflict, was widely regarded as the man who was "key in saving Korea," though others give the palm to MacArthur for his daring invasion at Inchon. In any case, MacArthur had gravely erred when he ignored indications that the Chinese were about to invade Korea from the north.[26]

Another prominent alumnus of the 15th Infantry was Lieutenant General Albert Coady Wedemeyer. John Keegan, the prominent British military his-

9. A Gallery of Generals

torian, wrote of him in the *New York Times* in 1987, saying he was "one of the most intellectual and farsighted military minds America has ever produced." Nonetheless, Wedemeyer was also a controversial figure for many reasons, especially late in his career.[27]

He was born in Omaha, Nebraska, on July 9, 1897, where his father was an army captain in the Quartermaster Corps. He graduated from West Point in 1919. Wedemeyer spent over three years at Fort Benning, Georgia, at the Infantry School and with the 29th Infantry. He then became aide-de-camp for Brigadier General Paul B. Malone at Fort Benning and followed him to Fort Sill, Oklahoma, and Fort Sam Houston, Texas. He subsequently served with the 31st and 57th Infantry regiments in the Philippines. This was followed by his being an aide-de-camp once more, this time for Brigadier H.O. Williams in Washington, D.C.[28]

In 1930, Wedemeyer arrived in Tientsin with his wife and two sons for service with the 15th Infantry Regiment, though he remained there for only two years. Tall and striking, even aristocratic in demeanor and appearance, his reputation as an up and coming soldier had preceded him to China, and he soon made an impression on the 15th for his military bearing and his skill on the rifle range. It was also of some notice that he was a baseball pitcher, which would certainly have been a point in his favor in the sports-minded 15th. It turned out that he had pitched for the army team at West Point.[29]

In 1932, he was ordered to serve as aide-de-camp for Major General Charles Evans Kilbourne on Corregidor in the Philippines. He later wrote that "my days at Tientsin and my ... tours of duty

Lieutenant General Albert Coady Wedemeyer, one of the 15th's more illustrious alumni. He replaced General Stilwell in China as commander of U.S. forces in the China Theater of Operations and on Chiang Kai-shek's staff. He was responsible for all U.S. military efforts in China in the last months of the war in Asia (official U.S. Army Signal Corps photograph).

in the Philippines gave me some insight into the ferment that was just about to shake the Orient."[30] From 1934 to 1936, he attended the Command and General Staff School at Fort Leavenworth and was promoted to captain.

Wedemeyer then entered upon a course that would greatly influence his thinking and actions for the remainder of his life. From 1936 to 1938, his most significant military schooling ensued. He was sent, as a U.S. military officer—only one of two ever to do so and the only one during those crucial years—to the German *Kriegsakademie*.[31] He there encountered the concept of grand strategy and its related tactics, new ideas as to armored infantry deployment, the use of air power and how these must be coordinated. In short, he encountered all aspects of the revolutionary form of warfare to be known as "blitzkrieg," so soon to be unleashed on an unsuspecting world. He witnessed a "hypothetical" invasion of Czechoslovakia soon to be implemented in reality. He learned about the relationship among political, diplomatic and military matters, with emphasis on "geopolitical" theories, with considerations of the importance of the Eurasian heartland, such as those advanced by the British thinker Sir Halford MacKinder and the German general Karl Ernst Haushofer, a geographer and geopolitician who lectured to the students at the school. The Germans also closely studied the lessons of World War I and were determined that they would learn from them. Instead of trench warfare, for instance, they sought to emphasize aggressiveness and highly mobile warfare. They also seemed to understand that the great industrial potential of the United States must be taken into account.

At the practical level, visits were made to various battlefields and Wedemeyer learned that the Germans, unlike the British, studied European military history and operations. The British, on the other hand, concentrated on the American Civil War. He was later to discover that many British officers knew much more about the American Civil War than did their U.S. counterparts. On one occasion, during exercises undertaken by the academy, Wedemeyer was given the opportunity to command a panzer division, thereby learning much about the capabilities of modern German armor. He noted that clearly the Germans were deep into preparations for a war, a fact that many elsewhere in Europe and United States had not grasped.

Many of his instructors and fellow German students were even then, or later, of importance in German affairs, and he met socially such men as Rudolf Hess, Joseph Goebbels, Hermann Goering, and Martin Bohrmann. He picked up on German attitudes then current, and was present in Vienna at the time of the *Anschluss*, witnessing the Storm Troopers, Brownshirts and Hitler Youth in action and the troops goose-stepping "between rows of excited people."

While in Germany, Wedemeyer prepared careful notes and compiled a 100-page report and discussed his experiences with many people, including General George C. Marshall, then chief of War Plans, who was considerably impressed with his account, and the chief of the Army General Staff, General Malin Craig. Asked to compare his own education at West Point and at the staff college at Fort Leavenworth, he drew many unfavorable comparisons between American and German military educational practices and points of view. He noted the vast differences in content in the courses, and also the much more arduous German school, and remarked upon the serious students and the sense of urgency that permeated the atmosphere. He recorded that the German school emphasized practical work rather than the highly theoretical problems that Leavenworth, for instance, emphasized. As a consequence of his experiences in Germany, Wedemeyer continued to analyze Germany's grand strategy and thinking, becoming, at the time, America's foremost authority on German military and political affairs.[32]

Following his return from Germany, he was assigned to the 29th Infantry Regiment at Fort Benning, Georgia. In 1940, he was promoted to major and assigned to the Training Section, Office of the Chief of Infantry. In May of 1941, General Marshall, who had read, with great interest and approval, Wedemeyer's report from his German experience, assigned him to the War Plans Division at the War Department in 1941. Wedemeyer's new appointment may also have been influenced by his father-in-law, Lieutenant General Stanley Dunbar Embick, the deputy chief of staff and director of the War Plans Division.

Subsequently, on July 9, 1941, President Roosevelt directed the secretaries of war and the navy to prepare a mobilization plan that might soon be needed as World War II developed. Accordingly, General Marshall instructed General Leonard T. Gerow, chair of the War Plans Division, to designate Wedemeyer, then a lieutenant colonel, to head up a team to write what was to be known as the "Victory Program," the most influential document in America's subsequent planning and waging of World War II. From the outset, the program indicated that Europe was to be the focus of American efforts, a position that was not altered, even after Pearl Harbor. Many observers (though there are dissenters) regard Wedemeyer's work in this regard as by far the most important development of his career because he was recognized as the major author of it.[33]

Wedemeyer, who had been promoted to brigadier general in 1942 and major general in 1943, was then assigned as the deputy chief of staff to Admiral Mountbatten, who commanded the Combined Anglo-American South East Asia Command. Wedemeyer also attended many of the subsequent conferences, such as Casablanca. He often accompanied General Marshall on such ventures. He also had a hand in the planning of Allied Mediterranean operations and "Overlord."

Then, on October 27, 1944, Wedemeyer was directed by General Marshall to proceed to China to replace General Joseph Stilwell, who had been dismissed from his command of U.S. forces in China on October 24, 1944. At the same time, the China Theater of Operations was formed, being therefore detached from the China-Burma-India Theater. Wedemeyer was also named chief of staff to Generalissimo Chiang Kai-shek. The major problem that he faced was that of attempting to persuade Chiang to form an alliance with the rapidly growing Communist forces to better resist the Japanese. Stilwell had sought this as well, but with much bitterness toward Chiang. Wedemeyer proved to be much more sympathetic to Chiang's position and became increasingly anticommunist.

Meanwhile, he expanded the Hump airlift operations and continued Stilwell's programs to train, equip, and modernize Chang's Nationalist Chinese Army. He had some success in his positioning of the Chinese to fight the Japanese and did extensive planning to use the South China coast as another staging area for operations against Japan. Wedemeyer was, during this time, promoted to lieutenant general. By 1945, however, the Allied effort against the Japanese was almost exclusively in the hands of others, especially General MacArthur and Admiral Nimitz. Pacific operations, by then, had relegated China to a distinct secondary role, which it was always considered to be by many Americans.

After the surrender of the Japanese, Wedemeyer moved his headquarters from Chungking to Shanghai, so as better to oversee operations when China's major cities were freed from Japanese control.[34] By this time, Wedemeyer had become increasingly anticommunist and was often at loggerheads with the American government, including President Truman and George C. Marshall, who headed a mission to China in December 1946 to early 1947, seeking to form an alliance between the Chinese Nationalists and the Communists. By now, as well, Wedemeyer was often being compared unfavorably with Stilwell by many army officers who served under him, they regarding him as too strongly opinionated and abrasive. One commentator who disdained him alleged that Wedemeyer had hired his own public relations representative to keep his public image burnished. A lieutenant colonel, who may well have been speaking for others, noted that indeed he "was a real dud. He had never had any command or combat experience, [and] he was universally disliked."[35] Immediately after Marshall left China he became U.S. secretary of state, pursuing, among other things, peace in China. Meanwhile, Wedemeyer had returned to the United States in April of 1946, leaving the command of the Chinese Theater in the hands of Lieutenant General Alvan C. Gillem.

Wedemeyer's subsequent career was an anticlimax. Initially, he commanded the Second Army in Baltimore, Maryland. He was then, in 1947 and 1948, director of the Plans and Operations Division in the General Staff. In 1948 and 1949, he was deputy chief of staff for Plans and Combat Operations, and from 1949 to 1951 commanding general of the 6th Army in San Francisco, California. He retired in 1951.

Earlier, in 1947, he was sent as a special envoy to China and Korea by President Truman. His report was, however, squelched by the secretary of state at that time, George Marshall, as being too controversial. The report favored much more assistance to Chiang than the Truman administration was willing to give. By this time, Wedemeyer was also closely allied with the China Lobby, an action group seeking to influence the American Congress. Wedemeyer openly voiced his criticism of those then being held responsible for the "loss of China" following the triumph of Mao's Communists in 1949. This group, and others, in 1951, after the outbreak of the Korean War, followed the lead of Senator Joseph R. McCarthy, with whom Wedemeyer sympathized. This witch hunt greatly damaged or destroyed the reputations and careers of many Americans both civilian and military. Wedemeyer died at Fort Belvoir, Virginia, on December 17, 1989, at age 92. He is buried in Arlington National Cemetery.

When considering officers associated with the 15th who became generals, one should also consider one chaplain, Luther Deck Miller, who was with the regiment from May 1925 to May 1928. An Episcopal priest, Miller was born in Leechburg, Pennsylvania, on June 14, 1890. He first attended Thiel College in Greenville, Pennsylvania, and obtained a BD degree from the Chicago Theological Seminary in 1917. He was commissioned a first lieutenant as an army chaplain in 1918.[36]

After service during World War I, Miller graduated from the U.S. Army's Chaplains School in 1922. He was then with the 15th Regiment in Tientsin from May 1925 to May 1928. He became an energetic addition to the officer corps. He took in hand the building of a new chapel. For many years, services had been held in the unsightly Recreation Hall. Miller soon had moved the chapel to a bare room over General Headquarters, transforming the accouterments of worship and establishing a choir. A Protestant, he made the services nonsectarian, which soon had a wide appeal. Late in 1927, he was instrumental in setting up a military religious and social order, or lodge, the "Can Do Fortress No. 5, Century of Cornelius," with Miller as its "Tribune."

Other officers of the organization included "Centurian," "Arareous," "Outer Sentry," and at the highest level, "Soldier." This was a military and naval organization that served armed forces personnel at home and abroad. Subsequently, both officers and enlisted men and their wives and guests participated in various social activities, including formal dances and debates. On one occasion the subject on the floor was "Resolved: that there is more pleasure in bachelor life than there is in married life."[37]

The regiment's newspaper, the *Sentinel*, did not neglect to note Miller's influence, once stating, "This regiment is indeed fortunate in the type of Chaplain assigned to it. He is a man [who] enjoys every sport, indulges [in] many himself, [and] he conducts himself toward enlisted men and officers as one of them and has worked hard and faithfully to build up a sprit among the men that will lead to living a clean and comfortable life while on duty in China." Upon his departure, the paper asserted that Miller's parishioners hated to see him go "because he is a 'man's man' and brings religion to us in a straightforward way," and "because he was 'one of us.'"[38]

Miller was also close to Marshall, the 15th's executive officer when they served in Tientsin. Marshall and his wife regularly attended chapel services and Marshall once reminisced about "the good, productive time with Luther Miller in Tientsin." He observed, "Between us we ran the church up from eight men to standing room only. I say us because I took a very active part in the arrangements." One of these "arrangements" consisted of Marshall's sentencing miscreants of the regiment for periods from a month to six-weeks' church attendance for minor infractions.[39]

Miller went from China to Fort Leavenworth, remaining there from 1928 to 1937. Eventually, as a major general, he became the army's chief of chaplains, serving from 1945 to November 1949, when he retired from the army. He then, until 1961, became canon precentor at Washington Cathedral. He continued as part-time canon, in which capacity he often officiated at funerals in Arlington National Cemetery, including that of General Marshall. Miller was himself buried at Arlington following his death on April 22, 1972, at age 81.

One man who was regarded as one of the more cerebral among the 15th's officers was Major Edwin Forrest Harding. It was said of him that he "he could quote T.S. Eliot or Tennyson or Kipling, and discuss history or astronomy like an Ivy League professor."[40] At Tientsin he was known as the "Poet Laureate of the American Forces in China," with good reason. He produced a publication, *Lays of the Mei-Kuo Ying-P'an*, published in Tientsin about 1927. These poems of the American Compound generally poked fun at members of the regiment and the current scene and were frequently cited and quoted as clever renditions that often squarely and cleverly hit their marks. Harding also fully participated in theatrical productions that occurred in the compound and attracted many of the outfit's thespians. On occasion, these even included the unit's executive officer, Lieutenant Colonel George C. Marshall, who, rather surprisingly on such occasions, revealed a lighter side to his usually more formal—even dour—personality.

One of Harding's most often repeated poems concerned the exploits of Captain William B. "Wild Bill" Tuttle, the commander of the regiment's Service Company. At Tientsin, on Christmas Day 1925, the regiment narrowly avoided an armed clash with the soldiers of the Kuom inchun—the army of the warlord Feng Yu-shiang. This force had deployed around Tientsin, threatening the Americans. Tuttle promptly faced down the commander, speaking to him in Chinese, which the officers in the regiment were required to study, and persuaded him to withdraw. Harding reported the matter in his poem "Tuttulius at the Dike":

> 'Twas then that Bill Tuttulius
> Made the play that won the war
> For on the Sullen Kuominchun
> He loosed his Chungua hus [hua]—erh.
> His tones were well nigh perfect
> and filled them with chagrin:
> The Army in awed silence stood
> While from Bill's lips poured forth a flood
> Of purest Mandarin.

Edwin Forrest Harding was born on September 18, 1886, in Franklin, Ohio. He was educated at Exeter Academy and at the Charles Braden Preparatory Academy for entry into West Point, graduating in 1909 with George S. Patton, Robert L. Eichelberger, and others of later note. In November 10, 1909, Harding joined the 14th Infantry Regiment, of Boxer Uprising fame, in the Philippines, assuming command of Company B. Because the 14th was scheduled to return to the United States in March 1910, Harding's overseas stint was a brief one.

From 1910 to May 1916, Harding remained with the 14th's 3rd Battalion at Fort Missoula, Montana. In May, the battalion was ordered to Douglas, Arizona, during the Pancho Villa episode. In June 1916, Harding was promoted to first lieutenant, and in August 1916, he was ordered to West Point to teach English and history. He was promoted to captain in 1917. In June 1918, Harding, strongly desiring to serve overseas with the AEF, was ordered from West Point to assume training duties at Camp Devens, Massachusetts, where he fervently hoped for a combat assignment in France. In September

1918, however, he was struck down by the flu epidemic, and then, contracting pneumonia, he remained in the hospital until December 20, 1918. His desires to serve overseas would not be realized.

In early 1919, Harding, still at Fort Devens, was ordered to a tour of the battlefields in France, as near as he would get to combat during the Great War. Sailing from New York on June 25, he returned to the United States on August 17, 1919, reporting, once more, to West Point, then under the command of General Douglas MacArthur. There, Harding taught modern languages from August 20, 1919, to August 28, 1921, shifting to economics and history from 1921 to August 24, 1923. During this period, he was promoted to major, on July 1, 1920.

After four years of teaching, Harding was ordered to the 15th Infantry at Tientsin, arriving on September 30, 1923. He returned to the United States in May 1927. While with the 15th, he commanded the 2nd Battalion, with a short temporary stint as the regiment's commanding officer from July 26 to September 9, 1924. He had a fine time in Tientsin and made numerous lifelong friends, including George C. Marshall, which would have numerous consequences for him later in life.

Following duty in China, in April 1927 Harding returned to the United States to further his own military education. In May 1927 he entered the advanced officers course at the Infantry School at Fort Benning, where Marshall was the chief of instruction from 1927 to 1932. Harding graduated from this course at Benning in June 1928 and proceeded to the army's Command and General Staff School, graduating in June 1929.

Harding promptly returned to Fort Benning to help Marshall revamp the Infantry School, assuming command of the Fourth Section of the advanced and company officers classes, and remained until June 25, 1933. Many of the officers who had served in China in the 15th Infantry arrived at Benning during this time. Then, abruptly, the Infantry School temporarily closed. One of the reasons was a consequence of the establishment of the Civilian Conservation Corps, dear to the heart of President Roosevelt. This required the mobilization of the resources of the U.S. Army to assist in its operations. Roosevelt, in April 1933, had ordered the army to set up and run the camps by enrolling thousands of young men. Harding recalled the tumult then in place and in yet another poem recalled something about "The Devastation of Benning," which stated in part:

> And all who had orders that took them away
> Were told to clear out by the last day of May
> And haste to their posts to become C.C.C.'s
> And forget about tactics and learn to plant trees.[41]

9. A Gallery of Generals 151

These events led Harding to seek other opportunities, as many others had to do. He chose to enter the War College at Washington Barracks, in the nation's capital, and graduated on June 26, 1934.

His next duty would require the exercise of his writing talents. It had been noted in some quarters that the army's prestigious *Infantry Journal*, published by the chief of infantry in Washington, D.C., was in dire need of renovation. Harding was assigned to assume this task, reporting to the Office of the Chief of Infantry on June 6, 1934. Shortly thereafter, on September 1, 1934, he was promoted to lieutenant colonel. He had been a major since 1920, not an unusual case for career American military officers between the world wars.

Having successfully revamped the *Journal*, and considerably enlarging its subscriber list, Harding at last found himself earmarked to take charge of troops. With his becoming a full colonel on August 1, 1938, he was eligible to take command of an infantry regiment. Accordingly, he was selected to assume command of the 27th Infantry Regiment at Schofield Barracks, Hawaii. This outfit was part of the Hawaiian Division, often called the "Haywire Division." It was an old four-battalion, square division of 28,000 troops, consisting of two brigades with two regiments each. Harding's 27th was called the "Wolfhound Regiment" and with the 21st Infantry made up the 22nd Brigade.

On September 16, 1940, FDR signed the conscription act, and the stage was set for a major increase in the nation's military strength. Among the needs then felt was for more officers, including generals. In this atmosphere of increasing concerns with developments, both in Asia, and Europe, Harding was promoted to brigadier general on October 1, 1940. This required his reassignment. He relinquished his command of the 27th Infantry on September 30, 1940, and on January 3, 1941, took over the office of assistant commanding general of the 9th Infantry Division, then at Fort Bragg, North Carolina. This was one of the newer three-battalion (triangular) divisions and had been activated at Fort Bragg on August 1, 1940. Harding's duties consisted of supervising the training of its three regiments: the 39th, 47th and 60th.

Just over a year later, on February 9, 1942, Harding took command of the 32nd "Red Arrow" Infantry Division at Camp Livingston, Louisiana, a Wisconsin-Minnesota National Guard outfit. His promotion to major general came through a few days later, when he was sworn in on February 19. Harding's division was supposed to have a year's training before it was shipped overseas. Originally scheduled to depart for Europe from Camp Devens, Massachusetts, on March 26, even before its training cycles were completed, the 32nd was ordered to sail from San Francisco bound for Australia and General

MacArthur's Southwest Pacific Area (SWPA). Arriving there on May 14, 1944, their ultimate destination was Port Moresby in New Guinea. From there, some of the troops set out over the extremely rugged Owen Stanley range bound for Buna, then in Japanese hands. Others were flown over the mountains. For those going on foot across the mountains, airlifts endeavored to keep them supplied, but this was a difficult task never fully accomplished. In any event, those who arrived near Buna were fatigued, depleted by diseases and ill equipped, especially lacking artillery support. In addition, many of the troops had been given inadequate training and were commanded by inexperienced officers.[42]

Nonetheless, they were scheduled to begin operations against Buna on November 19, 1942. Unfortunately, the Japanese defenses were much more substantial than had been anticipated and the Japanese troops were experienced and well armed. In addition, MacArthur relied on direct air support, instead of tanks or heavy artillery, which proved inadequate to assist his troops. A stalemate resulted. MacArthur, with growing impatience at the lack of progress, became convinced that the troops were poorly led and sent General Robert Eichelberger, commander of I Corps, to investigate and, if he deemed it necessary, to relieve the officers involved. He did so, alleging that there were gross examples of cowardice and widespread dereliction of duty. Eichelberger—who had graduated from West Point in 1909 in Harding's class—summarily relieved him of his command of the 32nd on December 2, 1944.

Harding's career subsequently fell under a cloud. He was undoubtedly the victim of adverse circumstances, as well as intrigues at MacArthur's headquarters. In any case, it was a severe strain on his strength and character. The blot on his escutcheon would continue to haunt him for the remainder of his life, though several historians, including Samuel Milner, who, in his *Victory in Papua* (1957), one of the army's official history of World War II volumes, pronounced in favor of Harding's assessments and actions regarding the engagement at Buna.

Meanwhile, MacArthur had promised Harding a new assignment elsewhere in the Southwest Pacific, but he dithered and failed to make a decision. Instead, Harding was recalled to the United States in early 1943. General Marshall, perhaps also in a dilemma as to his disposition, while allowing him to retain his two stars, significantly did not again place him in command of combat troops. Instead, on March 16, 1943, Harding became commander of the Panama Mobile Force in the Canal Zone. He remained in this backwater until August 19, 1944. He was then made commanding general of the Antilles Department, headquartered at San Juan, Puerto Rico, another zone far

9. A Gallery of Generals

removed from combat. He was at this post until June 28, 1945, when he was summoned to Washington as senior army member of the Joint Postwar Planning Committee of the Joint Chiefs of Staff. He remained until December 16, 1945. He then became director of the Historical Division of the General Staff Corps. There he supervised the launching of the army's prestigious official history of World War II series. Harding retired from the army on October 31, 1946. He died in Franklin, Ohio, on June 5, 1970, aged 83, and is buried at Franklin's Woodhill Cemetery.

Another prominent member of the 15th's alumni was Lieutenant General Richard Kerens Sutherland. He was born in Hancock, Maryland, on November 27, 1895, a son of Howard Sutherland, who was later a U.S. Senator from West Virginia. Richard Sutherland was educated first at Philips Academy and Yale, from which he graduated in 1911. He had joined the Reserve Officer Training Corps but was not commissioned at Yale. In 1916, he enlisted as a private in the Connecticut National Guard. When the national guard was federalized in that year, he served on the Mexican border during the Pancho Villa Expedition. At this time, he accepted a national guard commission as a second lieutenant in the field artillery. He soon exchanged his artillery commission for one in the infantry of the Regular Army. Promoted to captain in 1917, he was with the 2nd Division on the Western Front during World War I.

Following the war, Sutherland became an instructor at the United States Army Infantry School at Fort Benning from 1920 to 1923. From 1923 to 1928, he taught military science and tactics at the Shattuck Military Academy at Faribault, Minnesota. In 1928, he graduated from the Command and General Staff College, Fort Leavenworth, Kansas. Fluent in French, he attended the *École supérieure de guerre* in 1930. He studied at the U.S. Army War College from 1932 to 1933 and then served with the Operations and Training Division of the War Department General Staff.

In 1937, Sutherland was in Tientsin, China, serving as a battalion executive officer in the 15th Infantry. He remained only a year, going in March 1938—at which time he was promoted to major—to the Office of the Military Advisor to the Commonwealth Government of the Philippines, under General Douglas MacArthur. He was promoted to lieutenant colonel a few weeks later, in July 1938, and it has been alleged that he eased his superior, Lieutenant Colonel Dwight D. Eisenhower, out of his position as MacArthur's chief of staff.[43] In any case, Sutherland's subsequent career would closely follow that of MacArthur's. His promotions also came along rapidly. In 1941, he became a colonel, then, in the same year, was promoted to brigadier and major general. In August 1941, when MacArthur organized the United States Army of the Far East, he made General Sutherland his chief of staff. In this capacity, Sutherland accomplished the mobilization of the Philippine army and its assimilation into the U.S. Army of the Far East.

The early months of the war were hectic as the Japanese landed in the Philippines and MacArthur and Sutherland attempted to prevent the islands falling to the Japanese. They were eventually forced to flee Manila, moving the American headquarters into Malinta Tunnel on Corregidor. In view of the inevitable fall of Bataan and Corregidor, in March 1942 FDR ordered MacArthur and his staff to leave the Philippines and make their way to Australia. From there, the revival of Allied forces and the drive to their destination, at last, to Tokyo began. Sutherland's role was that of MacArthur's chief of staff throughout the war. Also, in 1943, led by Lieutenant General George C. Kenney, MacArthur's air force chief, and Senator Arthur H. Vandenberg, Republican from Michigan, there were attempts to promote General MacArthur's candidacy for the presidency. This came to nothing when MacArthur joined in criticism of Franklin D. Roosevelt, the details of which were published, to MacArthur's embarrassment. This forced him to disavow his bid, observing that he "did not covet" the Republican nomination nor would he accept it.

Sutherland remained controversial throughout his tenure. He incurred animosity, especially from Australians, for whom Sutherland had little respect, and from subordinate American officers. Sutherland was often MacArthur's "hatchet man," and bad news invariably came through Sutherland rather than from MacArthur himself. He also seems to have stirred up animosities among many people, sometimes with deleterious results. One officer described him as a "hard man" who was more feared than liked but who "would sometimes break the mask of hardness with a sardonic smile and curious flashes of humor."

More positively, Sutherland represented MacArthur before the Joint Chiefs of Staff in Washington and at various conferences and often made decisions attributed to his chief. MacArthur amply repaid Sutherland for his actions and loyalty. When MacArthur discovered that Eisenhower had promoted his chief of staff, Walter Bedell Smith, to lieutenant general in January 1944, he immediately arranged for Sutherland to be similarly elevated. Sutherland was often regarded as MacArthur's alter ego and the kingpin of his generalship, and many of MacArthur's ideas and actions seem to have originated in the office of his chief of staff. Nonetheless, animosity and misunderstandings grew between them, with much resulting bitterness, especially from Sutherland's viewpoint. In any event, Sutherland was with MacArthur from Manila and on to Corregidor and was evacuated from the Philippines to the moving headquarters, first at Melbourne and Brisbane, Australia, then on to Port Moresby, in New Guinea. He then followed the developing advance to Hollandia, also on New Guinea. MacArthur and Sutherland were frequently on shipboard, as on the cruiser *Nashville*, accompanying the advancing troops, MacArthur bestriding the embattled earth like the classic ancient colossus, sometimes in the thick of the action, often to the apprehensions and horror of his entourage. MacArthur was able to make good on his earlier promise to return to the Philippines and, after a substantial lapse, found himself once more in Manila.

In the meantime, Sutherland rendered much service, but he also clashed with MacArthur. One significant matter was Sutherland's affair with a Mrs. Elaine Bessemer Clarke, the daughter of Sir Norman Brookes, a famous Australian tennis champion, and whose husband was a prisoner of war of the Japanese. Sutherland had Mrs. Clarke appointed to the rank of captain in the U.S. Army's WACs and installed her in several of MacArthur's headquarters of the advancing U.S. forces. This caused a major rift between Sutherland and MacArthur, with far-reaching consequences.[44]

Ultimately, Sutherland did not long remain with MacArthur following the ending of World War II and played no role in MacArthur's governing of Japan for the next six years. He was, though, present at MacArthur's side on the occasion of the Japanese formal surrender on September 2, 1945, on the deck of the battleship *Missouri*. A few days later, Sutherland left Tokyo and was soon in the United States, there to be reconciled with his wife and family. He retired on November 30, 1946. He died at Walter Reed Hospital, Washington, D.C., on June 25, 1966, at age 73, and is buried at Arlington National Cemetery.

One of the best liked and respected of those associated with the 15th Infantry was the twenty-first colonel to command the regiment since its inception on May 4, 1861, Campbell King, who commanded it for 15 months in the early 1920s. He was born in Flat Rock, North Carolina, on August 30, 1871. His grandfather, Mitchell King, had arrived in Charleston, South Carolina, from Crail, Fifeshire, Scotland, in 1805. His grandmother was related to Richard Henry Lee, who had signed the American Declaration of Independence. Mitchell King became a prosperous lawyer, large landowner and planter in South Carolina, North Carolina and Georgia. Later, a writer included a poem, published in the regiment's troop newspaper, the *Sentinel*, that he thought was especially appropriate to King when he considered his heritage and later attainments:

> But it is not wealth, nor rank, nor state,
> But get-up-and-get that makes men great.

After high school, King attended the College of Charleston and Harvard University, from which he graduated. He afterwards studied law in Atlanta, and in 1897 he enlisted in the army as a private and soon-to-be corporal in Troop K of the 5th U.S. Cavalry, serving from July 31, 1897, to July 25, 1898. In July 1898, he was commissioned a second lieutenant in the 1st U.S. Infantry. He subsequently served in both Cuba and the Philippines during the Spanish-American War. In 1905, he was a distinguished graduate of the Infantry and Cavalry School. In 1906, he graduated from the U.S. Army Staff College and from the War College in 1911.

In World War I, promoted to brigadier general, King served first as chief of staff of the 1st Division, and then was chief of staff for both the 7th Army and the 3rd Army Corps. He was at the Battle of Verdun in August 1917, in the Aisne-Marne offensive, and the Saint Mihiel, and Meuse-Argonne operations. He also marched from the Meuse to the Rhine in 1919, where at Coblenz, he was with the U.S. Army of Occupation headquartered there. After the war, King was first sent to the General Staff College as an instructor and then to the War Plans Division of the Army General Staff in Washington. Also, in 1920, he was awarded an MA from Harvard.

King was then ordered to Tientsin to take over the command of the 15th Infantry Regiment. Arriving on April 12, 1923, the unit's troop newspaper, the *Sentinel*, observed, "When he arrived the morale of the regiment was low. We had been defeated in all branches of athletics for over a period of two years. The demoralizing effect of this was apparent." The regiment also suffered from the local turmoil resulting from Chinese civil war then raging in the country and the general isolation felt by the regiment. Accordingly, one of King's first priorities was "to put athletics on a sound and secure basis." He did this by requiring everyone in the command to engage in some form of sports during the afternoons. The result was an immediate improvement in morale. He did not stint on work, however, and put work and play on a well-balanced schedule.

After fifteen months and promotion to brigadier general, King was ordered to the Philippines. On the evening of August 11, 1924, the regiment honored the Kings at a reception at Tientsin's prestigious Astor House Hotel, presenting the new general and his wife with a large silver bowl embossed with dragons. The Kings departed on August 12, bound for Shanghai and a ship for Manila. Once in Manila, King assumed command of the coastal defenses of Manila and Subic Bay. He later became the assistant chief of the

9. A Gallery of Generals 157

Army Staff in Washington. On June 30, 1929, he assumed his duties as the commandant of the Infantry School at Fort Benning, Georgia. Promoted to major general in 1932, King retired from the army after 36 years of service, on July 1, 1933. He died at his home in Charleston, South Carolina, in 1953. He is buried at Flat Rock, North Carolina.[45]

Another colonel who commanded the 15th, and who was one of the more accomplished and effective of its commanders, was George Arthur Lynch. He was born at Blairstown, Iowa, on March 12, 1880. Appointed to West Point, he graduated in 1903 as an infantryman. Beginning on June 11, 1903, he served with the 17th Infantry, then engaged in service against the Moros in the Philippines. After they became "pacified," Lynch became district engineer of the District of Jolo, constructing bridges in the area. He then returned to West Point on August 22, 1905, as instructor in modern languages, remaining until August 13, 1909. He then served with the 29th Infantry at Governor's Island in New York, from 1909 to 1912. From 1913 to 1917, he was assistant to the chief of the Militia Bureau in Washington. He was made editor of the *Infantry Journal*. In 1917, Lynch went to France, serving on the general staff of Pershing's GHQ. There, he drafted the important *Infantry Drill and Combat Regulations* for the AEF.

Following the war, Lynch served in various capacities on the War Department's general staff, and in August 1922, he helped formulate the army's *Field Service Regulations of 1923*. From 1925 to 1929, he was attached to the army's Inspector Generals Department. He graduated from the Army War College in 1930. He was then ordered to the Philippines once more, and as a lieutenant colonel temporarily commanded the 31st Infantry Regiment, the "Polar Bears," from February 24, 1931, to June 17, 1931, at which time Colonel Lorenzo Dow Gasser assumed command. Lynch was then with the regiment when it served in China in 1932. Returning to Washington in 1933, Lynch was named assistant to the New Deal's National Recovery Administration's (NRA) chief, General Hugh S. Johnson, and was acting administrator of the organization from April to November 1934.[46] He then became assistant chief of staff, G-2, Second Corps Area, from which he was ordered to China to command the 15th Regiment, arriving on July 7, 1935.

Lynch made a strong impression on the men of the 15th, to whom he delivered frequent addresses calculated to influence their conduct and general attitudes. He came across as an organization man with a strong sense of order and a "by the book" approach. He had a strong appreciation for the soldierly virtues, once observing that "next to the bond of religious faith and closely allied to it, the military tie which bound them together was the strongest that unites the minds and actions of masses of men." Indeed, it was this "which most distinguishes a military unit from any merely assembled group."[47] He emphasized the regiment's fitness and virtues and stressed fair play towards the Chinese, noting that in addition to extolling their motto, "Can Do," they could add another: "Excelsior."

Lynch had been in command in Tientsin for almost two years when, in May 1937, FDR, over the heads of several other qualified officers, returned him to Washington as chief of infantry, with the rank of major general. He served in that office from May 24, 1937, to April 30, 1941, at which time he retired from the army with 40 years of service. He died in Winter Park, Florida, on August 10, 1962, at age 82, and was buried in Arlington National Cemetery.

That service in the crack 15th Infantry was regarded as important and highly desirable was demonstrated by the scramble of Regulars for assignments to China, both for themselves and their sons who had followed them in military careers. Two sons of prominent officers who attained general rank were Stephen Ogden Fuqua, Jr., and Joseph Warren Stilwell, Jr. Fuqua was the son of Major General Stephen Ogden Fuqua, who became the army's Chief of Infantry on March 28, 1929. Born on March 4, 1911, at Fort Clark, Texas, where his father was stationed, Fuqua Jr., graduated from West Point in 1933. He then served two years at Fort Benning and was at Fort Ontario until 1936, following which he was with the 15th Infantry in Tientsin, serving as a platoon leader and company commander. He returned from China with the 15th when it came home to Fort Lewis in Washington in 1938.

In May 1938, Fuqua was an instructor in the Department of Modern Language at West Point, teaching French and Portuguese. During this time he spent a year in Paris studying French. In 1942, following the outbreak of World War II, he was at the office of the U.S. military attaché in Lisbon and remained until 1946.

Fuqua then attended the Command and General Staff College at Fort Leavenworth, Kansas. Airborne training at Fort Benning followed, after which he joined the 11th Airborne Division at Fort Campbell. Before being ordered to Korea, he attended the Armed Forces Staff College. In Korea, he served in the G-2 sections of I Corps and the 8th Army. He then commanded the 38th Infantry of the 2nd Infantry Division. In 1954, he was at the National War College. Following this schooling, he was transferred to Heidelberg with Headquarters, U.S. Army, Europe. Promoted to brigadier general in 1960, he served as assistant division commander of the 6th Division in Germany in 1960 and 1961.

After serving in Europe, Fuqua was in the office of the assistant secretary of defense for International Security Affairs. There he was director for Military Assistance Programs and participated in numerous negotiations, often in cooperation with the Department of State. Many of the assistance programs concerned Iran, Greece and Turkey. He was involved with other matters pertaining to Libya and Ethiopia. He retired from the Army in 1963. He died on April 28, 1999, at Cornwell-on-Hudson, and is buried at the U.S. Military Academy cemetery.[48]

Another alumnus who was the son of a much more famous father was Joseph Warren Stilwell, Jr., born on March 6, 1912, in Syracuse, New York. He graduated from West Point in 1933, in the same class with Stephen Ogden Fuqua, Jr., and was with the 15th Infantry Regiment in 1937 as a first lieutenant. While there, he and several enlisted men obtained a Soldier's Medal, a peacetime decoration. This was awarded "for heroism at the risk of life not involving conflict with an armed enemy at East Station, Tientsin, China, July 29, 1937." This resulted in conjunction with the movement of the 3rd Battalion of the 15th Infantry when en route from Camp Burrowes, Chinwangtao, China, to Tientsin. There, when Chinese and Japanese troops were engaged in battle for possession of that station, a freight car carrying machine guns, ammunition and other valuable United States property arrived at the railroad freight yard. Its guard of enlisted men was thereupon cut off and stranded. Lieutenant Stilwell then arrived in charge of several trucks that removed the guard and property from the freight car and transported them to the American Compound. While underway, Stilwell and the detachment were subjected to sporadic rifle, machine-gun and mortar fire and were exposed to aerial bombs that fell nearby. Therefore, as the citation read, "by his heroic conduct in face of danger Lieutenant Stilwell aided materially in preventing the possible loss of human life and the destruction of Government property."[49]

During World War II, Stilwell served in his father's headquarters in the CBI. He became a colonel in 1944. In Korea, he was the commander of the 23rd Infantry Regiment. Following the Korean War, from 1959 to 1961, as a brigadier general, he became the deputy commanding general of the 18th Airborne Corps, at Fort Bragg, North Carolina. From 1961 to 1962, he was a brigade commander at Fort Devens, Massachusetts. During the Vietnam War, from 1962 to 1964, he was the commanding general, U.S. Army Support Group in Vietnam. Stilwell was made the deputy commanding general of the U.S. Army's JFK Special Warfare Center from 1964 to 1965. In 1965, he became its commanding officer.[50]

Stilwell was well known for being always eager for combat, and in Vietnam he often rode in helicopter gunships as gunner, leading to one of his nicknames, "Gunner Six." He could also be abrasive, as was his father, "Vinegar Joe," but, perhaps not being as "vinegary" as his father, he was styled a milder "Cider Joe." On July 25, 1966, he was lost at sea on a flight from San Francisco to Hawaii onboard a C-47. No trace of his aircraft was ever found. He was 54 years of age.

Another who served in the 15th infantry was Thomas S. Timberman. He was born on March 21, 1900, in New Jersey. Graduating from the U.S. Military Academy in 1923, he first served with the 5th Infantry Regiment, 1923–1925. From there, he proceeded to Tientsin, serving with the 15th Infantry from 1925 to 1928. He was closely involved with the Chinese language program in the regiment, assisting as an instructor.

He was then aide-de-camp for Brigadier General Harold B. Fiske, 1928–1930, as he would be again in the Panama Canal Department in 1935. In the meantime, Timberman was married to Virginia Fiske, daughter of Major General Fiske. In 1930 and 1931, he was a student at the Infantry School at Fort Benning. Then, perhaps having been influenced by his required study of Chinese with the 15th Infantry, he continued his studies of the Chinese language in Peking from 1931 to 1935. His lengthy preparation in the Chinese language and studies would play a major role in his subsequent military career.

Until then, however, he served in various locations, first as a company commander with the 30th Infantry Regiment, 1935–1938, then on special duty as the commander of the Provisional Golden Gate International Exposition Company, 1938–1939. Timberman then studied at the Command and General Staff School in 1939 and 1940. From 1940 to 1942, he was an instructor at the Infantry School, with a stint as a military observer in England in 1941.

With America's entry in World War II, Timberman was able to utilize his considerable knowledge of China and Asia to good effect. In 1942 and 1943, he was chief of the Asiatic Theater, Operations Division, War Department. He was then representative of the deputy supreme allied commander of the South East Asian Command in 1944. He subsequently commanded the Z-Forces Combat Team of Chinese troops in Kweilin, China. This was followed by his being commander, U.S. Forces, South East Asian Command, from 1944 to 1946.

When General George C. Marshall stepped down as U.S. Army chief of staff on November 18, 1945, he was promptly sent to China on a truce mission by President Truman, to seek some way to bring Chiang Kai-shek and Mao's

Communists into a peaceful settlement of China's internal turmoil. This he failed to do, and he returned to the U.S. empty-handed in early 1947. While in China, General Timberman served in the headquarters of Marshall's truce mission.

In the following three years, 1947–1950, Timberman was in the Office of the Army Assistant Chief of Staff, G-3. He then was assistant division commander of the 4th Infantry Division, 1950–1951, and, as a major general, commander of the 1st Infantry Division, 1951–1953. This was followed by his being the U.S. commandant in Berlin, 1953–1954.

Returning to the United States, he was first on the Joint Strategic Survey Committee of the Joint Chiefs of Staff, 1956–1958. His last service in the U.S. Army was as chief of the Army Security Agency, 1950–1960. He retired in 1960. He died on August 2, 1989, and is buried in Arlington National Cemetery.[51]

William Howard Arnold was born at Dyersburg, Tennessee, on January 18, 1901. Entering West Point Military Academy, he graduated in 1924 as an infantryman. In 1928, after various assignments, he graduated from the infantry officers course at Fort Benning. Following that, he spent two years at Schofield Barracks, Hawaii.

He was then ordered to Tientsin and served as Training and Operations Officer, S-3, for the 15th Infantry Regiment.[52] Back in the United States, in 1938, he graduated from the Command and General Staff College, Fort Leavenworth, Kansas.

During World War II, from 1942 to 1943, Arnold was assistant chief of staff for Training and Operations, G-3, for the IV U.S. Army Corps at Fort Lewis, Washington. Promoted to brigadier general in September 1943, he was assigned as chief of staff of the XIV Corps. In this capacity, he was responsible for the planning and carrying out of combat operations in Guadalcanal, and from there he was engaged in New Georgia and Bougainville.

Becoming a major general, in November 1944, Arnold became the commander of the 23rd (Americal) Infantry Division, leading it into combat in the southern Philippines. In August of 1945, Arnold presided over the surrender of the Japanese still engaged in operations on Cebu Island. On September 10, 1945, the Americal Division landed in Japan and took up occupation duties in the Yokohama-Yokosuka area. Returning to the United States on November 21, 1945, the division was deactivated on December 12, 1945.[53]

After the war, from 1950 to 1952, Arnold was the commander of the Joint Military Mission for Aid to Turkey. In 1953, he became the commander of

U.S. forces in Austria as a lieutenant general. He remained in Austria until 1955. Returning to the U.S., Arnold assumed command of the 5th United States Army, then headquartered in Chicago. He retired in 1961 and died in Lake Forest, Illinois, on September 30, 1976, at age 75. He is buried at Fort Sheridan, Illinois.[54]

Major General George Honnen was born on November 16, 1887, in Philadelphia. He enlisted in the army as a private in April of 1917. The following year, he was admitted to West Point, from which he graduated in 1922 as an infantry officer. Ordered to China with the 15th Infantry, he arrived in March of 1929, serving first as battalion adjutant and then as assistant adjutant of the regiment. That same year he coached the United States Army troops in China's baseball team. He departed China in March of 1931.[55]

Following his China service, Honnen was a professor of military science and tactics at the University of Hawaii. In the late 1930s, he was an assistant instructor at West Point. He would later become a graduate of the Infantry School at Fort Benning and the Command and General Staff School at Fort Leavenworth, Kansas.

Early in World War II, in 1941 and 1942, he was in Australia. He proceeded from there to serve as assistant division commander of the 79th Infantry Division in the United States, and in the period 1942–1943, was Chief of Staff of the 6th Army in the Southwest Pacific under General Walter Krueger. He followed this by becoming the Commandant of Cadets at West Point from 1943 to 1946.

During the Cold War, as a major general, Honnen was the commander of the American Zone in Berlin from August 5, 1954, to September 9, 1955, following which he was Chief of Staff of the United States Forces in Europe. Retiring from the army in 1957, Honnen went to the Citadel in 1959, serving as the administrative dean. He died on January 23, 1974, and is buried at the U.S. Military Academy Post Cemetery.

Robert Battey McClure was born in Rome, Georgia, on September 15, 1896. He entered the United States Naval Academy in 1916 but was unable to maintain the academic standards necessary to remain there. He thereupon entered the U.S. Army as a private. In November 1917, he was commissioned a second lieutenant, and during World War I, he fought with the famous 26th (Yankee) Infantry Division on the Western Front, first as a platoon commander, then company and battalion commander, winning a Distinguished Service Cross for valor. Remaining in the army following the armistice, for five years he was on duty at the New York Military Academy. Then he attended the U.S. Army Tank School at Fort Meade, Maryland, after which he remained as athletic officer. He successfully built up winning teams in basketball, baseball and football.[56]

He was next ordered to the 15th Infantry Regiment in China, remaining from 1927 to 1933. During this time, in June 1930, he was promoted to captain. He also served as athletic officer of the regiment, and he himself played baseball and coached the basketball team. Noted as a humorist, he was the originator of the "Krazy Kat Kwartette," which performed at regimental theatricals. Also while in Tientsin, he befriended a fellow officer, Albert Wedemeyer, under whom he would later serve in China during World War II. McClure was another of several of the 15th's veterans who put their knowledge of China to much use later.[57]

McClure graduated from the Army War College in 1938. Afterwards, he was on the staff of the 25th Infantry Division, where, as divisional G-4, he was in charge of logistics and supply. He remained with the division with the coming of World War II, assuming command of its 35th Infantry Regiment and leading it through the Guadalcanal and New Georgia campaigns. In 1943, McClure, by then a major general, returned to the United States to prepare his own division, the 84th Infantry, for combat in the European Theater. Six months later, he returned to the Solomon Islands as commander of the Americal Division, then engaged in action on Bougainville. He served in this role from April 1944 to October of that year. He was succeeded as commander by another alumnus of the 15th Regiment, Major General William H. Arnold.

In November of 1944, McClure returned to China as Chief of Staff to Lieutenant General Albert Coady Wedemeyer, who, on October 18, 1944, on the orders of FDR, replaced General Joseph Stilwell as commander of United States Forces in China and chief of staff of Generalissimo Chiang Kai-shek. McClure was also simultaneously deputy chief of staff to Chiang.

Wedemeyer understood the necessity of vigorous action being taken in China as World War II unwound in 1945. He proceeded to develop further Stilwell's earlier advances. Accordingly, in order more effectively to organize, train, supply and control operations of the Chinese army, in January of 1945 he created two organizations: the Chinese Combat Command and the Chinese Training Command. He appointed Major General Robert McClure head of the Chinese Combat Command. In this capacity, McClure was to closely advise and supervise, to the extent possible, Chinese army operations in the field.

After the war, in 1950, McClure returned once to the Far East Command Headquarters in Japan, becoming military governor and commanding general of the Ryukus Command, one of three major commands in the Far East

Command, the other two being the Eighth Army and Marianas-Bonin commands.

During the Korean War, in December of 1950, the commander of the 2nd Infantry Division, Major General Laurence "Dutch" Keiser, was relieved of his command in Korea. McClure became his replacement. Unfortunately, McClure's division was subsequently severely mauled and Major General Edward Almond, commander of x Corps, under which McClure served, in turn relieved him of his command on the grounds of a "lack of supervision" and evidence of "poor leadership." This came after only a month as divisional commander. McClure thereupon became the commanding general at Fort Ord, California, from early 1951 until May 1, 1954, when he retired from active duty. He died on his birthday, September 15, 1973, at Carmel, California, and is buried at Arlington National Cemetery.[58]

One of the better known officers who served with the 15th Infantry was Philip Edward Gallagher. He arrived in Tientsin in September 1923. As a first lieutenant he first commanded the howitzer platoon. In September 1924, he became adjutant of the 2nd battalion and personnel adjutant of the regiment. In April 1926, he became the regimental adjutant. When he departed Tientsin in September of 1926, the regiment's troop newspaper, the *Sentinel*, wrote that he had been closely involved in every phase of garrison life, and was an avid supporter of athletics and a participant in morale-building activities. One of these was regimental theatricals, and Gallagher was codirector and star performer in the celebrated regimental soldier show *Goofus Feathers*, which was performed for two consecutive years to much acclaim. As the paper further observed, he was "well-known as an entertainer … and his songs and eccentric dances are always in demand … [at gatherings] where informality is the rule and conscience the guide."[59]

Gallagher had graduated from West Point in 1918 and would return there as commandant of cadets in 1942 and 1943. In addition to his service in Tientsin in the 1920s, during World War II he served as commanding general of 1st Army of the Chinese Combat Command and was a senior U.S. adviser to the 1st Army. In 1946, he headed a military mission to Vietnam to attempt to deal with that state's fate following the war and opposed the moves being made by the French to regain their control over the area. He then proceeded to Europe as deputy director of the European Command (EUCOM) Constabulary from 1947 to 1948. From 1948 to 1951, he served as EUCOM director of Military Posts. Subsequently, he commanded the 6th Armored Division from 1951 to 1953. After a stint as the commander of Fort Holabird in Maryland in 1953, he was promoted to the rank of major general, becoming the

9. A Gallery of Generals 165

commanding general of Headquarters, the United States Army, Europe (USAREUR) Communications Zone from 1954 to 1956. Gallagher died in 1976.[60]

Donald Weldon Brann was born in Rushville, Indiana, on September 26, 1895. He was commissioned in the infantry, in the Officer Reserve Corps (ORC) in 1917, at Purdue University. He served in Tientsin as a first lieutenant from 1923 to 1927 and was a member of the regiment's polo team. From 1931 to 1933, he was an instructor at the Infantry School, where he joined several other members of "That Damned China Crowd" then "crowding" Fort Benning in some numbers. In the words of one observer, they were "thick on the ground" there. Brann subsequently graduated from the Command and General Staff School in Kansas in 1935. He proceeded from there to become professor of Military Science and Tactics at the University of Hawaii, 1935–1937. Once more in school, he graduated from the Army War College in 1938 and again was at Fort Benning as an instructor at the Infantry School in 1938 and 1939. His experience as an educator led him to duty with the Operations and Training Division of the War Department's General Staff from 1939 to 1942.

He was active in various operations in World War II, first as chief of staff of the 95th Infantry Division (1942–1943) while it was still in training in the United States. The division would later serve with distinction in the European Theater of Operations. Promoted to brigadier general in September 1943, Brann became assistant chief of staff for operations of the 5th Army in Italy. Following this, he was deputy chief of staff for the 15th Army Group, from December 1944 to December 1945. There he was involved in the group's capture of Rome on June 4, 1944, and in subsequent action in northern Italy until the war's end. Meanwhile, in June 1945, he was promoted to major general. Unfortunately, after the war, he fell from a cliff in the Tyrolean Alps on December 29, 1945. First buried in the American Cemetery in Florence, Italy, on January 3, 1946, he was later relocated to Arlington National Cemetery.[61]

Jens Anderson Doe was born in Chicago on June 20, 1891. Graduating from West Point, he was commissioned in the 11th Infantry on June 12, 1914, and served in Texas and Arizona. In World War I, he attended a machine gun training course at Fort Sill, and subsequently much of his career involved machine guns. He went to France in April 1918. Promoted to major on June 7, 1918, he assumed command of the 14th Machine Gun Battalion in July and participated in the Battle of Saint-Mihiel and the Meuse-Argonne offensive. At the end of World War I, he organized and instructed at the army Machine Gun School at Langres. Later instructing at the II Corps Schools, he became a student at the army's Artillery School. He returned to the United States with the 61st Infantry Regiment in June of 1919.

September of 1919 found him as an instructor at the Infantry School at Fort Benning, following which he was a student once more, attending the field officers' course there from 1921 to 1922. After stints with the 2nd Infantry at Fort Sheridan, Illinois, at Fort Custer, Michigan, and West Point, he attended the Command General Staff College at Fort Leavenworth from 1925 to 1926. This set the stage for his assignment to the 15th Infantry in Tientsin, where, as a major, he remained from 1926 to January 1930, serving as the commander of the regiment's 3rd Battalion for two years.

Back in the U.S., Doe commanded the Machine Gun School at Fort Dix, New Jersey, until 1932, leaving there to attend the U.S. Army War College. Promoted to lieutenant colonel on January 1, 1936, he became an instructor at the Command and General Staff College and then was professor of military science and tactics at the University of California at Berkeley.

As World War II began, Doe joined the newly reformed 7th Division at Fort Ord, California, in September 1940. Becoming a colonel on June 26, 1941, he took command of the division's 17th Infantry Regiment at Schofield Barracks, Hawaii. Following Pearl Harbor, in June 1942, he was sent to Australia to command the 163rd Infantry Regiment of the 41st Division. He was to be closely involved with the 41st throughout the remainder of the war.

Through the course of World War II in the Pacific, Doe was engaged with MacArthur's forces as they made their way first to Sanananda, New Guinea, and on to Aitape, the island of Wakde, and Biak, an island just off the coast of western New Guinea, and beyond. The first action at Sanananda in January 1943 led to Doe's becoming assistant division commander and being promoted to brigadier general on February 2, 1943. At the Battle of Biak, May 27 to August 17, 1944, the commander of the 41st Division, Major General Horace H. Fuller, was relieved of his post, whereupon Doe assumed command of the division, being promoted to major general on August 1, 1944. Subsequently, the 41st captured Palawan Island in the Philippines and proceeded to Zamboanga on the Philippine island of Mindanao, actions that occurred from February 1945 to April 1945.

After Mindanao was secured, further operations led to the conquest of the Sulu island chain and additional mopping up operations freed the southern Philippines from Japanese control. The 41st, still under Doe's command, then prepared for the anticipated invasion of Japan, which did not occur, because the war ended in August 1945. The 41st then performed occupation duty on the island of Honshu, following which, on December 31, 1945, the 41st was deactivated at Kure-Hiro, Japan.

Returning to the United States, Doe served a brief tour at the War Department, subsequently commanding the 5th Infantry and 3rd Infantry Divisions in the United States. He retired in February 1949 and died on February 24, 1971, at age 79 and is buried at the U.S. Military Academy Cemetery.[62]

It has been noted that Lieutenant General Richard Kerens Sutherland, an alumnus of the 15th, was a graduate of Yale University. Another veteran of the 15th, Lauen Lyman Williams, was also an "Eli." He was born on October 3, 1895, in Spokane, Washington. He began his military career as a member of the Reserve Officer Training Corps at Yale, being commissioned in the infantry in 1917. He served at various posts in the United States, including Camp Lee, Virginia, and Camp Fremont in California. He graduated from the Infantry School basic course at Fort Benning in 1921. In the mid–1920s, he was with the 15th Infantry Regiment in China. There, for several years, among other things he was editor of the regiment's troop newspaper, the *Sentinel*. Back in the U.S., he was then an ROTC instructor at the University of Washington. He then graduated from the army Tank School in 1930. In 1935, he was at Plattsburgh Barracks in New York. In 1939, he completed the Command and General Staff College in Kansas. On the eve of World War II, in 1940, Williams was at Fort Sam Houston in Texas. He was then at the Training and Operations office, serving on the War Department General Staff.

During World War II, Williams was commander of the 405th Infantry Regiment, of the 102nd Infantry Division. Later, he served as assistant division commander of the 29th Infantry Division. Remaining in Europe following the war, he served in the Intelligence Group of the U.S. Army's European Command.

The Korean War years found him serving as comptroller of the U.S. Army's Far East Command from 1949 to 1952. His experience as comptroller led to his being the assistant comptroller of the army in Washington, from 1953 to 1954. With his promotion to lieutenant general on March 1, 1955, he became the comptroller of the army, serving from 1955 to 1957. His last assignment was with the 6th U.S. Army at the Presidio, where he retired on June 30, 1957. He died on September 10, 1975, at age 79, in San Diego, California. He was cremated and his ashes were scattered at sea.[63]

One 15th alumnus with an unusually wide-ranging military career was that of Paul L. Freeman, Jr. He was one of the few to attain the rank of four-star general. He was born on June 29, 1907, in the Philippine Islands. He graduated from West Point in 1929. He was first assignment was with the 9th

Infantry Division at Fort Sam Houston, in Texas. In 1932, he attended the officers' course at the Infantry School at Fort Benning, Georgia, no doubt making acquaintances with several members of the 15th's "Old China Hands" then present there. He was then, in fact, assigned to the 15th Infantry Regiment in China, remaining until 1936. Returning to the U.S., Freeman served with the 12th Infantry Regiment at Fort Washington, Maryland, following which he attended a tank course at Fort Benning. He was then appointed company and battalion maintenance officer for the 66th Infantry Regiment.

No doubt drawing upon his experience with the 15th Regiment, Freeman was then a Chinese language student in Peking, serving simultaneously as assistant military attaché. His knowledge of Chinese led to his assignment to the U.S. Military Mission to China and then to the staff of the China-Burma-India Theater as an instructor of Chinese and Indian armies. He returned to Washington in September 1943 as a staff officer.

In 1944 he was sent to Rio de Janeiro, Brazil, as director of arms training for the Joint Brazil-U.S. Military Commission. He returned to Washington in 1947 to the army General Staff, working on Latin American affairs, including, from 1948 to 1950, as a member of the Joint Brazil-U.S. Military Commission and as a member of the U.S. Army delegation to the Inter-American Defense Board.

In the Korean War, as a colonel, he emerged as the commander of the 23rd Infantry Regiment of the 2nd Infantry Division. His most notable service in that struggle came in February of 1951, at the Battle of Chipyong-ni. At this time, his regiment was almost overwhelmed by massive Chinese attacks when five divisions assailed the 23rd Regiment, which in the face of furious attacks held out. He was wounded there and had to surrender his command of the regiment. His success in the battle helped turn the tide at that stage of the war in favor of the U.S. forces.[64]

Following the Korean War, in 1952, he attended the National War College. In 1955, he commanded the 2nd Infantry Division, in which he had served in Korea. In 1956 and 1957, Freeman assumed command of the 4th Infantry Division at Fort Lewis, Washington. In 1957, he was on the U.S. Army Weapons System Evaluation Group in Washington, D.C. Receiving his fourth star on May 1, 1962, he became the commander in chief of the Central Army Group of the U.S. Army Command in Europe.

His final command in the U.S. Army was as the commanding general of the U.S. Continental Army Command headquartered at Fort Monroe, Virginia, from 1965 to 1967. Freeman retired from the army in 1967. He died at Monterey, California, on April 17, 1988, at age 80 and is buried at Arlington National Cemetery.[65]

9. A Gallery of Generals 169

Another member of the 15th alumni to attain the rank of four-star general was Earle Gilmore "Bus" Wheeler, who was born on January 13, 1908, in Washington, D.C. He graduated from West Point in 1932. He was at first at Fort Benning with the 29th Infantry, from 1932 to 1936. He then graduated from the Infantry School in 1937. Following this, he went to China with the 15th Infantry as a first lieutenant and was among those who accompanied the unit back to Fort Lewis, Washington, in March 1938. He remained there until 1940. Wheeler was then engaged in various training assignments, one of which was to West Point in 1940 and 1941, where he was instructor of mathematics. In 1942, he attended the Command and General Staff School at Fort Leavenworth. There followed service as battalion commander of the 141st Infantry Regiment of the 36th Infantry Division. From 1942 to 1944, he was with the 99th Infantry Division. He went to Europe in November 1944 as chief of staff of the 63rd Infantry Division, which landed at Marseilles, France, and proceeded into Germany and action in the Rhineland until the end of World War II. In late 1945, Wheeler was back in the U.S. as an instructor at Fort Sill, Oklahoma, in the Artillery School, and then returned to Germany serving there from 1947 to 1949 with the U.S. Constabulary in occupied Germany.

Back once more in the U.S., Wheeler graduated from the National War College in 1950. In 1951 and 1952, he commanded the 351st Infantry Regiment in Italy. Promoted to brigadier general in November of 1952, he then served as assistant chief of staff for operations at Allied Forces Southern Europe Headquarters in Naples, Italy. In 1955, promoted to major general, he was director of plans in the office of the deputy chief of staff for Plans and Operations until 1957. In October 1958, he assumed command of the 2nd Armored Division at Fort Hood, Texas, and in the following year, in March 1959, he commanded the III U.S. Army Corps. In April 1960, as a lieutenant general, he was director of the Joint Chiefs of Staff in Washington. In March 1962, promoted to a four-star general, he was once more in Europe as deputy commander of the U.S. Forces in Europe. Later that year, he was named chief of staff of the U.S. Army, serving from October 1, 1962, to July 2, 1964.

As chief of staff, Wheeler oversaw many major developments, including a major reorganization of the army, the Cuban Missile Crisis, the use of the army during the school integrations conflict and the early stages of the divisive and controversial Vietnam War. Then, in July 1964, in the midst of the Vietnam War, he succeeded General Maxwell D. Taylor as chairman of the Joint Chiefs of Staff, continuing until July 1970, when he retired from the army. Serving for six years in that capacity, he had been chairman of the Joint

Chiefs of Staff longer than anyone else to date. His appointment was a controversial one, and many things that he did—or failed to do—such as the escalation or de-escalation of American involvement in the Vietnam War, were bones of contention throughout his tumultuous tenure. He died in Frederick, Maryland, on December 18, 1973, and is buried at Arlington National Cemetery.[66]

Frederick Mixon Harris was in the 15th in the 1920s.[67] He was born in Rockmart, Georgia, on June 29, 1900. He entered West Point on June 1, 1918, graduating on April 10, 1920. He was then assigned as a student at the Infantry School at Fort Benning. Following his graduation he was regimental adjutant at the 29th Infantry Regiment, also at Fort Benning.

In 1926, he was ordered to China with the 15th Infantry. By 1928, as a first lieutenant, he was commanding Company E. He has described in considerable detail what life was like in Tientsin in those "three happy years" he spent there. These accounts are in his papers now at the George C. Marshall Research Library in Lexington, Virginia. Following his return from China, during the 1930s, Harris was first assigned to the 16th Infantry at Plattsburg Barracks in New York. He then proceeded to teach at the Reserve Officer Training Corps at Drexel Institute in Philadelphia. From there he was assigned as regimental adjutant of the 65th Infantry Regiment in Puerto Rico, then of the 5th Infantry, stationed at Fort McKinley in Maine.

Early in World War II, Harris was assistant chief of staff in the Panama Canal Zone. His knowledge of this area brought him to a tour as chief, Special Intelligence Section, Latin-American Division, at the War Department. In 1943, having been made a brigadier general, he was appointed assistant division commander of the 63rd Infantry Division, known as the "Blood and Fire" Division. Later, for a short time, Harris was made commander of the 63rd. This outfit departed from the United States in November of 1944 and landed at Marseilles, France, on December 8, 1944. It then proceeded through the Siegfried Line to Worms, Mannheim, Heidelburg, and ended at Landsberg, Germany, in April 1945 on the eve of the end of the war in Europe on May 8, 1945.

After World War II, Harris became assistant chief of staff of First Army, at Fort Bragg, North Carolina. He then returned to Puerto Rico as the commanding officer, first of Fort Brooke, San Juan, and then of the Post, Port and General Depot, of the Antilles Command at Fort Buchanan, Puerto Rico. He was subsequently assigned to the Organization and Training Division of G3, Department of the Army, at the Pentagon. He went from there to being the commanding officer of Fort Meade, Maryland, following which he was in

Japan as the commanding officer of Camp Zama, where the headquarters of the U.S. Army Forces in the Far East were located. He returned to Fort Meade as special assistant to the deputy army commander of the Second Army. He retired on August 31, 1954. He continued, nevertheless, to serve in a military capacity as professor of Military Science and Tactics at Randolph-Macon Academy, at Fort Royal, Virginia. He died on April 10, 1969, at Fort Meade, Maryland. He is buried in the Saint Margaret's Episcopal Church cemetery near Annapolis.

Henry Balding "Monk" Lewis was born at Fort Wood, on Bedlow Island, New York, May 8, 1889, into a military family. His father was Major General Edward M. Lewis.[68] Monk Lewis graduated from West Point in 1913. The following year found him in Mexico as a company and battalion officer serving as aide-de-camp to General Bell. In 1915, Lewis was at Fort Benning. Following this, from 1919 to 1922, he was in Hawaii as assistant adjutant general at the Hawaiian Department. From 1926 to 1929, as a captain in the 15th Infantry, he was adjutant general of U.S. Army Forces in China in Tientsin. From 1929 to 1935, he was at Fort Benning, Georgia. He then attended the Command and General Staff School at Fort Leavenworth. With the coming of World War II, he was at the Presidio as adjutant general of the 4th Army. In 1942, he became adjutant general of the 12th Army Group in Europe, becoming deputy chief of staff to General Omar Bradley, its commander. The 12th Army Group, which controlled the majority of U.S. troops in Europe, consisted of the 1st Army, commanded by General Courtney H. Hodges; the 3rd, commanded by General George S. Patton; the 9th, under General William H. Simpson; and the 15th, commanded by General Leonard T. Gerow. The group numbered about 1.3 million U.S. troops.

At the end of World War II, Lewis became administrative advisor to General Omar Bradley, who was then the administrator of Veterans Affairs in Washington, D.C. In 1949, Lewis retired from the army as a major general. He died on May 21, 1966, in Alameda, California, and is buried in Arlington National Cemetery.

James Edward Moore, who became a four-star general, was born November 29, 1902, in New Bedford, Massachusetts. He was to have a far-ranging military career. He graduated from West Point in 1924 and for the next few years, until 1932, he was with the 5th and 10th Infantry regiments. He attended the Infantry School at Fort Benning from 1932 to 1933 and was then ordered to China, where, from 1933 to 1936, he was at first with a rifle company and was then personnel and assistant adjutant, as well as the provost marshal, in the 15th Infantry Regiment in Tientsin. Moore was pleased to be sent to China, noting that the officers were hand picked, and Tientsin was a prize station, and he was able to take his family with him.[69]

Moore was then at the Command and General Staff School and by 1940 had served as a company commander of the 29th Infantry Regiment. In the early 1940s, he was at first at the headquarters of the 2nd Infantry Division. During World War II, in succession, he served as the chief of staff of several organizations, culminating in 1945 and 1946, when he was chief of staff of the 9th U.S. Army, which consisted of over 200,000 men and was commanded by Lieutenant General William H. Simpson. Subsequently, Moore was the commanding general for the South Sector in the U.S. Army-Pacific. He was then secretary of the army General Staff from 1948 to 1950. He was commanding general of the 10th Mountain Division, in 1950 and 1951, following which he was at Fitzsimons Army Hospital, 1951–1953. He was then the commandant of the Army War College, 1953–1955.

From 1955 to 1958, Moore was the U.S. high commissioner of the Ryukyu Islands of Japan, and the commanding general of U.S. Army IX Corps located there. Summoned back to Washington, he became deputy army chief of staff for Military Operations, from 1958 to 1959. This was followed by his last command as chief of staff for the Supreme Headquarters Allied Powers Europe (SHAPE), from 1959 to 1963. He retired from the Army in 1963, having especially distinguished himself as a staff officer rather than as a combat commander. He died on January 28, 1986, at age 83, and is buried in Arlington National Cemetery.[70]

Charles Lawrence Bolte was born on May 8, 1895, in Chicago. In 1917, he graduated from the Illinois Institute of Technology, having majored in chemical engineering. In 1916, he earned a commission in the army as a second lieutenant. In 1918 he was in France in the 58th Infantry of the 4th Division that saw action in the Battle of St. Mihiel and the Mekuse-Argonne and Aisne-Marne offensives. On September 19, 1918, he was wounded in action.

Following the war, Bolte returned to attend the infantry advanced course, at Fort Benning, from which he graduated in 1930. He proceeded to the Command and General Staff School, graduating in 1932. He was then ordered to duty with the 15th Infantry Regiment in China as a company and battalion commander in 1933. In April 1936, he returned to the U.S. and commanded a battalion of the 13th Infantry Regiment at Fort Devens, Massachusetts. He then attended the Army War College, graduating in June of 1937, and remained as an instructor there until 1940.

With the coming of World War II, in 1941 Bolte headed a team of U.S.

Army observers in Britain. In 1942, he became the chief of staff of U.S. Forces in Britain. He returned to the U.S. in 1943, commanding the 69th Infantry Division in training in Mississippi. In July of 1944, as a major general, he assumed command of the 34th Infantry Division, then in action at the Arno River in Italy. He continued to lead the 34th in Italy in various operations in the Apennines culminating with the capture of Bologna and the surrender of Axis forces in Italy on April 29, 1945.

In the postwar period, Bolte served in several posts in Washington, D.C., including as Army Ground Forces chief of staff, the assistant chief of staff for operations, and deputy chief of staff for plans. In addition, he served as chairman of the Inter-American Defense Board. From August 1952 to April 1953, he commanded the 7th U.S. Army in West Germany. In 1953, as a lieutenant general, he was commander in chief of the U.S. Army, Europe, from April 1 to September 29. From 1953 to 1955, Bolte was the vice chief of staff of the United States Army under General Matthew B. Ridgway, retiring from service later in 1955 as a general. He died on February 11, 1989, aged 93. He is buried at Arlington National Cemetery.[71]

Harold LeMaire Boatner was born in New Orleans, Louisiana, on October 8, 1900. He graduated from West Point in 1924 and served first with the 29th U.S. Infantry Regiment, then proceeded to Tientsin, China, serving in the 15th U.S. Infantry Regiment. He was subsequently in the 30th and 38th Infantry regiments. He graduated from the Command and General Staff School in 1939. He then served in several capacities in China during World War II. In 1942, he was engaged in the training of Chinese soldiers at Ramgarh, India, a program that Stilwell had set up. Being promoted to brigadier general in November of 1942, Boatner became the chief of staff of the Chinese Army in Burma, 1942–1943, following which, in 1943 and 1944, he became the commanding general of combat troops in northwest Burma. In these commands he no doubt drew upon his experiences with China and the Chinese gained when he served with the 15th Infantry Regiment earlier in his career.

After General Albert Coady Wedemeyer took command of the Chinese Theater in October of 1944, when it had split off from the China-Burma-India Theater, Boatner became chief of staff of the newly created Chinese Combat Command, 1944–1945. During the Korean War, he is best known for his firm and skillful action and heroics in quelling a riot at a U.S. Chinese and Korean prisoner-of-war camp on Koje-do Island southwest of Pusan, South Korea.[72] He subsequently commanded the 3rd U.S. Infantry Division, from 1954 to 1955, at Fort Benning, Georgia. He then became provost marshal of the U.S. Army from November 19, 1957, to October 31, 1960. He retired in 1960 and died on May 29, 1977, at age 77. He is buried in Arlington National Cemetery.[73]

Paul Wyatt "Small Paul" Caraway was one of the more controversial of those who cycled through the ranks of the 15th Infantry while in China. His nickname, which came no doubt from his years at West Point, as was common among those of that brotherhood, referred to his height of five feet, five-and-one-half inches. Caraway was born on December 23, 1905, in Jonesboro, Arkansas. He was the son of well-known Arkansas United States senators. His father was Thaddeus H. Caraway and his mother was Hattie Ophelia Wyatt Caraway, the first woman to be elected to the U.S. Senate from Arkansas. She had replaced her husband on December 9 when he died in 1931. She went on to win two elections in her own right: a special election to fill her husband's office in 1932, and the general election in 1938. She lost her bid to return to the Senate in 1944.[74]

Caraway graduated from West Point in 1929. He then attended Georgetown University, graduating in 1933 with a law degree. From 1935 to 1937, he was with the 15th Infantry in Tientsin, China. From 1938 to 1942, he taught law at West Point. He then served on the General Staff of the United States Department of War from 1942 to 1944. He subsequently was deputy chief of staff to General Albert Coady Wedemeyer in the CBI in late World War II, and acting chief, Plans Section of Headquarters, U.S. Forces, in the China Theater. Promoted to brigadier general in 1945, he headed the Chungking Liaison Group from 1945 to 1946. When General Marshall, from December 1945 to early 1947, was on a mission from President Truman to attempt to form some unity between the Communists and Chiang Kai-shek in China, Caraway was on Marshall's staff. Back in the United States, in 1947, he was an instructor at the National War College. From 1949 to 1951, he commanded the 351st Infantry of the 88th Division in Trieste, Italy. Following this, he was with the NATO Defense College from 1951 to 1953. Back in the United States, as aide to Vice President Richard Nixon, he accompanied the vice president on an extended Asian tour in 1953, though he apparently disliked serving Nixon for undisclosed reasons. Following the end of the Korean War, Caraway was for a time head of U.S. Army Research and Development. From August 1955 to April 1956, he was once more in command of troops, this time as commander of the 7th Infantry Division in Korea. He proceeded from there to the Headquarters, Far East Command, in Japan and served from 1956 to 1958.

His greatest task by far was that of commanding general of the military forces and as high commissioner of the United States Civil Administration of the Ryukyu Islands in Japan. This was also the source of ongoing conflicts regarding numerous policies with such high officials as the U.S. ambassador to Japan, Edwin O. Reischauer, the Department of State, and President Kennedy himself.[75]

Throughout his career, Caraway was also subjected to opprobrium and even detestation because he had never been in combat. This was especially true regarding his promotion to lofty posts over the heads of seasoned combat veterans. A certain colonel, desiring to be promoted to brigadier general, noted that Caraway was rumored to possess a hatred of combat troops, because in his 33 years of service he had never "smelled smoke in combat." Hence, that colonel would no doubt never be promoted to flag rank, at least not by Caraway, who was denigrated as "our rose-growing, administration-loving general." In addition, Caraway was at least a mild eccentric who insisted that his men wear the same uniform he was wearing and prescribed the "uniform of the day" on a daily basis. He was also a well-known workaholic, though he did not insist that others be one as well.[76]

In 1964, at the end of his stint as high commissioner, Caraway retired from the military as a lieutenant general. For a time, he practiced law in Heber Springs, Arkansas, and taught at Benjamin Franklin University in Washington, D.C. He died on December 13, 1985, at age 79 and is buried at the West Point Cemetery.[77]

Another officer of the 15th Infantry who served with distinction was Major General Edwin Davies Patrick. His military career was unlike that of many of his cohorts, however, in that he, as a major general, was killed in action in World War II, being only one of three U.S. Army divisional commanders killed in combat in the conflict. Beyond this, Patrick also had a major U.S. naval vessel named for him, the details of which will be recounted below.

Edwin Davies Patrick was born on January 11, 1884, in Tell City, Indiana. Unlike many of the officers discussed, Patrick did not attend West Point. Instead, he was commissioned a second lieutenant of infantry on March 21, 1917, in the Indiana National Guard, which he had joined on February 11, 1915. He then joined the 14th Machine Gun Battalion in France and served with it in the St. Mihiel and Meuse-Argonne offensives. After service in Europe, in July 1919 Patrick returned to the United States and was stationed at various posts, notably at Fort Bliss in Texas. In May 1926, he arrived at Tientsin for service in the 15th Infantry. In May of 1927, he took command of that outfit's 2nd battalion, which had been commanded by Major Joseph

USNS *General Edwin D. Patrick* circa 1961. This ship was named for General Edwin D. Patrick, one of the prominent alumni of the 15th Infantry Regiment (courtesy of U.S. Naval History and Heritage Command).

Stilwell. He remained in China until July 1929, when he joined Marshall and Stilwell at the Infantry School at Fort Benning, Georgia.

With the coming of World War II, as a colonel, Patrick was transferred to the Southwest Pacific in December of 1942. He was first assigned to Admiral Halsey's staff, but soon, on April 26, 1943, being promoted to brigadier general, he became chief of staff of the 6th Army, engaged in operations in New Guinea. In May 1944, he was made a commander of a regimental combat team, following which he was promoted to major general. In August of 1944, he assumed command of the 6th Infantry Division. In January 1945, the 6th was engaged in the battle to liberate Luzon in the Philippines. There, Patrick was mortally wounded on March 15, 1945, killed by Japanese machine-gun fire in a battle near Mountain Mataba, south of Montalban, Luzon, the Philippines. He was first buried in the American Military Cemetery in Manila. His body was later returned to his home in Tell City, Indiana, where it was buried in the family plot in Greenwood Cemetery.

The ship that eventually bore the name of General Patrick was first laid down as an Admiral W.S. Benson Class naval transport. Its hull was begun on November 29, 1943, at the Bethlehem-Alameda Shipyards in Alameda, California. It was launched on July 27, 1944, and commissioned as the USS *Admiral C.F. Hughes* (AP-124) on January 31, 1945, under the command of a U.S. Coast Guard officer, Captain John Trebes. During the war, the ship transported passengers to both the Asiatic-Pacific areas and the Europe, Africa and Middle East theaters. On May 3, 1946, the ship was decommissioned and transferred to the Maritime Commission for reassignment to the U.S. Army Transportation Service. On August 30, 1946, it was formally recommissioned by the Military Sea Transportation Service (MSTS), as the USAT (U.S. Army Transport) *General Edwin D. Patrick*. Subsequently it was reacquired by the navy on March 1, 1950, and put into service as the USNS (United States Navy Ship) *General Edwin D. Patrick*. It regularly carried troops and supplies to American bases in Japan, Korea, Okinawa, the Marianas and the Philippines and was especially active during the Korean War, receiving three battle stars commemorating its service career at that time.

After the Korean War, from 1953 to 1965, the ship steamed to the Far East 110 times and was especially active during the early years of the Vietnam War. In December of 1966, she was overhauled in San Francisco and in 1967 placed in ready reserve status, though later in the year she was withdrawn from service. On September 30, 1968, she became part of the National Defense Reserve Fleet, at Suisun Bay in Benecia, California. In 2010, she was inspected for hull leaks. None being found, she was sold on March 18, 2010, to the firm of ESCO Marine, at Brownsville, Texas, for dismantling, which was accomplished beginning in July 2010 after her last voyage from San Francisco through the Panama Canal to south Texas.[78]

One of the alumni of the 15th Infantry, Paul Wilkins Kendall, also served in the American Siberian venture late in World War I, and shortly thereafter, before serving in China.[79] Kendall was born in Baldwin, Kansas, on July 17, 1898. He graduated from West Point on November 1, 1918, as a second lieutenant of infantry, at the time of the shortened course, the consequence of United States involvement in World War I. From 1918 to 1919, he attended the Infantry School of Arms at Fort Benning, Georgia. After graduating, he was assigned to the 27th Infantry Unit at Fort Benning and was then sent to Siberia in Russia, where he arrived in March 1919, to join American forces already involved. At this time, for several reasons President Wilson sent units of the U.S. Army to Russia. Some were in far northwest Russia; others, including the 27th, 31st, and 12th Infantry Regiments and other volunteers from the 13th and 62nd Infantry Regiments, were sent to Siberia.

Their mission was not altogether clear, though they were apparently to provide protection of American supplied property that had been sent into Russia earlier in support of the tsarist Russian government's war efforts on the Eastern Front. They were also to help the beleaguered Czechoslovakian legions attempting to evade Bolshevik forces along the Trans-Siberian Railroad by which they were bound for Vladivostok, and hopefully from there to be sent to the Western Front in France. Apparently there were no deliberate attempts to force clashes with Bolsheviks, though armed conflict did occur. The United States forces were also often at loggerheads with other Allied forces there, including the British, French and Japanese.

The first American troops arrived in August 1918, with General Graves appearing on September 4, 1918. The last of the U.S. forces left Siberia on April 1, 1920, having served for 19 months under arduous conditions and with 189 soldier deaths. One of the armed clashes involved Lieutenant Kendall. At Posolskaya, Siberia, on January 10, 1920, while in command of a detachment of the 27th Infantry, Kendall led his men into action when they were attacked by an armored train. In the words of his citation for the Distinguished Service Cross awarded to him later, "the detachment under his leadership and inspired by his example attacked and disabled the armored train and caused it to surrender."

Kendall returned to Manila in March 1920, still attached to the 27th Infantry. He was also still with the 27th Infantry when in January 1921 the regiment was reassigned to Fort Shafter in Hawaii. From March 1922 to July 1924, Kendall was with the 53rd Infantry Regiment in Wyoming and Colorado. In 1924, he served with the 38th Infantry Regiment, until, in December, he was appointed instructor at the U.S. Military Academy.

In September of 1929, Kendall entered the Infantry School at Fort Benning, graduating in June 1930. In August of 1934, he was at the Command and General Staff School at Fort Leavenworth, Kansas, graduating in June of 1936. Following these years of schooling, he joined the 15th Infantry in Tientsin, remaining from 1936 to 1938.

From March 1938 to August of 1940, he was engaged in various ways in the operations of the Civilian Conservation Corps in California. At the beginning of World War II, Kendall was assigned as chief of staff of the 85th Infantry Division at Camp Shelby, Mississippi.

Kendall's most important involvement during World War II was his command, from September 1944 to July of 1945, as a major general, when he commanded the 88th Infantry Division—the "Blue Devils"—leading them through Italy, where they obtained the capture of Vicenza and Verona. From July 1945 to May 1948, Kendall commanded units at Camp Roberts, California, and in April 1946 he became commanding general of the 2nd Infantry Division at Fort Lewis, Washington. In May of 1948, he went to Austria, assuming the post of commander of the United States Zone Command at Linz. In June 1950, he was elevated to the post of deputy commander of the U.S. Forces in Austria, headquartered at Salzburg.

Returning to the United States, Kendall was stationed at Fort Monroe in Virginia, and in April of 1951 he became the commander of the army's VI Corps at Camp Atterbury, Indiana. A year later, on September 16, 1952, he was promoted to lieutenant general and transferred to the U.S. Army Far East Command. On June 28, 1952, he assumed the command of I Corps, which was soon to be involved in the Korean War. In April 1953, shortly before the cease fire in Korea, Kendall was reassigned as deputy commanding general of the U.S. Army Forces Far East in Manila, Philippines. In the following year, 1954, he became the commander of Allied Land Forces Southeastern Europe, headquartered in Izmir, Turkey. He retired from the army in 1955, taking up residence at Palo Alto, California. He died on October 3, 1983, at age 85 and is buried at West Point.

One of the members of the 15th Infantry, John William Leonard, was earlier a cadet in the famous West Point class of 1915, the one that the "stars fell on." Leonard was born on January 25, 1890, in Toledo, Ohio.[80] He entered West Point in 1911, graduating in 1915 as a second lieutenant. He was assigned to the 6th Infantry Regiment at the Presidio in San Francisco. In March of 1916, the regiment was one of the two infantry regiments with General Pershing's punitive expedition in Mexico.

He was then detached from the 6th for officer training at Chickamauga Park, Tennessee. In March 1918, Leonard rejoined the 6th and sailed with it to France. There the 6th became part of the 10th Brigade of the 5th Infantry Division. It was first in action in early August of 1918, during the St. Mihiel Salient operations. This was followed by the Meuse-Argonne offensive. Wounded on October 16, Leonard was in a hospital until November 7, when he rejoined the 6th at the Meuse River.

Following the armistice, he was with the U.S. Army of Occupation in Coblenz, Germany. While there, Leonard, as a result of his several decorations, was made second in command and executive officer of the Third Army Composite Regiment, composed of highly decorated veterans assembled to accompany Pershing to victory celebrations in various capitals in Europe and in major cities in the U.S. following their return to the United States.

In 1919, Leonard was at the Artillery School at Fort Sill and then with tanks at Fort Meade, Maryland. In 1921, he was at the Infantry School at Fort Benning as an instructor on tanks and commanded the 15th Tank Battalion. From May 1923 to June 1926, Leonard was in the office of the chief of infantry in Washington, D.C. He was then returned to Fort Benning as a student for the advanced course in 1926. In 1928, he attended the Command General Staff School in Kansas. He then went to the Pennsylvania Military College to instruct ROTC cadets, remaining there from 1928 to 1933. In 1933, he became the commander of the 2nd Battalion of the 15th Infantry in Tientsin, taking his family with him to China. While there, in 1935, he became the regiment's executive officer.[81]

Returning to the United States in 1936, Leonard became senior instructor of the 5th National Guard Regiment of Maryland. Following this, in 1940, he was with the 2nd Infantry Division at Fort Sam Houston in Texas. In late 1941, he went with a survey team to Brazil to examine its defenses. In the same year, he participated in the U.S. Army's extensive maneuvers and also took command of the 6th Infantry, by then part of the 1st Armored Division, at Fort Knox. He was also promoted to brigadier general and transferred to the 4th Armored Division at Pine Camp, New York, and then to the 9th Armored Division being formed at Fort Riley, Kansas. After two years of training, in September 1944, the 9th Armored Division arrived in France and was assigned to the First Army, which became part of the VIII Corps. With the launching of the Battle of the Bulge, Leonard's forces were fully engaged. They then secured, and proceeded across, the bridge at Remagen. The 9th advanced into Germany, driving into the Ruhr industrial area. It went on to invade Czechoslovakia, then took up occupation duty in the Bayreuth area of Austria.

Leonard then became the commanding general of the 20th Armored Division, at Camp Cooke, California, where he was selected to lead it in the planned invasion of Japan. Following the Japanese surrender, however, the 20th was disbanded, and Leonard went to Camp Hood, Texas, to command the 2nd Armored. In 1948, he took command of the U.S. Army Armor Center at Fort Knox.

In 1950, Leonard became the military attaché in Great Britain. He was then sent to Fort Bragg, North Carolina, taking over as commander of V Corps. Not too long afterward, he took over the XVIII Airborne Corps. He retired from the army in 1952. He died on October 26, 1974, at age 84, and his wife, Eileen O' Brien Leonard, died in 1990. They are both buried at Arlington National Cemetery.

Certainly, service in China with the 15th Infantry Regiment was not the only criteria for attaining the rank of general. In any event, it is interesting to note that service therein was a springboard for many, both professionally and personally, and merits some consideration in any history of the U.S. Army in China, if only in a passing reference.

Part IV: The U.S. Army and the First "Shanghai Incident": With the 31st Infantry Regiment in China, January–June 1932

> We don't know Montezuma's Halls
> Or Tripoli's fair scenes,
> But we went to Shanghai once
> To save the U.S. Marines.[1]

10

INTRODUCTION

The men of the U.S. Army's 31st Infantry Regiment might be excused their braggadocio when the precipitant nature of their hasty departure from Manila in early February of 1932 is taken into account. This scurrying about no doubt conveyed the sense of a growing crisis, called in some circles the first "Shanghai Incident" (the second came in 1937), requiring their immediate assistance. Perhaps the Marines were in deep trouble in embattled Shanghai and only the "Polar Bears"—as the men of the regiment were called—could arrive in time to avert disaster.[1]

But there were assuredly other issues in 1932 pertaining to the 31st's deployment to China beyond "saving the U.S. Marines." On the face of it, the "incident" was a 33-day fight between Japanese and Chinese forces in the city of Shanghai and its environs. At any rate, it was a dress rehearsal for what was to come later in the 1930s, and was also pivotal to major military and political developments in China, Japan and the West.[2] It caused grave concern in Shanghai's "International Settlement," and fearing for their perceived national interests, several nations sent in military reinforcements. The United States was no exception, and the 31st Infantry Regiment, then stationed in Manila, was soon ordered to China. This resulted in the only U.S. Army intervention in Shanghai until late in World War II. To be sure, the U.S. Marine Corps had been there since 1927, so the 31st joined the fabled 4th Marines already on guard.[3]

The events in Shanghai in 1932 stemmed from actions of Japan in September 1931. At that time, the Japanese army launched a military campaign in Manchuria that within six months ended in Japan's gaining control of China's three northeastern provinces.[4] To assist in this venture, the Japanese used their Shanghai incursions as a diversion to induce the West to focus on Shanghai rather than Manchuria, where there was much more Western financial and commercial involvement and accordingly was regarded as being more important than Manchuria. Japanese aggression in Shanghai aroused strong anti–Japanese feeling throughout China, especially in Shanghai and Canton, already at a high pitch as a result of the Japanese machinations in Manchuria. Patriotic Chinese citizens organized societies, especially the Anti-Japanese National Salvation Association and the "Great Anti-Japanese Boycott," the latter, set up in Shanghai in July of 1931, called for boycotting the Japanese. These groups compelled Chinese merchants to refrain from using, or dealing in, Japanese products, threatening those who failed to comply with seizures of their goods and in extreme cases, being jailed.[5]

The Chinese went further: mobs launched violent attacks on Japanese citizens, dwellings and places of business. Early in January 1932, a Chinese newspaper in Shanghai, the *Min-kuo Jih-pao*, made derogatory references to the Japanese emperor and shortly thereafter, five Japanese monks were attacked in Shanghai, one of whom died of his wounds. This led to a street fight between Japanese civilians and Chinese police and the wounding of several persons on both sides. It is now known that much of the unrest was initiated by Japanese officials and army officers who, in various ways, sought to establish justification for further Japanese encroachment in China, Shanghai in particular. One of those most directly involved was apparently Japan's military attaché in the city, Major Tanaka Ryukichi, who had been given a slush fund of $20,000 to foment trouble. He had thus engaged Chinese thugs to attack the monks. The Japanese had also initially amassed about thirty ships with nearly seven thousand troops nearby to add force to any demands they might make. Throughout, they also, as one scholar has indicated, "revealed little capacity to associate Chinese feelings about Japanese with [their] aggression in Manchuria. This inability to empathize with Asians and foreigners in general became a flaw in Japanese dreams of hegemony." From their recent experience in Manchuria, the Japanese were certain that they "would make short and swift work" of the Shanghai situation.[6]

In addition to these events, difficulties within Shanghai had also evolved over the years. A prominent feature of central Shanghai, extending north and west of the famous Bund along the Whangpoo River, was the French Concession to the west of the "Old Chinese" city. More extensive was the International Settlement to the north of the French Concession, which, however, was not part of it. Soon after Shanghai became a treaty port on November 17, 1843, the Americans and British joined their concessions, forming the International Settlement. Other foreigners soon flocked to it. This new entity was administered by the Shanghai Municipal Council formed in 1854. Wholly foreign controlled, it maintained its own police force, fire brigade, and military reserve, the Shanghai Volunteer Corps. The council was staffed by many foreign nationalities, including some Japanese. The Chinese won the right to join the council in 1928. Chinese people could also reside in the settlement, and by 1932, more than a million Chinese lived there, usually having arrived to escape civil conflict or seeking better economic opportunities. With the rise of Nazi Germany, stateless Jews settled there as well. The Japanese presence in the settlement, which numbered about 30,000 residents, was mainly concentrated in the Hongkew District in its northern area, also known as "Little Tokyo," and the Yangtszepoo District in the eastern part. A major trouble spot, known as Chapei, abutted the settlement on the north. This had grown up around the terminal of the Shanghai-Nanking Railway. Chapei, about one-third of which was foreign owned, was an object of controversy between settlement and Chinese authorities because many of the foreign elements had long wished to add it to the settlement proper. Part of Chapei had been occupied by young, nationally minded—mainly Cantonese—Chinese who took pride in it, built mills and factories there, and even had their own electric power plant and water system. In addition, numerous Japanese had also settled there and they plainly wanted to add Chapei and the North Szechuan Road area—sometimes referred to as the "Tongue," in reference to its shape—projecting into the Chapei area, to the Japanese part of the settlement. (This area, a Settlement public park, was also called, Hongkew Park.)

As tensions increased in Shanghai, on January 20 a mass meeting of some 12,000 Japanese citizens in Chapei, apparently orchestrated to these ends, demanded that all anti–Japanese activities cease, and that the Chinese garrison in Chapei be withdrawn.[7] A few days later, on January 25, the local Japanese Residents' Association further insisted that the naval landing force in the Japanese Sector of the International Settlement, numbering about 3,000 troops, do something to protect them, failing which they would appeal to Tokyo to send army units to Shanghai. Rubbing salt into these wounds, they noted that the Japanese army was apparently having no difficulty in protecting their citizens in Manchuria. Perhaps the Japanese navy lacked ability or resolve? Clearly, as one scholar has noted, "the navy had launched its campaign partly out of jealousy, believing that the army had had a chance to run amok in Manchuria while the navy had had to remain restrained."[8]

Indeed, the perennially tense relations between the Japanese army and navy were well known. One observer noted that those allied against Japan should "play the Japanese army and navy against each other; they were very jealous partners, and each would try to outdo the other if cleverly handled." Unfortunately, this situation could also lead either Japan's army or navy to precipitate and sometimes disastrous action.[9]

10. Introduction

The Japanese naval landing force, usually referred to simply as the "marines," dated from the spring of 1927. It had arrived in Shanghai when Chinese forces threatened the International Settlement. British and American armed forces were also dispatched to Shanghai then and remained on permanent guard duty. For the Americans, this force was the 4th Marine Regiment. There was no marine corps in the Japanese navy. The landing force was made up of naval personnel who had received special training. Their general duties were similar to those of the other international forces stationed in Shanghai and were part of the "the joint international defense plan" in force in the International Settlement. These arrangements, however, had been made on the assumption that it might be necessary for the international forces—including the Japanese—to act in concert to defend the settlement against hostile Chinese. Under the plan, the Japanese were assigned the defense of the Hongkew and Yangtzopoo sections, where most of the Japanese nationals lived. The events of 1932, however, took quite another course; it would be the Japanese who emerged as the threat to the Chinese and Westerners alike.

The pressure from the Japanese civilians produced immediate results. The Japanese consul general in Shanghai, Murai Kuramatsu—after consulting with the commander of the Japanese naval forces in central China, Rear Admiral Shiozawa Kiochi—delivered an ultimatum on January 25 to the Chinese mayor of Shanghai, Wu T'ieh-ch'eng. The consul demanded that apologies be made to the Japanese, that anti-Japanese organizations and activities cease and that compensation be paid for the attack on the monks.[10] The mayor agreed to most of the Japanese demands, but Admiral Kiochi, to all appearances stung by the challenges presented by his countrymen, decided to act forthwith and ordered the marines to prepare for action at midnight the 28th of January. Simultaneously, he issued a proclamation that he was sending his forces into the Chapei area "to enforce law and order" as a "measure for the protection of their nationals and a part of the general defense scheme of the Settlement." He further expressed the pious hope that the Chinese troops would withdraw well to the west of the Shanghai-Woosung Railway and that all Chinese defenses in the area would be removed. The Chinese received this word just a few minutes before the Japanese acted (reminiscent of the situation just prior to the Pearl Harbor attack). The Japanese later excused this lapse, noting that their forces were acting in direct response to the declaration of the "state of emergency" issued by the Shanghai Municipal Council in the settlement at 4:00 p.m. on January 28.[11]

Indeed, the Shanghai Municipal Council had declared a state of emergency that day, and simultaneously deployed troops of the Shanghai Volunteer Corps—the SVC, the settlement's militia—to defend the foreign concessions there. This corps was first organized in the 19th century, coming under the control of the Shanghai City Council in 1870. It was composed of the various nationalities represented in the city, mainly people in business such as clerks and cashiers, but also including business executives. The senior officers were usually older citizens with a stake in the International Settlement. The corps' commander-in-chief was normally a regular British army officer, usually a major or a colonel. There were separate Scottish, Japanese, Italian, Jewish, Filipino, Chinese, Portuguese, and American companies, as well as a colorful White Russian unit, which, as one observer noted, was "superbly disciplined and impeccably turned out in British Army uniforms." The Scots were kilted and naturally equipped with their ubiquitous bagpipes. The American force, with an average of 110 men, boasted a mounted automatic weapons detachment equipped with eight Lewis machine guns. For some years, its commander was a Shanghai lawyer, Major H.D. Rodger. The troops sported American army campaign hats and American-style cavalry uniforms. All corps members wore khaki uniforms with a Shanghai Municipal Council insignia on the sleeve. As volunteers, they received no pay and normally mobilized for a few days at a time. They usually drilled once a week and regularly fired on a rifle range. The corps' arms were mainly supplied by the British, usually Lee-Enfield rifles, though there were some American Springfields on hand. The British companies included an artillery unit and an engineer and sapper outfit. The corps also had an intelligence detachment that sometimes employed paid Chinese agents.

When the Japanese landed their troops in Shanghai in 1932, the corps had about 1,525 members, the ranks growing to about 2,300 at the height of the crisis. The volunteers played a large role in guarding the entry points to the International Settlement and helped keep the Japanese at bay until reinforcements arrived, principally from Britain and the United States. The corps lasted until World War II. Notably, the Japanese did not enter the International Settlement beyond their own area until December 8, 1941.[12]

While the Chinese had sought to meet many of their demands, the Japanese were clearly bent upon military action and were not interested in any settlement.[13] Nonetheless, it became increasingly obvious to many observers that the Japanese had formed no clear plan for significant involvement. They simply attempted to use about 2,500 men of the naval landing party immediately available in their sector in the International Settlement to occupy Chapei, where the Chinese had stationed about 10,000 troops of the Cantonese-speaking 19th Route Army, which altogether numbered about 30,000 troops in three divisions scattered between Shanghai and Soochow. These could be quickly drawn upon to reinforce the forces in Shanghai.[14]

Among the Chinese advantages was the fact that they were defending a densely populated, well-built-up, metropolitan district that was rather easily defended. Furthermore, the area was near the International Settlement occupied by thousands of foreign residents who could count on their own military establishments for defense. In this regard, major weaknesses in the Japanese operational plans stand revealed: they had no definite information as to the condition, strength and morale of the Chinese units and they were convinced that the Chinese would immediately withdraw without opposition if challenged. In this instance, their relatively easy successes in Manchuria misled them.

As things developed, shortly before midnight on January 28 the Japanese mustered their forces, and together with "almost the entire Japanese civilian populace who had gathered to witness the occupation of Chapei," they began to advance along the North Szechuan Road, which paralleled the Shanghai-Woosung railway tracks. A knowledgeable commentator, one Colonel Thoms of the Shanghai Volunteer Corps, was present and noted that the Japanese treated the beginnings of the whole affair "in the light of a picnic ... with speeches, flashlight photography and general gayety." He had also observed the details of the Japanese assembly, the troops being brought up to their departure point at a certain public school by buses. From there, they departed, "at about a quarter to twelve," for various streets leading into Chapei. Thoms also had heard opinions that the Japanese navy "was jealous of the highly successful Manchurian expedition in which the Japanese army participated. The navy hoped to duplicate this success in Shanghai."[15]

Soon, after proceeding a few blocks, the Japanese bluejackets and their cheering companions, "many armed with cameras," were horrified to be met by heavy machine-gun fire from the Chinese sentinels, who were hardly willing simply to give way. Immediately, the Japanese sustained numerous casualties, both killed and wounded. In this way, as one analyst has concluded, "the 'Shanghai Incident of 1932' began. It was to cost the Japanese government an estimated 50,000,000 yen and several thousand lives and the Japanese, Chinese and other foreigners many times that amount in loss of property and trade." Japanese civilians were not alone on this occasion. Hallett Abend, a correspondent for the *New York Times* following a hunch that things were about to happen in Shanghai, had also arrived on the scene. If Admiral Shiozawa believed that the Chinese would run in panic before the Japanese Marines, "he was hideously mistaken," Abend wrote. He then reported on what he regarded as "one of the most bizarre developments of this incredible battle in the heart of a great city." Besides the crowd of Japanese civilians witnessing the events, Abend observed that automobiles began arriving in great numbers and then stopped "to disgorge chattering, laughing groups of American and European men and women in evening clothes." Coming from theaters, hotels and dinner parties, they were attracted by curiosity about the "skirmish" then unfolding. He noted that they "stood around the sloppy streets, smoking cigarettes, occasionally drinking liquor from bottles and enjoying sandwiches and hot coffee procured from nearby cafes which had not yet closed their doors." Many of these, whom Abend labeled as members of "imperialist-minded" Shanghailanders, expressed the hope that the Japanese would teach "the cocky Chinese a good lesson," thereby "saving the white man the job of bringing the Chinese to reason."[16]

The prompt Chinese military response left the Japanese bewildered and in disarray. Nonetheless, they rallied and a line of sorts was established in the maze of streets. This line that "was fixed two hours after the initial shots were fired remained in general unchanged throughout the fighting, which lasted more than a month."[17] The Japanese then quickly landed additional men from nearby ships and moved in some armored cars and began "digging in" with the usual sandbags and barbed wire. Hoping to blast the Chinese out of the area, on the 29th seaplanes began to bomb the Chapei District, causing an outcry in many parts of the world, including from Westerners who had earlier admired Japan. Though unnerved by the attacks, the Chinese defenders held firm.[18]

It was this growing conflict that persuaded various foreign nations, including the United States, to order additional troops to Shanghai. The American secretary of state, Henry L. Stimson, in a telegram to the American consul general at Shanghai, Edwin S. Cunningham, noted that American policy would be "to protect the legitimate rights and interests of American nationals and … to assist toward a settlement by and between the disputants of their differences as soon as possible."

In the meantime, the Western commanders ashore elected Brigadier General Fleming, the British senior officer present as coordinator of—though not the commander of—the International Settlement's defense. At the outset of hostilities these forces consisted of 1,264 American, 2,086 British, 1,008 French, 160 Italians, and 3,000 Japanese troops, and 1,746 members of the Shanghai Volunteer Corps, already being expanded with the influx of new volunteers. By the end of the "incident," the armed forces in the Shanghai area had been greatly increased. While the totals are difficult to ascertain with precision, a U.S. Marine commentator estimated that the number of Japanese troops in Shanghai eventually rose to almost 50 thousand. Other estimates range as high as 100,000. They were supported by 80 warships and more than 300 aircraft.[19]

10. Introduction

As for Shanghai, the new cockpit of war, in those years it had long been a storied place with a colorful past destined to continue to project its mystique into the 21st century. Within China, the city had a reputation for decadence, cosmopolitanism and pluralism, not to mention its "instincts for contrarianism." The American war correspondent Irene Corbally Kuhn, writing in 1945 in the U.S. Army's China (Shanghai) edition of *Stars and Stripes*, recounted something of its appearance and appeal for Westerners in the 1920s and 1930s, which she had witnessed firsthand as a journalist and radio commentator. She described the easy-money situation, with a favorable exchange rate and the methods of payment. One did not need much ready cash, she explained, except "small money," the "twenty cent pieces, the dimes, the coppers and the strings of punched brass discs called 'cash'—[which was] for rickshaw fare and alms." What one did need was "a pencil that always worked. You signed a chit for everything—including the tip for the boy." Collections came on the first day of the month, but one need not pay for months at a time. But then, "on the Chinese New Year—usually late in January—when all honest Chinese pay their bills, the foreign master and missy did too."[20]

A romantic aura permeated the atmosphere, and time evolved in "a graceful and gracious curve" in those years, Kuhn also remembered. And "the white man—and white missy—lived a champagne existence on a near-beer income." One could rent a fine house with modern fixtures and plumbing and a garden and servant's quarters for about thirty dollars a month. As many as eight servants went with the deal and their combined wages equaled the house rent. Shoes could be made to order by a shoe-tailor who came to the house and measured and fitted for shoes for about three dollars a pair. Another tailor made women's clothes of the finest silks. One "merely gave him a picture cut from *Vogue* or a Paris fashion magazine and said 'copy that.' He did. It was perfect—and it was loaded with handwork," all for about six dollars. Alcohol of any variety was plentiful and cheap, and while there were only a few nightclubs they were excellent. One was the original Del Monte, "where they sold ham and eggs at 4 a.m. after the gambling houses had closed downtown." When spring came to Shanghai, Kuhn further noted, "it came softly, on tiptoe. The soft green veiled the willows along Siccawei creek. Their misty green streamers swayed gently and the sun shone warmly." In the city, the Chinese ponies padded around the racecourse and the big sweepstakes fever was on. Every year someone drew a lucky ticket and won $100,000 or more. In other distractions, "houseboats ... [floated] up the canals and waterways to Soochow—the city of beautiful girls." Indeed, "love bloomed among the willows, and under the soft spring moon the Chinese street calls and the click of the food vendors' clappers mingled with the soft sighs of young people." It was, Kuhn concluded, "a lovely world, a lovely time, a lovely city … in those far off days."²¹

A more cynical view of Westerners in Shanghai was held by a certain "Proff. Bojack," who wrote for the journal *Shanghai Sports*. "Shanghai is a town of well lighted streets and well lit visitors," he wrote, and "champagne by the case costs less than hair tonic. And it is much more palatable to the prohibition-tried tourist," it being possible for one to "slip me something east of Suez" without worrying about prohibition officials. Also, he continued, "in spite of the fact that so many European Women are to be seen in Shanghai, it strikes one as a Man's Town. It's like a great big Club. Reminds one of Johannesburg, South Africa." He continued. "Obviously the thing that most impresses the stranger within the gates is the absolute freedom of everyone to do just [as they please]." Shanghai was a place where one would not endanger his social position "if he wears his shorts to church, plays golf in his morning coat, smokes a pipe with the soup course, or spends the evening with champagne, chickens and chat." To be sure, "lots of people go to the devil in Shanghai," he admitted, "but that is not Shanghai's fault." But Shanghai would change, Bojack correctly predicted, and "some day when China quits giving the world a three-reel imitation of the politics of the South American Republics of twenty years ago, she will become one of the world's mightiest industrial centres, and Shanghai will be a great towering city of wealth and learning." Until then, he concluded, suffice it to say "that already plenty of the good things of life are here for those know how to use them." For instance, there were "houseboys to dive under the bed for the elusive collar-button, and come up with it in their teeth and hand it reverentially to complaining Johnnies who never knew what a servant was before they came to Shanghai." These were the people who "used to wash their stiff respectable little necks in a tin basin out on the back stoop in the good Old Days." Indeed, "a family of two has eight servants in Shanghai, they say … more than Rockefeller has in America." When one could solve the servant problem as easily as that, "the dove of domestic harmony is apt to hang about the premises for quite awhile." [Therefore], "it is for the men and women in Shanghai to be grateful for the many things they can get [in China and] be merry and whistle in [their] bath."²² The literature describing the life of Westerners in China in the 1920s and 1930s is vast. One common theme was how rich, abundant and generally enjoyable life was for the average foreigner in those years.²³

Even beyond the interwar period, many, with deep senses of nostalgia, fondly recalled their time in Shanghai. In an article, Ron Gluckman, a reporter writing in the *Wall Street Journal* in September 1996, described a conference convened in Las Vegas which entertained over 1,000 persons from all over

10. Introduction

the world who had lived in China between the world wars. These Old China Hands enthusiastically reminisced about their experiences, especially in Shanghai. It seemed to have been generally accepted that Shanghai represented "the ultimate in excess, a Sodom of Sin on the China coast," though many of the former residents described "pre-war Shanghai as a wide open city of rogues, loose women and non-stop revelry [that] was, if anything, only too tame." They may have exaggerated but recalled that in this city of 40,000 foreigners "there were parties every night, grand parties." One attendee stated that he had traveled all over the world, "but there's nowhere like Shanghai." Another noted that, indeed, "Shanghai was the city that once was and never will be again" and it was in the memory of many "a special place and a special time." Another agreed, observing that "we lived our lives with great panache," and the Old China Hands were "a proud group of people, a diverse group, bound by a special camaraderie." He went on: "We had theater, culture, sports, everything. We didn't know we were magical then, but we were." An aviator who later flew missions during the war for the U.S. Army, and even later for the Nationalists of Chiang-Kai-shek against the Communists, observed that "through it all, we lived an Alice in Wonderland existence," and "we were flying when flying was dangerous and sex was safe." It was World War II that abruptly brought the enchanting arrangement "to a sudden and severe halt." To many Old China Hands, after December 8, 1941—which was December 7 in Pearl Harbor—those who had not escaped earlier, as many others did, were imprisoned by the Japanese and endured many horrors. Even so, others, much more fortunate, while having to exist for many years in a state of privation, found their situation bearable if not unduly oppressive. For some of these, "oddly enough," even their "memories were fond." In addition, during the 1940s, Shanghai became "a haven for Holocaust victims" and some 20,000 Jews from Europe poured in.[24]

Also during those years, Kuhn recalled, Shanghai was notably an American "navy town" and sailors "came tearing into [the city] when the fleet came up from Manila. The grey destroyers stood bow to stern in the Whangpoo off the Customs jetty." The Marines came down from Tientsin [in the late 1930s] once in a while "just to make things good."[25]

Shanghai at war, however, was not so idyllic, and it was into this maelstrom that the 31st Regiment was soon to be ordered. Combat was not unknown to the regiment. It had been created on August 13, 1916, in the Philippines, drawing its initial personnel from the 8th, 13th, 15th and 27th regiments. It took pride in the fact that it was never stationed in the United States in the years between the world wars and was sometimes called the "American Foreign Legion." Though remaining in the Philippines during the

Great War, with the dissolution of the Russian czarist army in the spring of 1918 in the midst of that conflict the Allied War Council decided to send Allied troops to Russia to assist in the withdrawal of Czech troops retreating in the face of Bolshevik forces, as well as to keep the Trans-Siberian railway open and to guard the huge stockpiles of supplies the Allies had shipped there for the Russian army.

A further reason was that Japan was taking advantage of the chaos and the power vacuum in Asiatic Russia. Over 70,000 Japanese troops had entered Siberia with the clear intent of taking control of the region. President Wilson decided to commit American troops, called the American North Russian Expeditionary Force [ANREF], totaling 5,500 men to Archangel in far northwest Russia, where they arrived on August 2, 1918. Additionally, Wilson ordered Major General William Sidney Graves, then commander of the Regular Army's 8th Infantry Division stationed at Camp Fremont, California, to take command of the American Expeditionary Force Siberia [AEFS]. He detached some 5,000 officers and men from the 8th Division and set sail from California on August 15, arriving in Vladivostok on September 1, 1918. In the meantime, two Regular Army infantry regiments, the 27th and the 31st, then stationed in the Philippines, sailed for Vladivostok, on the 27th with 1,590 troops, landing on August 16, and the 31st on August 21 with its 1,421 troops. They were soon in action, and as was true of all the American forces engaged in Russia, the service was arduous in the extreme. Indeed, the Siberian Expeditionary Force served under combat conditions longer than any other American force involved in the Great War. Its valor was recognized by the award of one Medal of Honor and fifteen Distinguished Service Crosses to individuals of the regiment. In its involvement in Siberia, the 31st lost at least one officer and twenty-nine enlisted men killed, with eight more dying of wounds received in action. Fifty-two more were wounded but recovered. Diseases and non-battle casualties claimed 135 additional lives.[26]

The outfit returned to the Philippines on April 1, 1920, and were ever after styled the "Polar Bears" in recognition of their Russian service. The return to Manila was not pleasant for many of the troops. Some had married Russian women in Siberia and had to arrange for their transportation to Manila, not an easy task. When they did get there, housing proved to be a problem that was only eventually sorted out.[27]

After returning from Russia, the 31st spent the ensuing eleven years in the usual duties of garrison life, though there was one notable exception. In August of 1923, Japan was wracked with a massive earthquake, a huge tidal wave and numerous fires which "nearly leveled the Japanese cities in the coastal area." Tokyo sent out frantic appeals to the world for relief. The U.S.

War Department responded, radioing headquarters of the 31st Infantry to dispatch a group of officers and men with supplies to Kobe and Yokohama. This the regiment did, though its records are sketchy as to the extent of its activities there. In any event, following this episode, a more or less somnolent era of existence then ensued, with little indication of what was to transpire abruptly in early 1932.[28]

11

THE 31ST UNITED STATES INFANTRY REGIMENT IN CHINA

The regiment's normal garrison activities in the Philippines included, among other things, field exercises. For example, on January 19, 1932, the outfit, for the occasion made up of thirty-five officers and 605 enlisted men and designated the "Red Force," engaged in maneuvers with a "Blue Force" near Manila. They continued until the evening of January 20, and the commander of the 31st, Colonel Lorenzo Dow Gasser, was pleased to report that, while his men and officers were "very tired," they nonetheless had maintained a "very high" morale and aggressive spirit throughout.[1]

Whatever might have been learned in the maneuvers, orders were soon received that would catapult the troops into a shooting war in an entirely different setting, further testing the men's "morale and aggressive spirit." On January 31, a conference was convened by President Herbert Hoover at the White House with the secretaries of state, war and navy and other key personnel to address the deteriorating situation in China. Specifically, they responded to the request of the American consul general in Shanghai, Edwin S. Cunningham, and ranking naval officers there, for further protection of American citizens in the International Settlement. Accordingly, the 31st Regiment was soon involved, together with 400 Marines. The cruiser *Houston* and six destroyers left Manila on January 31 in support. Orders for the 31st were conveyed to the Philippine Department on the same day—January 31—in a radiogram from the army chief of staff, General Douglas MacArthur. Addressed to the commanding general of the Philippine Department, Major General John L. Hines, it ordered the 31st to Shanghai "to protect the lives and property of United States citizens."[2]

The following morning, February 1, at 8:30, the officers of the regiment were issued a "verbal warning order" to execute the plan of movement. Quite complex, the order stipulated that the regiment's Post of Manila and its property, installations and records were to be placed in the custody of the 45th Infantry Regiment stationed at Fort McKinley, about seven miles distant from Manila. In addition, detachments from the Philippine Department's Medical, Signal, and Quartermaster corps, and Finance and Ordnance departments and personnel of the Chemical Warfare Service were attached to the 31st. Several junior officers from the units at Fort McKinley were also transferred to the regiment, bringing its officer strength up to the levels of the current tables of organization. Three days' field rations and medical combat equipment were drawn by S-4, and ammunition was issued in the amounts prescribed in the Tables of Basic Allowances, as were heavy tents, cots and mosquito bars. Finally, the regiment's vehicles, consisting of one staff car and eleven light trucks, were drawn and prepared for shipment.[3]

Moving expeditiously, the men embarked at 10:40 p.m. on February 1 on the Navy troop transport USS *Chaumont* (AP-5) and sailed at 4:10 on the following morning.[4] One report noted, "Thus, in the space of less than 12 hours, the regiment, which had been in the same barracks for 12 years, had effected a complete transition from a garrison duty status in the tropics to one [of] preparedness for field service in winter weather and in a foreign country." Their speedy preparations were a remarkable achievement by any standard and were accomplished "without confusion and with great zeal and enthusiasm."[5]

While the ship was underway, rations were supplied by the navy, and the feeding of the troops was handled by the ship, though the troops furnished the messing details. The ship also operated an excellent canteen and provided "talkie" movies on the aft-deck. Though rather crowded, as is common on troopships, the men were all furnished with standee bunks or cots and were generally comfortable. Morale was high, and an air of great expectancy prevailed. En route, the medical staff inoculated the troops against cholera. The men also received strict orders against the use of certain native foods in messes. The weather soon turned cold as the ship took up a northerly course around the west side of the Philippine Islands, and at reveille on February 4 the men changed their khaki uniforms for "ancient stocks of World War I woolens."[6]

Those in command, having gotten the trip underway, turned to the details of their mission in China. In a memorandum to the troops, Colonel Gasser stressed the international character of the work at hand, which under the circumstances was controlled by martial law. The 31st would be associated with the armed forces of other nations and also subjected to the critical scrutiny of these, as well as of foreign civilians. Accordingly, the strictest

USS *Chaumont*. This ship was a familiar troop carrier in the Far East in the 1920s and 1930s. The men of the 31st Infantry sailed from Manila to Shanghai on this ship in 1932 (courtesy of U.S. Naval History and Heritage Command).

discipline and soldierly conduct in the performance of their duties was expected.[7]

Information obtainable at sea of the situation in Shanghai was meager, especially regarding the International Settlement. The questions as to whether disturbances or riots were rampant could only be surmised. Similarly, much discussion resulted in the formation of a contingency plan for forcing a landing under fire, covered by machine-gun and howitzer support from the *Chaumont*. In addition, there was uncertainty regarding the site of docking. At 5:30 p.m. on February 4, however, debarkation orders were published. They directed the issuance of two sandwiches per man, the filling of canteens and the establishment of ammunition and ration distribution points. Pending final arrangements, the *Chaumont* dropped anchor at 10:55 a.m., February 5, eighteen miles out of Shanghai; but soon, at 1:15 p.m. she resumed her journey up the Whangpoo River. The last hours were filled with apprehension because the last few miles found the ship between the Chinese guns of Fort Woosung and the batteries of the Japanese warships with which the fort had been engaged. Japanese aircraft were also busily bombing parts of the city and the sound of gunfire was clearly audible "to the eagerly watching troops, who crowded the decks." Surprisingly, though, as one observer has recorded, "as if by mutual agreement, the opponents held all fire during the passage of the *Chaumont*, thus relieving the tension among the troops on board."[8] Then, without further ado, after traveling 1,122 miles, the *Chaumont* moored at the Commerce Company docks in Shanghai at 4:35 p.m. on February 5. There the regiment, which numbered sixty-five officers and 1,113 enlisted men, was placed under the commanding officer of the 4th United States Marines, Colonel R.S. Hooker, who was in charge of all American troops ashore. He was subordinate to the commander-in-chief, U.S. Asiatic Fleet, Admiral Montgomery M. Taylor, who was in command of all American Forces in Shanghai.[9]

The men thereupon began off-loading their supplies, while a contingent of troops charged with billet procurement was dispatched to the New World Building in the International Settlement to begin preparing it to receive troops the following day. After a busy but uneventful night, at 7:15 a.m., on February 6, the troops departed the ship. With the regiment's band playing at the head of the column, the men marched off the docks to their billets. They noted an air of ominous expectancy pervading the streets, which were "scantily peopled for such a populous city." Shops and stores were boarded up, and heavily armed police were everywhere. Most of the regiment established its billets at the New World Building, at the intersection of Nanking and Thibet roads, while the First Battalion continued one-half mile to another site under the main grandstand of the Shanghai Race Course.[10] Two days later, a historical event occurred when, at 3:00 p.m. on February 7, the first garrison flag ever to fly over a United States Army station in Shanghai was raised.[11]

Meanwhile, shortly after the United States Army forces in Shanghai—sometimes referred to as "Detachment 31st Infantry"—arrived, they were deployed, accompanied by the sound of Japanese and Chinese gunfire. The men were needed because the troops that had protected the settlement, notably men of the Shanghai Volunteer Corps, were exhausted. Plans were made to get the "Polar Bears" into action at once. They were initially distributed from the North Station and along Soochow Creek in the sector opposite Chapei, where the heaviest fighting was occurring.

Field Order No. 1, issued from regimental headquarters in the New World Building in the International Settlement and dated February 8, 1932, detailed the situation and what the regiment was expected to accomplish.[12] Therein the regimental commander, Colonel Lorenzo D. Gasser, surveyed the situation, noting that the Chinese and Japanese were engaged in armed conflict along the general line of the eastern edge of the Chapei District of

Shanghai. The Chinese had massed about 6,200 troops in the district with another force of about 3,800 in and around the Woosung Fort about ten miles north of the city. A Japanese force of approximately 4,500 was located in the Chapei and Hongkew districts within Shanghai, with another contingent of 3,000 just south of Woosung Creek near Fort Woosung. Defending the International Settlement was the Shanghai Volunteer Corps, situated on the left flank of the 31st and also in front of the right portion of the U.S. Army sector. The French were to the south of the Americans, with the 4th Marines to the west. Italian and British troops were west of the Marine Sector, in their respective sectors. The U.S. Army Sector was bounded on the east by the Honan Road, on the south by Avenue Edward VII—which was the northern boundary of the French Settlement. The west side included the Stone Bridge, Myburg Road and Mohawk Road. The northern boundary was formed by the infamously malodorous Soochow Creek. The mission was to "take over and protect American lives and property" within the sector known in the International Defense Scheme as the "U.S. Army Sector." They were to cooperate with the Shanghai Volunteer Corps, other foreign forces and the Municipal Police. The 31st took over its initial positions by relieving the Royal Scots Fusiliers on February 9, 1932, at 2:00 p.m.[13]

The U.S. Army Sector was subdivided into the "North Sector" and the "South Sector." In this setup, the 2nd Battalion occupied a line along the south bank of Soochow Creek, including the headquarters of the Sinza Police Station, the Louza Police Station and Tientsin Road. Its billets were then at 352 Bubbling Well Road. It was charged with defense along Soochow Creek and was to allow no one to cross that line, "except those permitted by the Municipal Police." In no case would armed persons, except those in the organized forces of the International Settlement, be allowed to pass. If Chinese soldiers retreated toward the line seeking protection, they were to be allowed to enter but were to be disarmed and turned over to the police.

In the area south of the same line, known as the "South Sector," the 1st Battalion, usually headquartered at the Temple of Heaven, was specifically charged with preventing the formation of mobs and were to protect lives and property in cooperation with the Municipal Police. It was also responsible for the local defense of regimental billets. The 3rd Battalion, which constituted the regimental reserve together with the howitzer platoon and regimental headquarters, had their billets in the New World Building.[14]

Throughout its time in Shanghai, the 31st, while not directly involved in action, did endure fire on numerous occasions when Chinese and Japanese troops fired wildly at each other around the settlement's perimeter, but no member of the regiment was ever hit. Had they been engaged, however, they were well organized and supplied and could have given a good account of themselves. The howitzer platoon had two 75 mm howitzers, the machine gun companies (D, H and M) each had sixteen .30 caliber water-cooled machine guns, and each rifle company had four air-cooled .30 caliber guns. An ammunition supply point was established near each blockhouse and an ammunition reserve was kept at each battalion headquarters. Extra rifle ammunition, grenades, tear gas candles and magazines for automatic rifles were kept in forward positions for each relief. The reinforcement routes were kept clear and guides were posted at key points to ensure that reinforcements could reach their stations by day or night. The "Regiment's Diary" routinely listed the rifle, machine gun and pistol ammunition the regiment possessed: 278,400 rounds of .30 caliber ball ammunition; 16,240 rounds of .30 caliber armor piercing; 15,000 rounds of .30 caliber, tracer; and 13,250 rounds of .45 caliber ball ammunition. Apparently the U.S. troops did not fire even one round in the course of the entire incident, as these figures, listed as "Ammunition Unexpended," were always unchanged. Other munitions on hand, such as grenades and howitzer shells, were not recorded in these reports.[15]

The men were able to use numerous buildings as guard posts, including several blockhouses, which were permanent defense installations in the International Settlement. Each was completely equipped with urinals, electric lights, telephones, searchlights and electric heaters. Some were of steel construction, though others were made of brick or reinforced concrete. They provided protection against small-arms fire but were of no value against artillery. The blockhouses were equipped with steel observation turrets, machine-gun mounts, rifle ports, and heavy steel sliding doors on all openings. Other sheltered sites included unoccupied or unfinished buildings or sandbag redoubts. Observation posts were set up on the roofs of prominent buildings such as an unoccupied Chinese hospital. The regiment's communications platoon established and maintained wiring systems keeping all units in close touch with each other. First-aid men from the medical detachment were attached to each front-line company, though it turned out there was no need for any medical care except minor treatments of the front-line troops as no casualties were suffered by the men from gunfire. Regular sick calls were attended by the surgeon stationed for front-line duty or in the rear area billets. If evacuations were needed, trucks were to be used to take casualties to the Shanghai General Hospital, though the regiment later set up its own hospital and was prepared to handle its own evacuations.[16]

As for conduct, Field Order No. 1 directed that every reasonable means was to be taken to avoid clashes. Gunfire was to be opened against mobs "only to save lives or prevent destruction of property, and then only as a means of last resort and at the discretion of a commissioned officer." If shooting was deemed necessary, it was "desirable to disable rather than kill." Throughout, the men were to use tact and diplomacy instead of bullets and bayonets if at all possible. This was in keeping with a directive in a radiogram from the chief of Naval Operations, Admiral William V. Pratt, to the commander-in-chief, U.S. Asiatic Fleet, Admiral Montgomery M. Taylor. This directive ordered all United States forces engaged in Shanghai to observe "utmost forbearance and make effort by conciliation to [re]move any friction that may develop between American and other defense units.... [The] United States Government desires that every reasonable means possible be taken to avoid clash[es] between American and Japanese forces."[17] The field order did stipulate, however, that batons or clubs could be used upon unarmed crowds and that bayonets were habitually to be fixed. All personnel leaving billets were to be armed and only two or more persons were to travel together. Command posts were also set up and details as to sentries, initial ammunition issues and reserves, and routine duty matters and dispositions were stipulated. In addition, each unit was to be prepared to relieve or support any other unit, and several specific city utilities, such as gas works, the telephone exchange, various pumping stations, and certain markets, were to be placed under guard by the regiment if requested by the Municipal Police.

In the midst of this action, the troops also had to rebuild barricades and string up wire and patrol and protect two miles of wire and fortifications, all the while maintaining order in the surrounding city overflowing with refugees whose numbers multiplied daily. This was done despite an occasional shell landing in the International Settlement or a ricocheting bullet "pinging down the streets." A curfew was in place in the troops' sector, making the nights easier, though the fighting opposite them became more intense after nightfall. They were often most uncomfortable when cold, drizzling rains descended, resulting in long, sleepless nights. To ease matters, hot meals were transported to the men at their posts by truck three times daily, and a Salvation Army car made the rounds with hot coffee and other refreshments for those on guard duty in the frigid weather.[18]

Within the International Settlement the situation was rather fluid as the weeks rolled by. One factor of considerable concern was that Japanese forces were using the sectors of other nations within the settlement for both offensive and defensive operations, thereby infringing upon the neutrality of the area. The United States and Britain strenuously protested. The Japanese did respond, and the British and American sectors were cleared of all Japanese posts and patrols by February 4, though the Japanese were guilty of sporadic encroachment.[19]

As time passed, another development intruded. Both Chinese and Japanese armed civilian irregulars began functioning as snipers and in other ways disrupted their foes' operations. These activities proved to be among the most effective of any taken in a more organized fashion, especially among the Chinese forces. Regarding these, one analyst has concluded, "It is not too much to say that the most important offensive actions taken by any Chinese forces during the whole 'Shanghai incident' were taken by these irregulars." In fact, he went on, "if their attacks, which were the only attacks worthy of the name, had been coordinated and timed with offensives by the Chinese troops in Chapei, the Japanese positions and lines could have been very seriously threatened." Among the Chinese civilians engaged there sprang up various patriotic societies that contributed money and food supplies to assist their soldiers. In addition, an anti-Japanese "dare to die" corps was formed to lend armed support to the 19th Route Army engaged in the action. Despite their successes, however, irregulars also caused disruptions and perpetrated excesses within the Chinese areas, sometimes using their arms to settle scores with their personal enemies.

Other disturbances were fomented by the Chinese. For instance, during the evening of March 4 considerable surprise was experienced when the sound of heavy explosions, which became increasingly frequent, was heard near the French Concession and around the waterfront of the Whangpoo River. There were fears of a major Chinese attack or an attack by Japanese destroyers. The noise, however, was the result of a monster firecracker demonstration by the Chinese inhabitants in the French Concession, celebrating the purported deaths of high Japanese military and naval authorities, great reverses inflicted on the field of battle by the Chinese 19th Route Army, and the sinking of numerous Japanese warships, "all a tissue of malicious falsehoods widely broadcast by countless gratuitous copies of the Chinese vernacular 'mosquito' press." The huge firecrackers were distributed from trucks that circulated through the city. The whole affair was an organized attempt by agitators to create disorder. Troops of the 31st were alerted for riot duty, but the Chinese Municipal Police handled the matter and dispersed the "good-natured crowds" to their homes.[20]

The Japanese also had trouble with their irregulars, accordingly decided that "armed civilians are a menace to even friendly forces," and discouraged their use, claiming that these "gangsters" were being sent back to Japan, though they were too valuable for both sides and they remained in use throughout the conflict.[21]

In the meantime, while the men of the 31st were en route and then getting situated, the fighting in Shanghai intensified, with artillery duels flaring up.

The Japanese mounted a general attack on February 3 with almost 6,000 men, many of whom had been hastily shipped in from Japan. The Chinese countered by sending an additional 4,000 troops from the 19th Route Army into the embattled areas. The attack began shortly after midnight (the Japanese favoring night actions), but it was beaten back with considerable Japanese losses and the Chinese held their positions. In the air, the Japanese continued some bombing attacks but also lost a few aircraft to Chinese fighter planes. The Japanese decided to remain chiefly on the defensive in the Chapei area, though they continued artillery bombardments.[22]

From February 9 through 13, just as the 31st was moving into position in the settlement, both the Chinese and Japanese intensified their artillery attacks and sought to cross Woosung Creek north of the city, but they met with "spirited resistance" and made little headway. Both sides brought up reinforcements, and the Japanese vice admiral Nomura arrived onboard his flag ship, the cruiser *Idzumo*, to replace Admiral Shiozawa in command of the Japanese forces in the Shanghai area.[23]

The Japanese then took control of the Hongkew District inside the settlement, which was heavily populated by Japanese. A reign of terror among the resident Chinese ensued and many executions and other excesses were committed by Japanese marines, reserves and irregulars, who were still present in some numbers. The irregulars, in particular, seemed largely motivated by a "spirit of revenge against the Chinese for earlier anti–Japanese activities." As a result, the non–Japanese population fled the area and all municipal activities of the settlement authorities in the district were curtailed, including that of the fire brigade.[24]

By the middle of February, the situation was stabilized, at least nominally, except for intermittent artillery, machine-gun and rifle fire. In fact, Shanghai was waiting—"in fear and trembling"—for the launching of an expected major Japanese drive calculated to force the Chinese army from the city. These apprehensions were not to be realized, however, because the Japanese failed to drive the Chinese out.

At this juncture it was decided in Tokyo that the Japanese army was to take over from the navy and marines in forcing events in the Shanghai area. On February 13, the Japanese 9th Division began landing just north of Shanghai. They changed their emphasis to targets between Shanghai and the Woosung Fort where the Whangpoo and Yangtze rivers join, and from February 20 to February 25 they especially focused on Chiangwan and Miaohang. Under the command of General Kenkichi Ueda, these forces, initially numbering over 7,000 men and supported by numerous ships and armored vehicles and artillery, hoped to succeed where the marines had failed. In general, regarding reinforcements, the Japanese had the better of it, as they had more aircraft, superior and heavier armaments, a world-class navy, adequate supplies of ammunition and greater discipline and military efficiency coupled with a "complete unity of purpose" calculated to prevail over the Chinese. Nonetheless, the Chinese countered with reinforcements. These were notably men under the direct command of Chiang, the 87th and 88th divisions of the 5th Army, an elite national guard outfit well equipped and ably advised by German military officers. The Chinese troops soon forced setbacks of the initial Japanese efforts in this area. Later in February further attempts by the Japanese army were repulsed and a request was made to Tokyo to send in two more divisions, the 11th and the 14th. The Chinese also began constructing elaborate new lines about twenty miles west of the fort to which they would soon retire.[25]

Meanwhile, the 31st Regiment, in the midst of the action in their close proximity, frequently rotated formations in their sector, always keeping one battalion in regimental reserve. They also periodically exchanged duty assignments with the Shanghai Volunteer Corps or men of the British Argylls, the Sutherland Highlanders, the Royal Scots Fusiliers, and other units.[26]

On February 20, 1932, an event typical of those that men of the regiment witnessed during these days was reported near the regiment's north sector. This broke out when a Japanese armored car took up station about ten feet from Blockhouse B, manned by men of the 31st. A "sharp engagement" broke out involving the 37 mm artillery piece, two machine guns which the armored car carried and Chinese machine guns in a nest in a second story of a nearby building. The Americans cheered on one Chinese machine gunner they had dubbed "Charlie Chan." They watched, appreciative of "Chan's" considerable skill with a machine gun and applauded his effective use of "potato-masher" grenades, with which he was plentifully supplied. After a sharp fight of some minutes, during which the bullets and grenade fragments frequently rained own on Blockhouse B, the Japanese withdrew, leaving "Chan" in command of the situation, to the gratification of the Americans, who subsequently referred to the battle site as "Windy Corner." Snipers then became active along most of the Regimental Sector during the early hours of darkness. Fortunately, there were no American casualties and, they being, of course, unengaged, they expended no ammunition.[27]

Four days later, February 24, 1932, moderate rifle, machine gun and trench mortar fire was heard throughout the night and the day, considerable shelling occurring in the vicinity of the north railway station. For about a quarter of an hour American troops located in Blockhouse C in their defense line came under fire and had to take cover from bursting shrapnel

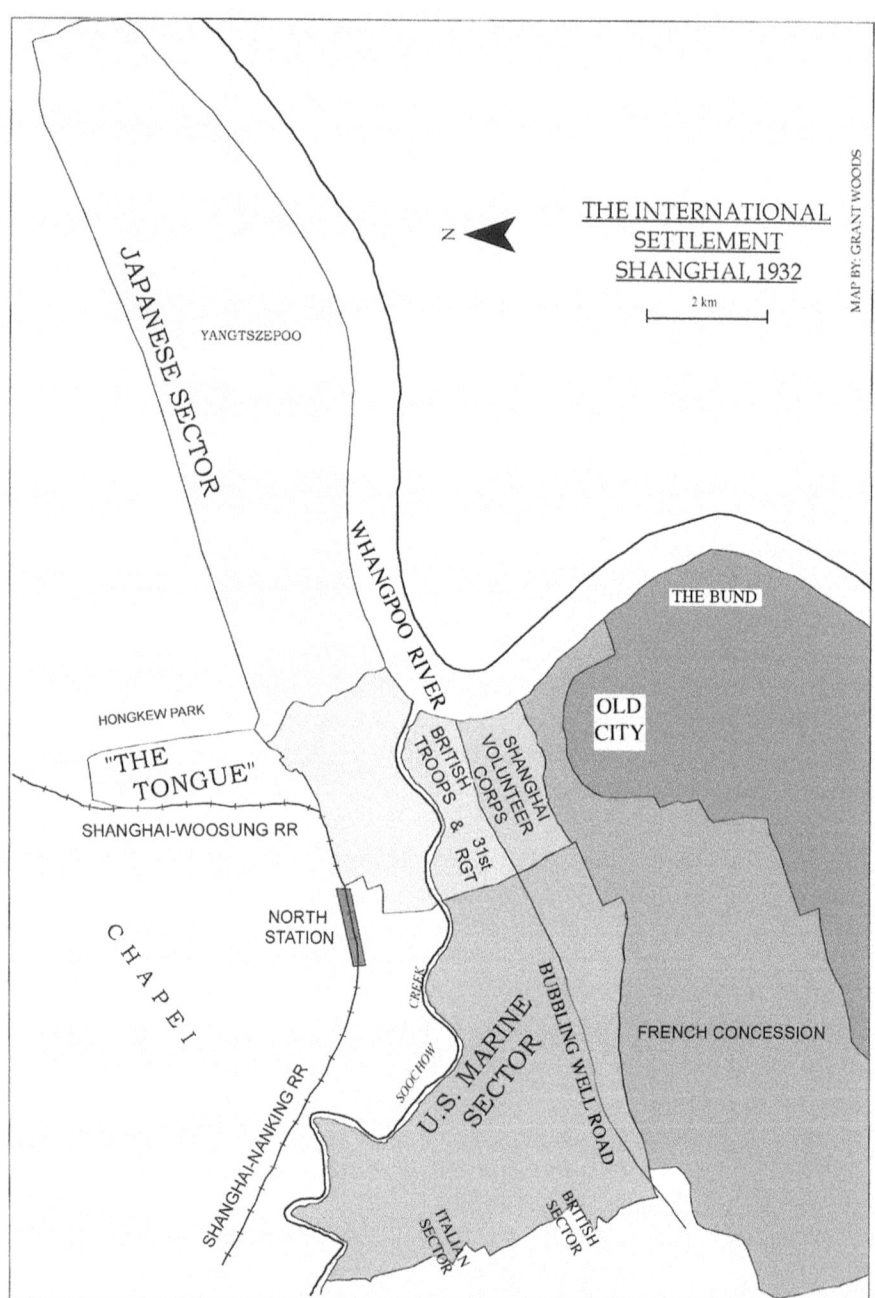

Map of the International Settlement as of 1932, where the 31st Infantry Regiment was engaged (map by Grant Woods).

in their area, but they sustained no casualties nor did they expend any ammunition.[28]

In other common occurrences, Western troops often "angrily watched barbarity and inhumanity taking place on a bewildering scale," but they were not allowed to intervene. Sometimes Chinese soldiers and police executed officials and others suspected of collaborating or fraternizing with the Japanese. Elsewhere, Japanese officers wielding Samurai swords could be seen beheading captured Chinese officers, suspected spies, snipers, and public officials. One historian has noted that, regarding the Japanese atrocities, "age and gender meant nothing. The Chinese people were victims of every side. Unless they lived inside the International Settlement, they had no one to turn to for protection."[29]

Meanwhile, the conditions of service for the 31st Regiment were governed by their initial restriction to quarters, which was apparently "received by all with a most commendable spirit." This was necessary because "the situation within and without the Settlement [was] so acute that the entire command had to be kept in readiness for employment at a moment's notice." In addition, intensive training, stressing the bayonet, exterior guard duty, riot control, and combat practice, was begun immediately and became ongoing, the nearby grounds of the Shanghai Race Course being used as a drill field. With an easing of the situation, beginning on February 13, passes were granted to half of the command for a time of 2:00 p.m. to 8:00 p.m.[30]

While the 31st's troops were engaged in their duties in Shanghai, one of their continuing activities involved upgrading their living quarters and enhancing their creature comforts. Their billets were at first haphazardly chosen and changes had to be made immediately. The first selection of a billeting committee had been the New World Building out on Nanking Road near the Shanghai Race Track. The building had been used for theatrical productions, and the winter winds "whistled in" through the ill-fitting windows. Only four small stoves, supposed to heat the entire structure, were installed. There was no running water nor conveniences or comforts of any kind. "Into this space, scarcely big enough for a battalion," the entire regiment was to fit. The men were first bunked almost shoulder to shoulder, with some overflowing into the corridors. Field ranges were speedily set up and other changes were made. As to improving their uniforms, the regiment, "with traditional American Army pride of service," began to employ "the ubiquitous Chinese tailor." Regarding the barracks, much-needed additions were soon secured. A large private house with a spacious garden out on Seymour Road was acquired for a hospital. Up Nanking Road, at 352 Bubbling Well Road, a "horse bazaar," with concrete main floor and wide, rough-board upper floors enclosed by storefronts, became the billet of the 2nd Battalion. Belying the name of the road it was located on, the building was initially without running water and just about anything else that might contribute to comfortable quarters. A little farther up the road, a large building with an open space in front became the billet of the 1st Battalion. All the quarters were less than 800 yards apart on Nanking Road, generally along the northern side of the midtown racetrack.[31]

As time went on, other improvements were made. On March 7, the men's footlockers, together with 159 replacements, arrived in Shanghai on board the U.S. Army transport *Grant*, both of which made their lives more tolerable. Bamboo bows were devised to hold individual mosquito nets in place. Soon, water was piped into the quarters, and showers and water closets, replacing wooden-seated bucket latrines, were installed. Chinese-made refrigerators were supplied. New stoves were improvised by using bricks to elevate the field ranges, and boiler plate, previously used as stove tops, were replaced by sheet-iron plates of large size, making as fine a stove as any "first class" cook could want. Corridors were modified into office spaces, and lumber was provided from which office tables, mess tables, typewriter and office desks were constructed. Chinese barbers and tailors were squeezed in where possible. An empty lot next door to the New World Building was cleared of rubbish and a battalion mess hall went up.[32]

As these events unfolded, at times the sentiments of the American officials in China regarding developing events surfaced. The minister to China, Nelson Trusler Johnson, in a telegram to the secretary of state, once advised that the U.S. government should make strong representations at Tokyo and challenge the arguments of the Japanese that they were defending the settlement against Chinese attack and that they therefore had a right to land forces there to protect Japanese life and property. In fact, Johnson argued, the International Settlement was not being attacked by the Chinese. While it was true that Japanese life and property were in danger, "this [was because] the Japanese [were] pursuing [a] policy here in Shanghai and elsewhere in China with which we have neither sympathy nor part." Without coupling such overtures with some threat of force or other coercive measures, this stance was quite weak, as was his other ploy, that of warning Tokyo that "we must hold [the] Japanese Government accountable for all damage done to American life and property in this area," of which Johnson indicated that there was already considerable and "a great deal more will be damaged or destroyed before this is over."[33]

Meanwhile, on February 19, the Japanese sent an ultimatum to General Tsai Ting-Kai, commander of the Chinese 19th Route Army, from the Japanese general Ueda, and Mayor Wu was sent another by the Japanese Consul General. The Japanese demanded a withdrawal of Chinese troops some twenty kilometers north and west of Shanghai and the removal of all fortifications and military works upon departure. The note to the mayor indicated that the present actions of the 19th Route Army were the consequence of his failure to carry out the immediate dissolution of the anti–Japanese movements as promised in his note of 28 January. In view of this lapse, the "Japanese authorities would be obliged to take such measures as they [thought] proper."[34]

In both cases, the Chinese rejected the demands, General Tsai simply indicating that Ueda's note was being "submitted to higher authority." The mayor's response was more pointed, reiterating that the "grave situation in Shanghai [was] due to the presence of your troops in violation of all international law." He stated further that "as acts of provocation by attack, bombing and bombardment, continue intensified, the indignation of our people remain united. Under the circumstances it is natural that anti–Japanese measures cannot fail to continue. The responsibility rests with you."[35]

These reactions reveal that the successes of the 19th Route Army, which had "won for itself the gratitude of the mass of Chinese," especially the Cantonese, had stiffened the Chinese resolve to resist the Japanese to a considerable degree, even among Chinese business men who had earlier opposed this course. The Japanese ultimatums and steadily increased use of force also caused a loss of sympathy for their cause among Americans and other nationals.[36]

It is noteworthy that the 19th Route Army was a Cantonese force and its successes created much envy and jealousy among other political leaders and military commanders within China, as well as tensions between the 19th's commanders and Chiang Kai-shek himself. These facts have to do with internal Chinese conflicts among the Communists, the Cantonese and the Nanking government as Chiang was struggling to establish his control over China.[37]

In the event, Chiang later hardly rewarded the 19th Route Army as it richly deserved. Its leaders were subsequently shipped to Foochow, in Fukien province, where, with little support, they nearly starved. A new rebellion thereupon arose in Foochow in December 1933 against Chiang's Nanking government. It was brutally crushed when Nanking employed air attacks (taking a lesson from the Japanese bombardment of Chapei the year before), which left a seething, bitter hatred of Chiang.[38]

Meanwhile, the Japanese were making little headway in their most recent military attempts to force the Chinese out. This put increasing pressure on

Japan, which wanted to get out of the Shanghai "mess" "if she could with honor but knew no way out, that she could not afford defeat." In any case, Japan factitiously argued that she "could not leave European nations in the lurch by retiring in the face of Chinese force"![39]

At the end of February, Cunningham surveyed the situation and drew some sweeping conclusions: "In initiating the Shanghai naval adventure with a handful of marines the Japanese naval commander completely misjudged the resistance of the Chinese and now in attempting to sweep the environs of Shanghai clear of the 19th Route Army ... they have blundered a second time." This came about because, although Chiang Kai-shek once again advocated nonresistance, the locally garrisoned 19th Route Army under Cai Tingkai fought back and put up a much better performance than the Japanese expected. Thus, "the penalty of the second miscalculation has been that the much heralded push of General Ueda with the 9th Division has come to a complete standstill and now the Japanese are awaiting the arrival of the 11th and 14th Divisions of approximately 30,000 men which are alleged to be on the way from Japan." These began arriving on February 28, landing north of Shanghai. In any case, the Japanese failures had relieved some of the anxieties of the citizens of Shanghai. Unlike the situation from the Japanese point of view, "in the defense of Shanghai the Chinese have attained a higher morale and a more complete coordination of military effort than has ever previously been realized." These successes had led, however, to Japanese frustration resulting in much brutality, and the Japanese killed many civilians, perhaps as many as 6,000. But the Japanese losses were also significant, perhaps as many as 2,000, many of them the victims of armed Chinese irregulars.[40]

In late February, some order was noted by the Americans by a report of "no change in the local situation," in the American Sector and the men busied themselves with routine maintenance of communications, the gathering of intelligence, and company administration, while the 2nd Battalion replaced some wire entanglements in the sector. The weather was cold, with snow developing. The men's health and morale were excellent and no casualties were reported.[41]

By now, both Japan and China were weary of hostilities, holding out hope for the end of the fighting. This led to a meeting on February 28 between Admiral Nomura and Yosuke Matsuoka, at their request, and their Chinese opposites. The meeting took place onboard the British ship HMS *Kent*, anchored at Shanghai, the initiators seeking a brokered agreement as to mutual and simultaneous evacuations, which was soon agreed to in principle.[42]

At about this juncture, Stella Benson, a well-known novelist and travel

Top: The Shanghai bund was a familiar sight to the men of the 31st Infantry Regiment when they served in that city in 1932 (courtesy of Virtual Shanghai Project, Image ID 126, http://virtualshanghai.net). *Bottom:* Soochow Creek, Shanghai, where the men of the 31st Regiment were most closely engaged in 1932. This view is in 2011 (photograph by the author).

writer who also served as a correspondent for *New Yorker* magazine, presented some rather cynical observations regarding the extent of the conflict in Shanghai, greatly downplaying events there and clearly writing after the fighting had ceased in the city. She had just returned from "the Seat of War, but nobody was sitting in it at the time," she primly declared. Many of her friends and associates had expressed concerns about her safety when they learned that she was there but she discounted their apprehensions, reporting that only a few weeks prior to her Shanghai visit, she had been in Kobe and Yokohama and heard no "clanking martial tread, no tocsin sounding to call the people to war, but only bicycle bells." Shortly after that, she "drove round a perfectly peaceful Shanghai, conscious of no tremors for the future more acute than my doubt whether the taxi would hold together." While many were elsewhere discussing the war clouds that hung heavily over Shanghai, she noticed only snow clouds and "the pall of imminent snow" over the city, where such flakes were rarely seen. As for the subjects of general conversation, she had heard much talk about golf and other mundane matters. She, in fact, did not notice any traces of war at all. During the night of her departure she did not hear guns in the distance as some might expect. Rather, she went on, "I heard nothing but the deafening crackings and bumpings of freight and baggage being put on board [a ship]." Furthermore, it was a Japanese ship and "surely Chinese waterside laborers wouldn't help to load a Japanese ship at a time of tension like that! I hate to disappoint you," she concluded, "but they did. Everybody seemed quite happy as they loaded. The coolies even sang a good deal." Benson had apparently not visited the Chapei District. Nonetheless, her report places the "Shanghai Incident" in a somewhat different perspective.[43]

Despite the truce talks, and now the truce having been reinforced, on February 29 the Japanese began massive operations starting at Chapei and extending north to the Yangtze River. The decisive action, however, came on March 1, when the newly arrived Japanese 11th Division launched a flanking attack near Liu Ho, at the mouth of the Liu River that flows into the Yangtze northwest of Shanghai. It was this event that caused dramatic developments in Shanghai. At 2:00 a.m., on March 2, the Chinese 19th Route Army and the two divisions of the 5th Army, realizing that they were now outflanked, chose voluntarily to begin withdrawing from Chapei and other territory north of Shanghai, taking up new substantial positions already prepared about twenty miles west of the city. This left the Japanese in control of the area around the International Settlement, except for isolated Chinese snipers. The strategic retreat was accomplished in secrecy and conducted in an orderly fashion without interference by the Japanese, who were taken completely by surprise.

This action greatly simplified the situation of the international forces in the settlement.[44]

As a consequence, on March 3, both the Chinese and Japanese high commands ordered cease-fires, each asserting that they would not resume hostile action unless attacked. Significantly, the Japanese, in late February, had announced the creation of the new Manchurian state of Manchukuo and on March 1 placed the Manchu Prince P'u Yi on the throne as the puppet emperor. Therefore, the diversion, which the Shanghai venture was in part, was no longer needed. Simultaneously, the Russians were massing troops on the Russian-Manchurian border, and the jittery Japanese had need for additional soldiers there. The Japanese stated that they had ceased hostilities "because they had attained their object; that the Chinese had retired [a] sufficient distance" as Japan had earlier demanded. Some sporadic actions did ensue subsequently, but as "the Asian Gods of War" had apparently "decided on a temporary recess" life rapidly returned to normal in Shanghai.[45]

Elsewhere, the coming of a cease-fire prompted the Assembly of the League of Nations, then in session in Geneva, to pass a resolution on the afternoon of March 4, 1932, calling upon China and Japan to "take immediately the necessary measures to ensure that the orders which ... had been issued by the military commanders on both sides for the cessation of hostilities, shall be made effective." It is clear, nonetheless, that the league, with its hands full with the Manchurian crisis, strongly desired that the Shanghai matter be settled locally. With no armed forces at its disposal and no nation inclined to intervene in the Sino-Japanese conflict, the assembly could only "recommend" that negotiations be entered into by the combatants "with the assistance of the military, naval and civilian authorities of the powers" interested in the Shanghai matter, i.e., Italy, Britain, France and the United States, toward seeking a permanent settlement. The outcome, though, would ultimately, after 1937, be as the Japanese willed it. Rather pathetically, and reflecting the weakness of the West at this time in China, Stimson gave pious lip service to China's well-being, hoping that throughout the proceedings "China's interests are not being jeopardized."[46]

Following the departure of the Chinese army from Shanghai, however, during the evening of March 4, fueled by rumors of Chinese military victories, Chinese mobs surged through the streets, the unrest apparently fomented by local Chinese Communists in the settlement for their own purposes. The 31st was ordered to stand by for possible riot duty, but the Municipal Police handled the situation and quiet was restored.[47]

Another incident that occurred on March 8 more directly involved the Americans in the conflict. Second Lieutenant Henry M. Bailey of the 1st

Battalion, in command of a patrol of Company B, rushed to break up a mob of Chinese attacking four Japanese civilians, who were rescued by Bailey and Warrant Officer Edward E. Kislow and taken to the Hongkew Police Station. The Japanese were then escorted to Japanese headquarters. On the following day, the chief of staff of the Japanese Naval Landing Forces, Captain Baron Samejima, called in person on Major Ross O. Baldwin, the battalion commander, to convey the appreciation and thanks of Rear Admiral Uyematsu, in command of the Japanese forces engaged "for the protection and assistance given their nationals."[48]

Also during this time, as a further sign of the easing of the situation, the regiment turned in its trench stores, earlier placed at the disposal of men in sentry posts and other advanced positions, to the regimental supply officer. In addition, the outposts and related patrol activity were reduced. At the same time in Shanghai, public utilities were again able to resume service to the public. Subsequently, after the weeks of conflict, a calm returned to the city, the Japanese holding their positions unmolested by Chinese forces.[49]

With these few exceptions, the ceasefire ushered in another phase of the "incident": that of negotiating a formal end to the conflict. On April 1, the British East Lancashire Regiment relieved the 31st north of Soochow Creek, which left the 31st with only internal patrol duties south of the creek. The regiment could then settle down to a duller routine of garrison life, and it was also possible for contingents of the international force to pay respects to each other with parades and reviews. In addition, sporting events, especially involving the 31st, the 4th Marines and British regiments, were held at the Shanghai racetrack. Even before the cessation of hostilities passes had sometimes been issued. They were now easily obtained, permitting the troops to wander about the International Settlement. There, "tea houses" with cheap Chinese beer and attractive "hostesses" beckoned just as they did around every military garrison worldwide. Several companies bought exclusive rights to certain brothels that agreed to serve no other customers. The regiment's surgeons made weekly inspections to ensure that the brothels maintained proper health and sanitation standards. Thus, what would have been illegal in the Philippines—an American possession—"seemed a virtue in Shanghai." Such controls were in place to help keep the VD rate in check. Venereal disease was a serious matter in the 1930s. Soldiers hospitalized—often up to a month—were heavily fined and had to pay the army additional time on their enlistments to make up for lost service. Officers who contracted VD were required to resign from the army. Regimental surgeons conducted monthly "short arm" inspections to detect any concealed infections.[50]

The interval of peace also permitted several of the regiment's officers to bring their families from Manila to join them. Some rented suites at the Cathay Mansions Hotel in the French Concession. The children were enrolled at the American Mission School and were taken there daily by rickshaw. The shopping opportunities were numerous and the wives spent happy hours in the shops seeking jade, silver and copper jewelry or housewares produced by skilled artisans. Most items could be bought at a fraction of their value in the Philippines or the States. When the regiment sailed for home in June of 1932, one account noted that the machine guns were wrapped in oriental rugs or heavily embroidered tablecloths and sets of fine china dishes were set aside for troop dining halls back in Manila. Every family carried back its own treasure trove of fine goods. Fortunately, the Philippine government gave the regiment "freedom of the port" for the occasion, so no customs checks were made.[51]

With the shooting apparently over, it now seemed possible that the 31st might be ordered home. Encouraged by the new situation, Colonel Gasser paid a visit to Cunningham on March 9, urging that his men be recalled to Manila, where the regiment "was very badly needed"—though he gave no details concerning these. After consulting with local Chinese officials, Cunningham was inclined to accede, but ever the cautious diplomat, he raised concerns that the 31st's departure would reduce the level of American forces in Shanghai "to its minimum," and this level should be maintained "until all differences between the Japanese and Chinese [had] been adjusted." He had further misgivings regarding the effect on the Japanese, "who are increasingly brutally arrogant and overbearing." There might also be adverse effects on "the Chinese mind," which might regard it as "a cessation of interest by the United States in the Sino-Japanese conflict."[52] All things considered, though, Cunningham was willing to support Gasser's request and took advantage of the occasion to express heartily the "appreciation on behalf of the entire community for the dispatch of the 31st Infantry at a time when conditions seemed so serious and also appreciation for the spirit of cooperation shown by Colonel Gasser [and] his staff."[53]

The matter was not left in Cunningham's hands, however, and Gasser's query made its way through the channels at the State Department. At length, it arrived at the desk of the chief of the Division of Far Eastern Affairs, Dr. Stanley K. Hornbeck, who conferred with General Douglas MacArthur, chief of the Army General Staff, about the unit's status. MacArthur reassured Hornbeck that "the 31st Regiment is absolutely at the disposal of the Department of State." Nonetheless, he thought that "the regiment [should] be kept at Shanghai until the situation is much more clear than at present" and feared that its removal would "give a bad impression." He noted that the 31st was getting on well in Shanghai, the men were comfortable, and furthermore, despite Gasser's assertions, were not then needed in Manila. It was decided to await further developments before a final decision was made.[54]

Subsequently, on May 5, a formal cessation of hostilities was agreed to following negotiations in Shanghai between the Chinese and Japanese and representatives of Britain, France, Italy and the United States. This provided for a permanent cease-fire and a mutual withdrawal of Chinese and Japanese troops from the combat areas. A neutral zone was also created around Shanghai, though the Chinese did not accept a total demobilization of the city, leaving the matter open for their later bringing troops into the city.[55] They were permitted to station special police forces in Shanghai. Therefore, the Japanese had obtained a temporary evacuation of Chinese troops in the Shanghai area, while they maintained the right to keep their forces in their concession area in the International Settlement, though on a restricted basis.[56]

While these positive developments might have conceivably resulted in the 31st's return to Manila, an incident occurred which prolonged its stay. The American minister to China, Nelson Trusler Johnson, did not regard the matter as serious, however, and thought that the generally improved situation in Shanghai warranted a reconsideration of the retention of the 31st at Shanghai and recommended "that the regiment be taken away."[57]

The event referred to occurred on the evening of May 3. Japanese sentries stationed on the We Chen Road bridge alleged that they were stoned by Chinese coolies, whereupon a Japanese patrol of about sixty men commanded by an officer crossed the bridge to the southern side of Soochow Creek, which was in the 31st's sector. The Japanese then clubbed and bayoneted Chinese civilians in the street and in nearby houses. Several Chinese were also seized by the Japanese, who endeavored to take them across the bridge. Assistance was requested from the 31st and a detachment, commanded by Major Gerow and accompanied by Chinese police, intervened. After much arguing, the Japanese officer in charge of the detachment was persuaded to withdraw his men and the Chinese who had been seized were released to the police. About ten Chinese had been injured. One immediate result was that all troops were withdrawn from the settlement border, leaving police to guard it. The troops were then confined to their billets and ordered to remain on alert.[58]

It then fell to the acting secretary of state, William R. Castle, Jr., in the absence of Secretary Stimson, who was on his way home from attending the league's General Disarmament Conference in Geneva, to make the decision about the 31st's status. Erring on the side of caution, Castle ordered Cunningham to take no further action until Stimson could act and further advised that "it would seem inadvisable to ... remove [the] 31st Infantry immediately on the heels of that incident."[59]

Stimson, following his return to Washington on May 14 and satisfying himself that the situation in Shanghai had indeed improved, decided to send the 31st back to Manila on the next army transport, scheduled to arrive in Shanghai the last week of June. His decision was underscored by the Shanghai City Council's withdrawing the state of emergency (which it had proclaimed on January 28), effective the morning of June 13, 1932. This removed the last obstacle to the 31st's return, and, accordingly, a change of station orders for the 31st Regiment was issued on June 17.[60]

Numerous tributes were paid to the 31st on the eve of its departure. These ranged from commendations from foreign and American civilians to a radiogram from General MacArthur, the U.S. Army chief of staff, which read: "Convey to all ranks of the regiment my earnest appreciation of the efficiency with which they have discharged a difficult and trying duty."[61] Also, plaques were exchanged by the 31st and men of the 4th Marines. The one from the 31st read: "Presented to the 4th Regiment U.S. Marines from the 31st Infantry in Commemoration of our Service Together. Shanghai, China—Feb. 5-June 30, 1932." In the *Walla Walla*, the 4th Marines troop paper published in Shanghai, the editor wrote that the paper, "on behalf of the fourth Marines, tender[ed] its sincere gratitude and good wishes to the officers and men of the 31st."[62]

To honor themselves, the sixty-six officers who had served with the regiment in Shanghai collected 1,600 Chinese silver dollars and instructed a Shanghai silversmith to make a silver bowl and sixty-six cups, one for each officer. The "Shanghai Bowl," as it was called, was officially presented to the regiment at Fort McKinley, near Manila, on July 5, 1932, by Lieutenant Colonel A.D. Davis, one of the officers who had been in China. A memento "of that unique service," the bowl subsequently became the center of ceremonies connected with the regiment.[63]

Shortly after the receipt of their orders, on June 30, 1932, the 31st left Shanghai. With Colonel Gasser at their head, the men fell in at the racecourse at 5:30 p.m. and began their march to the ship, the U.S. Army transport [USAT] *Republic*, led by the 4th Marine band. Five Shanghai Volunteer Corps armored cars, Sikh Troops, a 4th Marine contingent and the three British battalions present in Shanghai, the Wiltshire—and its band—the East Lancashire and Lincolnshire were drawn up to do honor as the Americans marched by. The line of march proceeded along Nanking Road, the Bund and Broadway, which were lined with many Chinese and foreigners who turned out en masse, as a guard of honor, and the foreign troops "rendered them a full salute as they passed in review for the last time along Shanghai's famous Bund." The wharf was also thronged with spectators from the international community, while the decks of the transport were crowded with those already aboard taking in the show. Colonel Gasser and his staff were then "at home" for a brief reception on board just prior to sailing, entertaining British Brigadier General Fleming, who commanded the Shanghai area, and other British officers. The ship sailed for Manila at 10 p.m.[64]

12
Dénouement

Not all of the men were happy about returning to somnolent Manila, though a few did want to get back to families and loved ones and welcome the "warmth of sunshine in contrast ... to the comparative chilliness of the Shanghai winter and spring." Indeed, those who "liked good, honest heat in their weather" found "very nearly their ideal in the [Philippine] Islands." A few others liked "to be stationed within hail of large numbers of their army friends and take pleasure on frequent social gatherings with them [and] also find enjoyment in a Philippine assignment." Then, too, there were always a certain number of higher-ranking officers who repeatedly asked for and received station in the Philippines, as they wished to "return. Nonetheless, the great majority of the "Polar Bears," especially the rank and file, were none too keen to return, because in their five months in Shanghai, they "grew to like China almost as well as the Can-Doers here in Tientsin," one account in the *Sentinel* noted. They too had grown accustomed to "the high exchange [rate] and inexpensiveness of almost anything money can buy, the temperateness of the climate, and the friendliness of the great cosmopolitan city," friendliness that included, no doubt, that of the Chinese "hostesses" with whom they had consorted. They had also seen some action and this was no doubt a heady tonic not easily forgotten.[1]

The regiment arrived at Manila on July 6, 1932, with forty-nine officers and 1,065 enlisted men on the roster. There were numerous other army personnel, including six officers, four army nurses, and forty-eight enlisted men attached to the regiment "for the journey only." Two days later, "Detachment 31st Infantry" was formally deactivated and the regiment resumed its status as a garrison force. The authority for the change of station was Paragraph 2, General Orders 24, Headquarters, Philippine Department, June 17, 1932. The discontinuing of the detachment came by verbal orders of Major General Ewing E. Booth, the commanding general of the Philippine Department, on July 8, 1932.[2]

Despite the feelings among the men about China and the desirability of service there, the regiment was well set up in Manila. It hardly returned to a hardship post and operated on a half-day schedule in deference to the heat of the tropics. In addition, the 31st was the officially designated ceremonial regiment of the Philippines, and, accordingly, particular emphasis was placed on close-order drill. It also furnished the guard for the U.S. Army Headquarters, the Philippine Department, at Fort Santiago in Manila.[3]

Officialdom expressed pleasure that the men had returned. Major General Ewing E. Booth, commanding the Philippine Department, in a letter of boiler plate language, welcomed the regiment "back to its home station with grateful appreciation that during its absence has performed a valued service in a manner which always should be a cause of pride to this command and to the entire Army." One trusts, too, that the establishments and haunts that the men had previously frequented in Manila, including the Metropolitan Theater, the Oriental Bar, and the Cummings Cafe, within the walled city—and elsewhere, Tom's Dixie Kitchen and the Poodle Dog—were as forthcoming in their "welcome backs."[4]

Much later, after the wheels of bureaucracy had ground out the authority, the War Department, in Bulletin No. 4, May 21, 1935, authorized, on the orders of the president, the issuance of the Yangtze Service Medal by the Marine Corps commandant to personnel of the 31st Infantry who served in Shanghai with the 4th Marines from February 5 to July 1, 1932. The medal, created by the Navy Department, was not to be awarded to any other Army personnel serving in China, a fact duly—and dourly—noted in Tientsin by men of the 15th Regiment.[5]

It was well that the men had some years to enjoy their posting in Manila. A cruel fate subsequently intervened, and exactly a decade after the "Shanghai Incident," in the spring of 1942, men of the 31st Infantry were to fight at Bataan and Corregidor and those who survived taken prisoner by the victorious Japanese. The Japanese bayonets and samurai swords would then be turned on the Americans who, with impotent rage, had earlier observed those same weapons being wielded against helpless Chinese victims in Shanghai. Subsequently, about half of the 1,600 men captured perished in captivity, an unfitting reward for the relief that they had provided the Japanese in 1923. Many of the men died of disease, torture and malnutrition in the prison camps in the Philippines, Formosa, Manchuria and Japan. On three occasions, hundreds more were wounded, killed or drowned when the prison ships

12. Dénouement

transporting them to Japan were torpedoed by American submarines unaware of the nature of their targets.[6]

Gasser, too, after 1932, had a substantial part of his military career ahead of him. In 1939 and 1940, he was the deputy chief of staff of the U.S. Army. Following his retirement in 1940, the coming of World War II led to his recall in 1941. As a major general, he was a key figure in the War Department's Manpower Board, which made significant decisions regarding the employment of the army's personnel. Retiring a second time in 1945, he died in 1955 and is buried in Arlington National Cemetery.

Regarding more immediate results and consequences of the "Shanghai Incident," undoubtedly the Japanese learned more than anyone else, at least in the military area. They undertook many studies of the "incident," some of which have been ably analyzed by Lieutenant Commander H.H. Smith-Hutton of the United States Navy.[7] He asserts that "the operations of the Japanese naval landing force at Shanghai during the period January-March 1932, form an interesting and important chapter in the history of the Japanese Navy." This was the first major land operation of the modern Japanese Navy. Accordingly, it aroused intense interest among all personnel of the naval forces and had a major influence on subsequent Japanese training and tactics. This included lessons on tactics, ship-to-shore operations, and the conduct of troops in the field. In addition, they learned how better to organize training programs, all of which paid off in later engagements, even on into World War II. They certainly learned what not to do in many instances. Another important thing learned was that Chinese soldiers could indeed fight as brave and resourceful opponents despite their failures in previous engagements with the Japanese. Smith-Hutton concluded that, in this regard, the Japanese singularly failed to estimate the odds against them and initially attempted an action with about 2,500 men that finally required twenty times that number to succeed. This resulted in considerable cost in men and money. But much more important, "at Shanghai, in 1932, the Japanese armed forces lost their reputation of being invincible," a serious loss of face. A much more significant factor in Asia than is generally recognized in the West, this loss stiffened Japanese resolve that in the future the Chinese would be forced to pay for that humiliation. While other factors were involved, this contributed to the severity of their occupation of Shanghai and much of eastern China, such as in Nanking, in the years just ahead. These atrocities still color relations between China and Japan, a significant long-standing legacy of the "Shanghai Incident" of 1932.[8]

Beyond this, the Japanese, who apparently wanted out of the Shanghai "mess," as they referred to it on several occasions, did not readily admit that the situation was largely of their own making. They had erred in incorrectly estimating the Chinese and could not, in their own view, agree to a settlement in Shanghai until they had recovered their lost prestige to the extent possible. A prescient assessment of certain Japanese attitudes was contained in a telegram sent from Peiping on January 29, 1932, by the assistant military attaché in China, Captain Parker G. Tenny, to the adjutant general of the army. Therein, Tenny concluded that the "Japanese General Staff is now war mad and it is believed it should be realized [that] it would not hesitate [to engage in] hostilities with [the] United States if blocked."[9]

Nonetheless, at the time, the Japanese attempted to put a "good face" on events and circumstances as far as possible. They always emphasized that they were acting on behalf of their own nationals and only with the concurrence of the Shanghai Council, which indeed went to great lengths to placate the Japanese. While the Chinese had acted lawlessly, the question as to why they were belligerent in the first place was often lost sight of. The emphasis was all too often on the violence fomented by "the irresponsible Chinese." Cunningham, in a telegram to the secretary of state on January 27, for instance, discussed the unreliability of the Chinese soldiers, composed mostly of "very young boys" who were almost bandits and a menace to everyone. This was only partially true. There were regular Chinese military forces in the field and the Japanese also had to contend with them in a major way.[10]

Surely the Westerners must have grasped that despite Japanese shortcomings they themselves thoroughly and painstakingly analyzed, Japan's definite arrival in east China and their growing professionalism and élan could only bode ill for themselves and for the civilized world. In fact, it was clear that the Japanese were developing their general aggressive stance vis-à-vis the Chinese, and much else besides, and it would require far more than a U.S. Army regiment, even the redoubtable "Polar Bears" or the 15th Infantry Regiment—the "Can Doers" in Tientsin—and a small, scattered force of Marines to stem the tides threatening to engulf that part of the world. It would eventually take the recruiting or drafting of millions of American service personnel, unprecedented production accomplishments, the mastering of mind-boggling logistical requirements, a war-winning strategy and two A-bombs to bring an end to the war in Asia.

Colonel James C. Breckinridge, commandant of the Marine Legation Guard in Peiping from 1931 to 1933, well exemplified the miscalculations and myopia that many Westerners manifested about the Japanese in the early 1930s. In his Marine headquarters in Peiping, Breckinridge had to work with the Japanese after the Manchurian takeover and noted considerable tension between the Japanese and the Americans, but both parties attempted to keep

12. Dénouement

things "proper" so as not to create any incidents. As far as he was personally concerned, "what they [the Japanese] are doing in China is their business, and does not differ from what others, including ourselves, have to do on other occasions. Their reasons seem to be about the same as our own in Nicaragua, Santo Domingo, [and] Haiti." The Japanese, Breckinridge contended, "said nothing to us when we did it!" The newspaper headlines tell of Japanese horrors but there was another side to the story, he went on. He was of the opinion that "the Japanese had to stop the 'nonsense,'" as he called it; and as he saw matters, "China and the Chinese had long been intolerable, utterly insufferable. As I have already said, we have kicked people for less cause." In his view, "China deserves all it is getting; every bit of it."

Though Breckinridge harbored some sympathy for what the Chinese suffered, he insisted that, while the Chinese were pitiable, certainly, they were also intolerable, as well as "corrupt, idiotic, stupid, sordid, vile, utterly horrid, and perpetually futile." They were, in addition, "plausible, suave, smooth, gentle, humorous, winning, deceitful and cunning." While they did not teach a philosophy, apart from perhaps Confucius, they lived another philosophy that was characterized as deceit being better than honesty and gaining the confidence of others in order to trick them. The Chinese, he said, would always yield to Westerners and then would trust to time and cunning to prevail eventually. They tended to tell people what they wanted to hear and never let them know what they really thought or intended to do. Life was essentially a "game of wits and deception." The stupid man was the one who allowed himself to be outwitted. But, their reasoning went, if you are outwitted, appear to have gained your end and then "wait your turn." Facts did not count for anything; appearances were everything. Truth, since it was not expected, was sometimes "the best deception." If one was found out to be deceitful, one should admit it, smile and plead misunderstanding, then win that man's friendship and "then deceive him for keeps."

The Japanese, however, were also at fault, Breckinridge acknowledged: "The chief criticism of [them concerns] their complete lack of tact; with a little tact they could, and would, have had most of the world with them. Now they are overdoing it all, and trying to play a clumsy western type of diplomacy at the same time. That is their mistake; that, and playing with China instead of simply smashing it at one fell swoop."

Within this context, Breckinridge had little sympathy for Westerners who continued to live in China, even when things got darker in 1931 and afterward, because they could "live lives of ease, with plenty of servants, where they could be perfectly safe in their own country but would have to do their own cooking and cleaning." This applied to missionaries as well, since "they all hang on to a safe income and cheap labor...." Back of their religious lives was "a large influence; it is servants, and ease, and plain laziness."[11]

Certainly, then, the main losers in the "Shanghai Incident" were the Chinese, as they were to continue to be for many years to come. They suffered heavy losses on the field of battle and were forced to withdraw their military forces from Shanghai. Though it was clear that the league was floundering and other instances of Western support of China was conspicuously lacking, nonetheless the Chinese at this time revealed a revitalized belief, faith and hope in world opinion to curb the Japanese, asking, for example, whether "we [the West] were going to simply allow the Japanese to get away with [it all]." What they found—not for the last time—was a mixed bag and a degree of disillusionment, the consequence of the West's inability or unwillingness to act decisively.

Though the West was greatly disturbed by Japanese intervention in Shanghai, many factors prevented any significant intervention against the Japanese. Among these was the worldwide depression, which forced a reduction of the maintenance of armed forces, especially in Britain and the United States. A general malaise prevailed and in America, particularly, a spirit of isolationism was deeply entrenched. In addition, the Western powers, though manifesting some sympathy toward the Chinese for the considerable damage and loss of life that they suffered, were more interested in damage to their own property in the settlement. Yet, there was surprise and admiration for the courageous and spirited defense the Chinese troops made against the much better equipped and trained Japanese forces, and the Chinese gained much prestige from it. Their orderly retreat in early March was also favorably commented on. In fact, as Professor Jordan has observed, after 1932 the United States rather sanguinely overestimated Chinese military power, "which distorted U.S. strategy until late in World War II."

What the West similarly failed to perceive about the course of action in 1932 was a Chinese proclivity to employ strategic retreats, which was at variance with Western views of the need always, if possible, to press offensive actions. This stance later caused much consternation in the minds of such as leaders as General "Vinegar Joe" Stilwell, who in World War II commanded Chinese troops in action. It also mystified the Japanese, who were schooled in samurai codes and Bushido concepts. As Professor Jordan has written, "The Japanese [also] should have studied the Chinese retreat, as it was to become China's modus operandi during the war that resumed in 1937." The Chinese views regarding retreats date at least as far back as the famous treatise *The Art of War*, by Sun Tzu, written about 500 BC. Therein, Sun Tzu noted that when the enemy was superior he should be evaded, and even retreat was acceptable. As he put it, "The general who advances without coveting fame and retreats without fearing disgrace, [and] whose only thought is to protect his country and do good service for his sovereign, is the jewel of the kingdom." Thus it must have appeared to Chinese commanders in March of 1932 at Shanghai. The Chinese seemed always willing to trade space for time, a strategy which was often quite costly to the Chinese in World War II, especially in civilian losses (perhaps fifteen million Chinese lost their lives in World War II), many of these being civilians caught by the Japanese in their occupied territory. Nonetheless, their actions did tie down millions of Japanese troops in China, which played a sometimes unappreciated role in aiding Allied forces to proceed toward Tokyo with reduced—though they were still formidable—Japanese forces with which to contend. Similar considerations seemed relevant in 1932 in that the Chinese retreat in March enabled the West to adjust to an understanding that it was Japan who was the aggressor and would over time rally otherwise neutral and other powers—some of which had earlier admired Japan—to the creation of an anti–Japanese bloc that would eventually emerge victorious in World War II in the Far East.

The West also failed to understand, as one Chinese governor had stated it, that many Chinese regarded Communism as "a disease of the heart, where the Japanese incursion was like a surface wound."[12] Accordingly, the "Shanghai Incident" exacerbated internal discord that already existed in China as, for example, among Chiang's Koumintang, the Cantonese, and the Communists. The West rarely understood the makeup and magnitude of these internal fissures. While a united front against the Japanese existed in certain circumstances and at various times for various reasons, this could never be counted on, either in the 1930s or during World War II. Nonetheless, it is clear that "nationalism [would be] expressed in a new and different way from 1931 onward and encouraged the replacement of 'imperialism' in general with Japan in particular as its chief target."[13]

As to the end of the conflict in 1932, another factor must be considered. After the truce was agreed to, support in China for the 19th Route Army dissipated, and the opposition toward the Japanese slackened, nor did it carry over to opposition in Manchuria as many had hoped. Nonetheless, the Shanghai episode had longer-range effects on the minds of Chinese, and Chinese nationalism grew apace. If it lapsed for a time following 1932, the events of 1937 aroused it to new fury.[14]

There were other dimensions of the Chinese response. These have been thoroughly discussed by Rana Mitter. For one thing, the Shanghai Incident was seized upon by many Chinese nationalist activists because of its far

The USAT *Republic* underway. The men of the 31st Infantry Regiment returned to Manila from Shanghai on this ship in the summer of 1932 (courtesy of U.S. Naval History and Heritage Command).

greater emotional impact, especially on foreigners, as well as on Chinese south of the Great Wall. Also, there was an awareness that Chinese activism in the 1920s aimed at imperialism was divided among several targets: Britain, Japan, France and the United States. But in the 1930s, events singled out Japan as "the sole target of attack, allowing China to turn from 'revolutionary diplomacy' to attempts to create international alliances."[15]

The Yangtze Medal. This U.S. Navy decoration was awarded to men of the U.S. armed forces who served, between the two World Wars, in Shanghai and the Yangtze River areas. This included the troops of the 31st Infantry Regiment for service in Shanghai in 1932 (courtesy of U.S. Naval Historical Society).

12. Dénouement

Regarding the 31st's deployment, some consideration should be given to the dispatch, smoothness and efficiency of their mobilization and transportation to China. Also, the regiment was not engaged any longer than seemed necessary. Altogether, "it was a good game they played there between the fire of two great nations where every minute was packed with danger lest some act of theirs plunge us all into another war," a member of the 15th Regiment in Tientsin, Charles M. Roland, wrote admiringly in the unit's newspaper, the *Sentinel*: "Not knowing who would be your friend or enemy the next day would fray the nerves of the most stoical of persons but they carried on. No regiment has ever faced a more difficult task. In ignorance of the people, the language and the customs of this strange country, they proceeded to their duties with a steady forthrightness that is truly remarkable." In addition, he pointed out, "year after year our training consists of the use of force but never diplomacy. Here then was a case that could not be treated in the usual manner," and by using "tact and diplomacy instead of bullets and bayonets," the men had faithfully carried out their orders." To the editor of the *Sentinel*, it seemed clear that "no regiment of the American Army has ever been more closely bound together by the ties of important duty and by loyalty to and admiration for its commanding officer than this one." To his mind, "the Shanghai performance of the Bears was a job well led and well done."[16]

To be sure, the presence of the 31st could have had an effect in directing hostilities in other directions than at the International Settlement. But, in fact, the consequences of the 31st Regiment's China deployment were negligible, and the combatants essentially proceeded along their own course. In the circumstances, the Western forces in China became increasingly peripheral and eventually superfluous. Concerned as they were with their own interests and the creature comforts that many Westerners had grown accustomed to in China, they were unaware that the Western Asian idyll was soon to be shattered, never to be restored. The Japanese increasingly took matters into their own hands and brazenly, with growing ferocity and cruelty, pursued their conquests in Asia. Accordingly, the American armed forces in Asia between the world wars simply became part of the general tragedy that overtook the Far East in the late 1930s and 1940s, culminating in many—including men of the 31st Regiment—becoming prisoners of war after Pearl Harbor. For the moment, in 1932, the men of the 31st had indeed done their duty well, but their accentuated sense of honor and enhanced martial traditions, the accolades, and other recognitions of their service in Shanghai, of prime interest to themselves, remained merely incidental to what was already a far larger and more profound course of events in the making.

As for China, subsequently, neither the best efforts of the Japanese nor of the Allies were able significantly to alter the course of its destiny. Dick Wilson, in his study, *When Tigers Fight*, has correctly stated, "The Sino-Japanese war is thus a one-off phenomenon, a tragic and wasteful episode which did no good to anyone, a negative example of the unwise use of military power," which in the end, "achieved nothing." As one of the initial engagements of this struggle, the first Shanghai Incident helped to set in motion a series of events that would not be ended until after World War II.[17]

On December 8, 1941, Japanese aircraft attacked Manila, and the 31st sustained its first casualty. It was not to be the last. After the Japanese landed in the Philippines, the 31st covered the retreat of American and Philippine forces to Bataan. It fought for four months until Bataan was surrendered on April 9, 1942. The regiment survived these horrors to rise again as a fighting unit. On January 19, 1946, General MacArthur resurrected the 31st in Korea and assigned it to the 7th Infantry Division on occupation duty. In 1948, when the occupation of Korea ended, the regiment moved to Hokkaido. When the Korean War began, the 31st was stripped of much of its personnel, who were sent to Korea when it was invaded in the summer of 1950. The remainder of the 31st, in the meantime, was reequipped and regrouped and used as part of the Inchon invasion force. When North Korea seemed defeated, the 31st pushed toward the Yalu River but was surrounded and virtually wiped out by the Chinese, who had by then entered the fray. What was left of the regiment was evacuated to Pusan, where it was once more reformed and participated in the battles that raged along the 38th parallel, such as at "Old Baldy," "Pork Chop Hill," "Triangle Hill" and others. The fierce action produced five Medals of Honor being awarded to the regiment.

After the Korean War, the U.S. Army reorganized its infantry regiments. Various units of the 31st were stationed in Korea and at various posts in the United States. Units of the regiment were then active in Vietnam in the spring of 1966 and lasting until 1970. Its operations in Vietnam produced two additional Medals of Honor. Various units were deactivated by 1995. Reactivated in April of 1996, some units were sent to Bosnia, and in May 2004 other men were engaged in "Operation Iraqi Freedom" and were back and forth into Iraq during 2009, returning to the U.S. in 2010. Troops of the 31st were then sent to Afghanistan. At the present time, it is headquartered at Fort Drum, New York.

The regiment was best known for its having been deployed outside of the U.S. throughout most of its career until recent times. Its motto is "Pro Patria" ("For the Country"), and it continued to use the nickname earned in Siberia, the "Polar Bears."[18]

In keeping with the format of this study, another legacy of the 31st

Infantry Regiment was Colonel Lorenzo Dow Gasser, who continued to serve with distinction in the U.S. Army. Born in Ohio on May 3, 1876, Gasser was appointed a captain in the 2nd Ohio Volunteer Infantry with the coming of the Spanish-American War. Mustered out of the Volunteers in 1901, Gasser was commissioned a 2nd lieutenant in the U.S. Infantry. In World War I, he served from 1918 to 1919 as assistant chief of staff, III Corps, on the Western Front and in 1919 became assistant chief of staff, 1st Army.

Following hostilities, from 1920 to 1921, Gasser attended the War College. He was then attached to the U.S. Army General Staff Corps, 1921–1925. Becoming a colonel in 1928, he assumed command of the 31st U.S. Infantry Regiment in the Philippines, which in 1932 served in Shanghai, China, as has been noted. Following service in the Philippines and China, Gasser became chief of staff, the General Staff Corps, in the IV Corps area, from 1934 to 1937, and was promoted to brigadier general in 1936. Ordered to Washington, he served as the assistant chief of staff from 1937 to 1939 and deputy chief of staff, 1939–1940. He retired in 1940, but with the coming of hostilities in World War II he was recalled in 1941. Promoted to major general in 1943, he became chairman of the important War Department Manpower Board established by General Marshall in January 1943, undoubtedly one of the most significant of his many assignments, in which he served from 1943 to 1945.

The Manpower Board was noteworthy because it was charged with combing out the army by releasing from active service or demoting those deemed ill-qualified, physically or mentally unable or unwilling to fight effectively, or those who were regarded as simply serving in the "overhead" as superfluous administration, communications and maintenance people and taking up slots that should to be filled with fully qualified personnel. Late in the war, as manpower needs swelled, training times were sometimes reduced, and infantrymen were sought in many other branches of the service. The board inevitably received numerous complaints as a result of its actions, which were often regarded as being far too arbitrary. Nonetheless, manpower needs were met in sufficient numbers to sustain American operations to the end of the war.

Gasser, retiring once more in 1945, died in Washington on October 29, 1955, and is buried at Arlington National Cemetery.

Conclusion

> New occasions teach new duties,
> Time makes ancient good uncouth;
> They must upward still and onward
> Who would keep abreast of truth.
> —James Russell Lowell (1819–1891)
>
> It's not what you look at that matters, it's what you see.
> —Henry David Thoreau (1817–1862)

Regarding East-West confrontations, the world by the 21st century has witnessed new developments. As the novelist Orhan Pamuk of Turkey has observed, East versus West is not now limited to a few countries but "is an expression of a new global phenomenon [involving the Middle East among other places] that we are only just coming to acknowledge and that we must now begin, however carefully, to address." The global canvas is now infinitely more complex. Accordingly, future leaders of the United States, whether political or military, must employ a greater understanding of long-range historical factors manifested in the East—in this case, China—for centuries.[1]

Kipling's famous statement "East is East, and West is West, and never the twain shall meet" did not ring true for the century from the 1840s to 1949 or so, during what is known in China as the "Century of Shame." In those years, there was much contact, and, notwithstanding Rudyard Kipling's further assertion that it was a danger to the West's health to try to "hustle" the East, both the "hustling" and "rustling" of Asia, especially China, occurred with reckless abandon. This led one journalist to assert that Kipling's line should now be rephrased as "East is East and West is West, and never the twain shall part." In addition, Kipling's views regarding dangers to the West were not valid in the short range, though no doubt possibly applicable in the longer term, as the world continues to seek the chimera of Churchill's "sunlit uplands." Meanwhile, the West greatly influenced the whole of China's checkered history, consisting of the long unraveling and then reknitting of Chinese life extending for over a century, from the middle of the 1800s to after World War II.

The West, including America, accomplished a great deal in that era "with signal success." Much of America's military efforts during this period were focused on the Boxer Uprising, the deployment of the 15th Infantry Regiment from 1912 to 1938, and the 31st Infantry Regiment's action in Shanghai in 1932. Much of this, however, was pernicious to the Chinese, though America's interests were upheld and defended and on occasion the Chinese were assisted as well, as they acknowledged in presenting the China Gate, or arch, to the 15th Infantry in Tientsin in 1924. Among the negative developments were that "Western businessmen pressed trade at the point of a gun to a degree unique in world commercial intercourse. The 'special treaties,' and extraterritoriality—extrality for short—a term indicating that foreigners could only be tried by their own courts, and not by those of China. Therefore, clearly, the Western world was living a privileged existence at the great expense of the Chinese." In addition, "missionaries in their thousands, zealous, self-sacrificing, well intentioned, and who often suffered privations, hardships and sickness, nonetheless, manifestly felt and acted superior to the 'heathen Chinee,' to the indignation of the Chinese who felt that what they considered culturally inferior people were attempting to foist on them inappropriate morals and dogma."[2]

These matters were further defined by the attitudes and goals of the Westerners. They had no aspirations to become part of Chinese life, unlike many of China's previous conquerors, who, sooner or later, were often absorbed into the Chinese world. But for Westerners, "deeming themselves more advanced societies, their goal was to exploit China for economic gain, not to join its way of life." Thus, "for the most part, the Western powers limited themselves to extracting economic concessions on the Chinese coast and demanding rights to free trade and missionary activity." There is a paradox here: the Europeans did not view all of this as a conquest at all. Rather, "they were not seeking to replace the existing dynasty—they simply imposed an entirely new world order essentially incompatible with the Chinese one."[3]

The actions and attitudes of Americans can be noted in a clear statement of U.S. views regarding the turn of the 20th century. These were contained in an oration extolling the virtues of Manifest Destiny by a young senator from Indiana, Albert Jeremiah Beveridge, entitled "The March of the Flag," which he delivered in numerous public appearances, as well as on the floor of the Senate. He asserted that "the Philippines are ours forever," and "just beyond them are China's illimitable markets. We will not retreat from either.... We will not abandon one opportunity in the Orient. We will not renounce our part of the mission of our race, trustee under God, of the civilization of the world."[4]

Similar attitudes were manifested by American troops engaged in the Boxer Uprising. One of their commanders, Brigadier General Aaron Simon Daggett, in a book about the U.S. forces there, stated, "Everyone felt that he was engaged in a righteous cause, and was stimulated to energetic exertion thereby." As to further heroics, Dagget asserted "the flag was honored, as it always has been where American soldiers have borne it." This matter of honor was clearly regarded as more important than the losses sustained by the Chinese—or Americans—whether or not they [the Americans] were right or wrong." This reflects the temper of the times, as well as the prevailing concept of "my country, right or wrong."[5]

Certainly, the "Century of Shame," even after the Boxer era, was a continuing source of rancor, extending to the years when Chiang ruled in China. Chiang, as was true of most Chinese, resented the unequal treaties and hoped for their abolition. In his view, their termination was one of the critical prerequisites for China to develop its economic potential. Thus, the key factor responsible for the sad state of the country, he alleged, was not internal decay or prior misrule by the Manchu (Ch'ing) dynasty but "the aggression of outsiders and their imposition of the unequal treaties." In the short run, however, it was Japanese invasion and World War II that ended the treaties, and it was Chinese resistance, endurance and persistence—though at the frightful cost of over fifteen million Chinese deaths between 1937 and 1945—that ultimately prevailed.[6]

Today's China, therefore, encountered the West in the "Century of Shame" in a way that "challenged the basic Chinese cosmology and left wounds still festering over a century later in an age of restored Chinese eminence." Indeed, "this reckoning," with the modern international system, designed along European and American lines, "would impose one of the most wrenching social, intellectual, and moral strains on Chinese society in its long history."[7]

In fact, there were key Chinese attributes and attitudes that developed along the way while China was in contact with the West that enabled China to persevere and eventually to emerge again as a world power. These views must still be considered in assessing China. Among these was a perennial idea of using barbarians to check barbarians. In addition, the Chinese have been shrewd practitioners of Realpolitik and have advanced a strategic doctrine distinctly different from that of the West: "A turbulent history has taught

Chinese leaders that not every problem has a solution and that too great an emphasis on total mastery over specific events could upset the harmony of the universe." Rarely did the Chinese risk the outcome of a conflict on a single all-or-nothing clash. They preferred multiyear maneuvers. While the West traditionally prized "the decisive clash of forces emphasizing feats of heroism the Chinese ideal stressed subtlety, indirection, and the patient accumulation of relative advantage." One way to understand this is to note the types of serious games played in China. In the West, chess was a major game. In China, the emphasis was on *wei qi*. This game featured longer-range activity with emphasis on actions with relative advantages and strategic encirclement rather than on precipitous confrontational action characterized by heroics.[8]

Similarly, in military theory, the emphasis was traditionally on avoidance of direct conflict, seeking, instead, psychological advantages. Key here is the thought of Sun Tzu ("Master Sun") presented in his military treatise, *The Art of War*. Western theorists test their maxims by victories in battles, with much preoccupation with heroes. The focus in China was on political and psychological positions so that battles need not be fought at all. War was not exalted; prudence was instead a major characteristic. Thus, there was an emphasis on roles of subterfuge, misinformation, deception or manipulation that are more humane and more economical than a triumph by superior force. Indeed, "perhaps Sun Tzu's most important insight was that in a military or strategic contest, everything is relevant and connected: weather, terrain, diplomacy, the reports of spies and double-agents, supplies and logistics, the balance of forces, historic perceptions, the intangibles of surprise and morale. Each factor influences the others, giving rise to subtle shifts in momentum and relative advantage. There are no isolated events."

These Chinese views followed from the notion that in the whole of creation no particular constellation is ever stationary. All patterns are ever evolving, never static, and therefore one must orient oneself to where things are at any given time and one must determine where things are going and set up one's own position in this evolving pattern, or *shi*. Growing from these considerations, one must ascertain and set up a proper time to strike to advantage.

Accordingly, "in general, Chinese statesmanship exhibits a tendency to view the entire strategic landscape as part of a single whole: good and evil, near and far, strength and weakness, past and future all interrelated. In contrast to the Western approach of treating history as a process of modernity achieving a series of absolute victories over evil and backwardness, the traditional Chinese view of history emphasized a cyclical process of decay and rectification, in which nature and the world can be understood but not completely mastered." Therefore, "the best that can be accomplished is to grow into harmony with it. Strategy and statecraft become means of 'combative coexistence' with opponents. The goal is to maneuver them into weakness while building up one's own *shi*, or strategic position."⁹

Undoubtedly, even Chiang, Mao and later Chinese leaders need to be considered in the context of this ancient Chinese thought, especially regarding withdrawal and the necessity of tying up opponents with longer and longer supply lines and the trading of space for time as well as by procrastination, understanding that often "all things get done when nothing is done." This is certainly counter to General Joseph Stilwell's views evident in World War II in China—notably when in command of Chinese troops, and those of the U.S. Army chief of staff, General George Marshall, regarding the war in Asia, borrowed from General Ulysses Grant in the American Civil War and later—that massive frontal attacks were needed to crush opponents. Sometimes, though, in Chinese history when the stakes were judged to be high enough or the situation seemed to require an all-out effort—as during the time of the Taiping Uprisings and, later, in the civil war of the 1940s—the Chinese could fight as ferociously as anyone, often with catastrophic loss of life.¹⁰

Barbara Tuchman, in her excellent study, *Stilwell and the American Experience in China, 1911-45*, elaborated regarding the West and China. In most instances, she asserted, the underlying assumption was always that, whatever the policy, Asia in general but China in particular was as "clay in the hands of the West." At the heart of the West's wrong assumptions was that the Chinese world could be changed and reformed along Western lines. After all, the Japanese had progressed far along this road in the nineteenth century and had emerged as a world power to be reckoned with. But demands by the West for change, such as the Chinese adopting the models of combat efficiency and inculcated with a Western offensive spirit, not to mention "Christianity and democracy offered by missionaries and foreign advisers"—sometimes referred to as American exceptionalism—failed because they "were not indigenous demands of the society and culture to which they were brought." Those in America who, in the years to come, so vociferously argued that many of their benighted countrymen had "lost" China failed to grasp that the West had never "found" China; it was never the West's to lose.¹¹

Other views as to why the West "lost" China included those of Colonel David D. Barrett, who summed it up neatly: "In all sincerity, at the risk of oversimplification, it is doubtful if anything could have prevented us from 'losing' China as we did as long as we remain essentially an anti-Communist country." Indeed, "China was doomed to go Communist as the sparks fly upward, as long as it was governed by the Kuomintang. The blind stupidity and arrogant stubbornness of Chiang Kai-shek did much to accelerate the loss of China to the Reds, and our well-meant but fumbling and poorly directed efforts to help were of little avail, and with the economy of the country in complete chaos, collapse of the government, which of course meant a take-over by the well-organized opposition, was inevitable."[12]

These views are reinforced by conclusions found in the U.S. State Department publication *The China White Paper* of August 1949, which stated that it was fully realized in Washington that "military considerations have been secondary to an earnest desire on our part to assist the Chinese people to achieve peace, prosperity and internal stability." To these ends, "the decisions and actions of our Government to promote these aims necessarily were taken on the basis of information available at the time." Indeed, "throughout this tragic period, it has been fully realized that the material aid, the military and technical assistance, and the good will of the United States, however abundant, could not of themselves put China on her feet." Therefore, "in the last analysis, that can be done only by China herself." The path the Chinese took led to the triumph of the communists and was largely the result of China's history and culture and the course of events and developments within China itself. Accordingly, "a realistic appraisal of conditions in China, past and present, leads to the conclusion that the only alternative open to the United States was full-scale intervention in behalf of a Government which had lost the confidence of its own troops and its own people." Unfortunately, this intervention "would have required the expenditure of even greater sums" and even lead to "the command of Nationalist armies by American officers, and the probable participation of American armed forces ... in the resulting war."

In addition, "intervention of such a scope and magnitude would have been resented by the mass of the Chinese people, would have diametrically reversed our historic policy, and would have been condemned by the American people." Therefore, "the unfortunate but inescapable fact is that the ominous result of the civil war in China was beyond the control of the government of the United States. Nothing that this country did or could have done within the reasonable limits of its capabilities could have changed that result; nothing that was left undone by this country has contributed to it. It was the product of internal Chinese forces, forces that this country tried to influence but could not. A decision was arrived at within China, if only a decision by default."[13]

Another Westerner who knew a great deal about China, the American writer Nora Waln, echoed Tuchman's and Barrett's views, writing in *The House of Exile* that to the Chinese there was the understanding that no foreigner could help them. "No foreigner can understand us, because no outsider can know our history or our system of homestead government, which is the government of the longest world history and the base of all Chinese government." This had to do with the families and clans and their deliberations and decisions.[14]

Clearly, then, despite many failures to comprehend much about China, the West has never lacked people who understood a great deal about it, its place in the world, and how it was failing or succeeding in making its way through time, even if their voices were either unknown or unheeded. Perhaps some of these observations should be reconsidered from time to time, with recognition of their historical contexts. Several experts' views are of long standing, such as those of the astute head of China's Imperial Customs Service, Sir Robert Hart. His considerations were candid, tempered judgments manifesting empathy coupled with realism, but with few illusions. For example, as early as November 13, 1882, he wrote to James Duncan Campbell, his associate and confidant, who, in 1873, established a London office of the Chinese Imperial Customs, that he recognized China's contacts with the West were sowing some seeds in fertile ground. These events indeed were laying "a new foundation ... for China's future history, and it is gradually rising through the waters just as steadily—and as unseen—as coral." Still, it had always been difficult for foreigners to control, and in addition, "China is a very big country and very hard to rub out!"[15]

Hart admitted, though, that as to China "there are ups and downs and in the end *physical forces* determine what is to be! China is *down* to-day but two hundred years hence she will be *up!*" He continued the theme in another letter three years later, stating that "the Chinese as a race have 'stay'—cannot be wiped out—and must come to the front sooner or later: of that I'm sure!" In another missive he concluded "if China will only do the right thing, she will be in a century the most powerful empire on earth—the least aggressive—the most tolerant—and the greatest patron of learning!" Clearly, Hart appreciated that longevity is a historical force that must be recognized. China's 5,000-year history as a viable civilization is not a negligible factor. Perhaps more to the point regarding foreigners in China, Hart advised that "in the far-off future it will all come right again for foreign domination will only end in making a greater China than ever."[16]

Hart warned, though, that the West should be ever cognizant that there would be a strong China in the future, but whether or not it would be "friendly or hostile would depend on the treatment received from the Western world during time of weakness—and I am sure the future will show this warning to have been right." But no matter what, there would be a rocky road ahead for both East and West. "Before China can settle down, as a great strong and powerful country—to enjoy all the advantages of western education and Christian civilisation, she will have to go through a series of sorrows, the natural consequences of little knowledge, much ignorance, many blunders, and misleading conceit, and her friends and well-wishers will have their share of the sufferings such troubles will surely entail."[17]

More of his usual caution about China came through in two letters to Campbell in 1895, one stating "there's no use in being surprised at anything China does, for it is like riding a dozen horses in the ring at the same time: somebody is sure to create confusion!" A few months later, he went on: "I am still by way of thinking that China has a big future ahead, but she'll take her own time and go her own pace, and it would be better to recognise this." In the following year, he continued the refrain, saying, "The Government of China is a puzzle: it to-day looks like a lot of quicksilver on a flat surface with little curleycues cutting across to join larger ones and these again splitting up and forming new centres without seeming rhyme and reason! but it's like the man with the three thimbles and the pea: you see the pea for a moment and you then swear it is under such a thimble—and lo it's not! There is a Govt. and it continually is felt, but it's more of an atmosphere than a body and there's no locating it for grappling purposes." He certainly grew tired of China's ever-so-slow pace of reform, because "it's like trying to make a fishing-line out of jade-stone!"[18]

In all of the backing and filling, however, Hart never lost his farsighted views of the Chinese. Though he was often weary of their situation, and their reluctance to effect needed reforms, especially following the Boxer Uprising, he admitted he "never los[t] heart," because, he noted with reference to Alfred Lord Tennyson, his "faith is large in Time, and that which shapes it to some perfect end." He was confident that circumstances "will force this Govt. to take action in various directions and in the end all will come right, but I am sure of one thing: China will grow strong and then international relations will be of another kind." A few years later, in 1904, after the unsettling Boxer Uprisings, he reasserted his faith in the unfolding of time: "The Chinese go very slowly—but they are bound to arrive!" These developments were destined to lie well beyond his own time but his faith was eventually justified.[19]

These themes were admirably advanced over a century later, in 2013, by Orville Schell and John Delury in their provocative study, *Wealth and Power: China's Long March to the Twenty-first Century*.[20] This study uses, as its point of departure, a quote from Wei Yuan, uttered in 1842: "When the country is humiliated, its spirit will be aroused." To Schell and Delury, it was the deep shame the Chinese have felt since the First Opium War and the era of the "unequal treaties" that has been utilized to undergird Chinese policy since that time, especially in the 20th and 21st centuries, i.e., from the Empress Dowager Cixi to Deng Xiaoping and beyond to the present. Thus, there is "a deep strain in the Chinese psyche, which the country's current leaders have inherited as part of their cultural DNA. To love China means to share a passionate commitment to overcoming the loss of face suffered in the 19th century, to ensure that the defeats of the past will never be suffered again." This deep desire has motivated those taking the path to wealth and power enjoyed by contemporary China. Thus, as the writer Joseph Kahn has asserted, "The constant through China's recent history is the persistent search for something—anything—that would bring restoration." Much of that restoration has been realized, at least for the present.[21]

Other voices include that of the American philosopher John Dewey, who, in 1926 advanced the view that there must be attempts made by the West to relate to the Chinese with a sense of understanding, a view which is still valid. He noted that "China is rapidly growing up.... It will henceforth resent more and more any assumption of parental tutelage, even of a professedly benevolent kind.... Politically, the Chinese no longer wish for any foreign guardianship.... In the next ten years we shall have to ... alter our traditional temper of patronage, conscious or unconscious, into one of respect and esteem for a cultural equal."[22]

Also as to China and the West, there is a penetrating and judgmental assessment by John Paton Davies, Jr., the controversial American State Department foreign service officer. At the end of his book *Dragon by the Tail*, he concluded: "The truth of the matter is that China has been since the fall of the Empire a huge and seductive practical joke. The western businessmen missionaries, and educators who had tried to modernize and Christianize it failed. The Japanese militarists who tried to conquer it failed. The American government which tried to democratize and unify it failed. The Soviet rulers who tried to insinuate control over it failed. Chiang failed. Mao failed." Davies might have asked, as we do, therefore, "Whither China?"[23]

For some keys to understanding what had happened during World War II in China one can turn to Rana Mitter's insightful study, *Forgotten Ally: China's World War II, 1937–1945*.[24] Therein he notes that China under Chiang did not submit to a militarily superior Japan. In fact, Chinese resistance proved crucial in the defeat of the Axis by tying down Japanese forces in what some have called the "Chinese Quagmire." Despite the widespread destruction of numerous cities and its countryside, together with the loss of perhaps 20 million Chinese, the nation in World War II had regained the sovereignty it had lost in 1842—a situation that had persisted through the "Century of Shame"—and assumed its role as one of the Big Four emerging into the latter years of the 20th century. Unfortunately, ahead there were horrific sufferings and man-made plagues under Mao's regime, resulting from the grievously misbegotten "Great Leap Forward" and "Cultural Revolution" programs, for example, before a sounder basis could be established.

In the long run, then, by the latter years of the 20th century China eventually "overcame its travails by its own efforts. Through a painful and often humiliating process, China's statesmen in the end preserved the moral and territorial claims of their disintegrating world order." How was this achieved? "To weather the storm, China relied not on technology or military power but instead on two deeply traditional resources: the analytical abilities of its diplomats, and the endurance and cultural confidence of its people." Throughout, there was also an "imperturbable self-confidence projected by Chinese officials charged with managing contacts with foreigners—a trait unchanged in the modern period.[25]

Nonetheless, concern with the "Century of Shame" is still not dead, often accompanied by a keen remembrance of the invasion of Chinese territory by the Eight-Nation Alliance in 1900, during the Boxer era, a major event that set a benchmark for outrages the Chinese suffered at the hands of the West.[26]

Despite what should be a clear understanding of what China has suffered, to many Westerners, especially Americans, there were continuing persistent puzzles regarding the Chinese enigma. There had been perpetually varying policies in mind-boggling, confusing array in the United States concerning what role China was to play, both during World War II and afterward. Many Westerners, again especially Americans, also found it inexplicable that the Chinese did not like them. "But," one observer asked, "why should they? They had been perennially put upon by outsiders—Mongols, Manchus, Japanese pirates, and then the 'Red Hairs'—who humiliated them and debauched them with opium." Sir Robert Hart, inspector general of the Chinese Maritime Customs, has written that "it is apparently beyond dispute that, however friendly individuals may have appeared or been, general intercourse had all along been simply tolerated and never welcome...."[27]

In many ways, the relations between China and the U.S. and the attitudes of Americans were rather more straightforward, if often misunderstood. The American foreign service officer John Paton Davies, Jr., an Old China Hand, summed it up as follows: "The approach of the American public to China, during the three years after Pearl Harbor, was largely subjective. It was a product of one hundred years of missionary compulsions and involvement, spiritual and emotional, of a sense of guilt that the United States had not gone to the rescue of China under attack from Japan and had sold war materiel to Japan, and of propaganda portraying the Chinese as heroically fighting on our behalf and wanting only American arms and know-how to drive the enemy into the sea." Of course, the latter views were not sound and would cause much grief and strife in China-U.S. relations in the years to follow.[28]

Some of America's misadventures in Asia earlier included the nation's involvement in the Chinese civil war which had begun immediately following the end of World War II, with the decision to ignore Communist claims to take the surrender of adjacent Japanese garrisons. The usual understanding was that only Chiang's forces were to effect this action. This was deepened with the American transport of half a million Nationalist troops by air and sea to sensitive areas to prevent the Russians from entering China and to prevent the Communists' exploitation of the developing situation to their advantage in North China. American Marines also sided with the Nationalists against the Communists and the U.S. supplied all manner of war materiel to Chiang's Nationalist forces. Davies described the American involvement as follows: "The decision—or perhaps, more accurately, absence of decision—grew out of a century of American evangelical, educational, philanthropic and business association with China."

The results were "a sentimental, condescending, proprietary love of fictional Chinese, who, Americans fancied, reciprocated with due gratitude, admiration and loyalty. Americans identified these mythic Chinese with the idealized Chiangs." Indeed, the violent transformation of China was especially upsetting to Americans. The "true Chinese—our Chinese—were being routed by the suspect, un–Chinese Communists," who "were hardly known to the American people. In so far as they were, they did not fit the prevailing American mythology about China." Americans were "also loath to recognize that [the transformation] was caused by Nationalist decadence and Communist vitality." Many in the U.S. concluded that some force outside of China was to blame, most likely that of international communism being masterminded from Moscow.[29]

James Lilley, former U.S. ambassador to China, has noted in his memoirs something about a common American attitude about China: "For some reason, many Americans think their personal experiences in China are fascinating and unique, and, like the Ancient Mariner, they must tell their tale to the end. Their idea is: I have seen China, and, therefore, it now exists. But this is a static view, shaped by subjective interpretation and woefully narrow in scope." Later, he continued, "I met American four-star generals who would get briefed on substantive issues before going into China. However, once they returned to the U.S. after their short trip, they would stop listening, thinking that they had China figured out. They became like one-way walkie-talkies that transmitted but didn't receive." This could be a harmless trait, he concluded, "but in generals it was dangerous."

He himself sought to eschew romanticism and excessive emotion about China. His later involvement was of a professional nature and not an emotional one. This stance was to protect himself and his judgments about China. There were many Americans who desired to see "their" China, as opposed to the one that existed. They were impressed by the country, but they did not seek to truly know it. As an example of his objectivity toward China, Lilley indicated that he himself did not "feel guilty about the historical role of foreigners in China." This view rested on the realization that the American guilt complex over wrongs done to China was often played on by Chinese: "We are weak [they would say]. You have caused this, so you owe us. Give us something." He knew that his views were conditioned by his roots in China. He left it when he was 12, "with an ingrained sense of the Chinese culled from interacting with wash-amah, hearing stories of my father's work with Chinese agents, seeing the country's weak position versus foreign powers, and other experiences. At that young age, I had begun to understand the Chinese as an appealing but manipulative people with kind of a raw, easily agitated nerve from having been squashed by foreigners." Lilley sensed that "China's mixture of grievances derive[d] from a self-centered nationalism—deeply rooted in the Chinese past—[could] assume an anti-foreign tone or cast. This is not to say that there isn't genuine resentment against foreign behavior, which in the nineteenth century was deeply offensive to China. But one must not lose sight of the former because he is emotionally wound up in the latter." Thus Lilley attempted to delineate the Chinese mosaic with its countless pieces, but he understood that a rich, detailed picture was ever present, and that there were, in fact, many Chinas.[30]

In 1949 or so, as one American admiral on the U.S. Navy's Yangtze patrol has observed, the foreign devils were gone, together with the missionaries and the opium. To be sure, the Christian legacy of the hospitals and universities "still shows through." Also, many Chinese students study in the U.S., and, finally, "the Chinese are indisputably an inherently industrious, clever, imaginative people who consider themselves superior to other races, with some justification. China can be our enemy or our friend—or both, or neither." But rest assured, he concluded, that whatever the choices, one can be wholly certain that they will be in "China's own best interests, while not necessarily America's."[31]

Ian Morris, in his book *Why the West Rules—For Now* stresses the clash between East and West, with emphasis on the U.S. versus China. He everywhere implies that the U.S. and China must find new ways to collaborate.

Like it or not, East and West are now in a common mess, and the next 40 years will be the most important in history. We must not see this as yet another confrontation but a golden opportunity—maybe the only one we will have—of working together."[32]

By the time of our own era, early in the 21st century, many in both East and West are recognizing major distinctions regarding relations between these two worlds. Tim Clissold has asserted, "We live in a monopolar world but this state can't last forever. Unless, by some bizarre turn of events, the people of Europe opt for real political union, the key global power balance in the next hundred years will probably be between the United States and China. The Americans and the Chinese have a lot more in common than they think. Acutely aware of their current disadvantage, many Chinese have consciously gone out to educate themselves about America. Their conclusions tend to be balanced and favorable. But so far, not so many Americans have shown an interest in China or made much effort to understand it." Still, there is a slow realization dawning that "Washington is going to have to deal with Beijing increasingly as an equal over the coming decades." He hoped in these conditions that "there might be a shortcut in the process of misunderstanding, conflict, and reconciliation" and that "these two great peoples can develop a relationship underpinned by their similarities and where differences are respected and enjoyed." This, indeed, "would be a source of great hope for everyone."[33]

Martin Jacques, a British journalist who writes for the *Guardian*, in his book *When China Rules the World: The End of the Western World and the Birth of a New Global Order*, goes further, arguing that China is destined to marginalize the West. If China reclaims its past primacy that lasted for centuries, it will demonstrate that the centuries of Western dominance were a mere historical blip. As for the present, as he states it, "China is the elephant in the room that no one is quite willing to recognize. As a result, an extraordinary shift in the balance of global power is taking place *sotto voce*, almost by stealth, except one would be hard-pressed to argue that any kind of deceit was involved either on the part of China or the United States."[34]

As Jacques further explained in a book review in the *New York Times*, America "must come to terms with the fact that China's rise and America's decline are not simply a result of a failure of policy but are rather one of those great—and highly infrequent historical shifts that governments can do relatively little to affect, let alone prevent." As Henry Kissinger has concluded, in the 21st century "a new era of Asian economic reform and prosperity [is] taking root—one that … may well return the region to its historic role as the world's most productive and prosperous continent."[35]

As events seem to be evolving in the 21st century, China will surely continue to enhance its power. Indeed, barring the unfortunate preoccupation with the Middle East, another observer has concluded that the most serious fact of international life today is the reemergence of China as a great power for the first time in two hundred years. This now looms "as the single greatest military-diplomatic challenge to the United States" and for many other nations around the globe.[36]

Not all observers, however, see China's burgeoning future as necessarily assured. Timothy Beardson, in a significant study, *Stumbling Giant: The Threats to China's Future*, suggests that, while China is certain to continue its rise on the world's stage, it faces threats "so serious and so widespread, and the domestic policy response [is] so timid, that it is inconceivable that China will overtake the United States this century." He included a long list of China's difficulties, alluding to its financial and economic weaknesses, and its need for substantial educational reforms, especially with an eye to emphasizing innovation and basic research. He further noted China's huge aging population, which will lead to China's overall population decline. There is need for far more comprehensive social programs. The nation must also cope with grave pollution problems regarding both air and water supplies. There are problems with a sufficient water supply and substantial drought and encroaching deserts. There is much evidence of area subsidence, the consequence of vast quantities of water being pumped from underground sources compounded by the massive construction of huge buildings, as in Shanghai, for example. In addition, China is engaged in enormous water diversion projects that cause alarm within China, as well as in several foreign countries, such as Burma, Vietnam, and Laos. Destructive landslides have resulted from the destabilization of soil caused by extensive dam building. There is an increase in the number of internal riots stemming from numerous causes. There is also much corruption at all levels of China's life both private and public. There are gender disparities, with many more males present in China than females, resulting in competition for brides and a measure of internal strife.[37]

A recent brief but cogent account by a self-styled "accidental sinologist," Mark Leonard, raises other interesting questions about China and the West. Leonard observes that the West knows little about contemporary Chinese thinkers and what they dream for their country, which, in turn, means a great deal of what the coming world will be like. As he observes, "Europeans and Americans, in particular, are ill-equipped to answer these questions. Since the time when French and British missionaries first travelled to the East, the West has focused on what it wanted from China—and how to convert the

Chinese to a Western way of life. People wrongly assumed that as China grew richer, it would also become more like us."[38] Leonard met many of China's intellectuals and watched fascinated as he "saw them take Western ideas and adapt them into a new Chinese approach for dealing with the world—joining an intellectual journey that China began when it first became entangled with the West in the nineteenth century."[39]

Leonard notes that China in the past has often manifested an intellectual insecurity that resulted in massive swings from one extreme ideology to the next, as in the Cultural Revolution, for instance, and in Marxism, then maybe back, at least to some extent, to Confucius, then once more to the Western political and economic thought and practice. This is certainly a case of the pendulum theory of history in practice. What the Chinese are learning is that following the West too far leads to chaos and to China's falling between the two stools of extremism in ways not conducive to the development of the good life for all Chinese. Leonard quotes a Tsinghua University professor, Cui Zhiyuan, who wrote a seminal article calling for a new "liberation of thought," arguing that after Chinese intellectuals had freed themselves from orthodox Marxism, they now "should liberate themselves from their unquestioning admiration of Western capitalism. Zhiyuan's goal was to break the boom and bust cycle that saw China embrace a new ideology every generation, and to encourage Chinese people to think for themselves." Leonard further concluded that China's development should be built on Beijing's terms and not those of the West.[40]

The author Pankaj Mishra, has similarly focused on modern Chinese thought. The question is "what to accept, adapt or reject from the West," which remains central in contemporary Asian politics. All of this seems to be necessary, because as Mishra observes, "the central event of the last century for the majority of the world's population was the intellectual and political awakening of Asia."[41]

In other ways, the Chinese have had to proceed along their own paths. One striking example regards Chinese Christians, revealing a decidedly mixed bag as to Western missionary activity and its consequences. The Chinese Christians today have an official Christian church but many are still underground. Others increasingly venture into the daylight, but there are still dangers of official harassment and even worse. Nonetheless, there are about 300,000,000 believers in Buddhism, Islam and Christianity, with something over 70,000,000 being Christians (about the same number of Chinese members of the Communist Party there). And many of the most thoughtful of Chinese Christians are determined to do things "their way." Many practice a blend of Chinese communism, Christianity, and capitalism. This places emphasis on trust and mutual respect, at least in theory, and communism, also at least in theory, as well as to a degree in practice. Christianity owes something to the widespread debunking of Confucius in the Cultural Revolution, though there has been a return to this as well in recent times. Christians also have to contend with a rampant—even rabid—capitalism that is widely recognized as debasing, if not eliminating, spiritual values, though some see congruence between capitalism and Christianity.

In view of the foregoing, a major question regarding China today is the following: "How quickly and competently will the new China now manage to capitalize on its early, historical promise?" There are others: How quickly can it overcome and recede from its horrific "Century of Shame" contacts with the West? Can these be subsumed, overcome and proceeded beyond? What will the new China look like? Will it be a danger to the West? There does not seem to be a lack of appreciation of all of the factors in play. Yet, as Simon Winchester notes in his book *The Man Who Loved China*, China has a very long, brilliant past. This brilliance persisted for thousands of years up to about AD 1500, when for some reason the Chinese "stopped trying" to further their creative path. This was the point at which the ball was passed to the West: the Renaissance, the rise of modern science and technology, then on down the road the industrial revolution and the modern age. In the 19th and 20th centuries, China was subsequently despised, regarded as retrograde, uncivilized, filthy, and was altogether detested. Consequently, since nothing intervened to stay their hand, it was systematically and thoroughly exploited by the West.

Then out of the chaos, there came modern China. This was partly the product of Western imperialism and missionary activity but also much else. Internally, there was chaos, but then, out of the incredible sufferings of China and her peoples, there came salvation, on Chinese terms and not to the liking of the West. Yet salvation was fraught with incredible shortcomings and backsliding and untold sacrifice and intense suffering by the Chinese people. There has persisted throughout something that seems "changeless" and something that "resists change and can only be described as an *attitude*. It is a *Chinese state of mind*," one which non–Chinese often find infuriating and insufferable "but which certainly exists, and at no great depth beneath the Chinese skin." This attitude is "of ineluctable and self-knowing Chinese *superiority*, and it results from the antiquity and the longevity of the Chinese people's endeavors."[42]

This sense of their seeming "unending achievement" has led to a sense of self-satisfaction and superiority, "a kind of national smugness" that contributed to its beginning to flounder, a hubris that is great in its magnitude and may result in dire consequences.[43]

Conclusion 245

In any event, China is neither poor nor backward anymore. It is surely one of the ironies of history that the success of modern China "derives in large measure from this very same sense" that had exasperated so many Westerners, that "peculiarly and infuriatingly *Chinese* sense ... of self-certainty, of an unshakable confidence about its position at the center of the world." So the smugness is returning. Will the Chinese have learned their lessons? The Chinese language remains intact essentially unaltered from its origins more than 3,000 years ago. While there was a hiatus of several hundred years, from about 1500 to the present, China has now profoundly changed yet again, and within two decades has "become so rich, energetic, freewheeling, awesome, and spectacular" that "it seems abundantly clear that creativity, true inventiveness, is starting to flow in China once again, with the new prosperity of the country." Thus, "no longer is China the sinkhole of decay and desuetude that it was. Nowadays, in every field—in science and technology on the one hand, in literature and the plastic arts on the other—the new China is entering a time of intense activity and entrepreneurial energy." Indeed, a "vast new China with vast new cities is emerging with an almost frightening speed and energy—fast turning itself into a global power the like of which it is almost impossible to imagine."[44]

Another writer, Robert McCrum, notes that this might seem to place China on a collision course with the U.S., as some in the Pentagon see it, maybe in a struggle over Taiwan. But this may be a misreading. As China watcher Joshua Cooper Ramo has noted, Sun Tzu, in his classic book, *The Art of War*, asserted "the goal for China is not conflict but the avoidance of conflict," because "the supreme act of war is to subdue the enemy without fighting." Therefore, for China, "true success in its strategy involves the successful manipulation of the situation to achieve an outcome that will inevitably favor Chinese interests." Finally, Sun Tzu had counseled that "every battle is won or lost before it is ever fought."[45]

An analysis of America's failures to understand the Chinese and their history and culture was presented by Senator J. William Fulbright, of the Senate Foreign Relations Committee. In February 1972, he further remarked on America's views: "For too many years Americans have found it difficult, if not impossible, to engage in rational, dispassionate discussion of China.... We consider ourselves uniquely qualified to play the role of China's savior." John S. Service, an American foreign service officer, also in February 1972, one week before Nixon went to China, stated, "I think that our involvement in Vietnam, our insistence on the need to contain China and to prevent what we thought was the spread of Communist influence in Southeast Asia, was based very largely on our misunderstanding and our lack of knowledge of the Chinese, the nature of the Chinese Communist movement and the intention of their leaders. We assumed that they were an aggressive country, and I don't believe that they really have been, and, therefore, I think we got into Vietnam largely, as I say, through the misinterpretation and misfounded fear of China."[46]

Yet another observer, Ian Morris, in his enlightening study, *Why the West Rules—For Now: The Patterns of History and What They Reveal About the Future*, asserts that the U.S. and China must find new ways to collaborate: "Like it or not East and West are now in a common mess, and 'the next 40 years will be the most important in history.'" This must not, however, be regarded as yet another confrontation but a golden opportunity, maybe the only one we will have, of working together.[47]

Our views of China are certainly changing. One scholar, Joseph Needham, of Cambridge University, in his book *Science in Traditional China: A Comparative Perspective*, has laid a substantial foundation upon which rests much fundamental reorientation about East and West, with particular attention to China. This book consists of several lectures delivered at New Asia College, the Chinese University at Shatin, Hong Kong, in 1979. Needham created the great study of Chinese science and medicine and began the publication of the multivolume study *Science and Civilisation in China*, which now consists of over 20 volumes. This work began in 1937, when several Chinese students arrived at Cambridge to study for their doctorates. Needham also served as scientific counselor at the British embassy in Chungking throughout World War II. By this time, he was fluent in Mandarin and had gathered much information about Chinese science and history. The center for this study, the great East Asian History of Science Library, is at Caius College, Cambridge. These lectures comprise studies of "Gun Powder and Firearms, Comparative Macrobiotics; Acupuncture and Moxibustion; and Attitudes Toward Time and Change." Needham began his writing career with one book, a history of science, technology and medicine in China.[48]

As to what Americans might now be doing regarding China, and why, the former U.S. secretary of state Henry Kissinger had some insights. He endeavored to put China into some sort of perspective: "The Chinese never generated a myth of cosmic creation. Their universe was created by the Chinese themselves, whose values, even when declared of universal applicability, were conceived of as Chinese in origin." China is perhaps best seen as a "civilization pretending to be a nation-state" and "Confucius best seen as one whose thinking affirmed a code of social conduct, not a roadmap to the afterlife." Central to much Chinese thought was that the Chinese Empire "should tower over its geographical sphere [which was] taken virtually as a law of nature, an expression of the Mandate of Heaven. For Chinese Emperors, the mandate did not necessarily imply an adversarial relationship with neighboring peoples; preferably it did not. Like the United States, China thought of itself as playing a special role. But it never espoused the American notion of universalism to spread its values around the world."[49]

In keeping with Kissinger's views, it might even be necessary, in the modern era, to dust off the old saws formulated in the 19th century by theoreticians, geopoliticians, and analysts such as the German-Prussian general Carl Philipp Gottfried von Clausewitz, who asserted that "diplomacy is the art of the possible" and suggested that "war is diplomacy by other means" and "diplomacy is war by other means." These approaches might once again be made integral to calculations as to our own considerations of whys and wherefores and what can legitimately be expected and anticipated in American involvement throughout the world.[50]

Whatever the legacies of the Westerners might be, there is no doubt that the unequal treaties and "extrality" were at the core of the "Century of Shame," which has continued to vex, perplex and haunt the Chinese even to this day. Long ago, Thucydides, in his *History of the Peloponnesian War*, had recounted what has been called the "Melian Dialogue." This occurred in the 27-year struggle (431–404 BC) between Athens and Sparta. During its course, in 416 and 415 BC, the Athenians had demanded that the people of Melos, a small island in the southern Aegean Sea, surrender their city and pay a tribute to prevent the destruction of their city. In the upshot, the people of Melos refused, noting that in such cases "the strong do what they will, and the weak suffer what they must." What they had to suffer was their own destruction, and their understanding of prevailing realities ever after was a definition of certain truisms in human conduct and affairs.

The Chinese found themselves in similar straits from 1839 to 1949, being "hustled" and "rustled" for a century or so. But on occasion many beleaguered sufferers not only endure but prevail and in the end become a force to be reckoned with, in this case, on a global scale. In this regard, a British official in China observed that the Chinese would eventually simply "be Chinese." "Not a race to be trifled with … they will go exactly their own way in conformity with their innate commonsense instinct." An American official in the Chinese Maritime Customs Service in the late 19th and early 20th centuries concurred, further observing, "There is no foreigner living who can advise the Chinese what is best for them. The Chinese 'breed true to type,' and they can never become free until the weight of the dead [Western] hand is completely removed."[51]

These developments can be closely observed in today's Nanjing

[Nanking]. There, in a tiny temple, the Jing Hui Shi, called simply the Nanjing Treaty Museum, the text of the Treaty of Nanking of August 29, 1842, which launched the "Century of Shame," "written in elegant calligraphy," is carefully preserved. The British traveler and man of letters Simon Winchester appeared at that temple in the mid-1990s. He met Professor Wang, director of the Nanjing Relics Bureau, who informed him that the humiliation of that century was almost over. Wang stated, "Now we have almost everything [that we lost] back. Manchuria is ours again. Shandong was taken back from the Germans. The Russians kicked out. So were the Japanese—the hateful Japanese. The Portuguese are leaving Macau." Soon Hong Kong would be returned, which would complete the picture, and, the professor continued, "maybe Taiwan, too." After that, the treaty would simply be a historic relic; but, he went on, the "people will not forget," and they would not let it happen again. He then concluded on a positive note: "Now, we must be friends. But equal friends. Not like before. We Chinese are at least the equal of you now, don't you agree? At the very least, equal."[52]

Presently, in the early 21st century, the institution of the ancient "Middle Kingdom," which had lasted for centuries, has returned; and the "Mandate of Heaven," which now once more bears the proud trademark "Made in China," is again to the fore.

In any case, as for the United States, there is recognition that China's 5,000-year civilization might be compared to the U.S.'s nearly 250-year history as a national state and its clearly significant status and accomplishments, though in one sense, it is still a youngster. There is also an appreciation of the differences in respect to population figures, though these are hardly the only factor in the formula of power. As someone in China has observed, China could match America's 300 million and still have a billion in reserve, though things are hardly that simple.

As to the last word regarding the impact of the West on China, it is difficult to quarrel with Barbara Tuchman's succinct and accurate conclusions in her fine study on Stilwell and the American experience in China. She argues that China—in the face of vast changes and monumental, massive sufferings resulting from its interminable contacts with the West, and its own internal struggles and strife—was ultimately "a problem for which there was no American [or Western] solution." In the end, she wrote, "China went her own way as if the Americans [and the West] had never come."[53]

Chapter Notes

Preface

1. Arthur Judson Brown, *New Forces in Old China: An Inevitable Awakening* (New York: Fleming H. Revell Company, 2nd ed. [1904; repr., Lititz, PA: Bibliobazzar, 2006], 19, 21).

2. Timothy Brook, *Vermeer's Hat: The Seventeenth Century and the Dawn of the Global World* (New York: Bloomsbury Press, 2008), 45–47, 53.

3. For a discussion of Barrett's views of the Chinese, see John N. Hart, *The Making of an Army "Old China Hand": A Memoir of Colonel David D: Barrett* (Berkeley: University of California Press, 1985), 8–9. For Buck, see her *My Several Worlds* (New York: John Day, 1954), 229.

4. Brian Power, *The Ford of Heaven* (New York: Michael Kesend, 1984), 20.

5. Nora Waln, *The House of Exile* (Boston: Little, Brown, 1933), 53–54.

6. Henry Kissinger, *On China* (New York: Penguin Press, 2011), 5–6, 13.

7. This appeared in the *Sentinel*, April 21, 1922. This publication was the troop news magazine of the 15th U.S. Infantry Regiment stationed in Tientsin, China, from 1912 to 1938. The author was related to an officer of the regiment.

8. Buck, *My Several Worlds*, 34.

Chapter 1

1. Robert McCrum, *Globish: How the English Language Became the World's Language* (New York: W.W. Norton, 2010), 15.

2. Pearl S. Buck, *My Several Worlds* (New York: John Day, 1954), 34, and Timothy Brook, *Vermeer's Hat: The Seventeenth Century and the Dawn of the Global World* (New York: Bloomsbury Press, 2008), 46–47, 53.

3. For studies of missionaries in China see Kenneth Scott Latourette, *A History of Christian Missions in China* (London: Society for Promoting Christian Knowledge 1929); Paul A. Varig, *Missionaries, Chinese, and Diplomats: The American Protestant Missionary Movement in China, 1890-1952* (Princeton: Princeton University Press, 1958); Jacques Genet, *China and the Christian Impact: A Conflict of Cultures* (Cambridge: Cambridge University Press, 1985); Arthur Judson Brown, *New Forces in Old China: An Inevitable Awakening* (New York: Fleming H. Revell, 2nd ed. [1904; repr., Lititz, PA: Bibliobazzar, 2006]); Hilary Spurling, *Pearl Buck in China: Journey to the Good Earth* (New York: Simon and Schuster, 2010); and John S. Service, ed., *Golden Inches: The China Memoir of Grace Service* (Berkeley: University of California Press, 1989).

4. Robert Hart, *"These from the Land of Sinim": Essays on the China Question* (London: Chapman and Hall, 1901), 119, 130–31, 134–35, 163. For information on Hart and his illustrious career see Juliet Bredon, *Sir Robert Hart: The Romance of a Great Career* (Reprint of the 1910 edition by Dodo Press, London, 2009). Juliet was a niece of Hester Jane Bredon, who married Robert in 1866 (see pp. 4–8). Also for Hart's career, see John King Fairbank, Katherine Frost Bruner, and Elizabeth MacLeod Matheson, eds., *The I.G. in Peking: Letters of Robert Hart, Chinese Maritime Customs, 1868-1907*, 2 vols. (Cambridge, MA: Harvard University Press, 1975), vol. 1, xiv, 1–9. These letters were addressed to James Duncan Campbell, Hart's associate and confidant, who in 1873 established a London office of the Chinese Maritime Customs. Hart wrote hundreds of informative letters to this official from that year until Campbell's death in 1907. For details, see especially ibid., xvi–xix, 8–9. For Hart's early years in China, and much about his private life in these years, see his journals published as *En-*

249

Notes—Chapter 1

tering China's Service: Robert Hart's Journals, 1854-1963, ed. Katherine F. Bruner, John K. Fairbank, and Richard J. Smith (Cambridge, MA: Harvard University Press, 1986).

5. Raymond Chang and Margaret Scrogin Chang, *Speaking Chinese: A Cultural History of the Chinese Language* (New York: W.W. Norton, 1978), paperback ed., 1983, note, pp. 50–51.

6. Simon Winchester, *The River at the Center of the World: A Journey Up the Yangtze, and Back in Chinese Time* (New York: Henry Holt, 1996), 101–102. Winchester is also author of the *Man Who Loved China: The Fantastic Story of the Eccentric Scientist Who Unlocked the Mysteries of the Middle Kingdom* (New York: Harper Perennial, 2009). For details of the early trade between the Chinese and Europeans, see Eric Jay Dolin, *When America First Met China* (New York: Liveright, 2012). For the impact of the opium wars on the Chinese, see Chang and Chang, *Speaking Chinese*, note, pp. 50–51. See also Arthur Judson Brown, *New Forces in Old China: An Inevitable Awakening* (New York: Fleming H. Revell, 2nd ed. [1904; repr., Lititz, PA: Bibliobazzar, 2006]).

7. Letters, Hart to Campbell, April 26, 1891, and September 15, 1895, in Fairbank et al., *The I.G. in Peking*, vol. 2, pp. 842, 1033. Extraterritorality, however, was not given up until the 20th century. The Germans and Austrians were forced out of China during World War I. The Soviet Union gave up Russian rights in 1924, after the Bolshevik Revolution. Italy and Japan lost their rights when they declared war on China in World War II. The British and Americans, in a bid to keep China in the war against Japan, gave up their rights in 1943. Portugal was the last nation to surrender rights, in 1946.

8. Quoted in Hart, "These from the Land of Sinim," 52–53, 68–69, 122.

9. Murat Halstead, *The Story of the Philippines: The Eldorado of the Orient* (Chicago: H.L. Barber, 1898).

10. Hart, "These from the Land of Sinim," 161–163, 165–166.

11. Letter, Hart to Campbell, October 1, 1891, in Fairbank et al., *The I.G. in Peking*, vol. 2, pp. 860–861.

12. Nora Waln, *The House of Exile* (Boston: Little, Brown, 1933), 91. See pp. 91–98 for details of theatricals in China.

13. For the Boxers, see the interesting account in a diary of Mrs. Edward Bangs Drew, in Lou Henry Hoover Papers, Subject File "Belgian Relief Correspondence, 1916–20, to Boxer Rebellion," Box 13, Folder 3, Boxer Rebellion Diaries, Herbert Hoover Presidential Library, West Branch, Iowa. Mrs. Drew noted that she wanted her coolie to see dead bodies of Boxers that were reported at the train station in Tientsin as proof that they did in fact get killed by bullets, but he refused to believe anything that she said and would not go. Mrs. Drew was the wife of Edward Bangs Drew, an American commissioner for the Imperial Chinese Customs Service in Tientsin, i.e., one of Sir Robert Hart's men. This diary focuses on the events in Tientsin, at the port of Tagu, and on board the U.S. Army transport USS *Logan*, which sailed to Nagasaki, Yokohama, and on to San Francisco.

14. Chang's version had been translated by missionaries in Shantung as *Death Blow to Corrupt Doctrines*. Letter, Hart to Campbell, July 30, 1891, in Fairbank et al., *The I.G. in Peking*, vol. 2, pp. 853–854. The tract was, in Hart's words, "spicy and clap-trap" and therefore effective among its Chinese readership.

15. See letters, Hart to Campbell, April 1, May 20 and 27, 1900, in Fairbank et al., *The I.G. in Peking*, vol. 2, pp. 1223–4, 1228–1230.

16. Joseph Esherick, *The Origins of the Boxer Uprising* (Berkeley: University of California Press, 1987), 299–300. See also discussion in Jonathan Spence, *The Search for Modern China* (New York: W.W. Norton, 1990), 232.

17. See the diary of W.E. Bainbridge, secretary to the U.S. minister to China, Edwin Hurd Conger, in the Lou Henry Hoover Papers, Subject File, "Belgian Relief to the Boxer Rebellion," Box 13, Folder: Boxer Rebellion Diaries of Mr. W.W. Bainbridge, Herbert Hoover Presidential Library, West Branch, Iowa, 3–4; David J. Silbey, *The Boxer Rebellion and the Great Game in China* (New York: Hill and Wang, 2012), 61–65.

18. Arnold Henry Savage Landor, *China and the Allies*, 2 vols. (New York: Charles Scribner's Sons, 1901), 240.

19. See quotes by John Patton Davies, Jr., an American Foreign Service officer who was born in Kiating, China, of missionary parents in 1908, in his book, *Dragon by the Tail: American, British, Japanese and Russian Encounters with China and One Another* (New York: W.W. Norton, 1972). See especially the chapter entitled "The Intruders," 71–83.

20. R.H. Mason and J.G. Caiger, *A History of Japan*, rev. ed. (Tokyo: Tuttle, 1997), 262. See also a discussion in Service, ed., *Golden Inches*, xv–xxi.

21. Arnold Henry Savage Landor, *China and the Allies*, 2 vols. (New York: Charles Scribner's Sons, 1901), vol. 1, p. 241.

22. Kemp Tolley, *The Yangtze Patrol: The U.S. Navy in China* (Annapolis, MD: Naval Institute Press, 1971), 55.

23. Madeleine Albright, *The Mighty and the Almighty: Reflections on America, God, and World Affairs* (New York: Harper, 2007), 24.

24. As quoted in Service, ed., *Golden Inches,* vii.

25. See volume one: *The Chinese Classics* (New York: John B. Alden, 1885). This includes *The Analects, The Great Learning* and *The Doctrine of the Mean.* The second part of the book consists of *The Works of Mencius.* Confucius lived from 551 to 479 BCE.

26. See Arthur Henderson Smith, *Chinese Characteristics,* reprint edition based on the 1894 edition, (Norwalk, Connecticut: Eastbridge Press, 2002), 1, reprint of the edition (Edinburgh: Oliphant, Anderson and Ferrier, 1900). The 1892 and 1894 reprint editions were each brought out in London and New York with a reduced text from the 1890 edition. In the much later 1998 Beijing edition, the eliminated chapters from the 1890 edition were reincorporated.

27. Ibid., 319–320; 330.

28. Hart, Robert. *"These From the Land of Sinim." Essays On the Chinese Question.* London: Chapman & Hall, 1903, p. 121.

29. Quoted in Brown, *New Forces in Old China,* 224–225.

30. As quoted in Benson Lee Grayson, ed., *The American Image of China* (New York: Frederick Ungar, 1979), 6.

31. L.C. Arlington, *Through the Dragon's Eyes: Fifty Years' Experiences of a Foreigner in the Chinese Government Service* (London: Constable, 1931), 276–7.

32. Hunter Thomas Gould, *An American in China, 1936-1939: A Memoir* (New York: Thomas and Sons Books, 2004), 208.

33. Signed by "Someone" of the 15th Infantry's Service Company, in the *Sentinel,* June 11, 1926.

34. They would have well understood a bon mot of an American soldier of the 15th Infantry who served in China in the 1920s: "It may be all very well while in Rome to do as the Romans do, but in China few of us would survive if we did as the Chinese do!" See the *Sentinel,* March 25, 1921.

35. For some aspects of Chinese hatred toward them and the suffering the missionaries endured, see books by Pearl Buck, such as *The Exile, The Fighting Angel,* and *The Exile's Daughter,* and the excellent study of her life by Hilary Spurling, *Pearl Buck in China: Journey to the Good Earth* (New York: Simon and Schuster, 2010), and Service, ed., *Golden Inches.*

36. For examples of missionary involvement in native lawsuits and their use of sedan chairs, see Brown, *New Forces in Old China,* 49–65, 215–22, and Hart, *"These From the Land of Sinim,"* 4–5.

37. Buck, *My Several Worlds,* 21, 132. See also Spurling, *Pearl Buck in China.*

38. Buck, *My Several Worlds,* 132. Note, therefore, the negative side of missionary activity there and the damage and collateral damage that they suffered as well. For more on losses of numerous family members, often to diseases, see Service, ed., *Golden Inches,* 28–29 and passim.

39. Buck, *My Several Worlds,* 109.

40. Ibid., 228–229.

41. Ibid., 119.

42. Goldsworthy Lowes Dickinson, *Letters from John Chinaman* (London, 1901), 32–40. As to the locusts, see Joel 2:25 in the Bible, which refers to "the years that the locusts hath eaten."

Chapter 2

1. Letters, Hart to Campbell, May 14, May 27, and June 4, 1891, in John King Fairbank, Katherine Frost Bruner, and Elizabeth MacLeod Matheson, eds., *The I.G. in Peking: Letters of Robert Hart Chinese Maritime Customs, 1868–1907,* 2 vols. (Cambridge, MA: Harvard University Press, 1975), vol. 2, pp. 844–847. On June 5, further attacks at Wuhsüeh resulted in the killing of two British citizens. See note 3, p. 847.

2. Ibid., 850–852, Letter, Hart to Campbell, July 9, 1891.

3. Ibid., 847, 854–855, 859–860, 860–61, Letters, Hart to Campbell, June 4, August 22, September 11, and October 1, 1891.

4. Ibid., 1022–23, 1027. See letters, Hart to Campbell, June 9 and August 4, 1895.

5. Some sources indicate that Brooks was slain by members of the *Ta-tao* (Big Sword) secret society.

6. Fairbank et al, *The I.G. in Peking,* vol. 2, pp. 1214–15, Letter, Hart to Campbell, January 6, 1900.

7. See p. 16 from "Besieged in Peking," the diary of William E. Bainbridge, second secretary of the American Legation in Peking, and secretary to the U.S. minister to China, Edwin Hurd Conger, Subject File "Belgian Relief Correspondence, 1916–20, to Boxer Rebellion," Folder: Boxer Rebellion Diaries, Box 13, in Lou Henry Hoover Papers, at the Herbert Hoover Presidential Library, West Branch, Iowa.

8. Boxer chant, quoted in Desmond Power, *Little Foreign Devil* (Vancouver: Pangli Imprint, 1996), i.

9. Details of the Battle of Tientsin are described in depth in the account by Lou Henry Hoover, the wife of the future U.S. president Herbert Hoover. Further regarding these events, Herbert Hoover rather pointedly stated that while the foreigners in Peking suffered a longer siege than did Tientsin they suffered fewer losses. At the same time as the Boxer Uprising, Britain's attention was focused on the South

African War and the dramatic sieges of Kimberley, Mafeking and Ladysmith that had just been lifted. But as Hoover rather primly put it, "the total losses of defenders in all three of these put together did not equal our white losses at Tientsin, to say nothing of the losses among the Chinese refugees." The reasons that the losses in South Africa and Peking were better known could be explained, Hoover asserting that "their publicity arrangements were better." See "Lou Henry Hoover's Story," Lou Henry Hoover Papers, Herbert Hoover Presidential Library, West Branch, Iowa. See also "The Memoirs of Herbert Hoover, Years of Adventure, 1874-1920," in the same source.

10. MacArthur was appointed the military governor-general in 1900, but his term ended in the following year because of clashes with the civilian governor-general and future U.S. president, William Howard Taft.

11. See the "Diary of Anna Drew," Subject File "Belgian Relief Correspondence, 1916–20, to Boxer Rebellion," Folder 3, Boxer Rebellion Diaries, Box 13, Lou Henry Hoover Papers, Herbert Hoover Presidential Library, West Branch, Iowa. The Americans were subsequently transported on the *Logan* to Nagasaki, Yokohama, and finally to San Francisco, courtesy of the U.S. Army.

12. For the 9th's history during this period, see the detailed study by its adjutant, Captain Fred Radford Brown, *The History of the Ninth U.S. Infantry, 1799-1909* (Chicago: R.R. Donnelley and Sons, 1909).

13. General Arthur MacArthur, from his Philippine post, suggested that the War Department might consider him for the leadership role. The secretary of war, Elihu Root, and the adjutant general, Henry C. Corbin, however, demurred, the latter politely but firmly stating his opinion "that the importance of the work that you have in hand is so great that your presence in Manila is demanded by the best interests of the service." See the study by Lieutenant Colonel Robert R. Leonhard, "The China Relief Expedition: Joint Coalition Warfare in China, Summer, 1900," 25–26.

14. Ibid., 37.

15. For the U.S. Army's involvement at this time, see the account by Brigadier General Aaron Simon Daggett, *America in the China Relief Expedition* (1903; rpr., Nashville TN: Battery Press, 1997). See also General Adna Romanza Chaffee, *Report on the China Relief Expedition*, excerpted from *Five Years of the War Department Following the War with Spain, 1899-1903*, (Washington, D.C.: U.S. War Department, 1904), 395–407. Chaffee was later promoted to lieutenant general in 1904. He subsequently served as chief of staff of the U.S. Army from 1904 to 1906.

16. As they marched, the melodious 9th Regiment, at least sometimes, reputedly sang: "The 9th is on the *Logan* to China for to go/ Where we may mix up, in a Oriental row/ Against Japanese and Germans we may have to make a stand/When it comes to dividing up, this Ancient China land."

17. Titus was awarded the Congressional Medal of Honor and an appointment to West Point. He subsequently graduated from there in 1905 and retired in 1903 as a lieutenant colonel.

18. For details of these events, see the *Armorer* (November 30, 2006); Monro MacCloskey, *Reilly's Battery; A Story of the Boxer Rebellion* (New York: R. Rosen Press, 1969), which also presents considerable detail regarding the Boxer Uprising in general; and Charles Pelot Summerall, *The Way of Duty, Honor, Country: The Memoir of General Charles Pelot Summerall*, edited and annotated by Timothy K. Nenninger (Lexington: University of Kentucky Press, 2010). Another American officer, Captain Joseph Theodore Dickman, who served in the 8th U.S. Cavalry in the China Relief Expedition, was a rare figure because the 8th was not a major unit of the U.S. Army involved in the campaign. Dickman, after the relief of the legations, was also on Chaffee's staff. He has provided his detailed account in an article, "Experiences in China," in the *Journal of the United States Cavalry Association* 13, no. 45 (July, 1902), 5–40. Dickman was destined for a much greater role in World War I. For an introduction to the U.S. Marines, who were also involved during the Boxer era, see the article by Trevor K. Plante, "U.S. Marines in the Boxer Rebellion," *Prologue* 31, no. 4 (Winter 1999). A useful summary of the U.S. Army's intervention in China is provided by Robert R. Leonhard, "The China Relief Expedition: Joint Coalition Warfare in China, Summer 1900" (Baltimore: Johns Hopkins University Applied Physics Laboratory, 2008.)

Chapter 3

1. David J. Silbey, *The Boxer Rebellion and the Great Game in China* (New York: Hill and Wang, 2012), 237.

2. Cixi has often been viewed negatively, especially in the West. For a recent, more sympathetic, revisionist study of the empress, with a close assessment of her views and actions during the Boxer era and her contributions to modern China, see Jung Chang, *Empress Dowager Cixi: The Concubine Who Launched Modern China* (New York: Alfred A. Knopf, 2013).

3. These provisions would later bring the U.S. 15th Infantry Regiment to China in 1912,

though there were other reasons for their deployment.

4. The empress dowager and her court had returned to Peking on January 7, 1902, after the protocol was signed.

5. For a solid account of the Boxer Uprising and its results, see Diana Preston, *The Boxer Rebellion: The Dramatic Story of China's War on Foreigners That Shook the World in the Summer of 1900* (New York: Berkley Books, 1999). For a useful more recent study, see David J. Silbey, *The Boxer Rebellion and the Great Game in China* (New York: Hill and Wang, 2012).

6. Arnold Henry Savage Landor, *China and the Allies*, 2 vols. (New York: Charles Scribner's Sons, 1901), vol. 1, pp. 200–205. Landor (1865–1924) was a famous English painter, explorer, writer and anthropologist and the author of numerous travel books set in such places as Tibet and many other exotic sites around the globe. Called by one writer "the ultimate stiff-upper-lipped English traveller in tweed," Landor was in Peking when the siege of the legations was lifted.

7. Captain Joseph Theodore Dickman, "Experiences in China," in the *Journal of the United States Cavalry Association* 13, no. 45 (July 1902), 5–40. Brigadier General Aaron Simon Daggett noted that there were over fifty of these expeditions in the winter and spring of 1900 and 1901. See his *America in the China Relief Expedition* (1903; rpr. Nashville TN: Battery Press, 1997), 115–116, 141–142.

8. This account was first published as "Christmas in China During the Boxer Rebellion, 1900," by Colonel William K. Naylor, ed. Alfred E. Cornebise, in *Military Collector and Historian: Journal of the Company of Military Historians* 54, no. 4 (Winter 2002–2003), 169–173.

9. For a discussion, see Captain Fred Radford Brown, *The History of the Ninth U.S. Infantry, 1799–1909* (Chicago: R.R. Donnelley and Sons, 1909), 532–536, passim.

Chapter 4

1. From "Besieged in Peking," diary of William E. Bainbridge, second secretary of the American Legation in Peking, and secretary to the U.S. minister to China Edwin Hurd Conger, Subject File "Belgian Relief Correspondence, 1916–20, to Boxer Rebellion," Folder, Boxer Rebellion Diaries, Box 13, Lou Henry Hoover Papers, Herbert Hoover Presidential Library, West Branch, Iowa.

2. The first five were published in London in a volume by Chapman and Hall in 1901 and in a revised edition appearing in 1903, which included his final article. These appeared under the title of *"These from the Land of Sinam": Essays on the Chinese Question*. The title was derived from the book of Isaiah, and Hart hoped that, "considering the kind of lay-missionary work I have been doing, and the messages I have been sending, I hope I shall not be considered irreverent in appropriating such words!" Letter, Hart to Campbell, February 6, 1901, in John King Fairbank, Katherine Frost Bruner, and Elizabeth MacLeod Matheson, eds., *The I.G. in Peking: Letters of Robert Hart Chinese Maritime Customs, 1868–1907*, 2 vols. (Cambridge, MA: Harvard University Press, 1975), vol. 2, pp. 1256–1259.

3. Letters, Hart to Campbell, November 15, and 26, 1900, in Fairbank et al., *The I.G. in Peking*, vol. 2, pp. 1247–1249.

4. Ibid., 1247–1248, 1256–1259, 1260–1261, 1313–1314, 1363, 1421, 1423, Letters, Hart to Campbell, November 15, 1900, February 6 and March 10, 1901.

5. Ibid., vol. 2, 1275, Letters, Hart to Campbell, September 1, 1901, June 1, 1902, June 15, 1903, July 10 and 18, 1904. See also *"These from the Land of Sinim,"* 49–52.

6. Kemp Tolley, *The Yangtze Partol: The U.S. Navy in China* (Annapolis, MD: Naval Institute Press, 1971), 67.

7. *China in a Convulsion*, 2 vols. (New York: Fleming H. Revell, 1901), x–xi.

8. Pearl L. Buck, *My Several Worlds* (New York: John Day, 1954), 52–54.

9. See comments in Han Han, *This Generation: Dispatches from China's Most Popular Literary Star (and Race Car Driver)*, trans. and ed. Allan H. Barr (New York: Simon and Schuster, 2012), 36. This work contains much about China's younger generations as of 2008 and following.

10. From the introduction to *The Analects of Confucius* (Norwalk, CT: Easton Press, 1976), translated from the Chinese, with an introduction and notes, by Lionel Giles (1875–1958). This translation was first published in 1933. Lionel Giles was born in Surrey, England, and educated in Belgium, Austria, Scotland at the University of Aberdeen, and Oxford at Wadham College. He earned an MA in 1902 and a Litt. D., in 1913. He was on the staff of the British Museum from 1900 to 1940. His father was Herbert A. Giles, a professor of classics at Cambridge and a foremost Sinologist of his day. He, together with Sir Thomas Francis Wade, developed the Wade-Giles system of Romanization of the Chinese spoken language.

11. Arthur Judson Brown, *New Forces in Old China: An Inevitable Awakening* (New York: Fleming H. Revell, 2nd ed. [1904; rpr., Lititz, PA: Bibliobazzar, 2006], 177).

12. Much has been written in the present age regarding American involvement in for-

eign wars, especially in view of American military ventures after World War II, widely regarded as the "Good War." Subsequent deployments have been less well appreciated and supported, either at home or abroad. See warnings from the former U.S. secretary of state Madeleine Albright in her memoir, *The Mighty and the Almighty: Reflections on America, God, and World Affairs* (New York: Harper, 2006); accounts by the former U.S. secretary of defense Robert M. Gates, *Duty: Memoirs of a Secretary at War* (New York: Alfred Knopf, 2014); and the provocative study by Chris Hedges, *War Is a Force That Gives Us Meaning* (New York: Anchor Books, 2002), among many others.

13. Brigadier General Aaron Simon Daggett, *America in the China Relief Expedition* (1903; rpr., Nashville: Battery Press, 1997), 36, 77.

14. The 15th Regiment maintains such memorabilia in its "China Room" at Fort Benning, Georgia. The 9th's is at Fort Drum, New York. For the Liscum monument and the Liscum Bowl, see Brown, *History of the Ninth U.S. Infantry, 1799–1909*, pp. 524, 840–841, and Appendices I and J.

15. Antoine Claire Thibaudeau, *Mémoire sur le Consulat, 1799 à 1804* (Paris: Chez Ponthieu el cie, 1827), 83–84. And so it remains true in the contemporary military universe. On the present scene, many U.S. service personnel are now top heavy with "scrambled eggs" on caps and a plethora of decorations, making them colorful billboards. Napoleon's idea, therefore, seems to have been carried to extremes.

16. He had earlier been with the 5th U.S. Field Artillery Regiment in the Philippines. See the memoirs of General Charles Pelot Summerall, published as *The Way of Duty, Honor, Country* (Lexington: University of Kentucky Press, 2010), edited and annotated by Timothy K. Nenninger. See 48–60, 76, 233.

17. Here see Alfred Emile Cornebise, *The Amaroc News* (Carbondale: Southern Illinois University Press, 1981).

18. See his memoirs: Major General Joseph Theodore Dickman, *The Great Crusade: A Narrative of the World War* (New York. D. Appleton, 1927).

Chapter 5

1. For the early history of the 15th Regiment, see Captain H.R. Brinkerhoff, "The Fifteenth Regiment of Infantry," 610–628, in *The Army of the United States: Historical Sketches of Staff and Line with Portraits of Generals-in-Chief*, ed. Theophilus Francis Rodenbough and William L. Haskin (New York: Maynard, Merrill, 1896), especially for its activities during the Civil War. For its later history, see G. Lee Cotter, *The Dragon Chronicle: History of the 15th Infantry from the Civil War to the Present* (Marceline, MO: Walsworth, 1981), which stresses the activities of the outfit in World War II and Korea; and *The Fifteenth Infantry Regiment, 1861–1953*, edited by Lieutenant Murray M. Olwell (n.p., c. 1953), which emphasizes the 15th's role in the Korean War. For a brief, useful summary of the 15th's history, see Timothy R. Stoy, "Fifteenth Infantry Regiment," *On Point: The Journal of Army History* 17, no. 1 (Summer 2011), 22–26. See also Aaron Philippe Toll, ed., *15th Infantry Regiment (United States)* (N.p.: Ceed, 2012). This consists principally of articles from Wikipedia and other online sources. One member of the regiment was 1st Lieutenant John McAuley Palmer of Company D, of the 1st Battalion. In his memoir, he provided information on the regiment's deployment and action in China. For the 15th's service in China at this time, see I.B. Holley, *General John M: Palmer, Citizen Soldiers, and the Army of a Democracy* (Westport: Greenwood Press, 1982), 102–128.

2. Holley, *General John M. Palmer*, 110.

3. Ibid., 111.

4. Charles Pelot Summerall, *The Way of Duty, Honor, Country: The Memoir of General Charles Pelot Summerall*, edited and annotated by Timothy K. Nenninger (Lexington: University of Kentucky Press, 2010), 57.

5. Goldsworthy Lowes Dickinson, *Letters from John Chinaman* (London, 1901), 43–44.

Chapter 6

1. For American early trade in China, see Eric Jay Dolin, *When America First Met China: An Exotic History of Tea, Drugs, and Money in the Age of Sail* (New York: W.W. Norton, 2012). For the history of the U.S. Navy in China, in the late 19th and early 20th centuries, see the important work by William Reynolds Braisted's *The United States Navy in the Pacific, 1897–1909* (Annapolis: Naval Institute Press, rpr. ed., 2008); *The United States Navy in the Pacific, 1909–1922* (Annapolis: Naval Institute Press, rpr. ed., 2008); and *Diplomats in Blue: U.S. Naval Officers in China, 1922–1933* (Gainesville: University of Florida Press, 2009).

2. See Chester M. Biggs, Jr., *The United States Marines in North China, 1894–1942* (Jefferson, NC: McFarland, 2003), 10–13.

3. Ibid., 13–14.

4. Much of the foregoing is based on Trevor K. Plante, "U.S. Marines in the Boxer Rebellion," *Prologue* 31, no. 4 (Winter 1999); and Biggs, *The United States Marines in North China*, 34–136.

5. For these developments, see Biggs, *The*

United States Marines in North China, 1894-1942, pp. 138–139, 142–148, 206.

6. See Hans Schmidt, *Maverick Marine: General Smedley D. Butler and the Contradictions of American Military History* (Lexington: University of Kentucky Press, 1987). See also Biggs, *The United States Marines in North China*, 151–167.

7. For a historical account of the 15th Regiment in China, see Alfred Emile Cornebise, *The United States 15th Infantry Regiment in China, 1912-1938* (Jefferson, NC: McFarland, 2004). This book has been translated into Chinese by Louie Liu, curator of the Tianjin Museum of Modern History and published by the Chinese Writers Publishing House, Beijing, on June 1, 2011. It fills in missing areas of Chinese history for the 1920s and 1930s era. For the early history of the 15th Regiment, see Captain H.R. Brinkerhoff, "The Fifteenth Regiment of Infantry," 610–628, in *The Army of the United States: Historical Sketches of Staff and Line with Portraits of Generals-in-Chief*, ed. Theophilus Francis Rodenbough and William L. Haskin. (New York: Maynard, Merrill, 1896), especially for its activities during the Civil War. For its later history, see G. Lee Cotter, *The Dragon Chronicle: History of the 15th Infantry from the Civil War to the Present* (Marceline, MO: Walsworth, 1981), which stresses the activities of the outfit in World War II and Korea, and *The Fifteenth Infantry Regiment, 1861-1953*, ed. Lieutenant Murray M. Olwell (c. 1953), which emphasizes the 15th's role in the Korean War.

8. Having been promoted to brigadier general on March 12, 1813, Pike was killed in the battle for York a few weeks later. He had earlier gained fame for his explorations in the American Southwest, giving his name to Colorado's Pikes Peak.

9. Victor Vogle, *Soldiers of the Old Army* (College Station: Texas A & M University Press, 1990), 8. Vogel himself enlisted in the 9th Infantry Regiment, in April 1934 in Texas. In World War II, he was commissioned a 1st Lieutenant in the U.S. Army. His book provides much insight into the nuts and bolts of the U.S. Army "Old Army" in the 1930s and 1940s.

10. See "Return of the 15th Regiment of Infantry" for the month of December 1911 in "Strength Returns of the Regiment" in Microcopy 665, Returns from Regular Army Regiments, June 1821-December 1916, Roll 172: Fifteenth Infantry, January 1910-December 1916, National Archives, Washington, D.C.

11. Historical account in the *Sentinel*, the 15th's troop newspaper, January 25, 1930, and data in the "Strength Returns of the Regiment," in Microcopy 665, Returns from Regular Army Infantry Regiments, June 1821-December 1916, Roll 172: Fifteenth Infantry, January 1910-December 1916, National Archives, Washington, D.C. See also Headquarters, U.S. Army Troops in China, *Conference Troop School, Officers, 28 Nov: '33—Mission and Objectives, U.S.A.T.C. (Syllabus), Tientsin, 1933*, and *Officers School Notes, U.S. Army Troops in China—School Years 1933-34, 1934-35 (Tientsin, 1935)*, as quoted in Charles W. Thomas Vol. 3, "The United States Army Troops in China, 1912-1937" (Stanford University, June 1937), 23–24 and passim (copy in United States Army Heritage and Education Center, Institute, Carlisle, Pennsylvania, hereinafter cited as Thomas, "The United States Army Troops in China, 1912-1917").

12. See the relevant documents for January 4, 12, 16, and March 16, 17, 1912, in folder "370.091—Guarding of Railroads, China," Entry 5960, RG 395. The American commander was further reminded that "the guarding of the railroad is not hostile to China, but is harmonious cooperation of the Powers concerned. You should strive to maintain the most cordial relations with the military representatives of these powers, as well as to safeguard the susceptibilities of the Chinese."

13. *Sentinel*, March 31, 1922, April 4, 1931.

14. Thomas, "The United States Army Troops in China, 1912-1917," 18.

15. Ibid., 19–20. Historical data in the "Strength Returns of the Regiment" in Microcopy 665, Returns from the Regular Army Infantry Regiments, June 1821-December 1916, Roll 172: Fifteenth Infantry, January 1910-December 1916, National Archives, Washington, D.C. Colonel Jones had been sick in quarters at Fort Douglas, Utah, since September 13, 1911. The regiment sailed for China on November 3, 1911, and on November 11 Jones was transferred to a military hospital in Hot Springs, Arkansas.

16. See an article by an old timer in the *Sentinel*, March 15 and 22, 1930.

17. G. Lee Cotter, *The Dragon Chronicle: History of the 15th Infantry from the Civil War to the Present* (Marceline, MO: Walsworth, 1981), 22; "Conditions of Service in China," *The Infantry Journal* 29 (August 1926), 167–174.

18. For example, the part of the old German barracks occupied by a German marine battalion in about 1913 was later occupied by the Chinese Bureau of the First Special Area, near the headquarters building of the 15th Regiment. See account in the *Sentinel*, November 11, 1933.

19. See accounts in the *Sentinel*, February 4, 1921, November 21 and 24, and December 8 and 15, 1922; "Annual Report, Headquarters, American Forces in China, Office of the Commanding Officer," Tientsin, China, August 24, 1923," to the Adjutant General of the Army, Washington, D.C., in RG 407, Adjutant Gen-

eral's Office, Folder: "Countries—American Forces in China, 123.61 to 333.3," Central Decimal Files Project Files, 1917-1925, Countries, American Forces in China to Cuba 350.2, Box No. 1350, AGO 1917-25.

20. See, for example, "Annual Report, Headquarters, American Forces in China, Office of the Commanding Officer, Tientsin, China, August 24, 1925," to the Adjutant General of the Army, Washington, D.C., in RG 407, Adjutant General's Office, Folder: "Countries—American Forces in China, 123.61-to 333.3," Central Decimal Files Project Files, 1917-1925, Countries, American Forces in China to Cuba 350.2, Box No. 1350 AGO 1917-25.

21. Among other things, the carpet for the new chapel was paid for by the popular explorer of the Gobi Desert and lecturer Roy Chapman Andrews, who turned over to Luther proceeds of lectures that he had presented in Tientsin. *Sentinel*, October 23, 1925; article in the April 22, 1927, issue; an article by H.C. Connette in *North China Star*, which recounted the history of the chapel's construction and furnishing; and Caspar Nannes, "A Visit With Chaplain Luther D. Miller," *The Chaplain* 26, no. 2 (March-April 1969), 9-12. There is additional information in the document "Chaplain Luther D. Miller—Marshall Bio," George C. Marshall Research Library Research File, Folder "Tientsin, China, 1924-1927." See also *Sentinel*, June 23 and October 13, 1928.

22. The coat of arms was approved by the office of the adjutant general on April 30, 1923, and the corresponding insignia, to be worn on the uniform, on April 22, 1924.

23. For Connor's role at the War College, see Major Mark Christian Bender, *Watershed at Leavenworth: Dwight D. Eisenhower and the Command and General Staff School* (Fort Leavenworth, KS: Combat Studies Institute, 1990). Earlier Connor authored an official publication of the War Department, *Military Railroads*, published in 1916. See accounts of Connor in *Sentinel*, April 20, 1923, August 14 and September 4, 1925 (misdated as August 4, 1925), May 13,1926. Connor died on June 16, 1960, and is buried at the West Point Post Cemetery.

24. Much of this information is from *The Official History of the Fifth Division U.S.A during the Period of Its Organization in the European War, 1917-1919* (Society of the Fifth Division, 1919), passim. The 5th was known as the Red Diamond (Meuse) Division. See also *Sentinel*, May 13, 1926, August 19, 1927.

25. Details are in the *Sentinel*, December 10 and 17, 1926, and *Infantry Journal* 29 (August 1926), 167-174. The 15th Infantry and the station hospital were authorized to organize and maintain a personnel section "under the provisions of Army Regulations."

26. *Sentinel*, March 16 and April 13, 1929. Subsequently, regimental headquarters moved to the former general headquarters, and the band moved into the former regimental offices.

27. *Sentinel*, April 13, 1929.

Chapter 7

1. Jefferson, NC: McFarland, 2004. *The United States 15th Infantry Regiment in China, 1912-1938* was translated into Chinese and published in that edition in June 2011 by the Chinese Writer's Publishing House in Beijing.

2. See letters, William R. Steele, to the newsletter of the Society of the 3rd Infantry Division, U.S. Army, *The Watch on the Rhine*, May 13, 1989, and to LTC Tim Stoy, November 18, 1994. Attachments include a facsimile photo of members of Company I of the 15th Infantry, as of 1936; copy of an official letter noting Steele's successful completion of the Chinese language exam, November 9, 1936; a facsimile of the certificate awarding Steele his "Chung." These are in the private collection of LTC Tim Stoy.

3. Breckinridge notes that this was written onboard the cruiser USS *Seattle*, at sea in about March 1926. See in "James C. Breckinridge Collection, Personal Correspondence, 1929-1933," http://www.mcu.usmc.mil/MCRCweb/ftw/files/pap2933.txt.

4. See James McCarthy, *A Papago Traveler: The Memories of James McCarthy* (Tucson: University of Arizona Press, 1985), 68-98.

5. Ibid., 96.

6. *Sentinel*, August 11 and October 13, 1922, May 13, 1927, May 4, 1929. For events during the Great War era, see W.R. Wheeler, "China Service," *Journal of the Military Service Institution of the United* States 59 (July-August, September-October, and November-December 1916): 80-93, 234-50, 378-93. For events of the early 1920s, see Anon., "An Officer of the China Expeditionary Forces, on the China Coast," *Infantry Journal* 19 (November 1921): 502-07.

7. "Nan Ta Ssu Memories," *Sentinel*, August 20,1926.

8. Letter, Howard W. Palm to Lieutenant Colonel Tim Stoy, December 23, 1994, from Stoy's private collection. Palm was an enlisted man in the 15th in the late 1930s. Stoy had served in the 15th in the 1950s. See also Tanaka Toshiyuki, *Japan's Comfort Women* (London: Routledge, 2001). What was the difference between U.S. soldiers here and those of World War II Japan? Perhaps it has to do with coercion. One needs to note that in the history of the 15th, attempts to control VD were perennial problems. A further discussion of these matters is in Cornebise, *The United States 15th Infantry Regiment in China*, 117-122. The exis-

tence of these houses was kept confidential, mainly for fears of what might be made of them by the citizenry in the United States.

9. The author is identified only as a "former cavalry soldier now a member of the 15th foot." The Hai Ho was a river running through Tientsin. "Beejoe" was a corruption of a Mandarin word for beer. This poem is in the *Sentinel*, September 10, 1932.

10. Though reprinted as it first appeared, there is no indication of the precise issue that it appeared in. Nor is Pvt. Haydock further identified.

11. See the typescript of his memoirs, "A Lucky Life," 3-16, describing the family's sojourn in China, in the John W. Leonard Papers, Box 1, United States Army Heritage and Education Center (USAHEC), Carlisle, Pennsylvania.

12. As to attitudes toward Koreans, the British scholar Rana Mitter has noted that the Japanese regarded them as "children to the Japanese adults" but mingled their "contempt for China's present with respect for its past" (quoted by Mitter in his *The Manchurian Myth: Nationalism, Resistance, and Collaboration in Modern China* [Berkeley: University of California Press, 2000], 167).

13. G. Lee Cotter, *The Dragon Chronicle: History of the 15th Infantry from the Civil War to the Present* (Marceline, MO: Walsworth, 1981), 22.

14. John Jr.'s father was John William Leonard, a professional soldier in the U.S. Army who retired with the rank of lieutenant general. For John, Jr.'s accounts, see his unpublished manuscript, "A Lucky Life," in the John W. Leonard Papers, Box 1, USAHEC, Carlisle, Pennsylvania. For details of Leonard's military career, see article by John W. Leonard, Jr., and Major General George Ruhlen, *Assembly* (March–April 2003), the bimonthly journal of the Association of Graduates, U.S. Military Academy. There is a further discussion of John William Leonard in part three of this study.

15. See account in Leslie Anders, *Gentle Knight: The Life and Times of Major General Edwin Forrest Harding* (Kent, OH: Kent State University Press, 1985), 116-122.

16. Ibid., 121-122.

17. See Cornebise, *The United States 15th Infantry Regiment in China*, 81-82, for a discussion of what Marshall, in particular, learned about training in China and the need to apply certain lessons to the U.S. Army schools at Benning.

Chapter 8

1. Mason's article in the *Dragon*, 15th Infantry Regiment Newsletter (April 2000), 8-9.

2. See the online publication *MilitaryTimes*' Hall of Valor column. The regiment's troop paper, *Sentinel*, did not ignore the growing menace and on August 7, 1937, published a double issue reporting on the Sino-Japanese conflict, especially as it affected Tientsin.

3. See the James E. Moore Papers, United States Army Heritage and Education Center, Carlisle, Pennsylvania, and documents in Folder "250.1, Disturbances," entry 5960, RG 395.

4. *Dragon*, 15th Infantry Regiment Newsletter (April 2000), 8-9. See also Manny T. Koginos, *The Panay Incident: Prelude to War* (Lafayette, IN: Purdue University Studies, 1967), and Hamilton Darby Perry, *The Panay Incident: Prelude to Pearl Harbor* (New York: Macmillan, 1969.)

5. See details in articles in the *New York Times*, February 5 and April 10, 1938.

6. See Koginos, *The Panay Incident*, 127.

7. Hull's speech is in the U.S. Department of State's Publication 1983, *Peace and War: United States Foreign Policy, 1931-1941* (Washington, D.C.: U.S. Government Printing Office, 1943), 407-18.

8. Akira Iriye, *Across the Pacific: An Inner History of American-East Asian Relations* (New York: Harcourt, Brace and World, 1967), 171-199.

9. Quoted in David M. Kennedy, *Freedom from Fear: The American People in Depression and War, 1929-1945* (New York: Oxford University Press, 1999), 502.

10. Article by Tom Mason, a member of the regiment in the late 1930s, in the *Dragon*, the 15th Infantry Regiment Association Newsletter (April 2000), 8-9.

11. For the tension and disturbances, see Record Group 395: "U.S. Army Overseas Operations and Commands, 1898-1942," Entry 5960, "U.S. Army Troops in China, 1912-38, General Records," Box 33, Decimal file, 250.1-250.413, Folder 250.1, "Disturbances." For the early withdrawal, see Box 90, Decimal file, 579.3-600, "Transports," Folder 579.3: "Passenger Assignments and Lists (USATC), March 2, 1938-24 March 1938," in U.S. National Archives II, Maryland.

12. See details in Cornebise, *The 15th Infantry Regiment*, 215-216, and Chester M. Biggs, Jr., *The United States Marines in North China, 1894-1942* (Jefferson, NC: McFarland, 2003), 178-180. Marines had served in Tientsin on two previous occasions. The first instance was in 1900 at the time of the Boxer Uprising. The second came in the late 1920s, when the United States and other Western powers sent military forces to Tientsin and Shanghai during Chiang Kai-shek's march into northern China and its attendant conflicts. Details of the Marines' arrival are in accounts in the *North-*

China Herald, March 9, 1938 and the *Peking Chronicle*, March 1, 4, 7, 1938. An analysis of the meaning of the 15th's withdrawal can be studied in the *China Weekly Review*, February 12, 1938, published in Shanghai. This emphasized that the Japanese were telling "the disheartened and discouraged Chinese that it was the Japanese Army which compelled America to withdrew its troops." While this contained an element of truth (the presence of Japan in eastern China was clearly a factor), the matter was more complicated.

13. Desmond Power, *Little Foreign Devil* (Vancouver: Pangli Imprint, 1996), 96–99; *North-China Herald*, March 9, 1938.

14. Frank Dorn, *The Sino-Japanese War, 1937–41: From the Marco Polo Bridge to Pearl Harbor* (New York: Macmillan, 1974), 96. The United States Sixth Marine Regiment had also departed from Shanghai on February 18, 1938, bound for San Diego, further reducing America's armed forces in China.

15. Power, *Foreign Devil*, 98. This memoir recounts the life of a British schoolboy born and bred in China who lived in the British Concession. Note excursions to Peitaiho for beach activities. Then, with the Japanese putting increasing pressure on the concessions, with Pearl Harbor and British and U.S. declarations of war, it was prison camps for all. For Desmond there were three, the final one at Weihsien, on the Shantung Peninsula, this one with his mother, who was called Tai-tai, his half-brother, Tony, and his half-sister, Betty. Rescued by U.S. air forces following the end of the war, Tai-tai went back home in Tientsin, with the impression that the Americans would maintain a concession and life could go on as before. What she, and so many other Westerners, could not or would not believe was that the Chinese would not tolerate their presence any longer, and even close Chinese friends would simply see them forever as "Foreign Devils." They would all be out within a year or two. Desmond could never forget, of course, an essence deep inside that he was Chinese born. There are also details of attitudes of rescuing Americans and events of the first few days of freedom. Note the heavy-handed American "rescue teams," orientation and newsreel movies as to Nazi camps, etc., in pp. 214–231.

16. This information is derived in part from the document "Strength Return of the 15th Infantry, as of Midnight, February 28, 1938, and Special Strength Return, March 2, 1938," in the box containing the Regular Army Organization Returns, Monthly Strength Returns, 1921–1939, 13th–15th Infantry Regiments, in RG 407.

17. See some details of the return voyage in a letter from Howard W. Palm to LTC Tim Stoy, December 23, 1994, in Stoy's private collection.

18. See articles and numerous photographs in the *Tacoma Times*, March 24, 1938.

19. Letter, Howard W. Palm to LTC Timothy Stoy, December 23, 1994, Stoy private collection.

20. Joan Power in the *Sentinel*, March 5, 1932.

21. Introduction to a discussion of the Old China Hands Archive at California State University at Northridge, http://library.csun.edu/Old China Hands. Other sources for the Old China Hands include *The Old China Hand Gazette*, edited by Tess Johnston and Deke Erh, in Shanghai and found online by its title. See this publication for pertinent book lists. Also, their Old China Research Service and Old China Hand Resources publish books and other materials devoted to this subject.

22. Pearl S. Buck, *My Several Worlds* (New York: John Day, 1954), 422.

23. The details of the ceremonies and of the gate are found in the *Sentinel*, May 1, 1925. Events concerning the gate's shipment to the United States and its relocation at Fort Benning are discussed in Cornebise, *The United States 15th Infantry Regiment in China*, 218–220. The 15th Regiment, however, was redeployed to Fort Lewis, Washington, so the men did not follow the gate to Fort Benning.

24. For the Eisenhowers' experiences at Fort Lewis, see the book *General Ike: A Personal Reminiscence* (Glencoe, IL: Free Press, 2003) by Eisenhower's son, John S.D. Eisenhower, who also later attained the rank of general. While at Fort Lewis he was a student at Tacoma's Stadium High School.

25. For many of these details see the article by Duane Colt Denfeld online at HistoryLink.org, *Free Online Encyclopedia of Washington State History*, April 7, 2013.

Chapter 9

1. Benjamin R. Beede, *The Small Wars of the United States: An Annotated Bibliography*, 2nd rev. ed. (London: Routledge, 2012), in a review of Alfred Emile Cornebise, *The United States 15th Infantry Regiment in China, 1912–1938* (Jefferson, NC: McFarland, 2004). To be sure, General Dwight David Eisenhower could have been included among the most famous of this group, but this presentation will be confined to those who served in China. Ike was with the 15th from February to September of 1940, after it had been withdrawn from China in March 1938 to Fort Lewis, Washington.

2. It is interesting that some army officers developed "a healthy antipathy" for those grad-

uates, describing them as belonging "to the Sacred Order of God's Anointed." This was the case with Colonel David Dean Barrett, who once remarked, regarding what he called "the Eleemosynary Institution on the Hudson," that "being a graduate of West Point admits one to the most sacrosanct lodge in the world, and one in which the material benefits are far greater than any branch of the Masons could ever offer." See John N. Hart, *The Making of an Army "Old China Hand": A Memoir of Colonel David D. Barrett* (Berkeley: University of California Press, 1985), 1–2.

3. See http://americanhistory.si.edu/westpoint/history_6b.html].

4. See Alfred Emile Cornebise, *The United States 15th Infantry Regiment in China, 1912–1938* (Jefferson, NC: McFarland, 2004), 70–71, and passim. For some indications that some of the 15th's officers did not get along with Connor very well, see Leslie Anders, *Gentle Knight: The Life and Times of Major General Edwin Forest Harding* (Kent, Ohio: Kent State University Press, 1985), 95–99, 102–104.

5. In 1916, Castner returned to Rutgers and obtained an MS degree.

6. *Sentinel*, August 19, November 25, 1927, and Charles G. Finney, *The Old China Hands* (Westport, CT: Greenwood, 1973), 57–76 and passim.

7. Finney, *The Old China Hands*, 57–76. See also *The Official History of the Fifth Division U.S.A: The Red Diamond (Meuse) Division* (Washington, D.C.: Society of the Fifth Division, 1919), 23–25, and the study by Scott Avedis Moomjian, *"Roaring Joe": The Life of Major General Joseph Compton Castner, 1869–1946* (San Diego: University of San Diego Press, 1993.)

8. For his tour in China, see letters and documents in Larry I. Bland and Sharon R. Ritenour, eds., *The Papers of George Catlett Marshall*, vol. 1, *"The Soldierly Spirit," December 1880–June 1939* (Baltimore: Johns Hopkins University Press, 1981), 263–205. For Marshall's life and career, see Forrest C. Pogue, with Gordon Harrison, *George C. Marshall: Education Of a General, 1880–1939* (London: MacGibbon and Kee, 1964), 246–254; Ed Cray, *General of the Army: George C: Marshall, Soldier and Statesman* (New York: W.W. Norton, 1990); Larry I. Bland and Sharon R. Ritenour, eds., *The Papers of George Catlett Marshall*, 7 vols. (Baltimore: Johns Hopkins University Press, 1981–); Forrest C. Pogue, *George C: Marshall*, vol. 1, *Education of a General, 1880–1939:* (New York: Viking, 1963); Forrest C. Pogue, *George C: Marshall*, vol. 2, *Ordeal and Hope, 1939–1942* (New York: Viking, 1966); Forrest C. Pogue, *George C. Marshall*, vol. 3, *Organizer of Victory, 1943–1945* (New York: Viking, 1973); Forrest C. Pogue, *George C. Marshall*, vol. 4, *Statesman, 1945–1959* (New York: Viking, 1987); John T. Nelsen, *General George C. Marshall: Strategic Leadership and the Challenges of Reconstituting the Army, 1939–1941* (electronic source) (Carlisle Barracks, PA: Strategic Studies Institute, U.S. Army War College, 1993); Marshall life timeline, http://www.marshallfoundation.org/about/timeline/timeline.html. See also the vast resources in the George C. Marshall Research Library, Lexington, Virginia.

9. See Katherine Tupper Marshall, *Together: Annals of an Army Wife* (New York: Tupper and Love, 1946). This book focuses on the private life of General Marshall, a welcome addition to the copious collections of official papers, documents and publications that exist from his life and career. *Together* also contains a brief biographical sketch.

10. David Hein article and lecture presented at the John Jay Institute, Philadelphia, May 8, 1913. The text is in an article, "In War for Peace: General C. Marshall's Core Convictions and Ethical Leadership," *Touchstone* 26, no. 2 (March–April 2013). See also the topic "Resources," "A Case Study in Principled Leadership: George C. Marshall's Core Beliefs," at the John Jay Institute online. On his teaching, see Larry I. Bland, "George C. Marshall and the Education of Army Leaders," *Military Review* 68 (October 1988), 27–37.

11. The army officers promoted were Marshall, Arnold, Eisenhower, and MacArthur. The naval admirals were Leahy, King, Nimitz and Halsey.

12. For his venture in China, see John Robinson Beal, *Marshall in China* (Garden City, NY: Doubleday, 1970); Larry I. Bland, *George C. Marshall's Mediation Mission to China, December 1945–January 1947* (Lexington, VA: George C. Marshall Foundation, 1998); and John Hart Caughey, *The Marshall Mission to China, 1945–1947: The Letters and Diary of Colonel John Hart Caughey*, ed., Rober B. Jeans (Lanham, MD: Rowman and Littlefield, 2011). Colonel Caughey was Marshall's executive officer while he was in China.

13. See Robert H. Ferrell, *George C. Marshall as Secretary of State, 1947–1949* (New York: Cooper Square, 1966), and Michael J. Hogan, *The Marshall Plan: America, Britain and the Reconstruction of Western Europe, 1947–1952* (Cambridge: Cambridge University Press, 1989.)

14. See Larry I. Bland and James B. Barber, *George C. Marshall: Soldier of Peace* (Baltimore, Johns Hopkins University Press, 1997). For insight into Marshall's key beliefs, see a lecture written and delivered by David Hein of Hood College, at the John Jay Institute, Philadelphia, May 8, 1913. The text is in an article, "In War

for Peace: General C. Marshall's Core Convictions and Ethical Leadership," *Touchstone* 26, no. 2 (March–April 2013), 41–48. See also the topic "Resources," "A Case Study in Principled Leadership: George C. Marshall's Core Beliefs," at the John Jay Institute online.

15. These accolades are quoted in Katherine Tupper Marshall, *Together: Annals of an Army Wife* (New York: Tupper and Love, 1946), 248–251.

16. See the fine study by Barbara W. Tuchman, *Stilwell and the American Experience in China, 1911-1945* (New York: Macmillan, 1971), 135–144.

17. Ibid., 157.

18. For Stilwell's escape, see the book by General Frank Dorn, Stilwell's aide, *Walkout with Stilwell in Burma* (New York: Thomas Y. Crowell, 1971), and another by a journalist, also with the Stilwell party, Jack Belden, *Retreat with Stilwell* (New York: Alfred A Knopf, 1943). See also the important collection regarding General Joseph W. Stilwell, *The Stilwell Papers*, ed. Theodore H. White (New York: William Sloane, 1948). These papers were assembled courtesy of Stilwell's wife, Winifred A. Stilwell, and they provide much insight into Stilwell's involvement in China during World War II. Also for Stilwell's role in China and Burma, see three volumes in the official United States Army in World War II series by Charles F. Romanus and Riley Sunderland, *Stilwell's Mission to China* (Washington: Chief of Military History, 1953); *Stilwell's Command Problems* (1956) and *Time Runs Out in CBI* (1990), and Frank Dorn, *The Sino-Japanese War, 1937-41: From Marco Polo Bridge to Pearl Harbor* (New York: Macmillan, 1974).

19. Dorn, *Walkout with Stilwell in Burma*, 243.

20. Stilwell also founded the CBI troop newspaper, *CBI Roundup*, an outstanding U.S. troop paper of World War II, which early in its career, at least, was a lively sheet that did not hesitate to criticize the high command. "If you can prove it, print it," Stilwell had informed its editors.

21. He could only conclude, "My God." See further discussion in *The Stilwell Papers*, 190–191; 317–319.

22. See George C. Mitchell, *Matthew B. Ridgway: Soldier, Statesman, Scholar, Citizen* (Mechanicsburg, PA: Stackpole Books, 2002); and Ridgway's memoirs, *The Korean War* (New York: Doubleday, 1967); and *Soldier: The Memoirs of Matthew B. Ridgway as told to Harold H. Martin* (Westport: Greenwood, 1974).

23. Quoted in Mitchell, *Matthew B. Ridgway*, 206.

24. See John S.D. Eisenhower, *Intervention! The United States and the Mexican Revolution, 1913-1917* (New York: W.W. Norton, 1995), and James W. Hurst, *Pancho Villa and Black Jack Pershing: The Punitive Expedition in Mexico* (Westport, CT: Praeger, 2008).

25. There is a photo of Walker made on the occasion of his arrival in Tientsin in the October 25, 1930, issue of the 15th's troop newspaper, *Sentinel*, 13.

26. For Walker's life and career, see Charles Province, *General Walton H. Walker: Forgotten Hero, the Man Who Saved Korea* (Online: CreateSpace Independent Publishing Platform, 2008), and Wilson Allen Heefner and Martin Blumenson, *Patton's Bulldog: The Life and Service of General H. Walker* (Shippensburg, PA: White Mane, 2002).

27. See Albert C. Wedemeyer, *Wedemeyer Reports* (New York: Henry Holt, 1958). For a recent favorable assessment of Wedemeyer, see John J. McLaughlin, *General Albert C. Wedemeyer: America's Unsung Strategist in World War II* (Philadelphia: Casemate Books, 2012).

28. In the Philippines, he met and married his wife, Elizabeth Dade Embrick, in 1925, the daughter of a colonel (later a general), Dunbar Embrick, who would have some influence upon Wedemeyer's career.

29. There is a photo of Wedemeyer, together with other newly arrived officers of the 15th Infantry, in its troop newspaper, *Sentinel*, March 22, 1930, 16.

30. *Wedemeyer Reports!*, 48.

31. Much of the foregoing is found in *Wedemeyer Reports!*, 44–62.

32. One of Wedemeyer's critics, who held that Wedemeyer "was a real dud" and difficult to get along with, would later allege that "probably a good deal of the worst of the German General Staff rubbed off on him." See W.J. Peterkin, *Inside China, 1943-1954: An Eyewitness Account of America's Mission in Yenan* (Baltimore: Gateway Press, 1992), 108.

33. For details of his work regarding the Victory Program, see *Wedemeyer Reports!*, 63–76, and MacLaughlin, 33–48.

34. For details of this time in China, see Alfred Emile Cornebise, *The Shanghai Stars and Stripes: Witness to the Transition to Peace, 1945-1946* (Jefferson, NC: McFarland, 2010).

35. W. J. Peterkin, *Inside China*, 106–109.

36. The *Sentinel*, October 23, 1925; Casper Nannes, "A Visit with Chaplain Luther D. Miller," *Chaplain* 26, no. 2 (March-April, 1969), 9–12; document, "Chaplain Luther D. Miller-Marshall Bio," George C. Marshall Library Research File, Folder "Tientsin, China, 1924–1927." For the role of chaplains in the U.S. Army, see the study by Chaplain Rodger R. Venzke, *Confidence in Battle, Inspiration in Peace: The United States Army Chaplaincy, 1945-1975* (Washington, D.C.: Office of the

Chief of Chaplains, Department of the Army, 1977).

37. See *Sentinel*, November 4, 1927, February 10 and 24, 1928, and March 16, 1929.

38. Ibid., December 17, 1926, May 4, 1928.

39. See "Chaplain Luther D. Miller–Marshall Bio," by Chaplain Luther D. Miller, in Folder "Tientsin, China, 1924–27," George C. Marshall Research Library. For Marshall's Christian faith (he was an Episcopalian), which is not often discussed in studies about him, see the article by David Hein, "In War for Peace: General George C. Marshall's Core Convictions and Ethical Leadership," *Touchstone* 26, no. 2 (March-April 2013), 41–48.

40. Leslie Anders, *Gentle Knight: The Life and Times of Major General Edwin Forrest Harding* (Kent, OH: Kent State University Press, 1985).

41. Ibid., pp. 137–139. Anders noted that this mobilization effort rivaled that required by the coming of the Spanish-American War in 1898.

42. Many commanders in the Regular Army did not hold National Guardsmen in very high repute, a factor in what then transpired regarding the 32nd Division.

43. Paul Rogers, *The Good Years: MacArthur and Sutherland* (New York: Praeger, 1990), 39–40.

44. For Sutherland and MacArthur in these years, see an extensive, intimate account of their odyssey by Paul Rogers, who served both generals throughout World War II as a stenographer: *The Good Years: MacArthur and Sutherland* (New York: Praeger, 1990), and *The Bitter Years: MacArthur and Sutherland* (New York: Praeger, 1991).

45. See the 15th's troop paper, *Sentinel*, April 20 and May 4, 1923, July 25 and August 15, 1924, March 9, 1929 and July 22, 1933, for accounts and photographs of King.

46. See folder "Biographical Information, George A. Lynch," George A. Lynch Papers, United States Army Heritage and Education Center (USAHEC), Carlisle, Pennsylvania.

47. See copies of several addresses in the George A. Lynch Papers.

48. Much of this information is from apps.westpointaog.org/Memorials/Article/9738.

49. See http://www.archive.or/stream/americandecorati02unit/_djvu.txt.

50. See http://www.findagrave.com/cgi-bin/fg.cgi?page=gr&GRid=22044.

51. See http://www.arlingtoncemetery.net/tstimberman.htm.

52. For some of his remembrances of service in Tientsin, see the William H. Arnold Papers, Recollections and Reflections, for text of an interview with Arnold, July–August 1975, Archives, USAHEC, Carlisle Barracks, Pennsylvania.

53. See http://www.militaryvetshop.com/History/americal.html for a history of the Americal Division.

54. For Arnold's military career, see the William H. Arnold Papers at the USAHEC, Carlisle, Pennsylvania.

55. For Honnen, see account of his service in the 15th and a photo in *Sentinel*, March 7, 1931.

56. For McClure, see http://www.cagenweb.com/montereybbs/viewtopic.php?p=17482&sid=ad570554a8f4aa6bb8187d46f5d22275. For McClure's service in China in World War II, see the study "China Offensive 1945," http://www.ibiblio.org/hyperwar/USA/USA-C-ChinaO/.

57. *Sentinel*, June 14, 1930.

58. For these developments in the Korean War, see T.R. Fehrenbach, *This Kind of War* (New York: Macmillan, 1963), 342–344.

59. For Gallagher, see beta.worldcat.org/archivegrid/data/51489183, and Alfred Emile Cornebise, *The United States 15th Infantry in China, 1912–1938* (Jefferson, NC: McFarland, 2004), 39, 79, 159, 220. Gallagher's papers are at the USAHEC, Carlisle, Pennsylvania.

60. *Sentinel*, January 11, 1924, March 14 and 21, 1924, February 6, 13, 20, and March 3, 6, 13, 1925.

61. For Brann see http://arlingtoncemetery.net/dwbrann.htm. See also book chapter "General Clark's Decision to Drive on Rome," by Sidney T. Mathews, http://www.history.army.mil/books/70-714.htm.

62. For Doe's military career, see William F. McCartney, *The Jungleers: A History of the 41st Infantry Division* (Washington, D.C.: Infantry Journal Press, 1948); biographical sketch, http://pwencycl.kgbudge.com/D/o/Doe_Jens_A.htm; http://en.wikipedia.org/wiki/Jens; A. Doe, R. Manning Ancell and Christin Miller, *The Biographical Dictionary of World War II Generals and Flag Officers: The U.S. Armed Forces* (Westport, CT: Greenwood Press, 1966), 86.

63. For Laurin Lyman Williams, see http://en.wikipedia.org/w/index.php?title=Laurin_Lyman_Williams&oldid=548877487.

64. For Freemen, see http://rokdrop.com/2007/02/12/heroes-of-the-korean-war-colonel-paul-freeman/; http://beta.worldcat.org/archivegrid/collection/data/48573935.

65. See account in T.R. Fehrenbach. *This Kind of War* (New York: Macmillan, 1963), 375–396, and an article in the *Los Angeles Times*, April 21, 1988.

66. See Herbert Y. Schandler, *The Unmaking of a President: Lyndon Johnson and Vietnam* (Princeton. Princeton University Press, 1977); Herbert Y. Schandler, *America in Vietnam: The War That Couldn't Be Won* (New York: Rowman and Littlefield, 2009); http://www.answers.com/topic/earle-wheeler and http://www.arlingtoncemetery.net/ewheeler.htm.

67. For Harris, see his papers for accounts

of service in the 15th Infantry in the mid–1920s, Frederick Harris Collection, Folder 9, George C. Marshall Research Library, Lexington, Virginia.

68. For Lewis, http://trees.ancestry.com/view/Military.aspx?pid=18002453006&vid=241a9f0e-f794-4296-bae0-bde0cf011786&tid=18782532, and Cornebise, *United States 15th Infantry in China, 1912–1938*, pp. 79–80.

69. For Moore, see his extensive interesting comments regarding service in China in the 1930s, in notes of an interview with him at the USAHEC, Carlisle, Pennsylvania, filed as part of the James E. Moore Papers there.

70. Also for Moore, see the article "Signatures of War, General James Edward Moore," by Niklas Wahlberg, http://signaturesofwar.com/id27.html; http://www.arlingtoncemetery.net/jemoore.htm.

71. For Bolte, see http://usacac.army.mil/cac2/cgsc/carl/resources/ftlvn/coldwar.pdf; http://www.arlingtoncemetery.net/clbolte.htm; Charles L. Bolte Papers, Archives, USAHEC, Carlisle, Pennsylvania.

72. For Boatner, see http://beta.worldcat.org/archivegrid/data/48039041; Haydon L. Boatner Papers, Archives, USAHEC, Carlisle, Pennsylvania; http://www.worldcat.org/title/barbara-tuchmans-stillwell-and-the-american-experience-in-china-a-statement-thereon-for-the-record/oclc/3228750&referer=brief_results; and http://www.arlingtoncemetery.net/hloboatner.htm. See also Charles F. Romanus and Riley Sunderland, *China-Burma-India Theater: Time Runs Out in CBI* (Washington, D.C.: Department of the Army, 1959); and the *CBI Roundup*, U.S. troop newspaper published in Delhi, India, vol. 1, no. 10, November 19, 1942, for an article concerning his being promoted to brigadier general. See also the PhD dissertation by Joseph G.D. Babb, "The Harmony of Yin and Yank: The American Military Advisory Effort in China, 1941–1951," University of Kansas, 2012, 119, 129, 130, 132, 135, 140 and 224. Some of Boatner's papers are at the Hoover Institution, Palo Alto, California.

73. For details, see http://rokdrop.com/2007/05/29/heroes-of-the-korean-war-general-haydon-boatner-part-1/.

74. She and her husband had another son, Forrest Caraway, who also graduated from West Point in 1931, became a general in the U.S. Army and had a substantial military career.

75. See details in George Kerr, *Okinawa: The History of an Island People*, rev. ed. (North Clarendon, VT: Tuttle, 2000) and Nicholas Evan Sarantakes, *Keystone: The American Occupation of Okinawa and U.S.–Japanese Relations* (College Station: Texas A&M University Press, 2000), 116–118.

76. For something of the animosity discussed here, see a provocative article by Jim Morris, "The Honorary Chinese Paratrooper," in *Soldier of Fortune* magazine, 2004.

77. See also the Paul W. Caraway Papers, Archives, USAHEC, Carlisle, Pennsylvania; and Paul W. Caraway Papers, Hoover Institution, Palo Alto, California.

78. For the career of Major General Edwin Davies Patrick, see the article by Ron Crooker at *MS Musings: Monthly Online Magazine*, www.msmusings.com/archive/138/Real,%20the%20patrick.html, and http://home.comcast.net/~83rd_artillery/Ed_Patrick/General_Edwin_Patrick.htm. For the ship, see Crooker's article and another at www.navsource.org/archives/09/22/22124.html and an article by Lieutenant Colonel Tim Stoy, in the *Dragon*, the journal of the 15th Infantry Organization, January, 2008, pp. 1–2. For the ship's final disposition, see photos by Mike Furgatch, the yard manager at ESCO Marine, Inc., in Brownsville, Texas, the photo dated July 28, 2010, depicting the ship in its final stages before being dismantled at Brownsville, Texas.

79. For Kendall's military career, see an article by James D. West, at http://www.indianamilitary.org/Camp%20Atterbury/Post%20Commanders/11-kendall.htm. For details of Kendall's papers and of his career, see account and information at http://beta.worldcat.org/archivegrid/data/706834057, and http://oac.cdlib.org/findaid/ark:/13030/kt4j49r8jc. There is an exhibit devoted to Kendall's service career in the 15th Infantry's China Room at Fort Benning, Georgia.

80. For much of Leonard's life and military career, see the article by John W. Leonard, Jr., and Major General George Ruhlen, "John W. Leonard '15: A Star in the Class the Stars Fell On," in *Assembly*, journal of the Association of Graduates USMA ("Home of the Long Gray Line"), March-April 2003, and an unpublished manuscript, "A Lucky Life," by John W. Leonard, Jr., and another typescript, "Volunteer World War II," John W. Leonard Papers, Box 1 of 3, USAHEC, Carlisle, Pennsylvania.

81. Much information about this posting is in John W. Leonard, Jr., "A Lucky Life."

Part IV

1. Anon., Pamphlet, *History of the 31st Infantry Regiment*, n.p., n.d., Folder: Joseph B. Longuevan Papers, United States Army Heritage and Education Center, Carlisle, Pennsylvania, hereinafter cited as Longuevan Papers, USAHEC.

Chapter 10

1. The regiment was styled the "Polar Bears" to commemorate its involvement in the Siberian venture of 1918-1919. The 31st had been formed at Ft. William McKinley in the Philippines on August 13, 1916. In the spring of 1918, it moved to Siberia together with the 27th Infantry Regiment, though their mission was not altogether clear. It was stated that they were to protect U.S. supplies sent to Vladivostok following the Bolshevik Revolution in 1917. In any case, they began a two-year-long deployment, during which they lost 32 men killed in action. They had taken on Manchurian and Cossack bandits, as well as roving Red revolutionists, and they also had to "check" eager Japanese troops bent upon taking over much of the territory there. In the course of these operations, the 31st became known as the "Polar Bears." Following its action in Siberia, the 31st returned to garrison the walled city of Manila until February 1932, when it was sent to Shanghai.

2. See detailed discussion in Donald A. Jordan, *China's Trial by Fire: The Shanghai War of 1932* (Ann Arbor: University of Michigan Press, 2001).

3. For the U.S. Military in China in this period, see Dennis L. Noble, *The Eagle and the Dragon: The United States Military in China, 1901-1937* (Westport, CT: Greenwood Press, 1990); Roy Kenneth Flint, "The United States Army on the Pacific Frontier, 1899-1939," in *The Proceedings of the Ninth Military History Symposium, United States Air Force Academy* (October 1980), 139-59; Louis Morton, "Army and Marines on the China Station," *Pacific Historical Review* 29, no. 1 (February 1960), 51-73; and Howard F.K. Cahill, "The Thirty-First Infantry in Shanghai," *Infantry Journal* 39 (May-June 1932), 165-75. For the 4th Marines, see Kenneth W. Condit and Edwin T. Turnbladh, *Hold High the Torch: A History of the 4th Marines* (Nashville: Battery Press, 1989). For the general situation in China at this time, see Parks M. Coble, *Facing Japan: Chinese Politics and Japanese Imperialism, 1931-1937* (Cambridge: Harvard University Press, 1991); James E. Sheridan, *China in Disintegration: The Republican Era in Chinese History, 1912-1949* (New York: Free Press, 1975); Henry L. Stimson, *The Far Eastern Crisis: Recollections and Observations* (New York: Harper and Brothers, 1936); and Rana Mitter, *The Manchurian Myth: Nationalism, Resistance, and Collaboration in Modern China* (Berkeley: University of California Press, 2000).

4. For a good background survey of these developments, see Stimson, *The Far Eastern Crisis*, 14-28. Stimson was at this time the U.S. secretary of state.

5. Jordan, *China's Trial by Fire*, 1. For the development of Chinese boycott practices, see Donald A. Jordan, *Chinese Boycotts Versus Japanese Bombs: The Failure of China's "Revolutionary Diplomacy," 1931-32* (Ann Arbor: University of Michigan Press, 1991).

6. See Jordan, *China's Trial by Fire*, 10-43, for a detailed discussion of the convoluted course of events that led to the initiation of the "Shanghai Incident." See also discussion in Jonathan Fenby, *Chiang Kai-shek: China's Generalissimo and the Nation He Lost* (New York: Carroll and Graf, 2003), 209. Further details of the growing unrest in Shanghai and the numerous violent incidents and activities of "irresponsible elements among both Chinese and Japanese" can be found in telegrams from the American consul general at Shanghai, Edwin S. Cunningham, to the American secretary of state Henry L. Stimson, on January 20 and January 29, in *Foreign Relations of the United States* [*FRUS*], 1932, vol. 3, *The Far East* (Washington: U.S. Government Printing Office, 1948), 39, 102. See also Hallett Abend, *My Life in China, 1926-1941* (New York: Harcourt, Brace, 1943), 186-193.

7. Telegram from the American consul in Shanghai, Cunningham, to the secretary of state, January 21, 1932, in *FRUS*, 1932, vol. 3, *The Far East*, 41-42.

8. Rana Mitter, *A Bitter Revolution: China's Struggle with the Modern World* (New York: Oxford University Press, 2004), 169.

9. See discussion in Kemp Tolley, *The Yangtze Partol: The U.S. Navy in China* (Annapolis, MD: Naval Institute Press, 1971), 274.

10. Telegram from Cunningham, consul, from Shanghai, to the secretary of state, January 25, 1932, *FRUS*, 1932, vol. 3, *The Far East*, 58.

11. See discussion of these events in a memorandum from the chief of the Division of Far Eastern Affairs in Washington, Dr. Stanley K. Hornbeck, of a conversation with the Japanese chargé, Kato, Washington, January 28, 1932, *FRUS*, 1932, vol. 3, *The Far East*, 88, and also explanatory note, 88-89; also in the same volume: telegram from the American minister in China, Nelson Trusler Johnson, to the secretary of state, from Peiping, January 28, 1932, p. 87, and telegram from Cunningham to the secretary of state, from Shanghai, January 29, 1932, p. 89.

12. See discussions of the SVC in Ralph Shaw, *Sin City* (New York: Time-Warner, 1992), passim. See also an interview with General Francis F. Vaughn of the U.S. Army. Before his military career, Vaughn had lived for some years in Shanghai. He first joined the Shanghai Volunteer Corps in 1916 because it was simply "the thing to do." Serving until mid-1917, he later rejoined for some months in 1922. A corporal, he especially prided himself on his skill

as a rifleman. He noted that the corps were adept at controlling streets by using barbed-wire-encased sawhorses, with which they could quickly close off the streets. Though Francis's middle initial was "F," his papers are officially listed as "Francis E. Vaughn Papers, 1919–1977," at the U.S. Heritage and Education Center, Carlisle, Pennsylvania.

13. Details of these convoluted events can be followed in Jordan, *China's Trial by Fire*, 10–43.

14. Some details of the 19th Route Army are in a telegram from Cunningham to the secretary of state, from Shanghai, February 3, 1932, *FRUS*, 1932, vol. 3, *The Far East*, 89–91.

15. See Thom's report in a memorandum by the American vice consul in Shanghai, Arthur R. Ringwalt, March 17, 1932, in *FRUS*, 1932, vol. 3, *The Far East*, 595–596. See also the telegram from Cunningham to the secretary of state, from Shanghai, January 29, 1932, *FRUS*, 1932, The Far East, VOL. 3, 89.

16. Abend, *My Life In China*, 190. Abend noted that later many of those "imperialist-minded" Westerners spent the years of World War II in Japanese concentration camps in Shanghai and had ample time to "wonder bitterly why they, and their governments, did not then learn a much-needed lesson which might have avoided the tragedies of the first three months of 1942" (195). See also Lieutenant Commander H.H. Smith-Hutton, "Lessons Learned at Shanghai in 1932," in *The Proceedings of the United States Naval Institute* 64 (August 1938), 1168–1169; telegram from Cunningham to secretary of state, from Shanghai, January 29, 1932, *FRUS*, 1932, vol. 3, *The Far East*, 96. Cunningham reported that in the first encounters, the Japanese casualties numbered 84 wounded and 11 killed. He did not indicate how many were civilians. He gave no figures for the Chinese casualties, though he felt that they "must be many times heavier," which, however, was not the case.

17. Smith-Hutton, "Lessons Learned at Shanghai in 1932," 1169.

18. Details of the air attacks and continued ground operations are in a telegram from Cunningham to the secretary of state, from Shanghai, January 30, 1932, *FRUS*, 1932, vol. 3, *The Far East*, 132–133. See also Hallett Abend's eyewitness account in his *My Life In China*, 191–193.

19. Telegram from Cunningham to the secretary of state, from Shanghai, January 28, 1932, *FRUS*, 1932, vol. 3, *The Far East*, 83–84; telegram from Stimson to Cunningham, from Washington, January 30, 1932, in *FRUS*, 1932, vol. 3, *The Far East*, 120–121. See discussion in C.H. Metcalf, "The Marines in China," *Marine Corps Gazette* 22 (September 1938), 56. Metcalf was a lieutenant colonel in the U.S. Marines (hereinafter cited as Metcalf, "The Marines in China").

20. *Shanghai Stars and Stripes,* September 28, 1945. Irene Corbally Kuhn (1900–1995) was a journalist and pioneer radio commentator in Paris and China in the 1920s and 1930s and a war correspondent for NBC and various newspapers reporting from the China-Burma-India (CBI) Theater during World War II and from Shanghai after the Japanese surrender in September 1945. See her memoirs, *Assigned to Adventure* (Philadelphia: J.B. Lippincott, 1938). Also, for Shanghai, see Mitter, *A Bitter Revolution,* 188; Shaw, *Sin City*; and Graham Earnshaw, *Tales of Old Shanghai* (Hong Kong: Earnshaw Books, 2003).

21. A U.S. Marine who served in Shanghai in those years recalled that they could purchase tailor-made civilian clothes and uniforms for a fraction of their cost at home. He noted that the "Chinese tailors custom made clothes from the finest chino khaki. Shirts, ties, camel-hair bathrobes (with dragon designs) ... and even silk underwear!" Ray Poppelman, "A China Marine: The Adventures of Ray Poppelman," *Leatherneck* (June 1992), 24.

22. From his article, "An Observer Observes," in the troop newspaper of the 15th U.S. Infantry Regiment, stationed in Tientsin, *Sentinel*, January 12, 1923, reprinted from *Shanghai Sports*.

23. See, among many others, *My Life in China*, by Abend, an Asian correspondent for the *New York Times*; *The Years That Were Fat: Peking, 1933–1940* (New York: Harper, 1952), by George N. Kates, a British author who, in a detailed account, discusses Chinese art and culture in some depth; *The Ford of Heaven* (New York: Michael Kesend, 1984), by Brian Power, who grew up in Tientsin, China, as a British teenager in the 1930s; *An American in China, 1936–1939: A Memoir* (New York: Thomas and Sons Books, 2004), by Hunter Thomas Gould, an American businessman who worked for Texaco Petroleum in China in the late 1930s and at several levels possessed considerable insight into relations between the Chinese and the West and also a detailed knowledge of the events leading to the coming of World War II in China; *My Several Worlds* (New York: John Day, 1954), by Pearl S. Buck, who has much to say about growing up in China as a child of missionaries (and also presents substantive analyses of Chinese-Western relations); *The House of Exile* (Boston: Little, Brown, 1933), by Nora Waln, a well-to-do American woman whose family had numerous business and social contacts in China, and who for some years lived with an upper-class Chinese family and describes the cycles of life and relationships among the upper strata of Chi-

nese society in the 1920s and early 1930s. See also Desmond Power, *Little Foreign Devil* (Vancouver, Canada: Pangli Imprint, 1996), 172–241.

24. See in Ron Gluckman, "From Shanghai to Vegas," *Wall Street Journal*, September 1996, reproduced online at http://www.gluckman.com/ShanghaiJews2.html.

25. For studies of the U.S. Navy in China between the world wars, see Kemp Tolley, *The Yangtze Partol: The U.S. Navy in China* (Annapolis, MD: Naval Institute Press, 1971); Dennis L. Noble, ed., *Gunboat on the Yangtze: The Diary of Captain Glenn F. Howell of the USS Palos, 1920–1921* (Jefferson, NC: McFarland, 2002). For the Marines, see Chester M. Biggs, Jr., *The United States Marines in North China, 1894–1942* (Jefferson, NC: McFarland, 2003); Alexander White, *The United States Marines in North China* (Millbrae, CA, 1974); and Robert H. Williams, *The Old Corps: A Portrait of the U.S. Marine Corps Between the Wars* (Annapolis: U.S. Naval Institute Press, 1982).

26. One historian, Colonel Karl H. Lowe, has recorded that also during the regiment's two-years in Siberia, 50 of its members deserted, "some simply melting into the polyglot international community where they could conceal their identities while others managed to sign on to the crews of departing commercial cargo ships or whalers."

27. See William Sidney Graves, *America's Siberian Adventure, 1918–1920* (New York: Jonathan Cape and Harrison Smith, 1931) and Gibson Bell Smith, "Guarding the Railroad, Taming the Cossacks: The U.S. Army in Russia, 1918–1920," *Prologue* 34, no. 4 (Winter 2002). Additional insight into the 31st's service in Russia can be gleaned from the pages of its troop paper, *Here and There with the 31st*, published during the unit's Russian sojourn in Valdivostok. This is discussed in Alfred Emile Cornebise, *Ranks and Columns: Armed Forces Newspapers in American Wars* (Westport, CT: Greenwood Press, 1993), 85–87. See also Warrant Officer Charles D. Brown, *Thirty-First U.S. Infantry Organization Day Twenty-Fifth Anniversary program*, published by the Regiment at Manila, August 13, 1941. See Lowe, chapters 1 and 2. For the American Expeditionary Force North Russian (AEFNR), E.M. Halliday, *Ignorant Armies* (New York: Bantam Books, 1990), and the same author's article "Where Ignorant Armies Clashed by Night," *American Heritage* 10, no. 1 (December 1958). For a history of the 339th Infantry Regiment and its involvement in North Russia, see Patrick Feng, "The 339th Infantry Regiment," *On Point: Journal of Army History* 18, no. 1 (Summer 2012), 21–26. Known as "Detroit's Own" because many of the unit's members were from that city and its environs, it was commanded by Colonel George Evans Stewart.

28. Details of life in Manila after the regiment's return are in "History of the 31st Infantry Regiment," Longuevan Papers, USAHEC, and in Lowe, "The 31st Infantry Regiment at War and Peace," chapter 3.

Chapter 11

1. The details of this exercise are in Record of Events, Diary of the 31st Infantry Regiment, entries for 19 and 20 January 1932, in Record Group 407, Records of the Adjutant General's Office, Monthly Strength Returns 1917–1921–1939, 31st and 32nd Infantry Regiments, Box 103, National Archives II (hereinafter cited as "Diary of the 31st Infantry Regiment, Record Group 407"). As a major general in World War II, Gasser was the head of the War Department's Manpower Board. See Roland G. Ruppenthal, *Logistical Support of the Armies*, vol. 2, *September 1944–May 1945*, The United States Army in World War II Series (Washington, D.C.: Government Printing Office, 1959).

2. Statement by the White House, in *Foreign Relations of the United States* (*FRUS*), vol. 3, *The Far East*, 146. MacArthur also wrote that the navy was ordered to furnish transportation "using *Chaumont* or other craft." The troops were to be equipped "for an indefinite stay and every emergency. All animals were to be left behind for the present. Upon arrival, the commanding officer of the regiment was to report to the senior American Officer ashore for instructions and duty." See text in Captain Howard F. K. Cahill, "The Thirty-First Infantry in Shanghai," *Infantry Journal* 39 (May-June 1932), 165. See also telegram from Cunningham to the secretary of state, from Shanghai, January 30, 1932, indicating that though he had earlier (in a telegram on January 27) concluded that the forces to protect the settlement were deemed adequate, he had then decided "that the exigencies justify my requesting that the landing forces from American vessels be increased at the earliest moment possible." Washington responded with more than he asked for. See in *FRUS*, 1932, vol. 3, 133; in the same source, see also Cunningham's telegram of January 27, p. 74. Major General John L. Hines commanded the Philippine Department from October, 1930 to May 31, 1932. He was replaced by Major General Ewing E. Booth. Hines's papers are at the U.S. Army Heritage and Education Center (USAHEC), Carlisle, Pennsylvania.

3. Cahill, "The Thirty-First Infantry in Shanghai," 165; U.S. Army, 4th Battalion (Mechanized) 31st Infantry, *History of the 31st U.S. Infantry* (Fort Sill, Oklahoma: By the Regiment, 1988), n.p., USAHEC.

4. The *Chaumont* was often involved in

various naval operations in Asia during these years. According to one account, she "was a Hog Island 'double ender,' her configuration calculated to confuse World War I German U-boaters as to which direction her all-out ten knots was taking her—a confusion shared by her passengers whenever a good head wind was blowing." Kemp Tolley, *Yangtze Patrol: The U.S. Navy in China* (Annapolis, MD: Naval Institute Press, 1971), 124.

5. Cahill, "The Thirty-First Infantry in Shanghai," 165–166, and U.S. Army. 4th Battalion (Mechanized) 31st Infantry, *History of the 31st U.S. Infantry*. See also an account of the 31st in Shanghai by Captain Elbridge Colby, a member of the 15th U.S. Infantry Regiment stationed in Tientsin, China, in the 15th's troop paper, *Sentinel*, July 9, 1932. Not surprisingly, the change in climate resulted in one of the first deaths—of the total of nine the unit suffered in the months ahead, all caused by disease—that of Technical Sergeant Miore L. Gordon of the Signal Corps, who died of pneumonia in the regiment.

6. Cahill, "The 31st Regiment in Shanghai," 166–167.

7. Ibid., 166.

8. Ibid.

9. U.S. Army. 4th Battalion (Mechanized), 31st Infantry, *History of the 31st U.S. Infantry*, n.p., and Regimental Diary, 31st Infantry (U.S. Army Forces in Shanghai, China), February 5, 1932, aboard USNT *Chaumont*, signed by Colonel L.D. Gasser, February 6, 1932, in Box 103, Record Group 407, Records of the Adjutant General's Office, 1917–Monthly Strength Returns, 1921–1939, 31st–32nd Infantry Regiments, National Archives II. In the official documents, the 31st was variously referred to as the "U.S. Army Troops in Shanghai" or as the "U.S. Army Forces in Shanghai," though no indication was given as to which term should be used or when.

10. The New World Building was not adequate for all of the billeting required. A bit later, the 2nd Battalion obtained quarters at the Studio Arts Building and along Bubbling Wells Road. Later, various other sites were also used as billets. The men were never under canvas, always being housed within buildings.

11. Cahill, "The 31st Regiment in Shanghai," 166–167, and Regimental Diary, February 5, 1932, Record Group 407, Box 103. Strength returns for this date recorded that the regiment had 65 officers and 1,113 men onboard.

12. Field Order No. 1, United States Army Forces in Shanghai, Office of the Commanding Officer, New World Building, Shanghai, China, February 8, 1932, Record Group 407, Box 103, National Archives II.

13. See map 1 in Cahill, "The 31st Regiment in Shanghai," 167. See also discussion in Benis M. Frank, "Shanghai's 4th Marines: The Glory Days of the Old Corps," *Shipmate* (November 1979), 16. Another account by a writer, Charles M. Roland, in the 15th Infantry's weekly paper published in Tientsin, also describes the deployment of the 31st (*Sentinel*, June 4, 1932).

14. Battalion command posts changed locations from time to time as required and included 352 Bubbling Well Road, the Temple of Heaven, the Studio D'Arts building and the New World Building among others.

15. Colonel Karl H. Lowe, "The 31st Regiment at War and Peace," http://www.31stinfantry.org/history.htm, chapter 4. Also regarding trench stores placed at the disposal of men in sentry posts and other advanced positions, see Field Order No. 6, 2nd Battalion, 31st Infantry, Shanghai, China, March 9, 1932, RG 407, Box 103, Diary, 1st Battalion, 31st Infantry, March 9, 1932, signed at its headquarters, the Temple of Heaven, March 10, 1932, by Major Ross O. Baldwin, commanding.

16. Cahill, "The 31st Regiment in Shanghai," 174–175.

17. The State Department issued a similar directive to the American consul in Shanghai (see in *FRUS*, vol. 3, *The Far East*, 124).

18. Further details are in the diary of the 31st Infantry (U.S. Army Forces in Shanghai, China), for February 9, 1932, signed by Colonel Gasser. These are in Record Group 407, Box 103, National Archives II. See also the account by Charles M. Roland, a soldier from the 15th U.S. Infantry stationed in Tientsin, China, writing in the June 4, 1932, *Sentinel*, the 15th's weekly paper.

19. Details of some of the Japanese activity are recorded in a telegram from the commander of the Fourth Regiment, United States Marines, Colonel R.S. Hooker, to the commander-in-chief, United States Asiatic Fleet, Admiral M. Taylor, from Shanghai, January 30, 1932, in *FRUS*, 1932, vol. 3, *The Far East*, 119–120; paper from the British embassy to the U.S. Department of State, Washington, January 31, 1932, in the same source, 146; telegram from commander-in-chief, United States Asiatic Fleet, Admiral Montgomery M. Taylor, to the Chief of Naval Operations, Admiral William V. Pratt, from Shanghai, February 4, 1932, in the same source, 205.

20. Cahill, "The 31st Regiment in Shanghai," 173.

21. Smith-Hutton, "Lessons Learned at Shanghai in 1932," 1170–1173. Details of the activities of the irregulars on both sides are in a telegram from Cunningham to the secretary of state, from Shanghai, February 3, 1932, *FRUS*, 1932, vol. 3, *The Far East*, 189–191; telegram from the U.S. ambassador in Japan, W. Cameron

Forbes, to the secretary of state, from Tokyo, February 7, 1932. Forbes reported on a conference with Japanese admiral Toyoda, who admitted that there was a Japanese "lawless element" present in Shanghai whom he described as "gangsters" but stated that they were being returned to Japan. Placing the blame on the Chinese for the difficulties in Shanghai, the admiral averred that the Japanese had negotiated two armistices in Shanghai in past days, both of which had been broken by the Chinese. He noted further that the Chinese were "mostly Cantonese and not under the control of Chang," though what difference this made was not clarified. The Japanese professed to believe that Red elements in the Chinese armies were responsible for the Shanghai unrest and sought to bring about a war between China and Japan. The Japanese, he stated, were only attempting to guard their own nationals and were prevented by these Chinese forces, and the new troop arrivals were mainly for the relief of the "exhausted forces of marines." The Chinese called the Japanese irregulars *ronin,* referring to traditional Japanese warriors who loved violence and acted outside of the law. For the various components of the irregular forces, see Jordan, *China's Trial by Fire,* 12; 79–82.

22. Telegrams from Cunningham to the secretary of state, from Shanghai, February 3, 1932; February 4, 1932; February 5, 1932; February 7, 1932, FRUS, 1932, vol. 3, *The Far East,* 189–191; 214–215; 225–226; 248–249.

23. Telegrams from Cunningham to the secretary of state, from Shanghai, February 9, 11, 13, in FRUS, 1932, vol. 3, *The Far East,* 265–266; 284–285; 320–321.

24. Telegram from Cunningham to the secretary of state, from Shanghai, February 15, 1932, FRUS, 1932, *The Far East,* vol. 3, p. 333.

25. For details of the military actions at this time, see Jordan, *China's Trial By Fire,* 123–170, and Telegram from Cunningham to the secretary of state, from Shanghai, February 15, 1932, FRUS, 1932, *The Far East,* vol. 3, 340.

26. See, for example, Field Orders No. 4, Headquarters, the United States Army Forces in Shanghai, then located at 325 Bubbling Well Road, February 18, 1932, in RG 407, Box 103; Record of Events (Diary) 31st Infantry (U.S. Army Forces in Shanghai, China), as of February 19, 1932, dated February 20, 1932 at the regimental command post, 352 Bubbling Well Road, Shanghai, China, and signed by Colonel Glasser, RG 407, Box 103; Record of Events (Diary), 31st Infantry (U.S. Army Forced in Shanghai, China), February 25, 1932, signed at the command post at 352 Bubbling Well Road, Shanghai, China, on February 26, 1932, Shanghai, China, by Colonel Gasser; Diary, 1st Battalion, 31st Infantry, February 25, 1932; Diary, 31st Infantry (U.S. Army Troops in Shanghai), March 11, 1932, signed at the command post at 352 Bubbling Well Road on March 12, by Colonel L.D. Gasser, in RG 407, Box 103. See also Field Order No. 6, 2nd Battalion, 31st Infantry, Shanghai, China, March 9, 1932 in the same source. The 2nd Battalion's headquarters were then at the Studio D'Arts Building, 190 Bubbling Well Road. It was commanded by Major R. Hartle.

27. Cahill, "The 31st Regiment in Shanghai," 172; Lowe, "The 31st Regiment at War and Peace," chapter 4.

28. Diary, 1st Battalion, 31st Infantry, February 24, 1932, signed by Major Ross O. Baldwin, commander, 1st Battalion, RG 407, Box 103, Record of Events (Diary), the 31st (U.S. Army Forces in Shanghai, China), February 20, 1932, signed at the regimental command post at 352 Bubbling Well Road, Shanghai, China, on February 21, 1932, by Colonel Gasser, RG 407, Box 103.

29. Metcalf, "The Marines in China," 56; Lowe, "The 31st Regiment at War and Peace," chapter 4.

30. Cahill, "The 31st Regiment in Shanghai," 167.

31. In order to get baths, in the early days, the men used the facilities of the navy YMCA and the foreign YMCA, across from the racetrack.

32. Captain Elbridge Colby, a soldier of the 15th Infantry Regiment stationed in Tientsin, China, described the deployment and billeting of the 31st in the July 9, 1932, issue of the unit's weekly paper, *Sentinel.* The *Grant* docked at the Dollar Line's docks. It departed the following day for Chinwangtao, where it supplied men of the 15th U.S. Infantry stationed in Tientsin (Record of Events [Diary], 31st Infantry [U.S. Troops in Shanghai], March 7 and 8, 1932, signed at the command post at 352 Bubbling Well Road, Shanghai, China, by Colonel Gasser on March 8 and 9, 1932; see RG 407, Box 103).

33. Telegram from Johnson to secretary of state, from Shanghai, February 19, 1932, FRUS, 1932, *The Far East,* vol. 3, pp. 393–394.

34. Telegram from Cunningham to the secretary of state, from Shanghai, February 19, 1932, FRUS, 1932, *The Far East,* vol. 3, pp. 399–400.

35. Telegram from Cunningham to the secretary of state, from Shanghai, February 19, 1932, FRUS, 1932, *The Far East,* vol. 3. 401.

36. Telegrams, Cunningham to the secretary of state, from Shanghai, February 20 and 28, 1932, FRUS, 1932, *The Far East,* vol. 3, 405–406; 464–465.

37. These developments are a main theme of Jordan's book, *China's Trial by Fire.* See also

a discussion of Chiang's attitude toward the 19th Army and his failure to support it fully can be followed in Jonathan Fenby, *Chiang Kai-shek: China's Generalissimo and the Nation He Lost* (New York: Carroll and Graf, 2003), 212–213.

38. Abend, *My Life in China*, 195.

39. Telegram from Johnson to the secretary of state, regarding conversation with Yosuke Matsuoka, from Shanghai, February 21, 1932, *FRUS*, 1932, *The Far East*, p. 412. There continued to be violations of the neutrality of the portion of the International Settlement assigned to the 4th Regiment, U.S. Marines. See discussions of these contacts and confrontations in telegrams from Cunningham to secretary of state, from Shanghai, February 21, 22 and 23, 1932, *FRUS*, 1932, *The Far East*, pp. 414, 417, 420–421.

40. Telegram from Cunningham to secretary of state, from Shanghai, February 25, 1932, *FRUS*, 1932, *The Far East*, vol. 3, pp. 443–444.

41. Record of Events (Diary) issued by Headquarters Company, 31st Infantry, on February 23 and 24, 1932, the New World Building, Shanghai, China, dated February 24 and 25, 1932, and signed by Captain H.N. Burkhalter, company commander, in RG 407, Box 103; Record of Events (Diary) 2nd Battalion, 31st Infantry, February 24, 1932, at the command post, the Studio D'Arts Building, Shanghai, China, February 2, 1932, Major R.Hartle, commanding, RG 407, Box 103.

42. Telegrams from Cunningham to the secretary of state, from Shanghai, February 28, 1932, *FRUS*, 1932, *The Far East*, vol. 3, pp. 464–465; Johnson to the secretary of state, from Shanghai, February 29, 1932, in the same source.

43. Reprinted in *Sentinel*, May 7, 1932.

44. Telegrams from Cunningham to the secretary of state, from Shanghai, March 2, 1932, *FRUS*, 1932, *The Far East*, vol. 3, pp. 490–491, 491–493; Regimental Diary, 31st Infantry (U.S. Army Forces in Shanghai, China), March 2 and 3, 1932, signed at the command post at 352 Bubbling Well Road, Shanghai, China, on March 3 and 4, 1932 by Colonel Gasser, RG 407, Box 103. See also Jordan, *China's Trial by Fire*, 171–182.

45. Telegrams from Cunningham to the secretary of state, from Shanghai, March 3, 4 and 7, 1932, *FRUS*, 1932, *The Far East*, vol. 3, pp. 497, 510, 523–524.

46. For the resolution, see telegram from the American consul at Geneva, Prentiss B. Gilbert, to the secretary of state, from Geneva, March 4, 1932, *FRUS*, 1932, *The Far East*, vol. 3, 515–516. For Stimson's views regarding China, see memorandum of a transatlantic telephone conversation between Stimson and Hugh Robert Wilson, the American minister to Switzerland, Geneva, March 4, 1932, in *FRUS*, 1932, *The Far East*, vol. 3, pp. 511–515.

47. Record of Events (Diary), 31st Infantry (U.S. Army Forces in Shanghai, China), March 4, 1932, Command Post, 352 Bubbling Well Road, Shanghai, China, signed by Colonel Gasser on March 5, 1932, in RG 407, Box 103.

48. Diary entries, March 8 and 9, 1932, 31st Infantry (U.S. Army Troops in Shanghai, China), signed at the regimental command post at 352 Bubbling Well Road by Colonel L.D. Gasser on March 9 and 10, 1932 (see RG 407, Box 103).

49. Field Order No. 6, 2nd Battalion, 31st Infantry, Shanghai, China, March 9, 1932, RG 407, Box 103; Diary, 1st Battalion, 31st Infantry, March 9, 1932, signed at its headquarters at the Temple of Heaven on 1 March 10, 1932, by Major Ross O. Baldwin, commanding, in the same source.

50. Account in Lowe, "The 31st Regiment at War and Peace," chapter 4.

51. Ibid.

52. With the departure of the 31st's 1,279 officers and men, the American forces in Shanghai would be reduced essentially to a standing force of 1,412 Marines and 200 additional Marines and sailors who could be "immediately landable if necessary." They could normally count on the support of approximately 3,000 British soldiers in the area and the Shanghai Volunteer Corps, there with about 2,239 officers and men. See Note 2, *FRUS*, 1932, *The Far East*, vol. 4, p. 2, quoting a telegram from Cunningham to the State Department, from Shanghai, May 13, 1932.

53. He also acknowledged "the buildings available for billeting were by no means modern so their stay has not been a fair-weather service." Telegram from Cunningham to the secretary of state, from Shanghai, March 9, 1932, *FRUS*, 1932, *The Far East*, vol. 3, pp. 541–542.

54. Memorandum by Hornbeck of a conversation with the chief of staff, United States Army, Washington, April 13, 1932, *FRUS*, 1932, *The Far East*, vol. 3, p. 691.

55. The dimensions of the Chinese stance regarding this matter, however, are not clear and various interpretations have emerged in the historical literature regarding it. See discussion in Jordan, *China's Trial by Fire*.

56. *Papers Relating to the Foreign Relations of the United States*, vol. 1, *Japan, 1931–1941* (Washington: Government Printing Office, 1943), 217–220.

57. Telegram from Johnson to acting secretary of state, William R. Castle, Jr., from Shanghai, May 5, 1932, *FRUS*, 1932, *The Far East*, vol. 3, pp. 753–754.

58. Details of this altercation were sent belatedly in a telegram by Cunningham to the

acting secretary of state, William R. Castle, Jr., from Shanghai, May 11, 1932, *FRUS, 1932, The Far East*, vol. 4, pp. 11–12.

59. Telegram from the acting secretary of state, William R. Castle, Jr., to Cunningham, from Washington, May 6, 1932, *FRUS, 1932, The Far East*, vol. 4, p. 2. Castle was the acting secretary of state from April 8 to May 14.

60. Telegram from Stimson to the American minister to China, Nelson Trusler Johnson, from Washington, June 7, 1932, *FRUS, 1932, The Far East*, vol. 4, p. 67; telegram from Cunningham to the secretary of state, from Shanghai, June 10, 1932, *FRUS, 1932, The Far East*, vol. 4, p. 72; Diary, 31st Infantry (U.S. Army Forces in Shanghai, China).

61. U.S. Army, 4th Battalion (Mechanized) 31st Infantry, *History of the 31st U.S. Infantry* (n.p.) USAHEC.

62. Quoted in *Sentinel*, August 6, 1932.

63. These details are in a pamphlet entitled "History of the 31st Infantry Regiment" (n.p., n.d., n.p.) Folder Joseph B. Longuevan Papers, USAHEC, Carlisle Barracks, Pennsylvania, and in a pamphlet by the U.S. Army 31st Infantry Regiment: *The Thirty-First United States Infantry* (Manila: Benipayo, c. 1939), 33–34, USAHEC. There are further details in Lowe, "The 31st Regiment at War and Peace, chapter 4.

64. Metcalf, "The Marines in China," 56; article in the English language Chinese newspaper *Peking and Tientsin Times*, reprinted in the 15th Infantry Regiment's weekly troop newspaper, *Sentinel*, July 16, 1932. In a diary entry of the regiment, First Lieutenant J. W. Dansby, the regiment's personnel adjutant, recorded that the 31st had "performed the usual camp duties and provost guard duty in the City of Shanghai, China, during the month." Little else had occurred (see diary of the regiment as of midnight, June 30, 1932, dated July 1, 1932, Shanghai, China, RG 407, Box 102). In the course of its deployment, the regiment had sustained the loss of nine men, all of the deaths attributed to disease. There were no combat deaths or serious injuries recorded.

Chapter 12

1. *Sentinel*, July 23, 1932. The 15th Infantry Regiment was the only other U.S. Army Regiment in service in China at that time. It had been based in Tientsin since 1912 and would only be withdrawn in March 1938. For a history of this outfit see Alfred Emile Cornebise's *The United States 15th Infantry Regiment in China, 1912–1938* (Jefferson, NC: McFarland, 2004).

2. See Diary, July 1, 1932, Shanghai, China, and Special Strength Returns, Post of Manila, July 6 and July 8, 1932, signed by First Lieutenant J.W. Dansby, the personnel adjutant of the 31st Regiment, RG 407, Box 102.

3. Details of the regiment's quarters, amenities, and conditions of service in general in the Philippines can be found in the pamphlet *History of the 31st Infantry Regiment* (n.p., n.d., n.p.), Folder: The Joseph B. Longuevan Papers, The United States Army Heritage and Education Center (USAHEC), Carlisle, Pennsylvania, and in a pamphlet by the U.S. Army, 31st Infantry Regiment: *The Thirty-First United States Infantry* (Manila: Benipayo, c. 1939), USAHEC. Of course, such spit-and-polish may well have been among the reasons that many soldiers preferred service in China.

4. U.S. Army, 4th Battalion (Mechanized) 31st Infantry, *History of the 31st U.S. Infantry* (Fort Sill, OK: By the Regiment, 1988), USAHEC, and the pamphlet *History of the 31st Infantry Regiment* (n.p., n.d., n.p.), Folder Longuevan Papers, USAHEC.

5. U.S. Army, 4th Battalion (Mechanized) 31st Infantry, *History of the 31st U.S. Infantry*, n.p., USAHEC, and see also Folder "220.31–220.48–Medals and Decorations," Entry 5960: General Correspondence, 1925–38, Record Group 395: General Records, U.S. Army Overseas Operations and Commands, 1898–1942, U.S. Army Troops in China, 1912–38, National Archives II.

6. See discussion in Colonel Karl H. Lowe, "The 31st Regiment at War and Peace," at http://www.31stinfantry.org/history.htm, chapter 7.

7. See his article "Lessons Learned at Shanghai In 1932," in *The Proceedings of the United States Naval Institute* 64 (August, 1938), 1167–1174.

8. Ibid., 1174.

9. Tenny's message was forwarded to the secretary of state by the War Department on the same day. See *FRUS, 1932, The Far East*, vol. 3, pp. 108–109; Memorandum by Nelson Trusler Johnson, the American minister to China, then for a time in Shanghai, regarding a meeting with prominent Chinese officials, including T.V. Soong, Shanghai, February 12, 1932, in *FRUS, 1932, The Far East*, vol. 3, pp. 309–310.

10. Telegram from Cunningham to the secretary of state, from Shanghai, January 27, 1932, *FRUS, 1932, The Far East*, vol. 3, pp. 74–75. Also, an undated *aide-memoire* from the British embassy sent to the Department of State, in *FRUS, 1932, The Far East*, vol. 3, pp. 99–100. See also telegram from Cunningham to the secretary of state, from Shanghai, January 29, 1932, *FRUS, 1932, The Far East*, 96.

11. For Breckenridge, see letter to his sister, Mary, Peiping, January 31, 1932, in "James C. Breckinridge Collection, Personal Correspondence, 1929–1933," http://www.mcu.usmc.mil/

MCRCweb/ftw/files/pap2933.txt. Breckenridge's cynicism regarding the Chinese no doubt resulted from personal experience, but by his own admission it was also gleaned from a book on Chinese characteristics by the American missionary, Arthur Henderson Smith, who, late in the 19th century, wrote several influential books derived from his long residency and experiences in China and his considerable insight into the Chinese people and their civilization in that era. Henderson's works reveal both negative and positive views of the Chinese. See his *Chinese Characteristics* (Norwalk, CT: Eastbridge Press, 2002), a reprint of the original published in Edinburgh, Scotland, by Oliphant, Anderson and Ferrier in 1900. See also Henderson's studies *China in Convulsion*, 2 vols. (New York: Fleming H. Revell, 1901); *Proverbs and Common Sayings from the Chinese* (New York: Dover, 1965), a reprint of the 1886 edition; and *Village Life in China: A Study in Sociology* (New York: Fleming H. Revell, 1899).

12. Quoted in Donald A. Jordan, *China's Trial by Fire: The Shanghai War of 1932* (Ann Arbor: University of Michigan Press, 2001), 103.

13. Rana Mitter, *A Bitter Revolution: China's Struggle with the Modern World* (New York: Oxford University Press, 2004), 3, 160, 166.

14. For details of the complications of Japanese-Chinese relations in Manchuria during this period, see Rana Mitter's fine study, *The Manchurian Myth: Nationalism, Resistance, and Collaboration in Modern China* (Berkeley: University of California Press, 2000), 130.

15. Mitter, *A Bitter Revolution*, 160, 169.

16. Roland's article is in the *Sentinel*, June 4, 1932. The editorial is in the July 23, 1932, issue.

17. Dick Wilson, *When Tigers Fight: The Story of the Sino-Japanese War, 1937–1945* (New York: Penguin Books, 1983), 255.

18. For a history of the regiment, see especially the online book by Colonel Karl H. Lowe, *The 31st Regiment at War and Peace*. Chapter 4 pertains to the regiment's employment in Shanghai in 1932.

Conclusion

1. Orhan Pamuk, *Other Colors: Essays and a Story* (New York: Alfred A. Knopf, 2007), 239. Pamuk won the Nobel Prize for literature in 2006.

2. Kemp Tolley, *The Yangtze Partol: The U.S. Navy in China* (Annapolis, MD: Naval Institute Press, 1971), 169, 304.

3. Henry Kissinger, *On China* (New York: Penguin, 2011), 57.

4. Quoted in Madeleine Albright, *The Mighty and the Almighty: Reflections on America, God, and World Affairs* (New York: HarperCollins, 2006), 24.

5. See account by Brigadier General Aaron Simon Daggett, *America in the China Relief Expedition* (1903; rpr., Nashville: Battery Press, 1997), 36, 77.

6. Gerhard L. Weinberg, *Visions of Victory: The Hopes of Eight World War II Leaders* (Cambridge, England: Cambridge University Press, 2005), 80.

7. Kissinger, *On China*, 34, 45.

8. Ibid., 20, 22–24.

9. Ibid., 23–31.

10. Ibid., passim.

11. (New York: Bantam Books, 1972), 678.

12. E.J. Kahn, Jr., *The China Hands: America's Foreign Service Officers and What Befell Them* (New York: Viking, 1975), note 5, 293.

13. Letter of Transmittal of *The Chinese White Paper*, Department of State, Washington, July 30, 1949, by U.S. secretary of state Dean Acheson.

14. Nora Waln, *The House of Exile* (Boston: Little, Brown, 1933), 258.

15. John King Fairbank, Katherine Frost Brunner, and Elizabeth Mac Leod Matheson, *The I.G. in Peking: Letters of Robert Hart Chinese Maritime Customs, 1868–1907* (Cambridge: Harvard University Press, 1975), letters to Campbell, November 13, 1881 (vol. 1, p. 393), and December 16, 1894 (vol. 2, p. 1001).

16. Ibid., letters to Campbell, September 27, and October 25, 1896 (vol. 2, pp. 1084, 1088), November 6, 1899, 1205, and April 29, 1900 (p. 1226).

17. Ibid., letters to Campbell of July 10, 1904, and J.A. Van Aalst (a clerk in the Peking office), August 21, 1905, (vol. 2, pp. 1421, 1479–1480).

18. Ibid., letters, Hart to Campbell, September 15, 1895 (vol. 2, p. 1033), November 17, 1895 (p. 1041), January 12, 1896 (p. 1047), September 7, 1902 (p. 1327), and June 15, 1903 (p. 1363).

19. Ibid., letters, Hart to Campbell, September 1, 1901, and July 18, 1904, (vol. 2, pp. 1275, 1423).

20. (New York: Random House, 2013).

21. Joseph Kahn, "Losing Face, Leaping Forward," *New York Times Book Review*, CXV 3, no. 29 (July 21, 2013), 18. The Chinese scholar Wei Yuan (1794–1857) was a leader of the "Statecraft School" of the earlier 19th century, which hoped to combine traditional scholarly knowledge with a practical approach. We wanted the Chinese to learn from the superior technology of the West, so as better to face the challenges this posed. He was concerned that China develop its maritime trade and frontier and border defenses. He was the author of *A Military*

History of the Qing Dynasty and *The Opium War*.

22. Michael Nylan and Thomas Wilson, *Lives of Confucius: Civilization's Greatest Sage Through the Ages* (New York: Doubleday, 2010), 241.

23. See Davies quoted in Khan, *The China Hands*, 59. It should be recorded that John Paton Davies, together with John Carter Vincent and John Stewart Service, so harshly castigated by the McCarthyites, were, in the words of Harvard professor John K. Fairbank, "true China specialists and we have no one like them today" (1967).

24. (New York: Houghton Mifflin Harcourt, 2013.)

25. Kissinger, *On China*, 59, 64.

26. See comments in Han Han, *This Generation: Dispatches from China's Most Popular Literary Star (and Race Car Driver)*: trans. and ed. Allan H. Barr (New York: Simon and Schuster, 2012), 36. This work reveals much about China's younger generations as of 2008 and later.

27. See discussion in Sir Robert Hart, "*These from the Land of Sinim*": *Essays on the Chinese Question* (London: Chapman & Hall, 1903), 161–163.

28. John Paton Davies, Jr., *China Hand: An Autobiography* (Philadelphia: University of Pennsylvania Press, 2012), 45. See also the important U.S. State Department publication *The China White Paper*, released in August 1949, and republished by Stanford University Press in 1967. This contains much information on Chinese-American relations from the early 19th century, with an emphasis on World War II and the immediate postwar period.

29. See discussions in Alfred Emile Cornebise, *The Shanghai Stars and Stripes: Witness to the Transition to Peace, 1945–1946* (Jefferson, NC: McFarland, 2011), 120–130, 136–146, passim; John Paton Davies, Jr., *China Hand: An Autobiography* (Philadelphia: University of Pennsylvania Press, 2012), 266–267; 291; and John J. McLaughlin, *General Albert C. Wedemeyer: America's Unsung Strategist in World War II* (Philadelphia: Casemate, 2012).

30. James Lilley, *China Hands: Nine Decades of Adventure, Espionage, and Diplomacy in Asia* (New York: Public Affairs, 2004), 170–171.

31. Tolley, *The Yangtze Partol*, 304.

32. *Why The West Rules—For Now: The Patterns of History and What They Reveal About the Future* (New York: Farrar, Straus and Giroux, 2010).

33. Tim Clissold, *Mr. China: A Memoir*, "An adventurous young man collides with a vast nation on the brink of capitalism" (New York: HarperCollins, 2005), author's note, 251–252. Clissold is British and educated at Cambridge in physics. He became interested in China, went to a university in Beijing and studied Mandarin for two years and then became an investment banker. He subsequently lived in Beijing for almost twenty years. Married with four children reared in China, he is hence an "Old China Hand" of a later generation. See also another fine book, by Rana Mitter, *A Bitter Revolution: China's Struggle with the Modern World* (New York: Oxford University Press, 2004).

34. (New York: Penguin, 2009), 429.

35. Jacques' book review is in the September 25, 2011, issue of the *New York Times*, p. 20; Kissinger, *On China*, 395.

36. Robert D. Kaplan, *Hog Pilots, Blue Water Grunts: The American Military in the Air, at Sea, and on the Ground* (New York: Random House, 2007), 49–50.

37. (New Haven: Yale University, 2013), 398.

38. Mark Leonard, *What Does China Think?* (New York: PublicAffairs, 2008), 7.

39. Ibid., 9.

40. Ibid., 14, 32–34.

41. Pankaj Mishra, *From the Ruins of Empire: The Intellectuals Who Remade Asia* (New York: Farrar, Straus and Giroux, 2012). See also a review of this book by Hari Kunzru, in *New York Times Book Review* 117, no. 39 (September 23, 2012), 10.

42. See Simon Winchester, *The Man Who Loved China: The Fantastic Story of the Eccentric Scientist Who Unlocked the Mysteries of the Middle Kingdom* (New York: HarperCollins, 2008), 258.

43. For further discussions of these matters see the views of Marine colonel James C. Breckenridge, from his post in Peiping in the 1930s, in "James C. Breckinridge Collection. Personal Correspondence, 1929–1933," http://www.mcu.usmc.mil/MCRCweb/ftw/files/pap2933.txt.

44. Winchester, *The Man Who Loved China*, pp. 257, 259, 262, and *The River at the Center of the World: A Journey Up the Yangtze and Back in Chinese Time* (New York: Picador, 2004), 398.

45. Sun Tzu, *The Art of War*, numerous editions.

46. See quoted in Kahn, *The China Hands*, 294–295.

47. (New York: Farrar, Straus and Giroux, 2010).

48. On Needham (Joseph Needham, b. 1900), see Simon Winchester, *The Man Who Loved China*. Needham's book was published by Harvard University Press in 1981.

49. See article by Robert D. Kaplan, "The Statesman: In Defense of Henry Kissinger," *Atlantic* 311, no. 4 (May 2013), 70–78, and Kissinger, *On China*, 11–17.

50. For Clausewitz, see his *On War*, translated and edited by Michael Eliot Howard and Peter Paret (Princeton: Princeton University Press, 1989); and Peter Paret, *Clausewitz and the State: The Man, His theories, and His Times:* (Princeton: Princeton University Press, 1976, and reprint, 2007).

51. For these remarks see E. Alabaster, foreword to L.C. Arlington, *Through The Dragon's Eyes: Fifty Years' Experiences of a Foreigner in the Chinese Government Service* (London: Constable, 1931), x, vol. 3, p. 274. Alabaster was a longtime commissioner of Chinese Customs who worked with Arlington, an American, for over forty years in the Chinese Maritime Customs Service.

52. Winchester, *The River at the Center of the World*, 135–139.

53. Barbara Tuchman, *Stilwell and the American Experience in China, 1911–45* (New York: Macmillan, 1970), 678.

Bibliography

Books

Abend, Hallett Edward. *My Life in China, 1926-1941*. New York: Harcourt, Brace, 1943.

Albright, Madeleine. *The Mighty and the Almighty: Reflections on America, God, and World Affairs*. With Bill Woodward. New York: Harper, 2006.

Ancell, R. Manning, and Christine Miller. *The Biographical Dictionary of World War II Generals and Flag Officers: The U.S. Armed Forces*. Westport, CT: Greenwood Press, 1996.

Anders, Leslie. *Gentle Knight: The Life and Times of Major General Edwin Forrest Harding*. Kent, OH: Kent State University Press, 1985.

Anderson, Terry H. *Bush's Wars*. New York: Oxford University Press, 2011.

A'Rabbitt, Shamus. *China Coast Ballads*. Shanghai: A.R. Hager, 1938.

Arlington, L.C. *Through the Dragon's Eyes: Fifty Years' Experiences of a Foreigner in the Chinese Government Service*. London: Constable, 1931.

Asbridge, Thomas. *The Crusades: The Authoritative History of the War for the Holy Land*. New York: HarperCollins, 2010.

Bacevich, Andrew J. *Breach of Trust: How Americans Failed Their Soldiers and Their Country*. New York: Metropolitan Books, 2013.

———. *The New American Militarism: How Americans Are Seduced by War*. New York: Oxford University Press, 2006, rev. ed., 2013.

Beal, John Robinson. *Marshall in China*. Garden City, New York: Doubleday, 1970.

Beardson, Timothy. *Stumbling Giant: The Threats to China's Future*. New Haven: Yale University Press, 2013.

Beede, Benjamin R. *The Small Wars of the United States, 1899-2009: An Annotated Bibliography*. 2nd rev. ed. London: Routledge, 2012.

Beinart, Peter. *The Icarus Syndrome: A History of American Hubris*. New York: Harper, 2010.

Belden, Jack. *Retreat with Stilwell*. New York: Alfred A. Knopf, 1943.

Bender, Major Mark Christian. *Watershed at Leavenworth: Dwight D. Eisenhower and the Command and General Staff School*. Fort Leavenworth, KS: Combat Studies Institute, 1990.

Biggs, Chester M., Jr. *The United States Marines in North China, 1894-1942*. Jefferson, NC: McFarland, 2003.

Bland, Larry I., ed. *George C. Marshall's Mediation Mission to China, December 1945-January 1947*. Lexington, VA: George C. Marshall Foundation, 1998.

Bland, Larry I., and James B. Barber. *George C. Marshall: Soldier of Peace*. Baltimore: Johns Hopkins University Press, 1997.

Bond, Charles R., Jr., and Terry Anderson. *A Flying Tiger's Diary*. College Station: Texas A&M University Press, 1984.

Bradley, James. *The Imperial Cruise: A Secret History of Empire and War*. New York: Little, Brown, 2009.

Braisted, William Reynolds. *Diplomats in Blue: U.S. Naval Officers in China, 1922-1933*. Gainesville: University of Florida Press, 2009.

———. *The United States Navy in the Pacific, 1897-1909*. Annapolis: Naval Institute Press, rpr., 2008.

———. *The United States Navy in the Pacific,*

1909-1922. Annapolis: Naval Institute Press, rpr., 2008.
Bredon, Juliet. *Sir Robert Hart: The Romance of a Great Career*. 1910; London: Dodo Press, 2009 (Juliet was a niece of Hester Jane Bredon, who married Robert in 1866).
Brook, Timothy. *Vermeer's Hat: The Seventeenth Century and the Dawn of the Global World*. New York: Bloomsbury Press, 2008.
Brown, Arthur Judson. *New Forces in Old China: An Inevitable Awakening*. 2nd ed. 1904; Lititz, PA: Bibliobazzar, 2006.
Cannadine, David. *The Undivided Past: Humanity Beyond Our Differences*. New York: Alfred A. Knopf, 2013.
Chandrasekaran, Rajiv. *Little America: The War Within the War for Afghanistan*. New York: Alfred A. Knopf, 2012.
Chang, Jung. *Empress Dowager Cixi: The Concubine Who Launched Modern China*. New York: Alfred A. Knopf, 2013.
Chang, Jung, and Jon Halliday. *Mao: The Unknown Story*. New York: Anchor, 2006.
Chang, Raymond, and Margaret Scrogin Chang. *Speaking Chinese: A Cultural History of the Chinese Language*. New York: W.W. Norton, 1978.
Clausewitz (General), Carl Phillip Gottfried von. *On War*. Translated and edited by Michael Eliot Howard and Peter Paret. Princeton: Princeton University Press, 1989.
Clissold, Tim. *Mr. China: A Memoir*. "An adventurous young man collides with a vast nation on the brink of capitalism." New York: HarperCollins, 2005.
Coble, Parks M. *Facing Japan: Chinese Politics and Japanese Imperialism, 1931-1937*. Cambridge: Harvard University Press, 1991.
Coffman, Edward M. *The Regulars: The American Army, 1898-1941*. Cambridge: Harvard University Press, 2004.
Cornebise, Alfred Emile. *The Amaroc News*. Carbondale: Southern Illinois University Press, 1981.
_____. *The Shanghai Stars and Stripes: Witness to the Transition to Peace, 1945-1946*. Jefferson, NC: McFarland, 2010.
_____. *The United States 15th Infantry Regiment in China, 1912-1938*. Jefferson, NC: McFarland, 2004.
Cotter, G. Lee. *The Dragon Chronicle: History of the 15th Infantry from the Civil War to the Present*. Marceline, MO: Walsworth, 1981.
Cray, Ed. *General of the Army: George C. Marshall, Soldier and Statesman*. New York: W.W. Norton, 1990.
Davies, John Paton. *China Hand: An Autobiography*. Philadelphia: University of Pennsylvania Press, 2012.
_____. *Dragon by the Tail: American, British, Japanese, and Russian Encounters with China and One Another*. New York: Norton, 1972.
Dickinson, G. Lowes. *Letters from John Chinaman*. 1901. London: George Allen and Unwin, 1946.
Dolin, Eric Jay. *When America First Met China: An Exotic History of Tea, Drugs, and Money in the Age of Sail*. New York: Liveright, 2012.
Dong, Stella. *Shanghai: The Rise and Fall of a Decadent City*. New York: Harper, 2001.
Dorn, General Frank. *Walkout with Stilwell in Burma*. New York: Thomas Y. Crowell, 1971.
Dreyer, Edward L. *China at War, 1901-1949*. New York: Longman, 1995.
Earnshaw, Graham, ed. *Tales of Old Shanghai*. Hong Kong: China Economic Review, 2008.
Eichelberger, Robert L. *Our Jungle Road to Tokyo*. New York: Viking Press, 1950.
Eiler, Keith E. *Wedemeyer on War and Peace*. Stanford: Hoover Institution Press, 1987.
Eisenhower, John S.D. *General Ike: A Personal Reminiscence*. Glencoe, IL: Free Press, 2003.
_____. *Intervention! The United States and the Mexican Revolution, 1913-1917*. New York: W.W. Norton, 1995.
Esherick, Joseph. *The Origins of the Boxer Uprising*. Berkeley: University of California Press, 1987.
Everett, Marshall. *Startling Experiences in the Three Wars: China, the Philippines, and South Africa*. Chicago: Educational, 1900.
Fairbank, John King. *Trade and Diplomacy on the China Coast: The Opening of the Treaty Ports, 1842-1854*. 2 vols. Cambridge, MA: Harvard University Press, 1953.
Fairbank, John King, Katherine Frost Bruner, and Elizabeth MacLeod Matheson, eds. *The I.G. in Peking": Letters of Robert Hart Chinese Maritime Customs, 1868-1907*. 2 vols. Cambridge, MA: Harvard University Press, 1975.
Fallows, Deborah. *Dreaming in Chinese*. New York: Walker, 2010.
Fallows, James. *Postcards from Tomorrow Square: Reports from China*. New York: Vintage, 2009.

Fehrenbach, T.R. *This Kind of War.* New York: Macmillan, 1963.
Fenby, Jonathan. *Chiang Kai-shek: China's Generalissimo and the Nation He Lost.* New York: Carroll and Graf, 2004.
Ferrell, Robert H. *George C. Marshall as Secretary of State, 1947–1949.* New York: Cooper Square, 1966.
Finkel, Davis. *The Good Soldiers.* Rpr. ed. New York: Picador, 2010.
_____. *Thank You for Your Service.* New York: Farrar, Straus and Giroux, 2013.
Finney, Charles G. *The Old China Hands.* Westport, CT: Greenwood, 1973.
Fleming, Peter. *The Siege of Peking.* New York: Harper and Row, 1959.
Ford, Daniel. *Flying Tigers.* Washington: Smithsonian Institution Press, 1991.
French, Paul. *Through the Looking Glass: China's Foreign Journalists from Opium Wars to Mao.* Hong Kong: Hong Kong University Press, 2009.
Friedman, Thomas L. *The World Is Flat.* New York: Picador, 2007.
Friedman, Thomas L., and Michael Mandelbaum. *That Used to Be Us: How America Fell Behind the World It Invented and How We Can Come Back.* New York: Farrar, Straus and Giroux, 2011.
Gates, Robert M. *Duty: Memoirs of a Secretary at War.* New York: Alfred Knopf, 2014.
Gernet, Jacques. *China and the Christian Impact: A Conflict of Cultures.* Cambridge: Cambridge University Press, 1985.
Girardot, Norman. *The Victorian Translation of China: James Legge's Oriental Pilgrimage.* Berkeley: University of California Press, 2002.
Goodman, Martin. *Rome and Jerusalem: The Clash of Ancient Civilizations.* New York: Vintage, 2008.
Gordon, Michael R., and Bernard E. Trainor. *The Endgame: The Inside Story of the Struggle for Iraq, from George W. Bush to Barack Obama.* New York: Pantheon Books, 2012.
Graves, William Sidney. *America's Siberian Adventure, 1918–1920.* New York: Jonathan Cape and Harrison Smith, 1931.
Grayson, Benson Lee, ed. *The American Image of China.* New York: Frederick Ungar, 1979.
Gulick, Edward V. *Peter Parker and the Opening of China.* Harvard Studies in American-East Asian Relations 3. Cambridge: Harvard University Press, 1973.
Hahn, Emily. *China to Me.* New York: Doubleday, 1944.
Halliday, E.M. *Ignorant Armies.* New York: Bantam Books, 1990.
Halstead, Murat. *The Story of the Philippines: The Eldorado of the Orient.* Chicago: Dominion, 1898 (a flamboyant presentation of American Manifest Destiny late in the 19th century).
Han Han. *This Generation: Dispatches from China's Most Popular Literary Star (and Race Car Driver).* Translated and edited by Allan H. Barr. New York: Simon and Schuster, 2012.
Hart, John N. *The Making of an Army "Old China Hand": A Memoir of Colonel David D. Barrett.* Berkeley: University of California Press, 1985.
Hart, Robert. *Entering China's Service: Robert Hart's Journals, 1854–1963.* Edited by Bruner, Katherine F. Bruner, John K. Fairbank, and Richard J. Smith. Cambridge, MA: Harvard University Press, 1986.
Hart, Robert. *"These from the Land of Sinim."* London: Chapman and Hall, 1903.
Hedges, Chris. *War Is a Force That Gives Us Meaning.* New York: Anchor Books, 2002.
Heefner, Wilson Allen, and Martin Blumenson. *Patton's Bulldog: The Life and Service of General H. Walker.* Shippensburg, PA: White Mane, 2002.
Herodotus. *The Histories.* Translated by Aubrey De Sélincourt. London: Penguin Books, 1954. Rev. ed., 2003.
Hessler, Peter. *Country Driving: A Journey Through China from Farm to Factory.* New York: HarperCollins, 2010.
Hogan, Michael J. *The Marshall Plan: America, Britain and the Reconstruction of Western Europe, 1947–1952.* Cambridge: Cambridge University Press, 1989.
Holley, I.B., Jr. *General John M. Palmer: Citizen Soldiers and the Army of a Democracy.* Westport: Greenwood, 1982.
Howell, Glenn F. *Gunboat on the Yangtze: The Diary of Captain Glenn F. Howell of the USS Palos, 1920–1921.* Edited by Dennis L. Noble. Jefferson, NC: McFarland, 2002.
Huebner, Andrew J. *The Warrior Image: Soldiers in American Culture from the Second World War to the Vietnam Era.* Chapel Hill: University of North Carolina Press, 2008.
Hump Pilots Association. *China Airlift: The Hump.* Dallas: Taylor, 1980.
Hunt, Michael. *The Making of a Special Relationship: The United States and China to 1914.* New York: Columbia University Press, 1986.

Hurst, James W. *Pancho Villa and Black Jack Pershing: The Punitive Expedition in Mexico*. Westport, CT: Praeger, 2008.

Iriye, Akira. *Across the Pacific: An Inner History of American-East Asian Relations*. New York: Harcourt, Brace and World, 1967.

Isaac, Harold. *Scratches on Our Minds: American Views of China and India*. New York: M.E. Sharpe, 1958, 1980. Includes a chart indicating U.S. views of China from 1840 to the present.

Jacques, Martin. *When China Rules the World: The End of the Western World and the Birth of a New Global Order*. New York: Penguin, 2009.

Jespersen, T. Christopher. *American Images of China, 1931–1949*. Stanford: Stanford University Press, 1996

Jisheng, Yang. *Tombstone: The Great Chinese Famine, 1958–1962*. Translated by Stacy Mosher and Guo Jian. New York: Farrar, Staus and Giroux, 2012.

Joiner, Lynne. *Honorable Survivor: Mao's China, McCarthy's America, and the Prosecution of John S. Service*. Annapolis, MD: Naval Institute Press, 2009.

Jordan, Donald A. *China's Trial by Fire: The Shanghai War of 1932*. Ann Arbor: University of Michigan Press, 1991, 2001.

Jordan, Donald A. *Chinese Boycotts Versus Japanese Bombs: The Failure of China's "Revolutionary Diplomacy," 1931–32*. Ann Arbor: University of Michigan Press, 1991.

Kahn, E.J., Jr. *The China Hands: America's Foreign Service Officers and What Befell Them*. New York: Viking, 1975.

Kaplan, Fred. *The Insurgents: David Petraeus and the Plot to Change the American Way of War*. New York: Simon and Schuster, 2012.

Kaplan, Robert D. *Hog Pilots, Blue Water Grunts: The American Military in the Air, at Sea, and on the Ground*. New York: Random House, 2007.

Kapuscinski, Ryszard. *Travels with Herodotus*. Translated by Klara Glowczewska. New York: Vintage Books, 2008.

Kates, George N. *The Years That Were Fat: Peking, 1933–1940*. New York: Harper, 1952.

Keay, John. *China: A History*. New York: Basic Books, 2009.

Kelly, Walt. *We Have Met the Enemy and He Is Us*. New York: Simon and Schuster, 1987.

Kerr, George. *Okinawa: The History of an Island People*. Rev. ed. North Clarendon, VT: Tuttle, 2000.

Kipling, Rudyard, and Wallcott Balestier. *The Naulahka: A Story of East and West*. London: Macmillan, 1892.

Kissinger, Henry. *On China*. New York: Penguin Press, 2011.

Koginos, Manny T. *The Panay Incident: Prelude to War*. Lafayette, IN: Purdue University Studies, 1967.

Kuhn, Irene Corbally. *Assigned to Adventure*. Philadelphia: J.B. Lippincott, 1938.

Landor, Arnold Henry Savage. *China and the Allies*. 2 vols. New York: Charles Scribner's Sons, 1901.

Latourette, Kenneth Scott. *A History of Christian Missions in China*. New York: Macmillan, 1929.

Lebovic, James H. *Limits of U.S. Military Capability: Lessons from Vietnam and Iraq*. Baltimore: Johns Hopkins Press, 2010.

Legge, James. *The Chinese Classics*. New York: John B. Alden, 1885.

Leonard, Mark. *What Does China Think?* New York: PublicAffairs, 2008.

Lilley, James. *China Hands: Nine Decades of Adventure, Espionage, and Diplomacy in Asia*. New York: Public Affairs, 2004.

Linn, Brian McAllister. *Guardians of Empire: The U.S. Army and the Pacific, 1902–1940*. Chapel Hill: University of North Carolina Press, 1997.

Logevell, Fredrik. *Choosing War: The Lost Chance for Peace and the Escalation of War in Vietnam*. Berkeley: University of California Press, 1999.

_____. *Embers of War: The Fall of an Empire and the Making of America's Vietnam*. New York: Random House, 2012.

Lutze, Thomas D. *China's Inevitable Revolution: Rethinking America's Loss to the Communists*. New York: Palgrave Macmillan, 2007.

MacCloskey, Monro. *Reilly's Battery: A Story of the Boxer Rebellion*. New York: Richards Rosen, 1969.

Macmillan, Margaret. *Nixon and Mao: The Week That Changed the World*. New York: Random House, 2007.

Marco Polo. *The Travels of Marco Polo*. Edited and revised by Manuel Komroff from William Marsden's translation. New York: Modern Library, 2001.

Marshall, Katherine Tupper. *Together: Annals of an Army Wife*. New York: Tupper and Love, 1946.

Mason, R.H.P., and J.G. Caiger. *A History of Japan*. Tokyo: Tuttle, 1997.

McCarthy, James. *A Papago Traveler: The Memories of James McCarthy*. Tucson: University of Arizona Press, 1985.

McCartney, William F. *The Jungleers: A History of the 41st Infantry Division*. Washington, D.C.: Infantry Journal Press, 1948.

McChrystal, Stanely. *My Share of the Task: A Memoir*. New York: Penguin, 2012.

McCrum, Robert. *Globish: How the English Language Became the World's Language*. New York: W.W. Norton, 2010.

McLaughlin, John J. *General Albert C. Wedemeyer: America's Unsung Strategist in World War II*. Philadelphia: Casemate, 2012.

McNamara, Robert. *In Retrospect: The Tragedy and Lessons of Vietnam*. With Brian VanDeMark. New York: Vintage Books, 1996.

Melby, John F. *The Mandate of Heaven: Record of a Civil War, China 1945-49*. Garden City, NY: Anchor Books 1971.

Mishra, Pankaj. *From the Ruins of Empire: The Intellectuals Who Remade Asia*. New York: Farrar, Straus and Giroux, 2012.

Mitchell, George C. *Matthew B. Ridgway: Soldier, Statesman, Scholar, Citizen*. Mechanicsburg, PA: Stackpole Books, 2002.

Mitter, Rana. *A Bitter Revolution: China's Struggle with the Modern World*. New York: Oxford University Press, 2004.

———. *Forgotten Ally: China's World War II, 1937-1945*. New York: Houghton Mifflin Harcourt, 2013.

———. *The Manchurian Myth: Nationalism, Resistance, and Collaboration in Modern China*. Berkeley: University of California Press, 2000.

Moomjian, Scott Avedis. *"Roaring Joe": The Life of Major General Joseph Compton Castner, 1869-1946*. San Diego: University of San Diego Press, 1993.

Morris, Ian. *Why the West Rules—For Now: The Patterns of History and What They Reveal About the Future*. New York: Farrar, Straus and Giroux, 2010.

Narbeth, C. *Admiral Seymour's Expedition and Taku Forts, 1900*. Chippenham, 1980.

Needham, Joseph. *Science in Traditional China: A Comparative Perspective*. Cambridge, MA: Harvard University Press, 1981.

Nelson, Robert L. *German Soldier Newspapers of the First World War*. Cambridge: Cambridge University Press, 2011.

Noble, Dannis L. *The Eagle and the Dragon: The United States Military in China, 1901-1937*. Westport, CT: Greenwood Press, 1990.

———. *Gunboat on the Yangtze: The Diary of Captain Glenn F. Howell of the USS Palos, 1920-1921*. Jefferson, NC: McFarland, 2002.

Nye, Joseph S., Jr. *Presidential Leadership and the Creation of the American Era*. Princeton: Princeton University Press, 2013.

Nylan, Michael, and Thomas Wilson. *Lives of Confucius: Civilization's Greatest Sage Through the Ages*. New York: Doubleday, 2010.

Odom, William O. *After the Trenches: The Transformation of U.S. Army Doctrine, 1918-1939*. College Station: Texas A&M University Press, 1999.

Oliphant, Nigel. *A Diary of the Siege of the Legations in Peking (1901)*. London: Longman, Green, 1901. Reprint edition, General Books, Danvers, MA, 2009.

Olwell (Lieutenant), Murray M. *The Fifteenth Infantry Regiment, 1861-1953*. N.p., circa 1953.

O'Reilly, Sean, James O'Reilly, and Larry Habegger, eds. *Travelers' Tales: China*. San Francisco: Travelers' Tales, 2004.

Packer, George. *The Assassins' Gate: America in Iraq*. New York: Farrar, Straus and Giroux, 2006.

Pamuk, Orhan. *Other Colors: Essays and a Story*. New York: Alfred A. Knopf, 2007.

Paret, Peter. *Clausewitz and the State: The Man, His Theories, and His Times*. Princeton: Princeton University Press, 1976, 2007.

Perry, Hamilton Darby. *The Panay Incident: Prelude to Pearl Harbor*. New York: Macmillan, 1969.

Peterkin, W.J. *Inside China, 1943-1954: An Eyewitness Account of America's Mission in Yenan*. Baltimore: Gateway Press, 1992.

Pfaelzer, Jean. *Driven Out: The Forgotten War Against Chinese Americans*. New York: Random House, 2008.

Phillips, Jonathan. *Holy Warriors: A Modern History of the Crusades*. New York: Random House, 2010.

Platt, Stephen R. *Autumn in the Heavenly Kingdom: China, the West, and the Epic Story of the Taiping Civil War*. New York: Knopf, 2012.

Pogue, Forrest C. *George C. Marshall*. Vol. 1, *Education of a General, 1880-1939*. New York: Viking, 1963.

———. *George C. Marshall*. Vol. 2, *Ordeal and Hope, 1939-1942*. New York: Viking, 1966.

———. *George C. Marshall*. Vol. 3, *Organizer of Victory, 1943-1945*. New York: Viking, 1973.

———, and Drew Middleton. *George C. Mar-*

shall: Statesman, 1945–1959. New York: Viking, 1987.
Pogue, Forrest C., Gordon Harrison, and George C. Marshall. *George C. Marshall.* London: MacGibbon & Kee, 1964.
Power, Brian. *The Ford of Heaven.* New York: Michael Kesend, 1984.
Power, Desmond. *Little Foreign Devil.* Vancouver: Pangli Imprint, 1996.
Preston, Diana. *The Boxer Rebellion: The Dramatic Story of China's War on Foreigners That Shook the World in the Summer of 1900.* New York: Berkley Books, 1999.
Price, Eva Jane. *China Journal, 1889–1900: An American Missionary Family During the Boxer Rebellion.* New York: Charles Scribner's Sons, 1989.
Province, Charles. *General Walton H. Walker: Forgotten Hero; The Man Who Saved Korea.* Online: CreateSpace Independent Platform, 2008.
Ricks, Thomas E. *Fiasco: The American Military Adventure in Iraq, 2003–2005.* New York: Penguin, rpr. ed., 2007.
Rodenbough, Theophilus Francis, and William L. Haskin, eds. *The Army of the United States: Historical Sketches of Staff and Line, with Portraits of Generals-in-Chief.* New York: Maynard, Merrill, 1896.
Rogers, Paul P. *The Bitter Years: MacArthur and Sutherland.* New York: Praeger, 1991.
_____. *The Good Years: MacArthur and Sutherland.* New York: Praeger, 1990.
Romanus, Charles F., and Riley Sunderland. *Stilwell's Command Problems.* Washington: Chief of Military History, 1956.
_____. *Stilwell's Mission to China.* Washington: Chief of Military History, 1953.
_____. *Time Runs Out in CBI.* Washington: Chief of Military History, 1990.
Ruppenthal, Roland G. *Logistical Support of the Armies.* Vol. 2, *September 1944–May 1945.* Washington, D.C.: Government Printing Office, 1959.
Sarantakes, Nicholas Evan. *Keystone: The American Occupation of Okinawa and U.S.–Japanese Relations.* College Station: Texas A&M University Press, 2000.
Schandler, Herbert Y. *America in Vietnam: The War That Couldn't Be Won.* New York: Rowman and Littlefield, 2009.
_____. *The Unmaking of a President: Lyndon Johnson and Vietnam.* Princeton: Princeton University Press, 1977.
Scheibert, J. *Der Krieg in China, 1900–1901.* Berlin, 1909.
Schell, Orville, and John Delury. *Wealth and Power: China's Long March to the Twenty-first Century.* New York: Random House, 2013.
Schmidt, Hans. *Maverick Marine: General Smedley D. Butler and the Contradictions of American Military History.* Lexington: University of Kentucky Press, 1987.
Scott, Robert L. *God Is My Co-Pilot.* New York: Charles Scribner's Sons, 1944.
Scully, Eileen P. *Bargaining with the State from Afar: American Citizenship in Treaty Port China, 1844–1942.* New York: Columbia University Press, 2001.
Service, Grace. *Golden Inches: The China Memoir of Grace Service.* Edited by John S. Service. Berkeley: University of California Press, 1989.
Shadid, Anthony. *Night Draws Near: Iraq's People in the Shadow of America's War.* New York: Picador Press, rpr. ed., 2006.
Shaw, Henry I., Jr. *The United States Marines in North China, 1945–1949.* Washington: Headquarters, U.S. Marine Corps, Historical Branch, 1960; rev. ed., 1962.
Shaw, Ralph. *Sin City.* New York: Time-Warner, 1992.
Sheridan, James E. *China in Disintegration: The Republican Era in Chinese History, 1912–1949.* New York: Free Press, 1975.
Shunxun, Nan, and Beverly Foit-Albert. *China's Sacred Sites.* Honesdale, PA: Himalayan Institute Press, 2007.
Silbey, David J. *The Boxer Rebellion and the Great Game in China.* New York: Hill and Wang, 2012.
Sledge, E.B. *China Marine: An Infantryman's Life After World War II.* New York: Oxford University Press, 2002.
Smith, Arthur Henderson. *China in Convulsion.* 2 vols. New York: Fleming H. Revell, 1901.
_____. *Chinese Characteristics.* Norwalk, CT: Eastbridge Press, 2002. Rpr. of Oliphant, Anderson and Ferrier, Edinburgh, 1900.
_____. *Proverbs and Common Sayings from the Chinese.* 1886. New York: Dover, 1965.
_____. *Village Life in China: A Study in Sociology.* New York: Fleming H. Revell, 1899.
Society of the Fifth Division. *The Official History of the Fifth Division U.S.A During the Period of Its Organization in the European War, 1917–1919.* Society of the Fifth Division, 1919.
Spence, Jonathan D. *God's Chinese Son: The Taiping Heavenly Kingdom of Hong Xiuquan.* New York: W.W. Norton, 1996.
_____. *The Search for Modern China.* New York: W.W. Norton, 1990.

Spurling, Hilary. *Pearl Buck in China: Journey to the Good Earth*. New York: Simon and Schuster, 2010.
Suri, Jeremi. *Liberty's Surest Guardian: American Nation-Building from the Founders to Obama*. New York: Free Press, 2011.
Sutton, F.A. *One-Arm Sutton*. New York: Viking Press, 1933.
Taylor, Jay. *The Generalissimo: Chiang Kai-shek and the Struggle for Modern China*. Cambridge, MA: Harvard University Press, 2009.
Thibaudeau, Antoline Claire. *Mémoire sur le Consulat, 1799 à 1804*. Paris: Chez Ponthieu et cie, 1827.
Toll, Aaron Philippe, ed. *15th Infantry Regiment (United States)*. Ceed, 2012.
Tolley, Kemp. *The Yangtze Patrol: The U.S. Navy in China*. Annapolis, MD: Naval Institute Press, 1971.
Toshiyuki, Tanaka. *Japan's Comfort Women*. London: Routledge, 2001.
Troost, J. Maarten. *Lost on Planet China*. New York: Broadway Books, 2008.
Tuchman, Barbara. *Stilwell and the American Experience in China, 1911-45*. New York: Macmillan, 1970.
Tunner, William H. *Over The Hump: The Story of General William H. Tunner*. New York: Duell, Sloan and Pierce, 1964.
Tzu, Sun. *The Art of War*. Mineola, New York: Dover Publications, 2002.
U.S. Army. 4th Battalion (Mechanized) 31st Infantry. *History of the 31st U.S. Infantry*. Fort Sill, OK: By the Regiment, 1988.
Varig, Paul A. *Missionaries, Chinese, and Diplomats: The American Protestant Missionary Movement in China, 1890-1952*. Princeton: Princeton University Press, 1958.
Venzke, Rodger R. *Confidence in Battle, Inspiration in Peace: The United States Army Chaplaincy, 1945-1975*. Washington, D.C.: Office of the Chief of Chaplains, Department of the Army, 1977.
Vogel, Victor. *Soldiers of the Old Army*. College Station: Texas A & M University Press, 1990.
Waln, Nora. *The House of Exile*. Boston: Little, Brown, 1933.
Weale, Bertram Lenox Putnam [Real name: Bertram Lenox Simpson] (1877-1930). *Indiscreet Letters from Peking*. New York: Bibliobazaar, 2007.
Wedemeyer, Arthur Coady. *Wedemeyer Reports!* New York: Henry Holt, 1958.
Wehrle, Edmund S. *Britain and the Antimissionary Riots, 1891-1900*. Minneapolis: University of Minnesota Press, 1966.
Weinberg, Gerhard L. *Visions of Victory: The Hopes of Eight World War II Leaders*. Cambridge, England: Cambridge University Press, 2005.
White, Alexander. *The United States Marines in North China*. Millbrae, CA, 1974.
White, Theodore H., and Annalee Jacoby. *Thunder Out of China*. New York: William Sloane, 1946.
Willett, Robert L. *Russian Sideshow: America's Undeclared War, 1918-1920*. Washington, D.C.: Brassey's Books, 2003.
Williams, Robert H. *The Old Corps: A Portrait of the U.S. Marine Corps Between the Wars*. Annapolis: U.S. Naval Institute Press, 1982.
Wilson, Dick. *When Tigers Fight: The Story of the Sino-Japanese War, 1937-1945*. New York: Penguin Books, 1983.
Winchester, Simon. *The Man Who Loved China: The Fantastic Story of the Eccentric Scientist Who Unlocked the Mysteries of the Middle Kingdom*. New York: HarperCollins, 2008.
_____. *The River at the Center of the World: A Journey Up the Yangtze and Back in Chinese Time*. New York: Henry Holt, 1996.
Wright, David C. *The History of China*. Westport, CT: Greenwood Press, 2001.
Yu-wen, Jen. *The Taiping Revolutionary Movement*. New Haven: Yale University Press, 1973.
Zhao Ziyang. *Prisoner of the State: The Secret Journal of Premier Zhao Ziyang*. Translated and edited by Bao Pu, Renee Chiang and Adi Ignatius. New York: Simon and Schuster, 2009.
ZZ [pseudonym]. *China High: My Fast Times in the 010; A Beijing Memoir*. New York: St. Martin's Press, 2009.

Articles

Brinkerhoff (Captain), H.R. "The Fifteenth Regiment of Infantry," 610-628. In *The Army of the United States: Historical Sketches of Staff and Line with Portraits of Generals-in-Chief*. Article edited by Theophilus Francis Rodenbough and William L. Haskin. New York: Maynard, Merrill, 1896.
Cahill, Howard F.K. "The Thirty-First Infantry in Shanghai." *Infantry Journal* 39 (May-June 1932), 165-75.
Cornebise, Alfred E. "Christmas in China During the Boxer Rebellion, 1900." *Mili-

tary Collector and Historian 54, no. 4 (Winter 2002–2003), 169–173.
Dickman, Joseph Theodore. "Experiences in China." *Journal of the United States Cavalry Association* 13, no. 45 (July 1902), 5–40.
Eiler, Keith E. "The Man Who Planned the Victory." *Hoover Digest*, no. 4 (2001).
———. "An Uncommon Soldier." *Hoover Digest*, no. 4 (2001).
Feng, Patrick. "The 339th Infantry Regiment." *On Point* 18, no. 1 (Summer 2012), 21–26.
Flint, Roy Kenneth. "The United States Army on the Pacific Frontier, 1899–1939." In *The Proceedings of the Ninth Military History Symposium, United States Air Force Academy* (October 1980), 139–59.
Frank, Benis M. "Shanghai's 4th Marines: The Glory Days of the Old Corps." *Shipmate* (November 1979), 16.
Gluckman, Ron. "From Shanghai to Vegas." *Wall Street Journal*, September, 1996.
Halliday, E.M. "Where Ignorant Armies Clashed by Night." *American Heritage* 10, no. 1 (December 1958).
Hein, David. "In War for Peace: General C. Marshall's Core Convictions and Ethical Leadership." *Touchstone* 26, no. 2 (March–April 2013).
Kaplan, Robert D. "The Statesman: In Defense of Henry Kissinger." *Atlantic* 311, no. 4 (May 2013), 70–78.
Leonard, John W., Jr., and Major General George Ruhlen. *Assembly* (March–April 2003).
Leonhard, Robert R. "The China Relief Expedition: Joint Coalition Warfare in China, Summer 1900." Baltimore: Johns Hopkins University Applied Physics Laboratory (2008).
Metcalf, C.H. "The Marines in China." Vol. 22 (September 1938), 56.
Morris, Jim. "The Honorary Chinese Paratrooper." *Soldier of Fortune* (2004).
Morton, Louis. "Army and Marines on the China Station." *Pacific Historical Review* 29, no. 1 (February 1960), 51–73.
Nannes, Caspar. "A Visit with Chaplain Luther D. Miller." *Chaplain* 26, no. 2 (March–April 1969), 9–12.
Naylor, Colonel William K. "Christmas in China During the Boxer Rebellion, 1900." Edited by Alfred E. Cornebise. *Military Collector and Historian* 54, no. 4 (Winter 2002–2003), 169–173.
Nye, Joseph S. "Do Presidents Matter?" *Atlantic* (June 2013), 13–15. This is an excerpt from Nye's book *Presidential Leadership and the Creation of the American Era*, Princeton University Press, 2013.
"An Officer of the China Expeditionary Forces, On the China Coast." *Infantry Journal* 19 (November 1921), 502–07.
Plante, Trevor K. "U.S. Marines in the Boxer Rebellion." *Prologue* 31, no. 4 (Winter 1999).
Poppelman, Ray. "A China Marine: The Adventures of Ray Poppelman." *Leatherneck* (June 1992).
Smith, Gibson Bell. "Guarding the Railroad, Taming the Cossacks: The U.S. Army in Russia, 1918–1920." *Prologue* 34, no. 4 (Winter 2002).
Smith-Hutton (Lieutenant Commander), H.H. "Lessons Learned at Shanghai in 1932." In *The Proceedings of the United States Naval Institute* 64 (August 1938), 1168–1169.
Stoy, Timothy R. "Fifteenth Infantry Regiment." *On Point* 17, no. 1 (Summer 2011), 22–26.
Twain, Mark. "To the Person Sitting in Darkness." *North American Review* 182, no. 531 (February 1901), 161–176.
Wheeler, W.R. "China Service." *Journal of the Military Service Institution of the United States* 59 (July-August, September–October, November–December 1916), 80–93, 234–50, 378–93.

Pamphlets

History of the 31st Infantry Regiment. N.p., n.d., Folder: Joseph B. Longuevan Papers, United States Army Military History Institute, Carlisle, Pennsylvania.

Selected Online Sources

"Breckinridge, James C. Collection. Personal Correspondence, 1929–1933. http://www.mcu.usmc.mil/MCRCweb/ftw/files/pap 2933.txt.
California State University, Northridge, Library. Introduction to a discussion of the Old China Hands Archive. http://library.csun.edu/Old China Hands.
Gluckman, Ron. "From Shanghai to Vegas." *Wall Street Journal*, September, 1996. http://www.gluckman.com/ShanghaiJews2.html.
Lowe, Colonel Karl H. "The 31st Regiment at War and Peace." http://www.31stinfantry.org/history.htm.
Thompson, Kensley Robert. Memoirs of Flight Officer Kensley Robert Thompson.

Documents and Primary Sources

Arnold, William H. Papers. Recollections and Reflections and text of an interview with Arnold, July–August, 1975. Archives, United States Army Heritage and Education Center, Carlisle, Pennsylvania.

Babb, Joseph G.D. "The Harmony of Yin and Yank: The American Military Advisory Effort in China, 1941–1951." PhD diss., University of Kansas, 2012.

Bainbridge, William E. "Besieged in Peking." Diary of the second secretary of the American Legation in Peking and secretary to the U.S. minister to China Edwin Hurd Conger. Subject file, "Belgian Relief Correspondence, 1916–20, to Boxer Rebellion," Folder, Boxer Rebellion Diaries, Box 13, Lou Henry Hoover Papers, Herbert Hoover Presidential Library, West Branch, Iowa.

Biggs, Chester M., Jr. *Behind the Barbed Wire: Memoir of a World War II U.S. Marine Captured in North China in 1941 and Imprisoned by the Japanese until 1945.* Jefferson, NC: McFarland, 2011.

Boatner, Haydon L. Papers. Archives, United States Heritage and Education Center, Carlisle, Pennsylvania, and the Hoover Institution, Palo Alto, California.

Brown (Warrant Officer), Charles D. "Thirty-First U.S. Infantry Organization Day Twenty-Fifth Anniversary Program, Published by the Regiment at Manila, August 13, 1941."

Caraway, Paul W. Papers. Archives, United States Army Heritage and Education Center, Carlisle, Pennsylvania, and Paul W. Caraway Papers, Hoover Institution, Palo Alto, California.

Caughey, John Hart. *The Marshall Mission to China, 1945–1947: The Letters and Diary of Colonel John Hart Caughey.* Edited by Rober B. Jeans. Lanham, MD: Rowman and Littlefield, 2011.

Chaffee (Major General), Adna Romanza. "Report on the China Relief Expedition." Excerpted from *U.S. War Department, Five Years of the War Department Following the War with Spain, 1899–1903.* Washington, D.C, 1904, pp. 395–407.

Daggett (Brigadier General), Aaron Simon. *America in the China Relief Expedition.* 2003 rpr. Nashville: Battery Press, 1997.

Drew, Anna. "Diary of Anna Drew." Subject file, "Belgian Relief Correspondence, 1916–20, to Boxer Rebellion," Folder 3, Boxer Rebellion Diaries, Box 13, Lou Henry Hoover Papers, Herbert Hoover Presidential Library, West Branch, Iowa. Mrs. Anna Drew was the wife of Edward Bangs Drew, an American commissioner for the Imperial Chinese Customs Service in Tientsin, i.e., one of Sir Robert Hart's men. This diary focuses on the events in Tientsin and at the port of Tagu and on board the U.S. Army transport USS *Logan*, which sailed to Nagasaki and then to the U.S.

Fairbank, John King, Katherine Frost Bruner, and Elizabeth MacLeod Matheson, eds. *The I.G. in Peking: Letters of Robert Hart Chinese Maritime Customs, 1868–1907.* 2 vols. Cambridge, MA: Harvard University Press, 1975.

Foreign Relations of the United States (FRUS). 1932. Vol. 3, *The Far East.* Washington, D.C.: Government Printing Office, 1948.

Gallagher, Philip E. Papers. Archives, United States Army Heritage and Education Center, Carlisle, Pennsylvania.

Gould, Hunter Thomas. *An American in China, 1936–1939: A Memoir.* New York: Thomas and Sons Books, 2004.

Harris, Frederick. Collection. Folder 9, George C. Marshall Research Library, Lexington, Virginia.

Hart, Robert. *Entering China's Service: Robert Hart's Journals, 1854–1963.* Edited by Katherine F. Bruner, John K. Fairbank, and Richard J. Smith. Cambridge, MA: Harvard University Press, 1986.

Hoover, Herbert. *The Memoirs of Herbert Hoover.* Vol. 1. New York: Macmillan, 1951.

Moore, James E. Papers. United States Army Heritage and Education Center, Carlisle, Pennsylvania.

Kautz Family. YMCA Archives, Elmer L. Anderson Library, University of Minnesota, Minneapolis.

Kennan, George F. *The Kennan Diaries.* New York: W.W. Norton, 2014.

Kuhn, Irene Corbally. *Assigned to Adventure.* Philadelphia: J.B. Lippincott, 1938.

"Lou Henry Hoover's Story." Lou Henry Hoover Papers, Herbert Hoover Presidential Library, West Branch, Iowa.

Lynch, George A. Papers. Archives, United States Army Heritage and Education Center, Carlisle, Pennsylvania.

Marshall, George C. *The Papers of George Catlett Marshall*. Vol. 1, *The Soldierly Spirit, December 1880-June 1939*. Edited by Bland, Larry I., and Sharon R. Ritenour. 7 vols. Baltimore: Johns Hopkins University Press, 1981– .

McCarthy, James. *A Papago Traveler: The Memories of James McCarthy*. Tucson: University of Arizona Press, 1985.

Moore, James E. Papers. United States Army Heritage and Education Center, Carlisle, Pennsylvania.

Ridgway, Matthew B. *The Korean War*. New York: Doubleday, 1967.

———. *Soldier: The Memoirs of Matthew B. Ridgway as Told to Harold H. Martin*. Westport, CT: Greenwood, 1974.

Stilwell (General), Joseph W. *The Stilwell Papers*. Edited by Theodore H. White. New York: William Sloane, 1948.

Stimson, Henry L. *The Far Eastern Crisis: Recollections and Observations*. New York: Harper and Brothers, 1936.

Summerall, Charles Pelot. *The Way of Duty, Honor, Country: The Memoir of General Charles Pelot Summerall*. Edited and annotated by Timothy K. Nenninger. Lexington: University of Kentucky Press, 2010.

U.S. Department of State. *The China White Paper, August 1949*. Reissue of *United States Relations with China with Special Reference to the Period 1944–1949*. Department of State Publication 3573, Foreign Eastern Series 80. 2 vols. Stanford: Stanford University Press, 1967.

Vaughn, Francis E. Papers, 1919–1977. Archives, U.S. Army Heritage and Education Center, Carlisle, Pennsylvania.

INDEX

Numbers in ***bold italics*** indicate pages with photographs.

Abend, Hallett 187–188
Allen, Gen. Henry Tureman 128
Almond, Gen. Edward M. 142
American Board of the Commissioners for Foreign Missions 23
American Expeditionary Force Siberia (AEFS) 192
American Forces in China 7, 75
An American in China, 1936-1939: A Memoir (book) 25
American Indians 82–86
American North Russian Expeditionary Force (ANREF) 192
American Relief Expedition 53–54
Anschluss 144
Arnold, Gen. William Howard 161–162
Arrasmith, Major James M. 72
The Art of War (book) 133, 222–223, 232, 245

Bainbridge, William E. 48
Barrett, Col. David D. 2, ***95***, 233–234
Battle of Tientsin (1900) 32–34
Beardson, Timothy, *Stumbling Giant: The Threats to China's Future* (book) 242
Beede, Benjamin R. 116
Bell, Gen. James Franklin 72, 122
Benjamin Franklin University 175
Benson, Stella (novelist) 208, 210
Beveridge, Albert Jeremiah (senator) 22, 230–231
Boatner, Gen. Harold LeMaire 116, 134, 173–174
Bogue, Treaty of (October 3, 1843) 13
Bolte, Gen. Charles Lawrence 99, 172–173
Bonaparte, Napoleon 55

Booth, Gen. Ewing E. (commanding general of the Philippine Department) 218
Boxer Uprising 4; Allied views 48–54; causes 18–22; consequences 48–58; early phases 19–21, 29, 32
Boxers 18–21; Allied attacks 29–32, 38–39, 51–53; Allies punitive expeditions 30–37, 40–46, 61–63; astrology 20–21; Protocol (September 7, 1901) 38–39, 72; views regarding 39–40, 49–52, 53–54, 58
Bradley, Gen. Omar 171
Brann, Gen. Donald Weldon 165
Breckinridge, Col. James C. (Marine Legation Guard, Peking) 82, 220–222
Brooks, Reverend Sidney M. 30
Brown, Arthur Judson (missionary) 24
Buck, Pearl S. 2, 23, 26–27, 108; *The Good Earth* (book) 26; *My Several Worlds* (book) 26–27; views of Chinese and the Boxer Uprising 51–52
Bullitt, William C. (American ambassador to France) 103
Burt, Col. Reynolds J. 100

Cairo-Yalta Conference (1943) 134–135
Calhoun, W.J. (American minister to China) 72, 73
Caraway, Gen. Paul Wyatt "Small Paul" 174–175
Castner, Gen. Joseph C. 77, 118, 119–121, 129
Chaffee, Gen. Adna Romanza 35, 37, 47, 57, 60, 65
Chapei (Shanghai district) 184, 185, 187, 188, 197, 198, 207, 208, 210
USAT *Chaumont* ***196***, 195–197
Chefoo Convention (1876) 14

284 Index

Chennault, Gen. Claire 132, 134, 136
Chiang Kai-shek 69, 125, 129, 132, 134, 143; Chinese Army 146, 207–208, 233–234; Gen. George C. Marshall 160–161, 174; government 137, 191, 237
China in a Convulsion (book) 51; *see also* Smith, Arthur Henderson
China Relief Expedition (U.S. Army, 1932), 35–37, 71–73
The China White Paper (U.S.) 234
China's Trial by Fire (book) 222
Chinese: appeal 2–3; "Century of Shame" 10, 53, 231, 237–238; Christians 243–244; Chung 81, **84**; civilization 10; communists 4, 51, 125, 191; language 2–3, 80, 81, 84, 98; 19th Route Army 186, 202, 206–208, 210–211, 223; pride and attitudes 11, 12; secret societies 19–21; views of warfare 134, 222–223, 232–233, 245; in Western eyes 2–4
Chinese Characteristics (book) 22; *see also* Smith, Arthur Henderson
Christianity 1, 11, 14, 18–19, 21–23
"Christmas in China During the Boxer Rebellion, 1900" (story) 41–47
Churchill, Winston 124, 126, 134, 229–230
Civilian Conservation Corps (CCC) 124, 150–151, 178
Cixi, Empress Dowager 18–19, 31–32, 38–39
Clausewitz, Carl Philipp Gottfried von 247
Clissold, Tim 241
Collins, Gen. J. Lawton 139
communism 211, 223, 239
Confucianism 1, 24, 28
Conger, Edwin Hurd (U.S. minister to China) 48
Connor, Gen. William Durward 75–77, 109–110, 118–119, 230
Cornebise, Alfred Emile, *The United States 15th Infantry Regiment in China, 1912–1938* (book) 5–6, 80
Craig, Gen. Malin 124
Cunningham, Edwin S. 188, 194, 213, 214

Daggett, Col. Aaron Simon 37, 53–54, 231
"Damned China Crowd" 98, 99, 116, 137, 165
Davies, John Paton, Jr. 237, 238–239
Delury, John, *Wealth and Power: China's Long March to the Twenty-first Century* (book) 236
Detachment Thirty-First Infantry 197, 217–218
Dewey, Commodore George 16

Dickinson, Goldsworthy Lowes, *Letters from John Chinaman* (book) 63
Dickman, Gen. Joseph Theodore 57–58
Doe, Gen. Jens Anderson 165–167
Dorn, Gen. Frank "Pinky" 105, 131
Dorward, Gen. Arthur 61
Drew, Anna 33–34
Drew, Edward Bangs 33
East India Company 12

East versus West 1–2, 7, 10, 11–12, 15, 16–17, 23, 52–54; consequences and assessment 230–248
Eight-Nation Alliance (1900) 18, 52
Eisenhower, Gen. Dwight David 12, 126, 140, 153, 154
Elder Brethren Association (*Ko-lao-hui*) 19
European Recovery Act (Marshall Plan) 125
extraterritoriality ("extrality") 14, 17, 19, 25, 68, 230

Field Service Regulations of 1923 157; *see also* Lynch, Gen. George Arthur
Fifteenth Infantry Regiment American China Expedition 72–79; arrival in China 60–61; billeting 73–77; Boxer Uprising and 60–66; coat of arms 6, 75; compound in Tientsin **49**, **65**, 74–77, **76**; concubines 86–88, 105; departure from China (1938) 104–108; early history 70–71; encounters with Japanese 100–103; Japanese tensions 100–101, 103–104; junks on the Pei Ho River 63, **64**, 65; later history 100–113; life 80–98; motto ("Can Do") 54, 75, 108; offices and men **66**; return to the U.S. 100–113; rifle range 86, 96–97, 100–101; service in Boxer Uprising 60–66; service in China (1912–1929) 71–79
Fifth Artillery 35
Finney, Charles G. 6–7; *The Old China Hands* (book) 120–121
First Opium War 4, 10, 12–13
First "Shanghai Incident" (1932): assessment 225–227; early development 184–188; forces engaged 188; later development 196–215; origins 182–184; results 219–225; "Shanghai Bowl" 215; Thirty-First Infantry Regiment 195–215
foreign devils 11, 18, 21
Forgotten Ally: China's World War II, 1937–1945 (book) 240; *see also* Mitter, Rana
Fort Benning (Georgia) 7, 98–99, 117, 123, 109–110, 113, 128–129, 131, 138, 140, 150,

Index

153, 157, 158, 160, 162, 166, 168, 169, 170, 171, 172, 178, 179
Fort Lewis (Washington) 107, 112, 121, 178
Fort McKinley (Manila) 83, 127, 192, 194–196, 217–218
Fortnightly Review (British journal) 49
Fourteenth Infantry Regiment: coat of arms 5; later history 55; nickname ("Golden Dragons") 54; service in China 35–41, 47, 54
Freeman, Gen. Paul L., Jr. 167–168
Fulbright, J. William (senator) 245
Fuqua, Gen. Stephen Ogden, Jr. 158–159

Gallagher, Gen. Philip Edward 164–165
Gaselee, Gen. Alfred 35
Gasser, Col. Lorenzo D. 157, 194, 195, 197, 213, 215–216, 227
USNS *General Edwin D. Partick* **176**
Georgetown University 174
The Good Earth (book) 26; *see also* Buck, Pearl S.
Gould, Hunter Thomas, *An American in China, 1936–1939: A Memoir* (book) 25
USAT *Grant* 206
Grant, Gen. Ulysses S. 206, 233
Graves, Gen. William Sidney 192

Halsey, Admiral William Frederick "Bull," Jr. 17
Halstead, Murat 16–17; *see also The Story of the Philippines: The Eldorado of the Orient* (book)
Harding, Gen. Edwin Forrest 98–99, 148–153
Harris, Gen. Frederick Mixon 170–171
Hart, Sir Robert 11, 12, 14, 18, 19, 48–50, 235–236
Harvard University 118, 125, 156
Haushofer, Gen. Karl Ernst 144
Hay, John 17–18
Haydock, Private 98; *see also* "His Belle of the Orient" (story)
Hines, Gen. John L. (commanding general of the Philippine Department) 194
"His Belle of the Orient" (story) 88–92; *see also* Haydock, Private
Honnen, Gen. George 162
Hoover, Herbert 194
Hornbeck, Stanley K. 213
"Horse Marines" (U.S. Marine Corps mounted detachment) 69, 81
House of Exile (book) 139–142, 234–235; *see also* Waln, Nora

Hull, Cordell 102, 103
The "Hump" 134, 135, 146

I Ho Tuan ("Righteous Fists of Harmony Society") 19; *see also* Boxers
Illinois Institute of Technology 172
Infantry Drill and Combat Regulations (AEF) 157; *see also* Lynch, Gen. George Arthur
Infantry Journal 151, 157

Jacques, Martin, *Why China Rules the World* (book) 241
James, Col. William C. (U.S. Marine commander in Tientsin) 104
Japanese in Shanghai 182–188
Jefferson, Thomas 16
Johnson, Gen. Hugh S. 157
Johnson, Nelson Trusler (U.S. minister to China) 206, 214
Jones, Col. Frank B. 73
Jordan, Donald A., *China's Trial by Fire* (book) 222

Keegan, John 142–143
Kendall, Gen. Paul Wilkins 177–179
Kennedy, John Fitzgerald 175
Kenney, Gen. George C. 154
Kettler, Baron Clemens von 32, 39
King, Gen. Campbell 99, 118, 155–157
Kipling, Rudyard 1–2, 25, 34, 52–53, 62–63, 229
Kissinger, Henry 3, 241, 246–247
Ko-lao-hui (Society of Brothers and Elders) 29
Kriegsakademie 144
Kuhn, Irene Corbally 189–191

Landor, Arnold Henry Savage 40
Lays of the Mei-Kuo Ying-P'an (book) 148; *see also* Harding, Gen. Edwin Forrest
League of Nations 211
Ledo Road (Stilwell Road) 135
legation guard (Peking) 30
Legge, James 22
Lejeune, Gen. John A. 69
lend-lease 132–133
Leonard, John William, Jr. 93–98
Leonard, Gen. John William, Sr. 93–97, 117, 179–180
Leonard, Mark 242–243
Letters from John Chinaman (book) 63
Lewis, Gen. Henry Balding "Monk" 171
Lewis and Clark Expedition 16
Liggett, Gen. Hunter 122
Lilley, James 239–240

Index

Liscum, Col. Emerson H. 32–33, 34–35, 54
"Liscum Bowl" *54*
"Little Tokyo" (Hongkew District of Shanghai) 184
USAT *Logan* 33, 72, 83
London Missionary Society 22, 30
looting 40–46, 61, 62, 63
Lynch, Gen. George Arthur 81, 100, 157–158

Ma Kien Chang (manager of China Merchant's Company) 20
Macao 10, 14
MacArthur, Gen. Douglas 32, 139, 142, 146, 152–155, 166, 194, 215, 226
MacKinder, Sir Halford 144
Madison, James 70
The Man Who Loved China (book) 244; *see also* Winchester, Simon
Mandate of Heaven 11, 247
Manifest Destiny 1–2, 15, 16, 17, 22, 53–54, 230
Mao Zedong 4, 10, 40, 51, 125, 147, 237
Marble China Gate (Tientsin, China and Fort Benning) 109–110, 230; *see also* Connor, Gen. William Durward
"The March of the Flag" (speech) 22, 230; *see also* Beveridge, Albert Jeremiah
Marco Polo 1–2, 11
Marshall, Gen. George Catlett 116–118, 121–126, 132, 141, 145–148, 152; Chiang Kai-shek 160–161, 174; Fort Benning 98–99, 129, 150, 176
Martin, Clarence D. (governor of Washington) 107
McAndrew, Col. Joseph A. 100
McCarthy, James 82–86
McCarthy, Joseph R. 147
McClure, Gen. Robert Battey 162–164
McCrum, Robert 245
McCunniff, Gen. Dennis 99
McKinley, William 15, 126
Medal of Honor 34, 54–55, 68, 75, 77, 109–110, 118–120, 129, 145, 192, 226
Mei-Kuo Ying-P'an (Fifteenth Infantry barracks in Tientsin) *49, 65,* 73–*76*
Merrill, Frank 135
Merrill, Gen. Thomas 107
"Merrill Marauders" 135
"A Military Soliloquy" (essay) 82; *see also* Breckinridge, Col. James C.
Miller, Luther D. 75, 147–148
Min-kuo Jih-pao (Chinese newspaper) 183
Mishra, Pankaj 243
missionaries 10, 11, 17, 19, 21–28, 29–30, 230

Mitter, Rana, *Forgotten Ally: China's World War II* (book) 237–238
Moale, Col. Edward 60
Moore, Gen. James Edward 171–172
Morris, Ian, *Why the West Rules—For Now* (book) 240–241, 246
Mountbatten, Admiral Lord Lewis 133, 135
Muslims 1
My Several Worlds (book) 26–27; *see also* Buck, Pearl S.

Nanking Treaty (August 29, 1842) 13, 15, 248
Napier, Lord 12
National Recovery Administration (NRA) 157
Naulahka: A Story of East and West (Kipling novel) 1
Naylor, Lt. William I. 41–46
Needham, Joseph, *Science in Traditional China: A Comparative Perspective* (book) 246
Nimitz, Adm. Chester 146
Ninth Infantry Regiment 32–35; coat of arms 5; early action in China 33–37; later history 55–56; motto "Keep up the fire, men" 34–35; nickname ("Manchus") 35; occupying Peking (1900) 41–46; service in China ends 47; Tientsin 34–35
Nixon, Richard 245
Nobel Peace Prize 125–126
North American Review (American journal) 49
North Atlantic Treaty Organization (NATO) 125
North China Daily News (Shanghai) 23

"Ocean People" 28
"Old China Hands" 6, 69, 75, 87, 98, 99, 101, 108–109, 116, 126, 191, 238
The Old China Hands (book) 120–121; *see also* Finney, Charles G.
Open Door Note (September 6, 1899) 17–18
Open Door Policy (U.S.) 18, 27, 67
"Operation Dragoon" 113
"Operation Torch" 112
Opie, Martha J. (poet) 3–4
opium 12–13, 15
Opium Wars 67

Palm, Pvt. Howard W. 87, 107
Palmer, Lt. John M. 61–62, 63–65
Pamuk, Orhan 229
Panay incident 101–103

Patrick, Gen. Edwin Davies 175–177, *176*
Patton, Gen. George S., Jr. 140–414
Peking, Conventions of (October 24–25, 1860) 13
Pershing, Gen. John J. "Blackjack" 58, 122, 123, 128, 140, 157
Philippines 10, 16, 22, 55, 71, 72
Pi-hsieh shih-lu (tract) 20; see also Ma Kien Chang
Pike, Col. Zebulon Montgomery 70
Portuguese 10, 14, 22
Power, Brian 2–3
Power, Desmond 104–105
Power, Joan (poet) 107–108
Pratt, Adm. William V. (chief of naval operations) 200
"Proff. Bojack" (*Shanghai Sports* columnist) 190
P'u Yi, Prince 71, 211
Purdue University 165

Ramgarh (India) 134
"Red Hairs" 28
"Red Lanterns Shining" (Boxer organization) 19
Reilly, Capt. Henry J. 35, 37, 57, 63
USAT *Republic* 215, **224**
Ridgway, Gen. Matthew Bunker 137–139
Robertson, Major Edgar B. 47
Rodger, Major H.D. (commander, Shanghai Volunteer Corps) 186
Roosevelt, Franklin Delano 100–101, 103, 124, 132, 133, 134, 142–143, 145, 150, 151, 154, 158
Russian-Chinese Treaty (1896) 17
Rutgers College 77, 118–119

Schaick, Col. Louis I. (U.S. Army inspector general) 120
Schell, Orville, *Wealth and Power: China's Long March to the Twenty-first Century* (book) 236
Science in Traditional China: A Comparative Perspective (book) 246
Scott, Gen. Winfield 70
"Scramble for Concessions" 17
Second Opium War (1856–60) 13
Second Treaty of Tientsin (June 9, 1885) 14
secret societies 29–30
Sentinel (Fifteenth Infantry troop newspaper) 3–4, 25–26, 41–46, 56, 86–92, 107–108, 121, 148, 155–156, 217, 225
"Sergeant Trooper" (U.S. Marine mascot) 104
Service, John S. 245–246
Seymour, Sir Edward 31–33, 36

Seymour Expediton 31–33, 36
Shanghai characterized 189–191
Shanghai Volunteer Corps 185–188, 197, 198, 203, 215
Shimonoseki, Treaty of (1895) 17
Sino-Japanese War (1894–95) 17
Sixth Cavalry Regiment 56
Slim, Field Marshall William 135
The Small Wars of the United States, 1899–2009 (book) 116
Smith, Arthur Henderson 22, 51; see also *China in a Convulsion*; *Chinese Characteristics*
Smith, Gen. Walter Bedell 154
Smith-Hutton, Lt. Cdr. H.H. 219
Smitley, George (Tacoma mayor) 107
Society for the Propagation of the Gospel in Foreign Parts 30
Society of Brothers and Elders (*Ko-lao-hui*) 29
Soldiers of the Old Army (book) 71
Sommerall, Gen. Charles Pelot 57, 63
Spanish-American War (1898) 15–16, 71
Steele, Private William R. 80–81
Stilwell, Gen. Joseph Warren, Jr. 81, 101, 116, 127, 136, 158–160
Stilwell, Gen. Joseph Warren, Sr. 98, 116, 126–137, *130*, 143, 146, 159, 163, 170, 233
Stilwell and the American Experience in China (book) 233; see also Tuchman, Barbara
Stimson, Henry L. (U.S. secretary of state) 188, 211, 214–215
The Story of the Philippines: The Eldorado of the Orient (book) 16–17
Stumbling Giant: The Threats to China's Future (book) 242
Sun Tzu (Master Sun), *The Art of War* (book) 133, 222–223, 232, 245
Sun Yat-sen 71–72
Sutherland, Gen. Richard Kerens 118, 153–155, 167

Tacoma, Washington 104–107, 110–112
Taku Forts 31, 33, 39, 73
Tao Kuang (emperor) 12–13
Taylor, Col. James D. 79, 100
Taylor, Gen. Maxwell D. 169
Taylor, Adm. Montgomery M. (commander-in-chief, U.S. Asiatic Fleet) 197, 200
Third Artillery 35
Thirty-First Infantry Regiment: "American Foreign Legion" 191; arrival in China 194–197; in China 182–218; coat of arms 6; departure from China 213–218; life in the Philippines 217–219; motto ("Pro Patria") 26, 226; nickname

("Polar Bears") 157, 182, 191–193, 217, 220, 226; operations in Shanghai 197–212; in Russian service (Siberia) 191–192; "Shanghai Bowl" 54; in World War II 218–219, 225–226
Timberman, Gen. Thomas S. 129, 160–161
Titus, Corporal Calvin P. 37
Tolley, Adm. Kemp 22, 50, 241
Treaties of Tientsin 13–14
Treaty of Paris (December 10, 1898) 15
Treaty Ports 12–13
Triad Society (*San-ho Hui*) 19
Trojans 1
Truman, Harry 125, 146, 147, 174
Tsai Ting-Kai, General 206
Tuchman, Barbara 233, 248
Tuttle, Capt. William B. "Wild Bill" 99, 149

United States Army 7; chief of staff 125, 131, 138, 139, 145, 154, 160, 169–170; Command and General Staff College (Fort Leavenworth, Kansas) 78, 117, 120, 129, 138, 140, 144, 145, 150, 153, 158, 162, 165, 167, 171, 172, 173; forces in China (USAFC) 77, 78, 118; Glenn Expedition (Alaska) 119; troops in China (USATC) 79; War College (Carlisle Barracks, Pennsylvania) 58, 77, 78, 117, 118, 119, 138, 141, 157, 158, 163, 165, 166, 168, 172, 174; War Plans Division 124, 145, 169, 173
The United States 15th Infantry Regiment in China, 1912–1938 (book) 5–6, 80
United States Marine Corps 30, 32, 34, 35, 47, 68–70, 82, 103, 104, 182, 194, 212, 218, 221
United States Navy 16, 67–68, 101–103, 191
United States Siberian Forces 177–178

venereal disease 80, 212
"Victory Program" 145; *see also* Wedemeyer, Gen. Albert Coady
Virginia Military Institute (VMI) 118, 121–122, 124, 139
Vogel, Victor 71

Waldersee, Gen. Alfred Graf von 35–36, 38, 41
Walker, Gen. Walton Harris 138–142
Wall Street Journal 190–191
Walla Walla (Fourth Marine Regiment troop paper) 215
Waln, Nora 3, 139–142, 234–235; *see also House of Exile* (book)
Wanghsia, Treaty of (1844) 15
Wealth and Power: China's Long March to the Twenty-first Century (book) 240; *see also* Delury, John; Schell, Orville
Wedemeyer, Gen. Albert Coady 116, 136, 142–147, **143**, 163, 173–174
Wen Hsiang (Chinese prime minister) 15
West Point 57, 65, 77, 117, 118, 119, 126, 127, 131, 138, 139, 140, 142, 143, 145, 149–150, 158, 159, 161, 162, 164, 165, 167, 169, 170, 171, 173, 174, 177, 179
Wheeler, Gen. Earle Gilmore "Bus" 169–170
When China Rules the World (book) 241
When Tigers Fight (book) 226
Williams, Gen. Lauen Lyman 167
Wilson, Dick, *When Tigers Fight* (book) 226
Winchester, Simon, *The Man Who Loved China* (book) 14, 244, 248

Yale University 118, 153, 167
Yalta Conference 134–135
Yangtze Service Medal 218, **224**